THE SANCTITY OF THE SEVENTH YEAR

Program in Judaic Studies
Brown University
BROWN JUDAIC STUDIES
Edited by
Jacob Neusner,
Wendell S. Dietrich, Ernest S. Frerichs,
Alan Zuckerman

Number 44

THE SANCTITY OF THE SEVENTH YEAR
A Study of Mishnah Tractate Shebiit

by
Louis E. Newman

THE SANCTITY
OF THE SEVENTH YEAR:
A STUDY
OF MISHNAH TRACTATE SHEBIIT

by
Louis E. Newman

Scholars Press
Chico, California

THE SANCTITY OF THE SEVENTH YEAR:
A STUDY OF MISHNAH TRACTATE SHEBIIT

by
Louis E. Newman

The publication of this book was made possible by support from Friends of Judaic Studies at Brown University.

Library of Congress Cataloging in Publication Data
Newman, Louis E.
   The sanctity of the seventh year.

   (Brown Judaic studies ; no. 44)
   Bibliography: p.
   Includes index.
   1. Mishnah. Shevi'it—Commentaries. 2. Sabbatical year
(Judaism). I. Mishnah. Shevi'it. II. Title. III. Series.
BM506.S63N48 1983   296.1'2306   83–8683
ISBN 0-89130-630-7

Printed in the United States of America

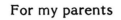

For my parents

CONTENTS

PREFACE

This study is a translation and exegesis of Tractate Shebiit (The Sabbatical Year) in Mishnah and in its corresponding document, Tosefta. The goal of my work is to explain the laws of this tractate as they were understood by those who redacted the document in Palestine in the late second century C.E. That is to say, I wish first and foremost to explain Mishnah's laws of the Sabbatical year as they have been formulated and compiled in their present context, not necessarily as later generations of rabbinic authorities interpreted them. By restricting the focus of my commentary in this way, I have attempted to expose the worldview of Mishnah's framers. My treatment of Mishnah's laws concerning the Sabbatical year also includes a translation and commentary to all of Tosefta Shebiit. This document supplies further valuable evidence concerning the concept of the Sabbatical year current during the period immediately following the formation of the Mishnah, and so forms a natural counterpart to my discussion of that document. This study, then, contributes to the larger task of understanding the concerns that occupy rabbinic Judaism in that early state in its development to which the Mishnah and related literature so richly attest.

The character of my translation and commentary reflects the goals outlined above. The translation, first, aims at reproducing in English, to the extent possible, the syntax of each ruling and the literary structure of each unit of law. This alerts the reader to the highly formalized modes of expression characteristic of Mishnah. Moreover, by high-lighting the literary constructions employed by Mishnah's authors, I am able to focus attention on the point which each pericope was designed to make. This is presented in the comment that follows each unit of law. Here I also explain any unarticulated principles that stand behind the law and indicate the broader implications of the law for our understanding of the worldview of Mishnah's framers.

The chapter introductions present the next stage in my analysis of the tractate's rules. There I discuss the larger thematic units, composed of sizeable blocks of material, around which the tractate as a whole is organized. Delineating the legal issues and principles addressed by these thematic units enables us to understand better the point made by each individual periciope. This discussion of thematic units prepares the way for the final portion of my commentary, presented in the introduction to the dissertation. That is, once each of the individual units of law has been explained, both in isolation and in its context within the document, it becomes possible for us to discern the central issues addressed by the tractate as a whole. This is accomplished, first, through an outline of the tractate, designed to reveal the logic of its entire discussion. This enables us to grasp the central points of the tractate as a whole, the message which its framers wished to convey through their discussion of the Sabbatical year. Also in my introduction I attempt

- 1 -

to explain the content of the tractate in its historical context. This entails a discussion of how Mishnah's conception of the Sabbatical year both carries forward and diverges from that implicit in Scripture. I thus show how Mishnah's authors, through their treatment of the Sabbatical year, both express their continuity with the past and frame their discussion in response to their own historical situation. Finally, the introduction contains a full account of the methods which I employ in my translation and commentary. There I explain the ways in which my form-analytical commentary serves the goals of my study, as well as how my approach to the interpretation of Mishnah differs from that of all previous exegetes.

ACKNOWLEDGEMENTS

I gratefully acknowledge my debt to the many teachers and colleagues who have contributed to my graduate education in general and to the preparation of this book in particular. Above all, I wish to thank Professor Jacob Neusner, my teacher, graduate advisor and dissertation director. His careful criticisms are reflected in every page of this study. By his example, he has taught me to appreciate not only the qualities of outstanding scholarship but also the character of the devoted teacher and colleague. I shall always be indebted to him for his generous support and persistent guidance. I also would like to express my appreciation to Professor Wendell Dietrich, Brown University. He has taken a special interest in my education, both inside and outside the classroom. For all that he has given me as a teacher and a friend I am very grateful. Finally, I wish to thank Professors Ernest Frerichs, Brown University, and Marvin Fox, Brandeis University, for serving as readers on my dissertation committee.

Fellow students in Professor Neusner's graduate seminar, in which my work was read and discussed, contributed to the improvement of this study through their many critical comments and suggestions. These students include Professor Alan Avery-Peck, Tulane University, Mr. Roger Brooks, Mr. Howard Schwartz, Ms. Judith Romney Wegner and Mr. Paul Flesher. Without their help and support, this thesis would be lacking in many matters both of substance and of detail. I also would like to acknowledge the work of Mr. Leonard Gordon, whose M.A. thesis (Brown University, 1980) on the first four chapters of Mishnah Shebiit was valuable to me in my study of the law.

I would like to thank Brown University for its generous support of me, in the form of University and Teaching Fellowships, throughout the years of my graduate education.

I thank Verbatim Word Processing for the typing and preparation of this manuscript and especially Catherine Hawkes for her diligent efforts. I also wish to acknowledge the fine work of Mr. Marc Rosen, who carefully proofread and corrected the entire first draft of this book.

My wife, Rosanne Zaidenweber, deserves the greatest measure of my gratitude. She has stood beside me, throughout the years of my graduate education, sharing in each of my successes and failures. She also has followed me, often sacrificing her personal gain and professional growth for the sake of my own; and she has walked ahead of me, by continually giving me new perspectives on the world outside my study and by inviting me to explore its possibilities with her. In many ways, this book and all that it represents belong to her as much as to me.

This book is dedicated to my parents, Marion and Annette Newman. Through their continuing patience and support, they have enabled me to pursue my goals, in education and in life. Their constant love is a blessing for which I shall always be grateful. By dedicating this book to them, I return to them only the smallest portion of what they have given me.

Louis E. Newman

Providence, Rhode Island
June 6, 1983

ABBREVIATIONS AND BIBLIOGRAPHY

Albeck
= H. Albeck, The Six Orders of the Mishnah (Jerusalem and Tel Aviv, 1957)

Aruch
= Alexander Kohut, ed., Aruch Completum, 8 vols. (Vienna, 1878-1892; second ed., 1926)

A.Z.
= Abodah Zarah

b.
= Babli, Babylonian Talmud, cited by tractate and folio number of ed. Romm (Vilna, 1886); ben, "son of," as in Simeon b. Gamaliel

B
= Mishnah Zeraim, MS. Berlin 93; see Sacks-Hutner, vol. 1, pp. 43, 77-78

B.B.
= Baba Batra

BDB
= F. Brown, S.R. Driver, and C.A. Briggs, eds., A Hebrew and English Lexicon of the Old Testament (1907; reprinted Oxford, 1952)

Bek.
= Bekhorot

Ber.
= Berakhot

Bert.
= Obadiah b. Abraham of Bertinoro (fifteenth century), Mishnah Commentary in Romm ed. of Mishnah (Vilna, 1908)

Bik.
= Bikkurim

Blackman
= Philip Blackman, Mishnayot, second ed., 6 vols. (New York, 1964)

B.M.
= Baba Mesia

Breuggemann
= Walter Breuggemann, The Land: Place as Gift, Promise and Challenge in Biblical Faith (Philadelphia, 1977)

B.Q.
= Baba Qamma

C
= Mishnah, early printed ed. of unknown origin, probably Constantinople or Pisaro, c. 1516; see Sacks-Hutner, vol. 1, pp. 64, 82-83

Ca
= Mishnah, MS. Cambridge 470, 1, printed in W.H. Lowe, The Mishnah On Which the Palestinian Talmud Rests (Cambridge, 1883; reprint: Jerusalem, 1967); see Sacks-Hutner, vol. 1, pp. 63, 67

Cahati
= Pinhas Cahati, Mishnayot, vol. 1: Seder Zeraim (Jerusalem, 1977)

Correns
= G. Beer, C. Holtzmann, eds., Die Mischna: Text, Übersetzung und ausfuhrliche Erklärung. Schebiit (Vom Sabbatjahr) Text, Ubersetzung und Erklarung nebst einem textkritischen anhang by Dietrich Correns (Berlin, 1960)

Dalman
= Gustav Dalman, Arbeit und Sitte in Palästina, 8 vols. (Gütersloh, 1928-42)

Danby
= The Mishnah, translated from the Hebrew with introduction and brief explanatory notes by Herbert Danby (London, 1933)

Davies   = W.D. Davies, The Territorial Dimension in Judaism (Berkeley, 1982)

Dem.   = Demai

Driver, Deuteronomy   = S.R. Driver, A Critical and Exegetical Commentary on Deuteronomy (New York, 1895)

Dt.   = Deuteronomy

E   = Tosefta, MS. Erfurt; see Lieberman, TZ, pp. 8-11

Ecc. R.   = Ecclesiastes Rabbah

Ed.   = Eduyyot

ed. princ.   = Tosefta, editio princeps (Venice, 1521)

EJ   = Encyclopedia Judaica, 16 vols. (Jerusalem, 1972), cited by volume and column (EJ, 9:119)

Epstein, Mabo   = Jacob Nahum Halevi Epstein, Prolegomena to the Text of the Mishnah (Heb.), 2 vols., ed. by E.Z. Melamed (Jerusalem and Tel Aviv, 1948; second ed., 1964)

Epstein, Mebo'ot   = Jacob Nahum Halevi Epstein, Prolegomena to the Tannaitic Literature (Heb.), 2 vols., ed. by E.Z. Melamed (Jerusalem and Tel Aviv, 1957)

Erub.   = Erubin

Ex.   = Exodus

Felix, Agriculture   = Yehuda Feliks, Agriculture in Palestine in the Period of the Mishna and Talmud (Heb.) (Jerusalem and Tel Aviv, 1963)

Feliks, Plant World   = Yehuda Feliks, The Plant World of the Bible (Heb.) (Tel Aviv, 1957)

Felix, Sabbatical   = Yehuda Feliks, Jerusalem Talmud Tractate Shebiit (Heb.) (Jerusalem, 1979)

Freimark   = Die Tosefta, Seder I: Zeraim, vol. 2, bersetzt und erklärt von Peter Freimark und Wolfgang-Friedrich Krämer (Stuttgart, 1971)

G (+ raised number)   = Mishnah MSS. fragments from the Cairo Genizah, listed and numbered in Sacks-Hutner, vol. 1, pp. 87-112

Gen.   = Genesis

Gereboff, Tarfon   = Joel Gereboff, Rabbi Tarfon: The Tradition, The Man, and Early Rabbinic Judaism (Missoula, 1979)

Git.   = Gittin

Gordon   = Leonard Gordon, A History of the Mishnaic Law of Agriculture Mishnah-Tosefta Shebiit: Translation and Commentary (unpublished M.A. thesis, Jacob Neusner, dir., Brown University)

GRA

= Elijah b. Solomon Zalman (or "Vilna Gaon;" Lithuania, 1720-1797), Mishnah commentary, in Romm ed. of Mishnah (Vilna, 1908, and numerous reprints); Tosefta emendations, in Romm ed. of Babylonian Talmud (Vilna, 1886, and numerous reprints)

Green, Approaches

= William S. Green, ed., Approaches to Ancient Judaism, vol. 1 (Missoula, 1978), vol. 2 (Chico, 1980), vol. 3 (Chico, 1981)

Green, Joshua

= William S. Green, The Traditions of Joshua ben Hananiah, Part I: The Early Legal Traditions (Leiden, 1981)

Haas, Second Tithe

= Peter Haas, A History of the Mishnaic Law of Agriculture: Tractate Maaser Sheni (Chico, 1980)

Hal.

= Hallah

HD

= Hasde David. David Samuel b. Jacob Pardo (Italy, Austria, Palestine, 1718-1790), Sefer Hasdé David [Tosefta commentary]. I. Seder Zeraim (Livorno, 1776; reprint: Jerusalem, 1970)

Hul.

= Hullin

HY

= Hazon Yehezqel. Yehezqel Abramsky (1886-1976), [Tosefta Commentary]; Hazon Yehezqel, Seder Zeraim (Vilna, 1925; second ed.: Jerusalem, 1971)

IDB

= The Interpreter's Dictionary of the Bible, 4 vols. (New York and Nashville, 1962), cited by volume and page (IDB 2:400)

Jaffee, Tithing

= Martin S. Jaffee, Mishnah's Theology of Tithing: A Study of Tractate Maaserot (Chico, 1981)

Jastrow

= Marcus Jastrow, A Dictionary of the Targumim, the Talmud Babli and Yerushalmi, and the Midrashic Literature, 2 vols. (New York, 1895-1903; reprint: New York, 1975), cited by page and entry (Jastrow, p. 623, s.v. kwsbr)

JE

= The Jewish Encyclopedia, 12 vols. (New York and London, 1901-1906; reprint: New York, 1975)

K

= Mishnah, MS. Kaufman A 50; photocopy: Georg Beer, Faksimile-Ausgabe des Mischnacodex Kaufmann A 50 (The Hague, 1929; reprint: Jerusalem, 1969); see Sacks-Hutner, vol. 1, pp. 63, 65-66

Kasovsky, Mishnah

= C.Y. Kasovsky, Thesaurus Mishnae: Concordantiae verborum etc., 4 vols. (Tel Aviv, 1957, rev. 1967)

Kasovksy, Tosefta

= C.Y. Kasovsky, Thesaurus Thosephthae: Concordantiae verborum etc., 6 vols. (Jerusalem, 1932-1961)

Kel.

= Kelim

Ket.

= Ketubot

Kid.

= Kiddushin

Kil.

= Kilayim

Klein

= Israel Klein, tr., The Code of Maimonides. Book Seven, the Book of Agriculture (New Haven, London, 1979)

KM   = <u>Kesef Mishnah</u>. Joseph b. Ephraim Karo (1488-1575).
                      Commentary to Maimonides' <u>Mishneh Torah</u>, in standard eds.
                      of the latter

L   = Palestinian Talmud, MS. Leiden; see Sacks-Hutner, vol. 1, pp.
                      63, 72

Lam. Rabbah   = Lamentations Rabbah

Lev.   = Leviticus

Levy   = Jacob Levy, <u>Neuhebräisches und Chaldäisches Wörterbuch</u>
                      <u>uber die Talmudim und Midraschim</u>, 4 vols. (Leipzig, 1876)

Loew, <u>Flora</u>   = Immanuel Loew, <u>Die Flora der Juden</u>, 4 vols. (Vienna and
                      Leipzig, 1926)

M   = Babylonian Talmud, Codex Munich 95; photocopy: Hermann
                      L. Strack, <u>Talmud Babylonicum Codicis Hebraica Monacensis</u>
                      <u>95</u> (Leiden, 1912; reprint: Jerusalem, 1971); see Sacks-
                      Hutner, vol. 1, pp. 63, 69-70

M.   = Mishnah. All references are to M. Shebiit unless otherwise
                      indicated.

Ma.   = Maaserot

Mak.   = Makkot

Maim., <u>Comm.</u>   = Maimonides (1135-1204), Mishnah Commentary; ed. used:
                      <u>Mishnah im perush rabbenu Moshe ben Maimon</u>, Hebrew
                      translation of the Arabic, introduction and notes by Joseph D.
                      Kappah, I. <u>Zeraim -- Moed</u> (Jerusalem, 1964)

Maimonides,   = <u>Hilkhot Shebiit veyovel</u> codifica-
Sabbatical   tion of laws of Sabbatical and Jubilee years in Maimonides'
                      <u>Mishnah Torah</u>, standard ed., cited by chapter and paragraph
                      (Sabb., 7:13). This ed. is also the source of references to
                      Maimonides, <u>Theft and Lost Objects</u>, <u>Borrower and Lender</u>,
                      and <u>Heave-Offering</u>.

Mandelbaum   = Irving Mandelbaum, <u>A History of the Mishnaic Law of</u>
                      <u>Agriculture: Kilayim</u> (Chico, 1982)

MB   = <u>Minhat Bikkurim</u>. Samuel Avigdor b. Abraham Karlin
                      (nineteenth century), Tosefta commentary (1842), in Romm
                      ed. of Babylonian Talmud

Men.   = Menahot

M.Q.   = Moed Qatan

MR   = <u>Mishnah Rishonah</u>. Ephraim Isaac of Premysla (Poland,
                      nineteenth century), Mishnah commentary (1882), in standard
                      eds. of Mishnah

MS   = <u>Meleket Shelomoh</u>. Solomon b. Joshua Adeni (Yemen and
                      Palestine, c. 1600), Mishnah commentary, in standard eds. of
                      Mishnah

M.S.   = Maaser Sheni

MS.   = manuscript

N	= Mishnah, ed. princ., Naples 1492; see Sachs-Hutner, vol. 1, pp. 64, 81-82
Ned.	= Nedarim
Neusner, Appointed Times	= J. Neusner, A History of the Mishnaic Law of Appointed Times, 5 vols. (Leiden, 1981)
Neusner, Cults	= J. Neusner, ed., Christianity, Judaism and Other Greco-Roman Cults: Studies for Morton Smith at Sixty, 4 vols. (Leiden, 1975)
Neusner, Damages	= J. Neusner, A History of the Mishnaic Law of Damages, 5 vols. (Leiden, 1982)
Neusner, Eliezer	= J. Neusner, Eliezer ben Hyrcanus: The Tradition and the Man, 2 vols. (Leiden, 1973)
Neusner, Holy Things	= J. Neusner, A History of the Mishnaic Law of Holy Things, 6 vols. (Leiden, 1978-79)
Neusner, Judaism	= J. Neusner, Judaism: The Evidence of the Mishnah (Chicago, 1981)
Neusner, Method	= J. Neusner, Method and Meaning in Ancient Judaism (Missoula, 1979), second series (Chico, 1981), third series (Chico, 1981)
Neusner, Modern Study	= J. Neusner, ed., The Modern Study of the Mishnah (Leiden, 1973)
Neusner, Pharisees	= J. Neusner, The Rabbinic Traditions about the Pharisees before 70, 3 vols. (Leiden, 1971)
Neusner, Purities	= J. Neusner, A History of the Mishnaic Law of Purities, 22 vols. (Leiden, 1974-77)
Neusner, "Redaction"	= J. Neusner, "Redaction, Formulation, and Form: The Case of Mishnah," Jewish Quarterly Review 70 (1980), pp. 1-22
Neusner, Tosefta	= J. Neusner, The Tosefta Translated from the Hebrew, 5 vols. (New York, 1977-81)
Neusner, Women	= J. Neusner, A History of the Mishnaic Law of Women, 5 vols. (Leiden, 1979-80)
Nid.	= Niddah
Noth	= Martin Noth, Leviticus (Philadelphia, 1963)
Num.	= Numbers
O^1	= MS. Oxford 366, Babylonian Talmud, Orders Zeraim and Moed; see Sacks-Hutner, vol. 1, pp. 63, 68-69
O^2	= MS. Oxford 393, Mishnah Zeraim, with Maimonides' commentary, autograph; see Sacks-Hutner, vol. 1, pp. 63, 76-77
Oh.	= Ohalot
Orl.	= Orlah

P   = Mishnah, MS. Parma DeRossi 138 (photocopy: Jerusalem, 1970); see Sacks-Hutner, vol. 1, pp. 63, 66-67

Pa   = Mishnah, MS. Paris 328-329 (photocopy: Jerusalem, 1970); see Sacks-Hutner, vol. 1, pp. 64, 79

Par.   = Parah

Peck, Priestly Gift   = Alan J. Peck, The Priestly Gift in Mishnah: A Study of Tractate Terumot (Chico, 1981)

Pes.   = Pesahim

PM   = Penei Moshe. Moses Margolioth (eighteenth century), commentary to the Jerusalem Talmud, Zhitomir ed.

Porter   = J.R. Porter, Leviticus (Cambridge, 1976)

Porton, "Dispute"   = Gary G. Porton, "The Artificial Dispute: Ishmael and Aqiba," in Neusner, Cults, vol. IV, pp. 18-29

Porton, Ishmael   = Gary G. Porton, The Traditions of Rabbi Ishmael, 4 vols. (Leiden, 1976-80)

Press   = Isaiah Press, A Topographical-Historical Encyclopedia of Palestine, 4 vols. (Jerusalem, 1955)

Primus, Aqiva   = Charles Primus, Aqiva's Contribution to the Law of Zeraᶜim (Leiden, 1977)

Qid.   = Qiddushin

R.   = Rabbi

Rabad   = Abraham b. David of Posquieres (ca. 1120-1198), glosses to Maimonides' Mishneh Torah, in standard eds. of the latter

Rashi   = Solomon b. Isaac of Troyes (France, 1040-1105), commentary to Babylonian Talmud, in standard eds. of the latter

RDBZ   = David ibn Zimra (1479-1589), supercommentary to Maimonides' Mishneh Torah, in standard eds. of the latter

R.H.   = Rosh Hashanah

Rosh   = Asher b. Yehiel (Germany and Spain, 1250-1327), Mishnah commentary, in standard eds. of Babylonian Talmud

S   = MS. British Museum 403, Palestinian Talmud, Zeraim, with commentary of Solomon of Sirillo (see Sirillo); see Sacks-Hutner, vol. 1, pp. 63, 73-75

Sa   = Mishnah Zeraim, MS. Sassoon 531; see Sacks-Hutner, vol. 1, pp. 63, 68

Sacks-Hutner   = The Mishnah with Variant Readings, Order Zeraim, 2 vols.; ed. by Nissan Sacks (Jerusalem, 1972-75). All references are to page numbers in vol. 2 unless otherwise indicated.

Sanh.   = Sanhedrin

Sarason, Demai   = Richard S. Sarason, A History of the Mishnaic Law of Agriculture: A Study of Tractate Demai, Part One (Leiden, 1979)

Shab.	= Shabbat
Sheb.	= Shebiit
Sheq.	= Sheqalim
Sens	= Samson b. Abraham of Sens (France, late twelfth - early thirteenth centuries), Mishnah commentary, in Romm ed. of Babylonian Talmud
Sifra	= Sifra debe Rab, hu Sefer Torat Kohanim, ed. I.H. Weiss (Vienna, 1862; reprint: New York, 1946)
Sifre Dt. (or Deut.)	= Siphre ad Deuteronomium, ed. L. Finkelstein, with H.S. Horovitz (Berlin, 1939)
Sifre Numbers	= Siphre de be Rab. Fasciculus primus: Siphre ad Numeros adjecto Siphre Zutta, ed. H.S. Horovitz (Leipzig, 1917; reprint: Jerusalem, 1966)
Sirillo	= Solomon b. Joseph Sirillo (d. 1558), Commentary to Palestinian Talmud, Zeraim (Jerusalem, 1963)
Sot.	= Sotah
Strack	= Hermann Strack, Introduction to the Talmud and Midrash (Philadelphia, 1931; reprint: 1976)
Suk.	= Sukkah
T.	= Tosefta. All references are to T. Shebiit unless otherwise indicated.
T^3	= Mishnah Zeraim, MS. Temani, New York 30/31; see Sacks-Hutner, vol. 2, p. 44
Ta.	= Taanit
Tcherikover	= Avigdor Tcherikover, Hellenistic Civilization and the Jews (Philadelphia, 1959)
Tem.	= Temurah
Ter.	= Terumot
Theophrastus, Enquiry	= Theophrastus, Enquiry into Plants, tr. Sir Arthur Hart, 2 vols. [Loeb Classical Library], (London, 1916), cited by book, chapter and paragraph (Enquiry, I, ii., 9-10)
TK	= Saul Lieberman, Tosefta Ki-fshuta: A Comprehensive Commentary on the Tosefta, I. Order Zeraim, 2 vols. (New York, 1955)
Toh.	= Tohorot
TYT	= Tosephot Yom Tob. Yom Tob Lippmann Heller (Austria, Bohemia, Poland, 1579-1654), Mishnah commentary, in standard eds. of Mishnah
TYY	= Tiferet Yisrael Yakin. Israel b. Gedaliah Lipschütz (Germany, 1782-1860), Mishnah commentary, in Romm ed. of Mishnah

TZ   = Saul Lieberman, ed., The Tosefta According to Codex Vienna
                              with Variants from Codex Erfurt, Genizah MSS. and Editio
                              Princeps, I. Order Zeraim, (New York, 1955)

Uqs.   = Uqsin

V   = Tosefta, MS. Vienna Heb. 20; see Lieberman, TZ pp. 11-12

de Vaux   = Roland de Vaux, Ancient Israel: Its Life and Institutions
                              (New York, 1961)

White   = K.D. White, Roman Farming (Ithaca, 1970)

y.   = Yerushalmi, Palestinian Talmud, ed. princ., Venice (1520-23),
                              cited by tractate, pericope, folio and column (y. Sheb. 3:1
                              [43c]). All references are to y. Shebiit unless otherwise
                              indicated.

Yeb.   = Yebamot

Z   = Mishnah, MS. Paris 362, with commentary of Sens; see
                              Sacks-Hutner, vol. 1, pp. 64, 79-80

Zeb.   = Zebahim

Zuckermandel   = Tosephta, based on the Erfurt and Vienna Codices, with
                              parallels and variants by Dr. M[oses] S[amuel] Zuckermandel
                              (Trier, 1881-82; revised ed. with supplement by Saul
                              Lieberman, Jerusalem, reprint: 1970)

Zahavy, Eleazar   = Tzvee Zahavy, The Traditions of Eleazar ben Azariah
                              (Missoula, 1977)

TRANSLITERATIONS

א	=	'	ל	=	l
ב	=	b	מ, ם	=	m
ג	=	g	נ, ן	=	n
ד	=	d	ס	=	s
ה	=	h	ע	=	c
ו	=	w	פ, ף	=	p
ז	=	z	צ, ץ	=	ṣ
ח	=	ḥ	ק	=	q
ט	=	ṭ	ר	=	r
י	=	y	שׁ	=	ś
כ, ך	=	k	שׂ	=	š

ת = t

Transliterations represent the consonantal structure of the Hebrew word, with no attempt made to vocalize. I do not distinguish between the spirantized and non-spirantized forms of b̲, g̲, d̲, k̲, p̲, and t̲.

INTRODUCTION

I.   The Issues of Tractate Shebiit

Tractate Shebiit (The Sabbatical Year) concerns the special agricultural and commerical restrictions which Israelites living in the Land of Israel must observe every seventh year. To understand the tractate's rules and the conception of the Sabbatical year expressed through them, we must turn first to Scripture's treatment of the topic. This is because, without the institution of the Sabbatical year as it is presented in the Pentateuchal codes, Mishnah's framers could not have created Tractate Shebiit. Since the very notion of a Sabbath for the land, together with the specific set of agricultural restrictions that flow from it, derive from Scripture, we must begin by laying out those rules that constitute the foundation of the tractate's discussion. Only after doing so will we be in a position to appreciate how Mishnah's framers contributed to the institution of the Sabbatical year above and beyond what they inherited from the authors of the Hebrew Bible.

The primary Scriptural injunction concerning the Sabbatical year[1] appears at Lev. 25:1-7, which reads:

1.   The Lord spoke to Moses on Mount Sinai:
2.   Speak to the Israelite people and say to them: When you enter the land that I give you, the land shall observe a sabbath of the Lord.
3.   Six years you may sow your field and six years you may prune your vineyard and gather in the yield.
4.   But in the seventh year the land shall have a sabbath of complete rest, a sabbath of the Lord: you shall not sow your field or prune your vineyard.
5.   You shall not reap the aftergrowth of your harvest or gather the grapes of your untrimmed vines; it shall be a year of complete rest for the land.
6.   But you may eat whatever the land during its sabbath will produce--you, your male and female slaves, the hired and bound laborers who live with you,
7.   and your cattle and the beasts in your land may eat all its yield.

For the priestly writer of Leviticus, the seventh year, like the seventh day, is sanctified. Just as God rested from the work of creation on the seventh day and sanctified it as a day of rest (Gen. 2:3), so too God has designated the seventh year for the land's rest.[2] Implicit in this view is the notion that the Land of Israel has human qualities and needs. It "must observe a Sabbath of the Lord" because, like the people of Israel and their God, it too experiences fatigue and requires a period of repose.[3] The Land of Israel, unlike all other countries, is enchanted, for it enjoys a unique relationship to God and to the people of Israel. That is to say, God sanctified this land by giving it to his chosen people as an exclusive possession. Israelites, in turn, are obligated to work the Land and to handle its produce in accordance with God's wishes. How so? During the year set aside by God for the land's rest, farmers must refrain from those agricultural activities by means of which, in other years, they assert their ownership over the land.[4] In this way, Israelite farmers every seventh year acknowledge that the Land of Israel ultimately belongs to God alone (see Lev. 25:23) and that they enjoy its fruit only as a gift from him.[5] Thus, for the priestly writer, Israelites must observe the restrictions of the seventh year as an affirmation of the unique bond between God's holy land and his chosen people.

A second, quite separate view of the Sabbatical year[6] emerges from Deut. 15:1-3.

1. Every seventh year you shall practice remission of debts.
2. This shall be the nature of the remission: every creditor shall remit the due that he claims from his neighbor; he shall not dun his neighbor or kinsman, for the remission proclaimed is of the Lord.
3. You may dun the foreigner; but you must remit whatever is due you from your kinsmen.

For the author of Deuteronomy, the restrictions of the seventh year concern economic relations between Israelites, rather than the relationship between the people of Israel and their land, as in the Holiness Code. Cancelling outstanding debts every seventh year serves to prevent poor Israelites from becoming destitute if they accumulate debts that they are unable to repay. The principle underlying this social legislation is that all Israelites have a right to share in the material benefits which God provides. Therefore, God takes a special interest in protecting the needy, those who do not enjoy the prosperity promised to all Israelites living in the Land. In particular, he requires Israelites periodically to restore equilibrium to their commercial transactions. They do this by relinquishing their claims over the economically disadvantaged members of the community every seventh year.[7]

As I said at the outset, these Biblical injunctions form the foundation of the entire tractate. Let me now elaborate upon that claim, by describing precisely how Mishnah Shebiit depends upon the rules of Leviticus and Deuteronomy for its fundamental conceptions, its agenda of issues, and its principle of organization. First, as we have seen, the very topic of the tractate, namely the sanctity of the seventh year, is Scriptural. Anyone familiar with Leviticus and Deuteronomy, upon opening our tractate, would have no difficulty in recognizing the institution that generates the tractate's discourse. Mishnah's framers, for their part, merely adopt views spelled out initially in Scripture.

Mishnah's program of inquiry into the Sabbatical year also is fully dictated by the information provided in Leviticus and Deuteronomy. That is to say, no topic raised by Scripture is ignored by Mishnah, and conversely, no concern addressed by Mishnah's framers is foreign to the Biblical sources. Rather, the authorities who stand behind Mishnah Shebiit are content to develop the rules of Leviticus and Deuteronomy by clarifying ambiguities or by addressing issues that Scripture leaves open, as we can readily see by briefly examining the broad outline of the tractate's discussion.

The tractate's opening chapters (One through Six) develop the prohibition of Lev. 25:1-5 against working the land during the seventh year. Where Leviticus speaks only of sowing and reaping in grain fields and in vineyards, Mishnah delineates a full range of forbidden agricultural activities. Mishnah's framers thus treat several other forms of cultivation, such as fertilizing and irrigating, and consider how the restrictions of the Sabbatical year apply to a wide variety of plants. In Chapters Seven through Nine,

Mishnah's authorities elaborate upon the rule of Lev. 25:6-7, that the yield of the seventh year is designated specifically as food for eating. In particular, Mishnah details the restrictions that apply to the handling of this produce and explain how the crop of the Sabbatical year differs from that of other years. The tractate's final chapter refines the injunction of Deut. 15:1-3 that the Sabbatical year cancels outstanding debts. Here Mishnah's framers clarify Scripture by defining the types of financial obligations governed by this rule and by specifying the circumstances under which it does and does not apply. In all, as I have said, the tractate addresses no topic which we could not have predicted on the basis of the verses cited above.

Finally, as we shall see when we consider the outline of the tractate in detail, even the order of Mishnah's discussion is determined by the sequence of the relevant Scriptural verses. Lev. 25:2-5 is taken up in Chapters One through Six, which detail the restrictions that apply to the cultivation of the land. The injunction of Lev. 25:6-7 occupies the second main unit of the tractate, Chapters Seven through Nine. These concern the restrictions that apply to the produce which grows during the seventh year. Chapter Ten, based directly upon the rule at Deut. 15:1-3, is devoted entirely to the cancellation of debts by the Sabbatical year. In conclusion, Mishnah's discussion of the Sabbatical year unfolds entirely within the framework established by Scripture. Its basic conception of the Sabbatical year as a period of rest for the land and of relief for the poor derives solely from the injunctions of Leviticus and Deuteronomy. Its set of concerns with respect to this institution is dictated entirely by information provided by Scripture. Finally, the tractate's organization follows directly the sequence of topics as they are presented in the Pentateuch.

From all that I have said, the reader now may feel that Mishnah Shebiit is merely the parrot of Scripture, repeating in its own idiom, with some minor amplifications, the words of the Biblical texts. Nothing could be further from the truth. Indeed, as I shall explain in a moment, the authors of Leviticus and Deuteronomy would have regarded Tractate Shebiit as a startling and unprecedented document. This is because Mishnah's framers, while treating topics inherited from Scripture, develop a theory of the Sabbatical year that differs in fundamental respects from the one we find in the Pentateuchal codes. Let me begin now to spell out this distinctive theory and to highlight the ways in which it diverges from Scripture's concept of the seventh year.

The cornerstone of Mishnah's theory of the Sabbatical year is that ordinary Israelites, through their actions and perceptions, play a role in determining how the agricultural restrictions of the Sabbatical year apply. That is to say, Israelite farmers and householders have the power within specified limits to decide when, how, and where the laws of the Sabbatical year take effect. To understand this complex and subtle view, we must begin by examining the ways in which Mishnah Shebiit clarifies, extends, and supplements Scripture's rules. As we analyze Mishnah's treatment of specific issues raised by Scripture, we will discover how, in each instance, Mishnah focuses its attention on the impact of Israelites' actions upon the restrictions of the Sabbatical year.

Mishnah's framers, as I indicated earlier, elaborate upon Scripture's injunctions in several ways. First, they refine Scriptural rules by applying a familiar principle to cases not mentioned in the Biblical text. Consider the following example. Mishnah's authorities recognize that, to prevent farmers from working the land during the seventh year, it is not sufficient to prohibit cultivation during that year alone. This is because under certain circumstances activities that a farmer performs during one year will be felt only during the year following. Accordingly, work that a farmer does during the sixth year that necessarily will benefit his field or its produce primarily after the seventh year has begun immediately becomes subject to the laws of the Sabbatical year. For example, people may not plow their fields or orchards toward the end of the sixth year, since this would have the effect of improving the crop that grows during the Sabbatical year alone (M. 1:1, 2:1). By the same token, a farmer may not plant a new tree during the last month of the sixth year, for this sapling would take root only after New Year of the seventh year (M. 2:6). Both of these rules represent straightforward extensions of Scripture's injunctions against cultivating during the seventh year. Yet, by extending the scope of the Sabbatical year in this way, Mishnah's framers introduce into its system of laws a new consider-ation--the actions of the Israelite farmer. When farmers work their land during the sixth year, they set in motion the restrictions pertaining to the seventh year. By taking into account the deeds of Israelite farmers and their long-term impact upon the land, Mishnah moves beyond the strictly calendrical conception of the Sabbatical year presented in Leviticus.[8] That is, while the priestly writer assumes that the Sabbatical year begins at a fixed time, determined only by the succession of seasons and years, in Mishnah's view, Israelites too play a role in determining when the restrictions of the Sabbatical year begin to take effect.

Mishnah's authorities also extend Scripture's rules by establishing a "fence around the law." That is, they enact secondary restrictions designed to preclude people from violating the basic prohibition of Leviticus against working the land during the seventh year. In particular, Mishnah's framers extend the prohibition against cultivating to include activities that would appear to other Israelites to be transgressions, even though they do not actually benefit the land. This prevents innocent observers from mistakenly concluding that such activities are permitted, which might lead them actually to violate the law. For example, people may not remove stones from their fields for use in construction if it would seem to someone else that they were clearing the land for planting (M. 3:5-4:1). Similarly, an Israelite who stockpiles manure during the seventh year must take precautions to avoid the appearance of fertilizing his field (M. 3:1-4). The point in both cases is that appearing to improve the land during the seventh year, even if one does not actually do so, itself constitutes a transgression. These rules, as I indicated, may be viewed merely as secondary expansions of Leviticus' prohibition against working the land during the seventh year. Yet, it is important to note the underlying principle expressed through them. In the view of Mishnah's framers, the way things appear to the average Israelite is decisive. Quite apart from the actual impact of the farmer's activity upon the land, the perceptions of Israelites play an important role in defining what farmers may not do during the seventh year.

Finally, Mishnah's authorities supplement Scripture by addressing issues left open in the Biblical text. The priestly writer of Leviticus, for instance, never specifies the boundaries of the Land of Israel within which the restrictions of the seventh year apply. Mishnah's framers fill out Scripture's law by delineating several distinct geographical regions of the Land within which the various restrictions of the Sabbatical year take effect (M. 6:1). The central principle of their discussion is that those regions which have been inhabited by Israelites for the longest period of time (both before and after the Babylonian exile) are subject to the greatest number of restrictions. Areas of the Land occupied for a shorter period of time (before the exile, but not afterward) are subject to fewer restrictions. Why? Mishnah's authors believe that Israelites, by dwelling in the Land, make it holy. It follows that areas in which Israelites have lived for longer periods of time are holier, and so are subject to more rigorous restrictions. Thus, Mishnah's sages, while addressing a topic dictated in the first place by Scripture, reinterpret the priestly view of the Land's holiness. In Leviticus, the Land is sanctified by God alone, who dwells in it and who has given it to Israel, his people. Mishnah's framers, by contrast, claim that Israelites also play an active part in sanctifying their land.

We see, then, that the authorities who stand behind Mishnah Shebiit, in the course of developing Scripture's rules, interpret the institution of the Sabbatical year in a new and striking way. The recurring theme of the tractate is that the sanctity of the seventh year depends in the last analysis upon the actions and will of the people of Israel. They are the instruments of sanctification. The Israelite farmer when he cultivates his field during the sixth year helps to determine when the restrictions of the seventh year first take effect. The perceptions of Israelites when they see others who appear to be violating the law play a role in defining what, in fact, is permitted behavior. Finally, Israelites, merely by dwelling in their Land, increase its holiness. To be sure, Mishnah's authors, no less than the writer of Leviticus, believe that God has sanctified the seventh year by setting it apart from all others as a year of rest for the Land. And certainly, in Mishnah, as in Scripture, observing the laws of the seventh year affirms God's ownership of the Land, and so, its intrinsic holiness. Yet, in striking contrast to Leviticus, Mishnah affirms that what Israelites do to their land is decisive, the way in which they perceive the world is definitive. The message of Tractate Shebiit, then, is that the sanctity of the seventh year is activated and regulated by the thoughts and deeds of the community of Israel.[9]

Let us now turn briefly from the content of our tractate to its historical context. For it is not sufficient merely to describe Mishnah's theory of the Sabbatical year and to examine the relationship of this structure to its Scriptural foundations. To appreciate fully the views which Mishnah's authorities held, as well as the choices they made, we must address two fundamental questions. First, why did Mishnah's authorities devote a tractate to the subject of the Sabbatical year at all? The significance of the question becomes apparent when we consider that, within the whole range of literature left to us from late antiquity, no other authors dealt with the Sabbatical year.[10] The apocryphal writers, the scribes at Qumran, and the early Christian writers make no mention of it whatsoever. Yet, Mishnah's sages deem it worthy of sustained attention. We wish to know then why Mishnah's framers broke centuries of silence concerning the Sabbatical year in order to reaffirm the priestly conception that the land's holiness endures. Second, we must consider why Mishnah's authorities, having decided to treat the Sabbatical year, chose to say just these things about it. That is, we must attempt to explain why Mishnah, within the framework of a discussion dictated entirely by Scripture's rules and conceptions, continually focuses upon the power of Israelites to affect the application of laws relating to the Sabbatical year. The answers to these questions, I believe, emerge only when we turn to the synchronic context of the document. For, as I shall now explain, Mishnah's worldview constitutes a response to, and a judgment upon, the events of its own time and place.

Mishnah, completed in Palestine at the end of the second century C.E., came into being at a time of crisis in the life of Israel. The Temple, which had stood as the symbol of God's presence in the Land, lay in ruins. The last desperate attempt to rebel against the Roman forces, led by Bar Kokhba (132-135 C.E.), had been crushed. As a thoroughly defeated people, Israelites had little hope of regaining their former political autonomy. Indeed, Israelites living in the Land in the aftermath of this destruction could hardly have avoided the conclusion that God had abandoned them. In the face of this catastrophe, Mishnah's assertion that all Israelites still are obligated to observe the ancient laws of the Sabbatical year represents a striking repudiation of the events of history. For Mishnah's framers, the destruction of the Temple and the loss of Israelite control over the Land did not sever the bond between God, his Land and his people. In their view, the Land of Israel, now war-torn and under foreign domination, still belongs to God. It retains its holiness and so remains subject to the agricultural restrictions set forth in Scripture. Moreover, they believe that the unique relationship between the Land and the people of Israel remains unaltered. Every seventh year Israelites still must leave their fields fallow, thereby affirming that they are God's chosen people, to whom this Land has been given as an eternal possession. This reaffirmation of Scripture's view that the Land and the Sabbatical year are sanctified constitutes a powerful statement that the holy life of Israel is eternal, that it remains essentially unaltered by the forces of history.

Within the context of the situation prevailing in second-century Palestine, we also can make sense of Mishnah's persistent concern with the power of Israelites' actions and perceptions. At a time when Israelites had lost control of their Land, Mishnah affirmed that, merely by dwelling there, they had the power to make it sacred. Although Israelites no longer controlled their destiny, Mishnah asserted that their perceptions determined what ultimately mattered to God. Indeed, by placing Israelites at the very center of its theory of the Sabbatical year, Mishnah emphasizes that they are the sole surviving source of sanctification. They can overcome their defeat on the stage of history through the exercise of their will. In answer to the despair which must have been prevalent among Jews in second-century Palestine, Mishnah offers a message of hope that, despite overwhelming evidence to the contrary, Israelites still can control their world.

II.   The Structure of Tractate Shebiit

Tractate Shebiit's concern with the actions and perceptions of Israelites constitutes the common thread which unites its diverse topics. That is, although the framers' agenda of issues, as I said above, is dictated by Scripture, this fresh and unprecedented concern emerges at each stage of their inquiry. To illustrate this point, let me now briefly review the tractate's main thematic units and indicate how the perceptions and actions of Israelite farmers and householders form the focus of interest at nearly every point in the tractate's discussion.

Unit I deals first with the restrictions that apply to cultivation of the land during the sixth year, before the Sabbatical year itself has begun. The central principle of the entire discussion is that during the sixth year Israelites may not engage in any agricultural activity that would have the primary effect of improving the land or its produce during the seventh year. Thus, in the view of Mishnah's framers, Israelites through their actions during the sixth year can invoke the taboos of the seventh year. The next main segment of the discussion concerns the restrictions that apply to agricultural activity during the Sabbatical year itself. Here, as I explained above, Mishnah's framers rule that Israelites may not perform any agricultural activity that others would perceive to be a transgression. The perceptions of Israelites, in other words, help to define what is forbidden during the seventh year. Moreover, Mishnah's authors make the point that under certain circumstances, Israelites may engage in activities during the seventh year even though they have the secondary effect of improving the soil. So long as their primary intention is to engage in a permitted activity, the secondary effects of their actions are deemed to be of no consequence. Thus, the intentions of Israelites, in part, determine what is permitted during the seventh year as well.

Unit II of the tractate, as we shall see, addresses three quite distinct topics. One of these, which concerns the regions within the Land of Israel in which the laws of the seventh year apply, quite clearly carries forward the thrust of the previous material. The main point, which I elucidated above, is that the regions of the Land in which Israelites have dwelled for longer periods of time are subject during the Sabbatical year to more stringent restrictions. This means that Israelites, by dwelling in the Land, play a role in sanctifying it. Their actions have an impact on where and how the restrictions of the Sabbatical year take effect.

The tractate's third main unit begins by defining the species of produce subject to the special restrictions of the Sabbatical year. Not surprisingly, the actions of Israelite householders again are decisive. Only those types of produce that, during other years of the Sabbatical cycle, Israelites trade in the marketplace--edibles, animal feed, and dyeing matter--are subject to the restrictions of the Sabbatical year. That is to say, species of produce that Israelites generally use during other years for commercial purposes are regarded as ownerless during the Sabbatical year. The law of removal, discussed in detail in Chapter Nine, likewise focuses on the actions and needs of Israelites. This law provides that when all produce of a certain species has disappeared from the field, so that it no longer is available for Israelites to gather, people must physically remove from their homes all produce of that type which they have stored there. This enables all to share in the limited quantity of food that grows uncultivated during the seventh year. The point at which Israelites no longer can gather crops growing in the fields determines when the law of removal takes effect. We see once again that the way in which laws apply depends upon the action of Israelites.

The last segment of the tractate concerns the cancellation of debts by the Sabbatical year. Its central point is that the injunction of Dt. 15:1-3 does not preclude Israelite merchants and laborers from earning their livelihoods. This means that the prohibition against collecting outstanding debts after the beginning of the Sabbatical year does not apply to commercial credit extended by Israelite businessmen. The need of Israelites to conduct their business in a normal fashion defines the scope of Scripture's injunction.

In all, the central point of the tractate is clear. What Israelites do to their land and its crops, the way that they perceive the actions of fellow Israelites, and the intentions with which they perform their agricultural activities--these determine when, how, and where the restrictions of the Sabbatical year apply. To be sure, not every rule in the tractate can be said to make just this point. In this sense, the tractate as a whole does not comprise a cogent essay with a single protracted argument in which each section plays an integral and logically necessary part. Yet, as we have seen, a single point of emphasis unites the tractate's thematically diverse materials into a coherent discussion.

With this point in hand, let us now examine in detail the logic that governs the tractate's arrangement of materials. As I noted, the overall outline follows the order of topics as presented in the Pentateuch. Unit I deals with the prohibition against working the land (Lev. 25:2-5). A transitional unit (II) forms a bridge to a discussion of the restrictions that apply to using produce of the seventh year (Lev. 25:6-7), the topic of Unit III. Unit IV deals with the cancellation of debts by the Sabbatical year, based on the injunction of Dt. 15:1-3. The sub-units that comprise each of these sections of the tractate are delineated in the following outline.

Outline of Mishnah Tractate Shebiit

I.   A Sabbath for the Land: Allowing the Land to rest during the seventh year (1:1-4:10)

    A.   The Sixth Year: The earliest point at which the laws of the seventh year take effect (1:1-2:10)

        1.   Prohibited labor: agricultural activities the effects of which are felt primarily during the seventh year (1:1-2:1)

            a.   Plowing orchards of fully-grown trees (1:1-5)

                1:1   When during the sixth year must farmers cease plowing an orchard? Shammaites: when it no longer will benefit fruit of the sixth year; Hillelites: Pentecost (+ gloss)

                1:2   Definition of the area of land that constitutes an orchard-- three trees in a seah-space that yield 30 maneh of pressed figs

                1:3   Extention of definition at 1:2 to non-fig trees

1:4
A-H Gray areas with respect to the definition at 1:2-3; if one of more of the trees is barren, yet three together yield 30 maneh (+ rules for ten trees and over)

I-L Excursus: Scriptural prooftext for the principle that restrictions of the seventh year may take effect during the sixth year (as at 1:1-4) or continue into the eighth year (+ Ishmael's gloss)

1:5 Further gray areas: three trees belonging to three separate owners (+ Gamaliel's gloss)

b. Plowing orchards of saplings (1:6-8)

1:6 Ten saplings form an orchard and may be plowed until New Year of the Sabbatical year

1:7 Gourds join with saplings to constitute an orchard (+ Simeon b. Gamaliel's gloss)

1:8 Distinguishing saplings from mature trees (dispute: Eleazar b. Azariah, Joshua, Aqiba; + Simeon's rule regarding shoots that sprout from a tree stump)

c. Plowing grain fields (2:1)

2:1 When during the sixth year must farmers cease plowing grain fields?--when people generally quit plowing fields of gourds (+ dispute: Simeon)

2. Permitted labor: agricultural activities the effects of which are felt primarily during the sixth year (2:2-5)

2:2-5 They manure and hoe in fields of chate-melons and gourds until New Year of the Sabbatical year (+ 15 other activities permitted throughout the sixth year; several glosses and disputes)

3. Ambiguous cases: agricultural activities the effects of which might be felt during either the sixth year or the seventh year (2:6-10)

2:6 Planting or transplanting within thirty days of New Year of the Sabbatical year (+ dispute: Judah, Yose/Simeon)

2:7-9 Crops, such as rice and durra, planted during the sixth year which may take root either during that year, and so be subject to the tithes of the sixth year, or during the seventh year, and so be subject to the special rules of that year (+ related glosses and disputes)

2:10
A-G Principle of 2:7-9 applied to gourds that grow from the sixth year into the seventh year

H-K Miscellaneous rules: irrigation of grain fields and flooding of rice paddies during the Sabbatical year

B. The Seventh Year: The prohibition against working the Land (3:1-4:10)

1. Appearing to cultivate the land (3:1-4:1)

a. Appearing to fertilize a field (3:1-3:4)

3:1   When during the seventh year may farmers store manure in their fields without thereby fertilizing the land? (dispute: Meir, Judah, Yose)

3:2   How to store manure in a field without appearing to fertilize (+ dispute, Simeon)

3:3   Further disputes on the proper way to store manure

3:4   The farmer who makes his field into a fold for animals must indicate that he does not do so in order to fertilize the land (+ gloss, Simeon b. Gamaliel)

b.   Appearing to clear the field for planting (3:5-4:1)

3:5   Opening a stone quarry in a field without appearing to clear the land for cultivation

3:6   One who tears down a stone fence in his field may remove only the large stones, to indicate that he is not clearing the land (+ qualifications)

3:7   Further applications of the principle of 3:6

3:8-9   One may repair a terrace during the Sabbatical year to prepare the land for planting during the eighth year, but not during the sixth year, to prepare for the seventh year (+ rules for doing so without appearing to engage in forbidden cultivation)

4:1   Summary of the law on removing stones from a field ("At first they ruled . . . when transgressors increased, they ordained . . .")

2.   Actually cultivating the land (4:2-10)

a.   Prohibited labor: deriving benefit from the transgressions of others (4:2-3)

4:2   A field cultivated during the Sabbatical year may not be sown during the year following (+ two complementary Houses-disputes; Judah's gloss)

4:3   A field plowed by gentiles during the Sabbatical year may be leased for sowing during the eighth year; one plowed by Israelites may not be leased

b.   Permitted labor: activities that farmers may perform even though they have the secondary effect of cultivating the land (4:4-6)

4:4   One who thins out the shoots that grow between olive trees--Shammaites: he cuts them off; Hillelites: he uproots them (+ clarification and qualifications)

4:5   One who truncates an olive or sycamore tree to obtain wood must do so in an abnormal manner, to indicate that he does not cultivate new branches (+ dispute, Judah)

4:6   One who cuts off vines and reeds--Yose the Galilean: he does so in an unusual manner; Aqiba: in the usual way (+ gloss and separate rule for the care of trees)

c.   Appendix: other activities, unrelated to cultivation, that are prohibited during the Sabbatical year (4:7-10)

4:7-9   The prohibition against gathering fruit of the Sabbatical year until it is fully ripe, to assure that it becomes available for its designated use, as food (spelled out for figs, grapes and olives)

4:10   The prohibition against cutting down a fruitbearing tree during the Sabbatical year; Houses dispute the point at which the prohibition takes effect (+ related rule)

The discussion of Leviticus' prohibition against working the land during the seventh year unfolds in a chronological manner. Mishnah's framers first consider the way in which this prohibition applies during the sixth year (A) and then turn to the restrictions that apply during the seventh year itself (B). The sub-units that make up each section of this discussion also are presented in a thoroughly logical fashion. The sages consider first activities that certainly are prohibited (A1), then those that certainly are permitted (A2), and finally, those that may or may not be permitted (A3). Only two units of law appear out of place. M. 1:4A-H presents a Scriptural prooftext for the view that the restrictions of the seventh year can begin to take effect during the sixth year. I cannot explain why this has been placed in the middle of the discussion on plowing orchards during the sixth year, rather than at its beginning or end. The rulings regarding the irrigation of fields and rice paddies, at M. 2:10H-K, do not belong with the restrictions that apply during the sixth year. It appears that they have been placed at the conclusion of A3 only because the cultivation of rice is discussed earlier in the same section. Unit B, concerned with the prohibition against working the land during the seventh year itself, follows a sensible redactional scheme. Before dealing with the prohibition against actually cultivating the land (B2), Mishnah's framers take up the prohibition against appearing to do so (B2), surely a logically prior question.

II.   Transition: Rules related both to working the Land and to using its produce during the seventh year (5:1-6:6)

A.   Special problems: produce that grows over two or more calendar years (5:1-5)

5:1   White figs that appear during the Sabbatical year are subject to the restrictions of the law when they become fully ripe, two years later (+ dispute over Persian figs)

5:2   How to store arum during the Sabbatical year to prevent it from sprouting (dispute: Meir, sages)

5:3   The status of leaves that sprout from arum tubers during the Sabbatical year (dispute: Eliezer, Joshua)

5:4   How to uproot arum during the Sabbatical year; with wooden rakes; Hillelites: with metal spades

5:5   When during the eighth year people may assume that arum in the market no longer is from the crop of the seventh year (dispute: Judah, sages)

B.   Assisting others in harvesting crops or processing produce during the seventh year (5:6-9)

5:6   The artisan may not sell during the Sabbatical year a plow and all its accessories, a yoke, etc., but he may sell a hand sickle, etc. (+ general rule)

> 5:7   The potter sells to an individual only as many containers as one usually needs to store produce gathered in accordance with the law
>
> 5:8   One does not sell a plowing heifer during the Sabbatical year, so Shammaites; Hillelites: permit (+ related rules)
>
> 5:9   A woman lends to a neighbor suspected of violating the laws of the Sabbatical year a sifter, sieve, etc., but she may not sift or grind with her (+ related rules)

C. Geographical areas within which the laws of the Sabbatical year apply (6:1-6)

> 6:1   Three areas delineated with respect to the laws for working the land and using its produce
>
> 6:2   Comparison between laws operative in Land of Israel and Syria
>
> 6:3-4 Digression: produce that grows over two calendar years
>
>> 6:3   Onions that sprouted--if their leaves are dark, they are subject; if light, they are exempt (+ dispute, Hanina b. Antigonos)
>>
>> 6:4   When during the eighth year people may assume that vegetables in the market no longer are from the crop of the seventh year (+ rule for crops that ripen earlier in one part of the Land than in another)
>
> 6:5-6 The ambiguous status of Syria with respect to the importation and exportation of crops of the Sabbatical year and heave-offering

The tractate's second main unit is problematic, for it has no discernable unifying issue or principle. Moreover, there is no apparent logic to the order of the units or, in general, to the order of pericopae within them. The only thematic coherence that I can identify among the three sub-units, which discuss crops that grow over two calendar years (A), benefiting from the transgressions of others (B), and the regions of the Land within which the laws of the seventh year apply (C) respectively, is that all concern both cultivating the land and handling its produce. The redactor thus may have intended this material as a transition between Units I and III. As to the sequence of these sub-units, it may be that A, which deals in part with restrictions that apply during the eighth year, has been placed first so as to carry forward the earlier discussion of restrictions in effect during the sixth, and then during the seventh years. Even this observation, however, does not account for the entire content of A, much of which appears to be an independent essay on the arum plant, nor, of course, does it explain why the same issue, addressed at M. 6:3-4, does not appear together with this material. In all, this segment of the tractate appears to be a catalog of miscellaneous rules placed here as an interlude in the treatment of those larger blocks of materials that address problems of central interest.

III. The Land's Yield: Restrictions governing the use of produce that grows during the Sabbatical year (7:1-9:9)

A. Definitions: species of produce invested with the sanctity of the seventh year (7:1-7:7)

1. General rules (7:1-2)

   7:1   That which is fit for human consumption, animal consumption, or a type of dyeing matter and which is an annual--is subject to the restrictions of the Sabbatical year... and is subject to removal... (+ examples)

   7:2   That which is fit for human consumption, etc., and which is a perennial--is subject to the restrictions of the Sabbatical year... and is exempt from removal... (+ examples)

2. Examples (7:3-7)

   7:3
   A-C   Species of dyeing matter (husk and blossom of pomegranate, etc. are subject to the restrictions of the Sabbatical year, etc.)

   7:3D-7:4Q
        Excursus: rule governing dyeing with produce of the Sabbatical year, followed by unit of law on prohibition against doing business with such produce (+ dispute, Judah and sages)

   7:5-6   Other plants that meet criteria of M. 7:1-2 (Young sprouts of the service tree, ...rose, etc., are subject to the restrictions of the Sabbatical year, etc. + dispute, Simeon)

   7:7   Excursus: rule governing rose petals of the Sabbatical year that become mixed with produce of other years.

B. Restrictions: using the sanctified produce of the Sabbatical year (8:1-9:1)

   1. The proper use (8:1-2)

      8:1   General rule: that which is used during other years exclusively as food for man, may be used only as food.

      8:2   Expansion of the foregoing rule

   2. Improper uses (8:3-7)

      8:3   They do not sell produce of the Sabbatical year in the usual manner, by volume, weight, or fixed quantity (+ Houses-dispute)

      8:4   Using produce of the Sabbatical year to remit a debt

      8:5   Illustration of rule at 8:4

      8:6   Prohibition against processing this produce in the usual manner

      8:7
      A-C   Prohibition against cooking produce of the Sabbatical year in a way that may cause some to be wasted

      8:7
      D-E   Produce of the Sabbatical year never is deconsecrated when exchanged for money or other produce.

   3. Penalties for misusing produce of the Sabbatical year (8:8-9:1)

      8:8   They do not buy slaves, etc., with produce of the Sabbatical year, and if one did, he purchases and eats other produce to replace it.

      8:9
      A-C   Dispute on the principle of 8:8 (Eliezer and sages)

8:9D-8:10G
Excursus: Aqiba's interpretation of Eliezer's position at 8:9B and of another rule of Eliezer's

8:11   Using a bath illegally heated with straw of the Sabbatical year is permitted.

9:1   Types of produce that grow wild may be bought from anyone during the Sabbatical year, for one may assume that they have not been cultivated (+ dispute: Judah, Simeon, sages)

C.   The Law of Removal: sharing equally produce of the Sabbatical year (9:2-9)

1.   The scope of the law: the geographical areas within which it applies (9:2-3)

9:2-3   Delineation of three areas of the Land of Israel and their sub-regions (+ dispute, Simeon)

2.   Ambiguous cases (9:4-7)

9:4   Whether the law applies when vegetables are growing only in private courtyards, where they are not available to all (+ dispute, Yose)

Whether the law applies when winter fruit is growing in the field, which is not available until after the Sabbatical year has ended (+ gloss, Judah)

9:5   How the law applies to three species of produce that have been pickled together in a single jar (dispute: Joshua, Gamaliel, Simeon)

9:6   How the law applies to a single species of produce harvested at two distinct seasons of the year (fresh herbs--when the ground dries out; dry herbs--at the time of the second rainfall)

9:7   Excursus: other rules for which the time of the second rainfall is decisive.

3.   Procedures for observing the law of removal and penalties imposed for violating it (9:8-9)

9:8   When the time for removal comes, one sets aside food for three meals, followed by dispute concerning who eats this food (Judah: only the poor; Yose: also the rich)

9:9   Penalties imposed for retaining produce in one's home after the time for its removal (dispute: Eliezer, sages; + penalty for eating dough of the Sabbatical year from which dough offering has not been removed)

The tractate's third main unit amplifies the injunction of Leviticus 26:6-7, that the produce of the seventh year is designated for eating. Mishnah's framers develop this rule, first by delineating the types of produce to which it applies (A). This serves as the foundation for the subsequent discussion of the rules which prohibit Israelites from using these types of produce for any purpose other than eating (B) and which assure that produce will be distributed equally within the community and so be available for all to use as food (C). The sub-units within each of these sections unfold in a thoroughly logical manner. A1 supplies a pair of general rules that specify the types of produce subject to the special restrictions of the Sabbatical year. This draws in its wake a catalog (A2) of the various species of produce that meet the criteria spelled out at A1. B opens with the general rule that all edible produce of the Sabbatical year may be used only as food. This positive injunction is followed by prohibitions against using this produce for purposes other than eating (B2). The discussion reaches its logical culmination at B3, which considers the consequences of using produce of the seventh year in violation of the rules set forth at B2. C's exposition of the law of removal, which prevents Israelites from stockpiling edible produce and thus depriving others of their access to it, likewise is organized in a straightforward manner. The redactor begins with the broadest consideration, the way in which the law of removal applies within the distinct geographical areas of the Land of Israel (C1). This sets the stage for the discussion of ambiguous cases, at C2. As in the preceding unit, the discussion draws to a close with a consideration of the consequences of violating the rules spelled out above (C3).

IV.   The Cancellation of Debts by the Sabbatical year (10:1-9)

    A.   Definitions: The types of financial obligations subject to cancellation (10:1-2)

        10:1   Sabbatical year cancels loans, not commercial credit. Commercial credit that has been converted into a loan is cancelled (+ Judah and Yose gloss)

        10:2   Other debts not cancelled by the Sabbatical year

    B.   The prozbul: a document by which a lender turns outstanding loans over to a court for collection and thereby circumvents Scripture's prohibition against his collecting this money after the Sabbatical year has begun (10:3-7)

        1.   The origin and substance of the prozbul (10:3-4)

            10:3   Prozbul is not cancelled, followed by the story of Hillel's invention of this institution

            10:4   Text of the prozbul

        2.   Conditions for writing a prozbul (10:5-7)

            10:5
            A-D   Prozbul may be pre-dated, but not post-dated (+ contrasting rule for bonds)

            E-F   Each creditor must write his own prozbul, though a single document may include loans owed by several borrowers

            10:6   The debtor must own real estate (+ qualifications)

            10:7   What constitutes real estate for purposes of writing a prozbul

    C.   Repaying debts cancelled by the Sabbatical year (10:8-9)

        10:8   The creditor must verbally acknowledge that he has no legal right to this payment.

        10:9   The debtor who repays his loans, even though he has no legal duty to do so--the sages are pleased with him (+ related rules)

The tractate closes with an essay, entirely independent of the foregoing, devoted to the cancellation of debts by the Sabbatical year, the topic of Dt. 15:1-3. The main principle is that the Sabbatical year does not cancel payments which would prevent Israelite merchants from conducting their business. This central refinement of Scripture's rule, spelled out at A, lays the groundwork for a discussion of a legal fiction, the prozbul, by which Israelites circumvent Scripture's injunction. The section on the prozbul, which comprises the bulk of this unit of the tractate, begins logically with the purpose and nature of the document (B1) and proceeds to the details of when and how it may be written (B2). The essay concludes, appropriately, with a discussion (C) of repaying debts even after the Sabbatical year has cancelled the debtor's obligation to do so. That is, having delineated the limits of Scripture's injunction and established a procedure for circumventing it, Mishnah's framers close by acknowledging the value of exceeding one's legal duty by repaying a debt which the Sabbatical year has cancelled.

Standing back from the outline of the tractate as a whole, it is apparent that there is a deep tension between its structure and its underlying message. For the tractate throughout addresses topics drawn from Scripture and, indeed, discusses them in an order dictated by the sequence of Scriptural verses. Yet, its point of emphasis is strikingly non-Scriptural. The view that Israelites control the sanctity of the seventh year, suggested nowhere in the Hebrew Bible, emerges again and again as the central point of Mishnah's discussion. So we see that Mishnah's authors both reaffirm and transform the legacy that they inherit from the Pentateuch. For them, Scripture's laws concerning the Sabbatical year provide the structure and agenda for their treatment of the topic, surely a powerful assertion that the priestly conception of the land's holiness, embodied in Leviticus' injunctions, remains deeply embedded in their thought. Nonetheless, the worldview that emerges from the details of their laws is by no means confined to the views implicit in Scripture. Rather Mishnah's framers invest Scripture's laws with new meaning and reformulate them to convey their own message.

III. The Exegesis of Tractate Shebiit: An Explanation of this Translation and Commentary

The conclusions I have just presented about the meaning and structure of Mishnah Shebiit derive from my exegesis of the tractate's rules. This commentary, its methods and the larger purpose that it is designed to serve, now must be explained. To begin at the heart of the matter, my goal in this study is to discern the meaning of Mishnah Shebiit for those late second-century authorities who created the document. That is, I claim to present the original meaning of Mishnah's rules, the thoughts its authors intended their words to convey. Let me unpack this fundamental assertion by explaining what it is that I claim to know and how I claim to know it. The answers to these questions constitute the epistemological foundations of my work, on which rests the validity of the entire interpretive enterprise.

The methodology of my commentary rests upon two premises. First, I claim that Mishnah's framers wrote their rules to convey some determinate meaning. The message of this text is a function of the ideas that its authors wanted to express, which must be distinguished from other interpretations which the language of the text will support, but which its authors did not intend to convey. Second, I maintain that there are objective criteria, provided by the language of the text itself, which enable us to render judgments about the original meaning of Mishnah's rules. It is this point which I want now to clarify, for it is one thing to assert that Mishnah's rules have some determinate meaning, and quite another to propose, as I have, that this meaning is within our grasp. In particular, I wish to explain how I think it is possible for us to discover from the character of the document the specific ideas which Mishnah's framers wanted to communicate to their audience.

Mishnah's framers express everything they say in a few highly formulaic grammatical constructions and well-defined literary forms. These clearly indicate the way in which they meant their words and sentences to be construed. How so? First, they present all of their rules in only a small number of set syntactic formulations (e.g., "one who does x, lo, he is exempt").[11] These syntactic constructions mark the beginning and end of each complete thought, thereby delineating distinct phrases and sentences. More important, Mishnah's framers arrange sequences of these syntactic units in a limited number of fixed patterns (e.g., "one who does x is liable, one who does y is exempt"). These literary forms clearly define the relationship of one thought or rule to another and so point to the issue which each unit of law was constructed to address. In all, Mishnah's authorities carefully specify the meaning which they wished their words to convey by imposing upon them a very small repertoire of syntactic patterns and literary forms. It follows that analysis of these literary conventions is a necessary step in discovering the meaning of the ideas expressed through them.[12] Let me now explain in detail how this literary analysis works.

We begin by examining the dispute, a common Mishnaic form consisting of a superscription, followed by two or more contrasting rulings.

A.   A hide which one rubbed with oil of the Sabbatical year --
B.   R. Eliezer says, "It must be burned."

C.   But sages say, "One must [purchase and] eat [produce] of equal value." (M. 8:9)

The importance of the dispute is that it illustrates how Mishnah's formal traits provide the principles required for the exegesis of its rules. First, the superscription (A) points to the legal issue that gives rise to the dispute. In the case at hand, the owner of the hide has misused this oil, for he should have consumed it (see M. 8:2). Second, the contrasting rulings themselves (B, C) express alternative ways of resolving the problem raised by the superscription. Finally, from the statement of the problem, together with the opposing rulings, we can deduce the principle that the dispute as a whole was constructed to convey. That is, the juxtaposition of two alternative responses to a single issue points toward the principle upon which the disputants agree, the common ground from which their disagreement arises. In the case at hand, the main point of the entire discussion is that people who misuse produce of the Sabbatical year must be penalized for their violation of the law. In short, to glean the information which this unit of law was intended to provide, one must understand the function of the dispute form, namely, the fixed relationships of each opinion to the other and of both to the superscription. This analysis of Mishnah's particular literary conventions enables the exegete to discover the meaning of its rules.

A second common literary form employed by Mishnah's authors is the list. As its name implies, this is composed of a series of items subsumed under a single super-scription, as at M. 5:6:

A.   These are the tools which the artisan is not permitted to sell during the Sabbatical year:
B.   1.   a plow and all its accessories,
      2.   a yoke,
      3.   a pitchfork,
      4.   and a mattock.

The structure of the list indicates the manner in which its framer wishes us to interpret it. By grouping diverse items beneath a single rubric, the redactor indicates that one principle unites the list. The exegete's task then is to determine what the items on the list have in common and how the group as a whole relates to the prohibition set forth in the superscription. This will yield the principle which the list was constructed to convey. As in the case of the dispute, formal analysis serves as a tool for discerning the meaning of Mishnah's rules.

The framers of our tractate do not always express their ideas in the form of disputes and lists. Very often the simple repetition or contrast of syntactic constructions guides us to the point of the law. For example, we sometimes find a series of rulings composed of three distinct protases each followed by a single repeated apodosis. This is the case at M. 10:9, which exhibits the following formulary pattern:

one who does x--the sages are pleased with him
one who does y--the sages are pleased with him
one who does z--the sages are pleased with him

By presenting these cases in parallel language, Mishnah's framer tells us that he views all three as illustrative of a single principle. To discover the point of the unit as a whole, we must focus our attention on the feature common to all three cases. Similarly, contrasting

syntactic constructions illustrated by the rule at M. 8:6, also help the exegete to discern
the meaning of Mishnah's rules.

  A.   Figs of the Sabbatical year--
  B.   they do not dry them in the drying place,
  C.   but one does dry them in a deserted place.
  D.   They do not trample grapes in a vat,
  E.   but one does trample them in a trough.

The contrasting syntactic constructions at B and C ("they do not do x, but one does do y"),
repeated at D and E, carry the message of the unit as a whole. To discover the point
which Mishnah's authors wanted to convey by framing matters in just this way, we must
determine how a "drying place" (B) differs from a "deserted place" (C) and how that
distinction parallels the difference between a "vat" (E) and a "trough" (F). We see again
how Mishnah's framers articulate legal principles through the use of formulaic constructions and why we, in turn, must allow these literary conventions to guide us to their main
point.

        From all that I have said, it now should be clear that to understand Mishnah's rules
we must allow its mode of expression to dictate our methods of interpretation. This
principle forms the cornerstone of my commentary, in which I systematically analyze the
literary structure of the tractate from its smallest to its largest components. This
analysis proceeds in four stages, which now may be explained in detail.

        My fresh translation of the tractate forms the first part of my form-analytical
commentary.[13] Its goal is to reveal to the English reader the highly formalized traits of
Mishnah's rhetoric which, as I indicated, are of critical importance for the interpretation of its rules. I accomplish this by replicating, insofar as English grammar permits,
the word-order of the Hebrew and by identifying, with a letter of the English alphabet,
each separate syntactic unit of the pericope. How does this constitute a commentary on
the text? First, by breaking down each pericope into its component stichs, I show how the
very formulaic syntax of the text indicates the beginning and end of each discrete
thought. This enables me to recognize the literary forms and formulary patterns,
discussed above, which the redactor has used to convey his point. In addition, isolating
each separate syntactic unit highlights the presence of doublets or triplets, that is, series
of rules expressed in a single, repeated syntactic pattern. These groupings of parallel
rules, which I have marked for easy identification with Roman numerals, were formulated
by Mishnah's authors to be read as one extended unit of law. Finally, by exposing the
formal traits of Mishnah's rules, I am able readily to discern those stichs which break with
the established patterns. These generally are either glosses, added to clarify or develop a
point, or independent rules, appended to the central unit of law because they are relevant
to its theme.

        This literal translation is supplemented in a few important ways. To begin with the
most obvious addition, I supply in brackets certain explanatory language not in the Hebrew
text. These interpolations serve to create coherent English sentences by making explicit
in English what is implied in the Hebrew. Frequently I also indicate in brackets the legal
principles that stand behind Mishnah's rules. This alerts the reader to the issues at hand,
which I discuss at greater length in the comment following the translation of each

pericope. Second, Hebrew words or phrases which do not lend themselves to literal translation have been transliterated in parentheses. Here, of necessity, my translation is idiomatic. Finally, I indicate in parentheses important textual variants.[14] Those which have a bearing on the meaning of Mishnah's rules are discussed either in the comment to that pericope or in the footnotes.[15] In short, my translation gives the reader full access to the textual and linguistic problems of the document, to the basic conceptions of the law, and to the literary forms through which they are expressed.[16]

Following my translation of each pericope, the reader will find my extended discussion of the law. This generally begins with a clear statement of the central point of that pericope. After spelling out what I believe to be the meaning of the law, I retrace my steps, indicating how these conclusions emerge from my literary analysis of the rules and from their conceptual content. In particular, I draw attention to the literary forms and formulatory patterns exhibited by the pericope and show how these guide my interpretation of its rules. I also bring to bear on the pericope at hand any principles or other rules, not explicitly stated, which the reader needs to know in order to understand the law. Where more than one reading of the law is defensible on formal and substantive grounds, I spell out the exegetical possibilities in detail. I then offer my own judgment about the point which Mishnah's authorities most likely wished this rule to express. Finally, whenever possible, I point out the wider implications of the law by showing how the rules under discussion contribute to our understanding of the worldview of Mishnah's framers.

Explaining the main point of each discrete pericope sets the stage for the next step of my exegesis. This entails examining the ways in which Mishnah's redactor has arranged individual pericopae into larger blocks of material.[17] As the outline of the tractate provided above indicates, Mishnah Shebiit presents a well-organized exposition of a series of logically arranged topics. This means that Mishnah's redactors often express their legal principles as much by the way they organize larger units of law as by the manner in which they formulate individual rules. To understand fully the point of any individual pericope, then, we must indicate how it contributes to the unfolding of the larger thematic unit of which it is an integral part. Moreover, viewing a pericope in its larger context often provides clues to the meaning of a rule which otherwise would remain obscure. That is, when a particular ruling is open to more than one interpretation, its setting often indicates the point its redactor intended to make. My expositions of the tractate's thematic units appear in the chapter introductions, so that the reader can get an overview of the topics and issues under discussion before turning to the details of the individual rules. It should be noted, however, that these thematic units do not invariably correspond to the chapter divisions as they appear in standard printed texts of Mishnah. These traditional chapter markings, by dividing the tractate into manageable sections, merely provide periodic opportunities to review the unfolding of the tractate's discussion.

My explanation of the meaning of Mishnah Shebiit as a whole, presented in earlier sections of this introduction, constitutes the final step in my interpretation of the tractate. Here I lay out the tractate's structure, by providing a detailed outline which delineates its thematic units. This enables us to grasp the central points of the tractate's entire discussion, the message its framers wished to convey, by dealing with these specific topics and issues and by organizing them in precisely this way. Yet, there is one further stage of analysis, for to understand the tractate as a whole we must explain not only its content, but also its historical context. This is, we must attempt to relate the central points of the tractate's discussion to the historical setting in which its authors lived. We wish specifically to explain both how Mishnah's authorities viewed their own cultural heritage, embodied in Scripture's laws of the Sabbatical year, and how their interests and viewpoints were shaped by the events of their own day. By placing the content of the tractate in a diachronic and synchronic context, we gain important evidence about the worldview of Mishnah's framers. These conclusions, then, represent the fruit for the historian of Judaism of the extended exegetical work that occupies the bulk of this study.

The methodology of my commentary, now fully exposed, represents only one approach, among others, to the interpretation of the tractate's rules. Indeed, Mishnah Shebiit, together with the rest of Mishnah, has been the subject of centuries of rabbinic commentary from the second century to our own day. Let me now place my commentary in the context of this long exegetical tradition, by explaining how my methods and goals differ from those of all previous commentators. To begin with, they approach the text with a set of assumptions quite different from my own. In particular, they invariably view Mishnah as one part of the eternally valid oral law. To them, the whole of Mishnah, no less than Scripture, represents the word of God as communicated to Moses, subsequently transmitted to scribes and sages, and ultimately recorded by Mishnah's authorities. This theological orientation generates the questions they deem central to the exegesis of the tractate, which differ from the issues I address in two important respects. First, the particular literary form in which Mishnah expresses itself, so central to my commentary, is of no particular concern to them. Since the peculiar formal traits of Mishnah's rules bear no special meaning for these exegetes, they feel free to interpret pericopae in isolation from their particular setting within the document. This means that groups of laws which have been formulated as a single unit often are treated as a series of essentially unrelated rules. As a result, the point that a particular rule makes within a larger literary and conceptual construction is lost, as is an overview of the structure and message of the tractate as a whole. Moreover, rabbinic exegetes make no effort to explain the document as a whole in its historical context. Since, for them, Mishnah is merely one repository, among others, of revealed law (halakhah), questions about the relationship between the ideas of Mishnah's authors and the historical setting in which they lived are of no consequence. My commentary, on the other hand, focuses exclusively on these literary and historical questions in an attempt to discover the meaning which Mishnah's rules held for their authors.

It also is important to note that traditional rabbinic commentators feel compelled to raise certain questions which I do not deem critical. For instance, they often attempt to reconcile apparent contradictions between one rule and another. Proving the internal consistency of Mishnah's rules is of the utmost importance for those who assume that Mishnah records revealed law. By the same token, these exegetes often focus on the implications of one legal principle for the scope and application of other rules, whether elsewhere in the tractate, or in other tractates altogether. In my commentary, by contrast, I am content to point out divergent positions held by Mishnah's authorities and to indicate the divergent theories or principles which they represent as they appear in their present context.

But the reader should not conclude from this comparison that the traditional commentators make no contribution to my exegesis of the tractate. Indeed, insofar as I share with them the desire to understand the logic of Mishnah's rules, I am indebted to their comments. Often my interpretation of a difficult passage relies upon the insights of the many exegetes and legal authorities who have gone before me. Their knowledge of the whole of Mishnaic law has enabled me to make sense of rules which otherwise would have remained obscure. Moreover, they often present the entire range of exegetical possibilities for a given unit of law. In such cases, I can only attempt to show, on form-analytical grounds, why one reading more likely represents the view of Mishnah's framers than another. In all, my commentary both builds upon the work of these traditional commentaries and contributes to the exegesis of the tractate by bringing to the text an agenda of fresh literary and historical critical questions.[18]

One traditional commentary, Tosefta Shebiit, has been of particular value to me and so deserves special attention. This compilation of laws, redacted between the third and fifth centuries C.E., stands closer to Mishnah than any other rabbinic legal text in time and literary form. Specifically, it both employs Mishnah's peculiar rhetorical style and attributes rules to Mishnaic authorities. It most often contributes to our understanding of Mishnah by citing and glossing its rules, thereby clarifying a point which Mishnah does not make explicit. Frequently, Tosefta also provides rulings, independent of those in Mishnah, which apply principles elicited from Mishnah's rules to new sets of facts. In doing so, it helps us to pinpoint the meaning of Mishnah's laws and to specify the principles expressed through them.

For these reasons, I have translated and commented upon the whole of Tosefta Shebiit, placing each pericope of Tosefta after the unit of Mishnah to which it is relevant.[19] My translation of Tosefta employs the same methods which I use in translating Mishnah, with one minor exception. I underscore direct quotes of passages from Mishnah in order to draw the reader's attention to the many points at which Tosefta cites and then clarifies Mishnaic rules. My comments to Tosefta have a rather limited purpose, to explain how each of its pericopae helps us to understand the related pericope of Mishnah. Other issues related to the interpretation of Tosefta's rules, including questions of its formulation and redaction, are addressed only insofar as they serve this goal. My interpretation of Tosefta and its relationship to Mishnah has benefitted greatly from Saul Lieberman's critical text of the document, TZ, and his masterful commentary to it, TK.

CHAPTER ONE

Shebiit Chapter One

The chapter begins a protracted essay on the prohibition against working the Land during the seventh year. The foundation of Mishnah's discussion is the injunction of Lev. 25:4 that, ". . .in the seventh year the land shall have a sabbath of complete rest." Mishnah's authors begin their treatment of this law in a logical manner, by considering the earliest point during the Sabbatical cycle when the restrictions of the seventh year could take effect. As we shall see, the framers of our tractate assume that late in the sixth year, even before the Sabbatical year itself has begun, farmers may not engage in certain agricultural activities. Let me begin by explaining this striking conception, for though it underlies the chapter before us, Mishnah's framers never fully articulate it. The central principle is that Israelites may not work the Land during the sixth year if their labor will benefit the ground or its yield during the Sabbatical year itself. Any agricultural activity that has the effect of improving the Land during the seventh year would violate Scripture's injunction that during this year the Land must have "a sabbath of complete rest." For example, during the final months of the sixth year the farmer may not plow a field of trees, for this would have the effect of strengthening the trees and thereby improving the crop of the seventh year. This is forbidden because, as I have said, Mishnah's authorities forbid Israelite farmers from engaging in any labor that would benefit the Land or its yield during the seventh year.

This general notion, known in later rabbinic sources as tosefet shebiit (lit., "the addition to the Sabbatical year"), underlies the question posed at M. 1:1A and generates the problematic of the chapter.[1] At what point during the sixth year must the farmer quit plowing his orchard? The answer, endorsed by both the Hillelites and Shammaites, is that farmers may continue to plow only until they begin to harvest the fruit of the sixth year. After this time, further plowing clearly will not benefit the fruit of the sixth year, which already is ripe and ready for harvest. Rather, the farmer's plowing will improve only the crop of the Sabbatical year, which is forbidden (M. 1:1). This opening unit draws in its wake two ancillary questions. First, we wish to know how to determine the boundaries of an orchard, that area of land within which the prohibition against plowing applies (M. 1:2-5). Second, we investigate how orchards of fully-grown trees differ from orchards of saplings (M. 1:6-8). With the central point and overall structure of the chapter in hand, we turn now to a brief summary of the details of the law.

An orchard is defined as an area the size of a seah-space (approximately 784 square meters)[2] which contains at least three trees. This tract of land constitutes a single unit because the trees growing within it extend their roots throughout this area. Plowing anywhere within this plot of land aerates the roots of the trees and is permitted only until the farmer begins harvesting the crop of the sixth year. This basic definition is subject to an important qualification. Trees that produce a small yield or trees that are unevenly distributed within the seah-space do not fill the entire area with their roots. In such cases, the tract as a whole does not constitute an orchard, so that farmers are not free to plow until harvest time throughout the entire seah-space. Instead, they may plow only the land immediately surrounding each tree, where the roots of that tree are located (M. 1:2-1:4, 1:5).

At M. 1:6-7, the discussion shifts to fields of saplings. Young trees, unlike mature ones, have small, delicate root systems. Mishnah's authorities thus rule that ten saplings, which together extend their roots throughout a seah-space, constitute an orchard. Moreover, farmers may plow orchards planted with saplings and gourds until New Year of the Sabbatical year. This insures that these delicate plants do not die during the dry, summer months (M. 1:6-7). The chapter concludes appropriately with a discussion of the point at which saplings become fully-grown trees (M. 1:8).

As we have seen then the redactor of this chapter has arranged his discussion in a thoroughly logical fashion. He begins by introducing the prohibition of plowing an orchard late in the sixth year, turns next to the definition of an orchard, and finally, considers special types of orchards, those that contain saplings. This well-structured essay is interrupted only at M. 1:4I-L, which offers Ex. 34:21 as the Scriptural prooftext for the concept of tosefet shebiit. I cannot account for the placement of this unit in the middle of this discussion, rather than at the outset or conclusion.

1:1

A.   Until what time do they plow an orchard [of fruitbearing trees] (śdh 'yln) during the
       sixth year [of the Sabbatical
       cycle] (ᶜrb šbyᶜyt)?

B.   The House of Shammai say, "[One may continue to plow] so long as [the plowing
       continues] to benefit the produce (yph lpry) [of the sixth year. That is, after the
       crop of the sixth year has ripened and been harvested, the farmer no longer may
       plow in his orchard]."

C.   But the House of Hillel say, "[One may continue to plow] until Pentecost [of the
       sixth year]."

D.   And the opinion of the one is close to the opinion of the other.

M. 1:1 (b. M.Q. 3b)

During the sixth year of the Sabbatical cycle, Israelites may not engage in agricultural activities that have the effect of benefiting the Land during the following year. Improving a field in this way would violate the injunction of Lev. 25:1-7, that during the Sabbatical year the Land of Israel must be allowed to rest. This notion, that certain prohibitions against working the Land during the seventh year start to take effect even before that year beings, gives rise to the Houses-dispute at A-B vs. C. Both parties agree that late in the sixth year a farmer may not plow his orchard. This would aerate the roots of the trees and so improve the harvest of the following year. The Houses' disagreement focuses upon a secondary issue: at what point during the sixth year does plowing in an orchard become forbidden? According to the Shammaites, as soon as a farmer begins to harvest the crop of the sixth year, he may no longer plow in his orchard. Any further cultivation would benefit only the yield of the Sabbatical year, which is forbidden. It follows from the Shammaite position that the prohibition against plowing will take effect at different times in various locations, as the farmers of each region begin harvesting their orchards. Since the Shammaites recognize that fruit ripens and is harvested earlier in some orchards than in others, they do not set a date at which farmers must stop plowing. The Hillelites, C, on the other hand, rule that after Pentecost of the sixth year all farmers must stop plowing their orchards. This marks the official beginning of the new harvest season, when Israelites bring the first fruit of the new crop as a gift to the Temple (see M. Bik. 1:3). After Pentecost of the sixth year a farmer may not plow his orchard, for this would benefit only the crop which ripens during the Sabbatical year. The Hillelites, in contrast to the Shammaites, wish to assure that Israelites throughout the Land begin observing the restrictions of the Sabbatical year at the same time. They therefore fix a specific date when the prohibition against plowing takes effect.

Despite the opposing positions of the Houses, there is little practical difference between their views, as the gloss at D notes. This is because Pentecost, in fact, is when farmers generally begin to harvest their fruit.

1:2-3

A. What is [considered] an orchard [and so may not be plowed after Pentecost of the sixth year,[3] in accordance with the rule of M. 1:1]?

B. Any [field in which there are at least] three trees [growing] within a <u>seah</u>-space, [that is within an area large enough to plant a <u>seah</u> of seed].[4]

C. If [the trees referred to at B] are capable of producing a loaf of pressed figs weighing sixty <u>maneh</u> according to the Italian [measurement,[5] such that the roots of these trees extend throughout the entire area,]

D. they plow the entire <u>seah</u>-space for [the trees'] benefit. [That is, the entire area constitutes an orchard. In accordance with the rule of M. 1:1, a farmer may plow this land only until Pentecost of the sixth year.]

E. [But if the trees referred to at B yield] less than this [amount of produce, such that their roots do not fill the <u>seah</u>-space,]

F. they plow [until Pentecost of the sixth year] for [the trees'] benefit only as far out [from each tree] as [the place where] the gatherer [stands] with his basket behind him. [That is, only the area in the immediate vicinity of these trees, where their roots are located, is subject to the prohibition against plowing in an orchard after Pentecost. The remainder of the <u>seah</u>-space, where the trees' roots do not reach, is subject to the rules governing the plowing of grain fields during the sixth year; see M. 2:1.]

M. 1:2

G. The same [law, C-F, applies] both to non-fruitbearing trees ('yln srq) [which do not yield edible produce]⁶ and to fruitbearing trees [other than the fig trees referred to at C-F]--

H. [in either case,] they view them as if they were fig trees. [That is, they compare the size of these trees to that of fig trees in order to apply the rule of C-F].

I. If [three of these trees growing in a seah-space are the same size as three fig trees, which would be] capable of producing a loaf of pressed figs weighing sixty maneh according to the Italian [measurement,]

J. [the rule of C-D applies, so that] they plow the entire seah-space for [the trees'] benefit [until Pentecost of the sixth year].

K. [If three of these trees are the size of fig trees which would produce] less that this [amount of produce,]

L. [the rule of E-F applies, such that] they plow them [until Pentecost of the sixth year] only according to [the trees'] need, [that is, only in the immediate vicinity of the trees, where their roots are located].⁷

M. 1:3

A farmer must know how to determine the boundaries of his orchard, since it is forbidden for him to plow within this area of land after Pentecost of the sixth year. As we know from M. 1:1, further plowing after this time will have the effect of benefiting the roots of his trees and so will improve the crop of the seventh year. This would be forbidden. Since the primary concern of Mishnah's authorities is to prevent the farmer from aerating the roots of his trees, only that area of land which is filled by the trees' roots is regarded as part of the orchard.⁸ This conception of the boundaries of an orchard is presented in the rule at B and further developed in the discussion that follows, at C-F and G-L. Mishnah's framers claim that three trees planted within a seah-space of land will spread their roots throughout that entire area. Plowing anywhere within this plot of land therefore would benefit the roots of the trees. This is forbidden after Pentecost of the sixth year, in accordance with the rule of M. 1:1.

At C-F, Mishnah's authorities refine this basic definition by distinguishing large trees, with expansive root systems, from smaller ones, the roots of which remain close to the trees. The extensiveness of the trees' roots is indicated by their yield. If three fig trees produce a combined yield of 60 maneh of dried pressed figs, a farmer may assume that their roots extend throughout the entire seah-space. Since plowing anywhere within this area would benefit the trees, he may not do so after Pentecost of the sixth year (C-D). Trees which yield less produce have smaller root systems. Since their roots extend only a short distance, the prohibition against plowing after Pentecost applies only to the area near the base of each tree (E-F).

The definition of an orchard presented at C-D, as we have seen, refers explicitly to the yield of fig trees. This poses a problem, for it is not clear how to determine the size of orchards containing other types of trees. The answer, provided at I-L, is that one compares the size of these trees to the size of fig trees which would be capable of producing the quantity of fruit specified at C. We then apply the rule of C-F to all other types of trees.

1:4

A.   [If] one [of three trees planted in a seah-space, as at M. 1:2-3,] yields a loaf of pressed figs [weighing sixty maneh according to the Italian measurement,] but [the other] two do not [yield anything,]

B.   or [if] two [of the trees] yield [the required amount] and [the other] one does not [yield anything]--

C.   they plow for [each of] them only according to their need. [That is, the prohibition against plowing after Pentecost of the sixth year applies only in the vicinity of the trees themselves, not to the seah-space as a whole.]

D.   [This law applies in cases of] (^{C}d $\v{s}$yhyw) from three to nine trees.

E.   [If] there were ten [trees,]

F.   [or] upwards of ten,

G.   whether or not they [together] yield [the required amount]--

H.   they plow the entire seah-space for [the trees'] benefit. [It is assumed that ten or more trees will extend their roots throughout the seah-space. This area in its entirety constitutes an orchard and so may be plowed only until Pentecost of the sixth year.]

I.   [I-J provide a Scriptural prooftext for the notion that some restrictions of the Sabbatical year apply during the sixth year, see M. 1:1A-1:4H, or during the eighth year, see Chapters Eight and Nine.] As it says in Scripture, ["For six days you shall work, but on the seventh day you shall cease work;] even at plowing time and harvesting time you shall cease work" (Ex. 34:21).

J.   There is no need [for Scripture] to mention plowing and harvesting during the Sabbatical year [itself, for these expressly are prohibited by Lev. 25:4-5]. Rather, [Ex. 34:21 refers to] plowing during the sixth year [the benefits of which] extend into (nkns) the Sabbatical year and to harvesting during the Sabbatical year [the crop of which continues to be subject to certain restrictions] into (yws') the year following the Sabbatical; [see Chapters Eight and Nine].

K.   R. Ishmael says, "[This is not the correct interpretation of Ex. 34:21. Rather, the verse teaches us that] just as plowing, [which] is a voluntary act, [is prohibited on the Sabbath,] so [only an act of] harvesting [which likewise] is voluntary [is prohibited on the Sabbath].

L.   "This excludes harvesting the first sheaf (h^{C}mr) (Pa adds: which is obligatory) [and is therefore permitted even on the Sabbath; see M. Men. 10:9]."

M. 1:4 (I-J: b. R.H. 9a; I-L: b. M.Q. 3b; b. Mak. 8b)

In the opening unit of law, A-C+D-H, three trees planted within a seah-space in the aggregate yield a loaf of pressed figs, yet one or more of these trees produces no figs whatsoever. The question is whether the seah-space in which these trees are growing constitutes an orchard, as defined at M. 1:2-3. On the one hand, the combined yield of the three trees may be decisive. In that case, the trees in question do form an orchard, for together they produce the requisite quantity of figs (M. 1:2C). The seah-space as a whole then should be subject to the prohibition against plowing after Pentecost of the sixth year. On the other hand, the fact that one or two of these trees are barren may be determinative. Since the roots of a barren tree extend only a short distance from its base, some portion of this seah-space is not filled with the roots of any of the three trees. The prohibition against plowing therefore should apply only to the area immediately surrounding each tree. The rule at C, which resolves the ambiguity, makes the point that the extent of the trees' roots is probative. Since the roots of these trees together do not fill the entire seah-space, the tract does not constitute an orchard. The prohibition against plowing after Pentecost applies only in the area around the base of each tree, where its roots are located.

Let us stand back from this unit of law for a moment and see how it qualifies the basic definition of an orchard provided at M. 1:2-3. Those pericopae, as we recall, specify that three trees form an orchard if together they produce a large quantity of fruit. The case at hand presents an exception to this rule. Three trees, as at A, that formally satisfy the definition of M. 1:2-3, yet for some reason do not extend their roots throughout a seah-space, do not constitute an orchard. Rather, each tree is viewed as a separate entity. In such cases, the prohibition against plowing after Pentecost of the sixth year applies only in the area surrounding each tree.

The gloss at D-H reinforces the main point of the preceding discussion, that a group of trees which spread their roots throughout a seah-space constitute an orchard. A large number of trees, which of necessity are planted closely together within a seah-space, clearly will extend their roots throughout this area. This is the case whether or not these trees together yield the volume of fruit specified by M. 1:2C. It follows that a seah-space which contains ten or more trees will be subject to the rules governing orchards.

At I-J, Mishnah's authors provide a Scriptural prooftext for the principle that some restrictions of the Sabbatical year apply during the preceding or the following year as well. During the sixth year, for example, a farmer may not plow if his labor benefits only crops of the Sabbatical year (see M. 1:1A-1:4H). Moreover, during the year following the Sabbatical, certain restrictions apply to the edible produce that grew during the seventh year itself. This is because crops of the Sabbatical year inherently are sanctified and so must be consumed and distributed in accordance with the rules presented in detail in Chapters Eight and Nine. Mishnah's authorities derive this notion of extending the restrictions of the Sabbatical year (tosefet shebiit), which never is mentioned explicitly in Scripture, from the prohibition of Ex. 34:21, ". . . at plowing and harvesting time you shall cease work." To understand their exegesis of this verse, we must recall that, according to Mishnah's authors, two Scriptural passages never teach the same rule. On the basis of this principle, they deduce first that Ex. 34:21 cannot refer to the prohibition against plowing and harvesting on the Sabbath, since this already is prohibited by Ex. 20:10.[9] Similarly, the point of Ex. 34:21 cannot be to prohibit such agricultural activities during the Sabbatical year itself, for Lev. 25:4-5 explicitly forbids this. Mishnah's authors thus conclude that this verse provides the basis for those agricultural restrictions that apply either before or after the Sabbatical year.

Ishmael, K-L, rejects this reading of Ex. 34:21 entirely. He holds that the verse relates to the laws of the Sabbath, not to those of the Sabbatical year. The point of the verse, on his view, emerges from the juxtaposition of the words "plowing" and "harvesting." Both of these activities are performed by farmers at a time of their choice. Since there is no set time at which farmers are obligated to plow or harvest, they may not choose to engage in these activities on the Sabbath, which Scripture enjoins as a day of rest. The act of harvesting the first sheaf (omer), however, is prescribed by Scripture (Lev. 23:10-11), and in this respect differs from all other agricultural activities. Since this act of harvesting is mandatory, not voluntary, it may be performed even on the Sabbath, when ordinary agricultural activities are prohibited.

1:5

A. Three trees [growing in a seah-space] belonging to three persons,

B. lo, these [trees] join together [to form a single orchard, in accordance with the definition stated at M. 1:2E-F,]

C. and [therefore any of the three owners mentioned at A] plows the entire seah-space for [the trees'] benefit [until Pentecost of the sixth year].

D. And how much [space] must there be between [the three trees, so that the roots will extend throughout the seah-space, rendering the entire area subject to the rules of M. 1:2-4]?

E. Rabban Simeon b. Gamaliel says, "Enough [space] so that an ox with its yoke may pass [between the trees]."

M. 1:5 (A-C: b. B.B. 26b; D-E: T. B.B. 4:11; E: T. B.B. 1:14)

At issue is whether the trees referred to at A meet the definition of an orchard presented at M. 1:2-4. The ambiguity arises because a single individual does not own all three of the trees. If ownership is decisive, then each tree will be viewed as growing in a distinct plot of land, owned by a separate person. The tract in its entirety therefore will not comprise an orchard. Alternatively, we might take account of the fact that the three trees together fill the entire seah-space with their roots. The area as a whole thus satisfies the definition of an orchard provided at M. 1:2A-D, even though the trees belong to separate individuals. B-C resolves the problem by asserting that the ownership of the trees is of no concern. The critical consideration, as the discussion of M. 1:2-4 has indicated, is whether the trees together spread their roots throughout the seah-space. The three trees at A thus form an orchard, which may be plowed only until Pentecost of the sixth year (B-C).

The formally separate unit of law at D-E concludes the chapter's discussion of the definition of an orchard by reaffirming the central principle of all that has gone before. Three trees in a seah-space constitute an orchard only if their roots fill this entire area. Simeon b. Gamaliel therefore specifies that the trees must be planted at a certain minimum distance from one another. On his view, if an ox with its yoke can pass between the trees, the farmer may assume that their roots extend throughout the area.

A.   [As regards] three trees within a seah-space--

B.   lo, these join together [to form an orchard],

C.   and they plow the entire seah-space for [the trees'] sake [until Pentecost of the sixth year; cf. M. 1:2A-D].

D.   "But [this rule applies] only if they [the three trees] are planted as would be ten trees (mt_tn mmt_) in a seah-space, [that is, only if they are evenly spaced throughout the area,] the words of R. Meir and R. Judah.

E.   R. Yose and R. Simeon (E omits: R. Simeon) say, "They plow for them [i.e., the trees] only according to their need. [That is, plowing is permitted until Pentecost only in the area surrounding each tree, but not in the field as a whole; cf. M. 1:2-3]."

F.   How much space must there be between them?

G.   Rabban Simeon b. Gamaliel says, "[Enough space] so that an ox with its yoke may pass [between the trees; =M. 1:5D-E].

H.   Rabban Gamaliel and his court ordained that working the land be permitted until the New Year [of the Sabbatical year].

I.   [If] one tree (so Lieberman, TZ, p. 165, who reads with E: 'hd; V reads: 'hr) stands within [an area of] two qab (byt qbyym), and two [other trees] stand within [an area of] four qab--

J.   they plow for them only according to their need.

K.   If three trees belong to three individuals [=M. 1:5A with slight variations],

L.   and the field belongs to someone [else] (so ed. princ. which reads: 'hr; E, V, read: 'hd)

M.   even though the owner of the field plows for the needs of his field [and not for the sake of the trees],

N.   he is permitted [to plow the entire seah-space until Pentecost of the sixth year].

T. 1:1 (F-G: T. B.B. 4:11; H: y. Shab. 1:4 [3d], b. M.Q. 3b)

Three trees within a seah-space constitute an orchard and may be plowed only until the summer of the sixth year (A-C). This rule, which summarizes the law of M. 1:2A-C, sets the stage for the discussion which follows, at D vs. E, F-G and I-J. The central theory of the pericope is that three trees comprise an orchard only if they are evenly distributed within the seah-space. This assures that the trees' roots extend throughout the area. Since plowing anywhere within the seah-space benefits the trees, it is permitted until Pentecost of the sixth year. This theory, first attributed to Meir and Judah (D), is augmented by Simeon b. Gamaliel, who offers his own criterion for the spacing of the trees (F-G). At I-J, we consider the opposing case, three trees which are unevenly planted within a seah-space. One tree stands in one-third of the area (two qab) while the other two stand next to one another in the other two-thirds of the seah-space.[10] The result is that a farmer may plow until Pentecost only in the area which will benefit the trees, at the base of each tree.

Yose and Simeon, E, reject the general rule at A-C as well as the qualification that the trees must be planted at a certain distance from one another. Their view is that, under all circumstances, a farmer may plow only in the vicinity of each tree. The assumption underlying this position is that trees generally extend their roots only a short distance. Farmers, therefore, never are permitted to plow an entire orchard, irrespective of the spacing of the trees.

Two further units of law, H and K-N, each concern plowing during the sixth year, but neither contributes to the foregoing discussion. Rabban Gamaliel, H, holds that Scripture's prohibition against working the land during the Sabbatical year applies only during the seventh year itself. He thus rejects the notion of tosefet shebiit, that plowing an orchard is prohibited during the summer of the sixth year (see M. 1:1-5). This view, attributed to Rabban Gamaliel alone, never again is referred to in M.-T.[11] I cannot account for the redactor's placement of Gamaliel's ruling here, in the midst of a discussion with which he could not concur.

We turn, finally, to a case in which an individual owns a field containing trees that belong to other people (K-N). The issue concerns when in the sixth year the owner of the field may plow his land. That is to say, farmers ordinarily may plow their fields only until Passover of the sixth year (see M. 2:1). Yet, as we know from M. 1:1, an orchard may be plowed until Pentecost of the sixth year. We now ask whether the landowner may continue to plow this area until Pentecost, despite the fact that he does not own the orchard. T. rules that he may, since his plowing has the effect of benefiting the trees. The fact that he plows in order to improve his land, not the yield of the trees, is of no consequence. It is noteworthy that this ruling in no way is dependent on the facts of M. 1:5, stipulated at K. The ruling would be the same even if all the trees were owned by a single person. Lieberman, on the basis of y. Sheb. 1:4, hypothesizes that originally K was followed by materials relevant to the case of M. 1:5.

1:6-7

A. [As regards] ten saplings which are spread out [evenly] within a seah-space--
B. they plow the entire seah-space for [the saplings'] sake until the New Year [of the Sabbatical year. Since the saplings together spread their roots throughout the seah-space, the area a whole is deemed an orchard, as at M. 1:2C-D].
C. [But as regards ten saplings which] were formed in a line or in a semi-circle (mwqpwt ᶜtrh)[12]--
D. they plow for them [until New Year of the Sabbatical year] only according to [the saplings'] need, [that is, only in the vicinity of each tree. The roots of these saplings

do not fill the entire seah-space, so that the tract as a whole is not deemed an orchard, as at M. 1:2E-F].

M. 1:6 (b. B.B. 26b)

E.   Saplings and gourds[13] join together [to make up ten plants] within a seah-space [which permit one to plow the entire area until Pentecost of the sixth year].

F.   Rabban Simeon b. Gamaliel says, "[If] all (eight MSS. omit: all) ten [of the plants] in a seah-space are gourds [that is, if the seah-space contains no saplings at all,]

G.   "they plow the entire seah-space until the New Year [of the Sabbatical year]."

M. 1:7

Saplings have small, delicate roots, which distinguish them from fully-grown trees. As a result, young trees can survive the dry, summer months only if farmers continue to aerate their roots after Pentecost of the sixth year.[14] Mishnah's authorities therefore permit farmers to plow fields of saplings up until the very beginning of the Sabbatical year. Moreover, it takes ten saplings, as against three mature trees, to fill a seah-space with roots. An area of this size containing ten saplings thus constitutes an orchard. It may be plowed in its entirety until the end of the sixth year. With this basic information in hand, we can understand the pericope's central point, expressed in the contrast between A-B and C-D. The spacing of the saplings determines whether the area as a whole is subject to the rules governing orchards. If the saplings are evenly planted within the seah-space, they may be assumed to extend their roots throughout this entire plot of land. It therefore comprises an orchard and may be plowed until the beginning of the Sabbatical year (A-B). On the other hand, saplings distributed unevenly within a seah-space do not fill the whole area with their roots. Plowing, therefore, is permitted only in the vicinity of each tree, not throughout the entire seah-space (C-D) (see M. 1:5D-E).

Gourds pose a problem with respect to the foregoing rules. Like saplings, they have thin roots and so should be subject to the same rules as young trees. On the other hand, gourds are not a type of tree. The rules governing orchards of saplings therefore should not apply to gourds. At E, the surroundings in which these plants are growing resolves their ambiguous status. Gourds that grow alongside saplings in an orchard are treated like young trees, for their roots, together with those of the saplings, fill the seah-space. A field containing both saplings and gourds, ten plants in all, is subject to the same rules as an orchard composed entirely of saplings (E).[15] Simeon's lemma, formally independent of the preceding rule, presents a separate theory of the matter. He holds that gourds are fully analogous to saplings, for their root systems are similar in character. It follows that a seah-space containing ten gourds, but no saplings at all, likewise constitutes an orchard (F-G).

A. Three chate-melons, three gourds, and four saplings [planted in a seah-space],

B. lo, these join together [to make the requisite ten items which comprise a field of saplings; cf. M. 1:7E].

C. (E adds: and they plow the entire seah-space for their sake).

D. But only if they are planted as would be ten trees within a seah-space, [that is, provided they are evenly distributed.]

E. How much space must there be between them?

F. Rabban Simeon b. Gamaliel says, "[There is sufficient space] as long as [the area] underneath and around [the melons, gourds, and saplings permits] a pair of joined oxen with their yokes [to pass between them; cf. M. 1:5, T. 1:1].

T. 1:3a

The ten plants referred to at A all have delicate roots. Together they comprise an orchard which may be plowed in its entirety until New Year of the Sabbatical year, in accordance with M. 1:6A-B, E.[16] Like any other orchard, the plants must be distributed evenly so that the roots extend throughout the area (D). This rule is followed, at E-F, by a reprise of Simeon's lemma with respect to the spacing of fully-grown trees (cf. M. 1:5D-E, T. 1:1F-G). If a pair of oxen can pass between the plants, he assumes that their roots spread throughout the seah-space.

1:8

A. Until what [stage of growth are trees] called "saplings?"

B. R. Eleazar b. Azariah says, "Until they become permitted for common use (ᶜd ꞌsyhlw) [that is, until they are five years old; see Lev. 19:23-25 which forbids the consumption of fruit in the first four years of a tree's growth]."[17]

C. R. Joshua says, "(Eight MSS. add: Until) [they are] seven years old (two MSS. read: nine years old)."

D. R. Aqiba says, "A sapling [must be understood] according to its [common] meaning."

E. "[As regards] a tree which has been cut down, [the stump of which] produces shoots--

F. (1)   "[if the stump is] one handbreadth [tall] or less, [the shoot is treated] as a sapling;

   (2)   "[if the stump is] one handbreadth [tall] or more, [the shoot is treated] as a tree,"

G. the words of R. Simeon.

M. 1:8

The Israelite farmer must know when saplings take on the status of fully-grown trees, for quite distinct rules govern plowing during the sixth year in these two types of orchards. Three separate theories of the point at which saplings become mature trees are presented in the dispute at A-D. Eleazar holds that a tree becomes mature only in its fifth year of growth, when the householder first freely may gather and eat its fruit.[18]

This position is based upon the injunction of Lev. 19:23-25, that during the first three years of a tree's growth its yield may not be consumed at all, while in the fourth year the fruit is sanctified and must be brought to Jerusalem and consumed there. Joshua, C, rules that a sapling becomes a tree only after seven years, for certain types of trees take that many years to mature and produce fruit.[19] Aqiba, D, unlike Eleazar and Joshua, takes account of the fact that not all trees develop at the same rate. He therefore rejects the notion that all saplings become fully-grown after a set number of years, but rather, turns to public consensus to resolve the issue. Any tree that people commonly refer to as a sapling may be plowed until New Year of the Sabbatical year, in accordance with the rules governing orchards of young trees (M. 1:6-7).

Simeon, E-G, considers a separate problem with respect to the definition of a sapling. What is the status of a shoot that grows from the stump of an older tree? We might view the shoot either as a new growth, that is, as a sapling, or alternatively, as a remnant of the former tree. Simeon holds that the height of the stump determines the status of the shoot. If the tree has been razed to the ground, so that only one handbreadth of the former stump remains, then the original tree no longer exists. The new shoot is viewed as if it had grown directly from the ground so that it is subject to the rules pertaining to saplings. If more of the original stump remains, however, the shoot constitutes a continuation of the old tree. It therefore is governed by the rules for mature trees.

A. A mature tree (zqnh) which resembles a sapling, [that is, if it is small and yields little fruit],

B. lo, it is [subject to the same law] as a sapling.

C. And a sapling which resembles a mature tree, [that is, if it is large and yields much fruit],

D. lo, it is [subject to the same law] as a mature tree.

E. What is the difference between [the law regarding] a mature tree and [that regarding] a sapling?

F. A mature tree [may be plowed] until Pentecost [cf. M. 1:1C]

G. and a sapling [may be plowed] until New Year [cf. M. 1:6].

H. A mature tree [must be one of] three [trees within a seah-space in order to be plowed until Pentecost] (m^{c}yn šlšh) [cf. M. 1:2].

I. A sapling [must be one of] ten [saplings within a seah-space in order to be plowed until New Year; cf. M. 1:6].

J. And a field of reeds is considered (ndwnt) as [a field of] saplings.

T. 1:2

T. investigates the distinction between saplings and fully-grown trees, the topic of M. 1:8. The first unit of law, A-D, develops the definition of a sapling attributed to Aqiba (M. 1:8D). The way a tree looks, that is, its size and yield, determine whether it is a sapling or a mature tree. This definition clearly is consistent with the principle underlying Mishnah's entire discussion. The extensiveness of a tree's roots, indicated by its size and yield, determines which rules apply to it.[20] This ruling, A-D, brings in its wake a brief summary of Mishnah's rules for saplings and fully-grown trees (E-I).

A formally and substantively independent ruling, J, makes a simple point. Reeds, like saplings, have small roots and so require plowing throughout the summer of the sixth year. This rule has no bearing on the foregoing discussion and actually belongs with T. 1:3's rules concerning plants analogous to saplings.

G.   What is considered a sapling? [=M. 1:8A with slight variations]

H.   R. Joshua says, "A five year old [tree], a six year old [tree], a seven year old [tree;" cf. M. 1:8C].

I.   (V omits: I) Said Rabbi, "Why did they say, 'A five year old tree, a six year old tree, a seven year old tree?'

J.   "Rather I [would] phrase ('wmr 'ny) [the rule as follows]: grapevines [are considered saplings until they are] five years old, and fig trees [are considered saplings until they are] six years old, and olive trees [are considered saplings until they are] seven years old."

T. 1:3b

Joshua offers three different dates at which saplings become trees (H). Rabbi explains his lemma, suggesting that each time period refers to a different type of tree (I-J). This interpretation of Joshua elucidates his ruling at M. 1:8C, that a sapling becomes a fully-grown tree in its seventh year of growth. That ruling, which applies to all trees, is based on the case of olive trees, which take the longest time to mature.

CHAPTER TWO

Shebiit Chapter Two

The central principle of the chapter, familiar from what has gone before, is that during the sixth year farmers may not engage in any labor that improves primarily crops of the Sabbatical year. This would violate the prohibition against working the Land during the seventh year (see Chapter One, Introduction). The bulk of the chapter, comprising three formally separate units of law (M. 2:1, 2:2-5, 2:6), carries forward the discussion of the preceding chapter by delineating several distinct types of agricultural activity and specifying when during the sixth year each becomes forbidden. Let us turn now to the details of these rules.

First, farmers may not plow a field of grain during the sixth year after the ground has dried out. Since by this time they have begun reaping the grain of the sixth year, further plowing clearly would benefit only the crop of the Sabbatical year, which is forbidden (M. 2:1). At M. 2:2-5, we consider types of activity, such as pruning vines, that yield immediate as well as long-term benefits. Mishnah's authors rule that the farmer may engage in such activities right up until the beginning of the Sabbatical year. That is to say, they regard as primary the immediate benefits of such activity, which are felt during the sixth year itself. A farmer therefore may prune his vines until the very end of the sixth year, even though this has the secondary effect of improving his plants during the Sabbatical year as well. Finally, during the last thirty days of the sixth year farmers may not plant new trees or graft branches. By starting new plants a full month before the New Year, a farmer makes certain that the new shoots take root before the seventh year begins, when planting becomes forbidden (M. 2:6).

The remainder of the chapter, M. 2:7-10, substantively quite separate from the foregoing, again concerns the critical boundary between the sixth and seventh years.[1] At issue now is how to determine the status of rice and other types of grain that take root during the sixth year, but which farmers harvest both during that year and into the year following. Is such produce subject to the tithes which must be separated from the crop of the sixth year, or is it governed by the special restrictions that apply to sanctified food of the Sabbatical year?[2] Mishnah's authorities rule that the year during which the rice takes root is determinative, with the result that the entire crop is subject to the restrictions of that year alone. The fact that some of this rice is gathered and eaten during the following year is of no consequence. This principle, presented at M. 2:7, draws in its wake a discussion of ambiguous cases, at M. 2:8-10. Egyptian beans, for example, could fall into the category of rice, in which case they are subject to the restrictions of the year during which they take root. Alternatively, we might regard these beans as vegetables, which are governed by the restrictions of the year during which they are harvested. In such cases of ambiguity, Mishnah characteristically rules that the intention of the individual farmer determines the status of the produce. Beans which a farmer cultivates as a vegetable for eating are treated accordingly.

The chapter concludes with a dispute (M. 2:1OH,J vs. I,K) concerning whether farmers may irrigate their fields during the Sabbatical year. This material bears no formal or substantive relationship to that which precedes. It may have been included here because it deals with activities prohibited during the Sabbatical year itself, the topic of Chapter Three.

2:1

A.   Until what time do they plow in a field of grain (śdh hlbn) (lit., a white field)[3] during the year preceding the Sabbatical year?

B.   Until the moisture [in the ground] is gone,

C.   [that is], as long as people plow in order to plant chate-melons and gourds.[4]

D.   Said R. Simeon, "You have put the law into the hands of each and every individual,

E.   "Rather, [one may plow] in a field of grain until Passover [of the sixth year, when Israelites offer the first sheaf of new grain at the Temple; cf. Lev. 23:10]

F.   "and [in accord with M. 1:1L, one may plow] in an orchard until Pentecost [of the sixth year, when they present the first-fruits; cf. Ex. 23:19].

M. 2:1 (b. M.Q. 3b)

Plowing a field of grain late in the sixth year is forbidden, since this would improve the crop that grows during the Sabbatical year. This rule, which parallels that concerning orchards at M. 1:1, underlies the question at A.[5] We wish to know when during the sixth year the prohibition against plowing a grain field takes effect. B specifies that the decisive point in time is when the ground moisture from the winter rains has dried up. Further plowing after this time could no longer benefit the crop of the sixth year, which the farmer by then has begun to reap. Rather, this plowing would serve to improve only the crop of the Sabbatical year, which the farmer may not do. The gloss at C reformulates B's answer in terms of the growing season of chate-melons and gourds. Farmers plant these vegetables early in the season, when the level of ground moisture is sufficient for the development of their delicate roots. Once the ground has dried out and farmers no longer plant these crops, plowing in fields of grain becomes forbidden.

Simeon (D-E) disputes the rule at A-C, for it provides that plowing will become forbidden in each field at a somewhat different time, in accordance with the prevailing climate and ground conditions. In order to assure that all Israelites begin to observe the restrictions of the Sabbatical year at the same time, he proposes exact dates on which the prohibition against plowing takes effect. After Israelites bring to the Temple the new crops of grain and fruit, on Passover and on Pentecost respectively, they no longer may plow fields and orchards. This would aid the crop of the seventh year alone, which is forbidden.

2:2-5

I.   A.   They (1) manure and (2) hoe

      B.   in fields of chate-melons and in fields of gourds

      C.   until New Year [of the Sabbatical year].

      D.   And likewise: [they manure and hoe] in an irrigated field [until New Year of the Sabbatical year].

II.   E.   They (3) cut off dry twigs, (4) strip off leaves, (5) cover [the roots] with dust, and (6) fumigate

      F.   until New Year [of the Sabbatical year].

      G.   R. Simeon says, "Also: one may remove [dead] leaves from a grape-cluster during the Sabbatical year itself."

M. 2:2

III. H.   They (7) remove stones [from a field]

      I.   until New Year [of the Sabbatical year].

IV.   J.   They (8) cut back [shoots that grow from the roots of trees,] (9) clip [branches] and (10) prune [trees]

      K.   until New Year [of the Sabbatical year].

      L.   R. Joshua (Ca omits: Joshua) says, "[In contrast to the rule at J-K,] just as [the actions of] clipping and pruning [trees, in order to care for the fruit of] the fifth year [generally continue into the sixth year,] so too [the clipping and pruning of trees, in order to care for the fruit of] the sixth year [may be continued into the seventh year. That is, during the seventh year farmers may continue to cultivate fruit that they began pruning during the preceding year]."

      M.   R. Simeon says, "As long as I am permitted to care for the tree, I am permitted to prune it, [that is to say, throughout the Sabbatical year]."

M. 2:3

V.   N.   They (11) smear the saplings [with oil,] (12) wrap them, (13) cover them with ash (qwtmyn), (14) make shelters for them, and (15) water them

      O.   until New Year [of the Sabbatical year].

      P.   R. Eleazar bar R. Sadoq says, "Also: [with respect to watering trees,] one may water the leaves during the Sabbatical year itself, but [one may] not [water] the roots [directly]."

M. 2:4 (N-O: b. A.Z. 50b)

VI.   Q.   They (16) pour oil on unripe figs and (17) pierce them [which improves the quality of the fruit]

      R.   until New Year [of the Sabbatical year].

S.   Unripe figs [which began growing] during the year preceding the Sabbatical and
      which continued growing [and ultimately became ripe] during the Sabbatical
      year itself,

T.   [as well as unripe figs which began growing] during the Sabbatical year and
      which continued growing [and ultimately became ripe] during the year
      following the Sabbatical--

U.   they neither pour oil [on them] nor pierce them [during the Sabbatical year, for
      one may not process the fruit which grows during the Sabbatical year.]

V.   R. Judah says, "Where it is customary to pour oil [on unripe figs,] they do not
      pour oil [during the Sabbatical year,]

W.   "because it is [considered to be the normal way in which such crops are]
      processed (mpny šhy' ᶜbwdh).

X.   "[But] where it is not customary to pour oil [on unripe figs,] they may pour oil,
      [because there it is not deemed to be a normal agricultural activity].

Y.   R. Simeon permits [pouring oil on] the tree [itself, as well as on the fruit,]

Z.   because one is permitted to tend a tree [during the Sabbatical year].

M. 2:5 (Q-R: b. A.Z. 50b)

Throughout the sixth year farmers may perform any agricultural activity that
provides an immediate benefit to the produce of that year. The farmer may continue to
do such work until the beginning of the Sabbatical year itself, even though his labor also
will benefit the crop of the seventh year. The effect of this cultivation upon the produce
of the Sabbatical year is regarded by Mishnah's authorities as secondary and of no
consequence. Seventeen agricultural activities of this type are presented in a formally
unitary construction consisting of six parts (present participle + "until the New Year").
The list as a whole is punctuated by several glosses and units of secondary material, at D,
G, L-M, P and S-Z. Let us now turn to the details of the laws before us.

Chate-melons and gourds have tender roots which require special care in order to
survive the dry, summer months (see M. 1:7). Spreading manure and hoeing preserve the
moisture in the ground and so benefit these crops during the sixth year itself (A-C).[6] D
extends this rule to plants growing in an irrigated field, even though these do not require
additional moisture. In this case, manuring helps the plants by replenishing the fertility of
the soil.[7]

Farmers must care for vines throughout the sixth year in order to prevent them
from dying (E-F). They must trim dead leaves and branches, so that the healthy ones can
develop normally. In addition, spreading dust at the base of a vine protects any exposed
roots, while fumigating exterminates harmful insects. Simeon, G, permits farmers to
remove dead leaves from grape-clusters even during the Sabbatical year itself. This is
necessary to prevent vines from becoming tangled, which would cause the grapes to die.[8]

Removing stones from an orchard and pruning trees are permitted throughout the
sixth year, since these activities enable the trees to grow normally (H-I, J-K). Joshua, at

L, claims that during the Sabbatical year farmers may prune fruit that began to grow during the preceding year. Since the farmer already began tending this fruit during the sixth year, it is clear that he is not engaged in cultivating the crop of the Sabbatical year, which would be forbidden.[9] Simeon, M, like Joshua, permits pruning during the Sabbatical year, but for an entirely different reason. He views pruning as one aspect of tending a tree. Farmers may care for their trees throughout the Sabbatical year, since this is necessary to prevent irreparable damage (see Simeon's lemma below, Y-Z).[10]

At N-O, the discussion shifts to saplings. All types of labor that prevent young trees from dying are permitted until the New Year of the Sabbatical year (N-O) (see M. 1:6-7). Eleazar bar Sadoq, P, claims that farmers may water saplings during the Sabbatical year itself, for this assures that their roots receive the necessary moisture to develop properly. Farmers must water saplings, however, in a manner which indicates that they intend to benefit only the tree, not the field as a whole. They do this by pouring water on the leaves and allowing it to drip down to the roots.

Oiling and piercing unripe figs are permitted throughout the sixth year, for they hasten the ripening process and improve the quality of the fruit (Q). Two further rulings, S-U and V-X, carry forward the discussion of oiling unripe figs. We consider first the case of figs that grow over a period of two years, either from the sixth year into the seventh, or from the seventh into the eighth year. Since half or more of this fruit's growth occurs during the Sabbatical year, it is subject to the restrictions governing the produce of that year. Such figs, therefore, may not be oiled, for it is forbidden to process fruit of the Sabbatical year (see M. 8:6). Judah, V-X, qualifies this rule. He takes account of the fact that oiling figs is not a common agricultural practice in all places. He thus permits farmers who do not ordinarily oil their figs to do so during the Sabbatical year. In such cases, this does not constitute a forbidden act of cultivation.

Simeon, Y-Z, holds that all aspects of caring for a tree, including spreading oil on the trunk, are permitted throughout the Sabbatical year. This is because neglecting a tree for an extended period of time would result in permanent damage.

A.   In the year preceding the Sabbatical, they sell manure to, and bring it out [to the field of,] an Israelite who is suspected [of transgressing the laws] of the Sabbatical year. [But they do not do these things after the beginning of the Sabbatical year].

B.   And [with regard to selling manure to, or bringing it out to the field of,] a gentile or a Samaritan--

C.   even during the Sabbatical year, it is permitted.

D.   Until what time is it permitted to manure [a field belonging to an Israelite]?

E.   As long as one is permitted to plow, one is permitted to manure.

T. 1:4

One may not assist Israelites who are suspected of violating the laws of the Sabbatical year, for one thereby becomes an accomplice to their transgressions. It thus is forbidden to sell manure to such people during the Sabbatical year, since they will use it in violation of the law. Selling manure during the sixth year, however, is permitted, for it is assumed that the buyer will spread the manure immediately, when doing so is permitted (see M. 2:2) (A). Since gentiles and Samaritans are not obligated to observe the restrictions of the Sabbatical year, Israelites who sell them manure during that year commit no transgression (B-C).

A formally independent unit of law, D-E, supplements this discussion. Plowing and spreading manure both are agricultural activities which preserve plants during the dry, summer months. Since both serve the same function, they are permitted during the same period of time, until the beginning of the Sabbatical year (see M. 1:7, 2:2).

A.   They water saplings

B.   until the New Year [of the Sabbatical year; =M. 2:4N(15) with variation].

C.   R. Yose b. Kiper says in the name of R. Eliezer,

D.   "The House of Shammai say, 'One waters the foliage and [the water] falls on the root.'

E.   "The House of Hillel say, '[One waters both] on the foliage and on the root.'

F.   "Said the House of Hillel to the House of Shammai, 'If you permit him [i.e., the Israelite farmer, to do] part [of the labor], permit him [to do] all [of it]. If you do not permit him [to do] all, do not permit him [to do] part.'"

T. 1:5

The Houses dispute how farmers should water their trees during the sixth year, an agricultural activity permitted by the rule of M. 2:4N.[11] The Shammaites hold that immediately preceding the Sabbatical year farmers must avoid the appearance of irrigating their orchards, for this activity is forbidden during the Sabbatical year itself. They may water saplings only indirectly, not in the normal manner (D). The Hillelites argue that watering trees during the sixth year is permitted and so may be done in the usual way (E). Their retort to the Shammaites at F indicates that the redactor of T. deems their view authoritative. It should be noted that this dispute probably is not original to the Houses. The fact that Yose b. Kiper, an Ushan, is the tradent, and that the Shammaite position is presented at M. 2:4P by Eleazar b. Sadoq, another Ushan, suggests that this is an Ushan dispute attributed pseudepigraphically to the Houses.[12]

A.   (And) they straighten the saplings

B.   until the New Year [of the Sabbatical year].

C.   R. Judah says, "If they were wrapped (reading with E: mkwrkwt; V, ed. princ. read: mbwrkwt) [in order to straighten out the saplings] before the Sabbatical year,

D.   "he removes them [i.e., the bindings] even during the Sabbatical year [itself]."

T. 1:6

T. adds to Mishnah's list of agricultural activities permitted throughout the sixth year. Straightening saplings assures that they grow properly. Since this benefits the tree immediately, it is permitted until the beginning of the Sabbatical year (A-B). Judah's point is clear. Once the tree has begun to grow straight, the wrappings no longer are needed. They may be removed at any time, for this in no way benefits the tree (C-D).

A.   What are ('lw) the channels (ᶜwgywt) [in a vineyard which, according to M. M.Q. 1:1, people may not dig during the Sabbatical year]?

B.   These are the ditches [which people dig] around the roots of trees [in order to irrigate them].

C.   [During the Sabbatical year] they thin out and detach [vines that grow above] the reeds [since this activity benefits the grapes of the sixth year which remain on the vine].

D.   Where it is customary to thin out and detach vines before Tabernacles [throughout the years of the Sabbatical cycle,]

E.   they thin out and detach [vines only] before Tabernacles [of the Sabbatical year].

F.   [Where it is customary to thin out and detach vines] after Tabernacles [throughout the years of the Sabbatical cycle,]

G.   they [also] thin out and detach [vines] after Tabernacles [of the Sabbatical year].[13]

T. 1:7 (A-C = T. M.Q. 1:2A-C; y. M.Q. 1:1[80b]; b. M.Q. 4b)

Only the second of the pericope's two units of law, A-B and C+D-F, relates directly to Mishnah, so we turn to it first. Joshua's ruling of M. 2:3L is applied to the case of vines. As we recall, Joshua holds that during the Sabbatical year farmers may trim and prune trees. This activity is permitted for it benefits fruit of the sixth year which remains on the branch into the following year (C). For the same reason, farmers also may prune vines during the Sabbatical year. The qualification of this rule at D-G is clear. Farmers trim vines during the Sabbatical year only as long as they ordinarily do so during other years. This assures that their labor benefits the crop of the sixth year alone, not the grapes which appear on the vine during the Sabbatical year itself.

These rulings are preceded, at A-B, by a quite separate unit of law. People may not dig irrigation ditches during the Sabbatical year, for this is considered an act of cultivation. This rule bears no relation to the discussion of M. 2:2-5. It appears to have been transferred here from T. M.Q. 1:2 because of C, which rules on the pruning of vineyards during the Sabbatical year.

A.   Unripe figs [which began growing] during the year preceding the Sabbatical year and which continued growing [and ultimately became ripe] during the Sabbatical year itself-- [=M. 2:5S]

B.   R. Judah says, "Where it is customary to pour oil [on unripe figs], they do not pour oil [during the Sabbatical year],

C.   "because it is [considered] an ordinary agricultural activity (^{C}bwdh).

D.   "[But] where it is not customary to pour oil, they may pour oil, [because there it is not deemed to be a normal agricultural task]" [=M. 2:5V-X].

E.   [Unripe figs which began growing] during the Sabbatical year and which continued growing [and ultimately became ripe] during the year following the Sabbatical,

F.   all authorities agree that

G.   they neither pour oil on them nor pierce them [during the Sabbatical year] [=M. 2:5T-U with slight variations].

H.   And similarly, R. Judah said, "One who buys an unripe fig from his fellow during the first six years of the Sabbatical cycle (bšr šny šbw^C) [and then the Sabbatical year arrives],

I.   "even where it is customary to pour oil [on unripe figs during the first six years of the Sabbatical cycle],

J.   "they pour oil [on these figs during the Sabbatical year].

K.   One may not smear resin over the roots

L.   because it makes [the root] softer [i.e., it causes the root to deteriorate].

M.   But one may smear the leaves [with resin].

T. 1:8

T. offers its own version of the rules concerning tending figs during the Sabbatical year (M. 2:5S-X). Judah's ruling of M. 2:5V-X here refers only to figs which begin growing during the sixth year. These figs are deemed to be produce of the sixth, not of the seventh, year. They may be pierced and oiled during the Sabbatical year so long as this is not regarded as an ordinary agricultural activity (B-D). Figs which grow from the Sabbatical year into the year following are another matter. This fruit is sanctified and may not be cultivated during the Sabbatical year.

A separate qualification of Judah's ruling follows at H-J. Figs harvested and sold before the beginning of the Sabbatical year are part of the crop of the sixth year. Since they are not subject to the restrictions of the Sabbatical year at all, farmers are free to oil and pierce them.

K-M, an independent ruling, has no bearing on the foregoing discussion. Smearing resin on the roots of a tree destroys them.[14] This is forbidden during the Sabbatical year, for uprooting a tree is considered cultivation of the land. Farmers may, however, defoliate a tree with resin. This has the same effect as pruning, an activity which is permitted during the Sabbatical year itself (cf. T. 1:7C, T. 1:11).

A.   A fig tree the bark of which peeled off--

B.   they do not coat it with mud (tyt) [during the Sabbatical year,]

C.   because it is an ordinary agricultural activity (ml'kth).

D.   [During the Sabbatical year] they do not (1) hang wild figs on a fig tree

E.   and they do not (2) graft [branches] onto a fig tree,

F.   because it is an ordinary agricultural activity (^{C}bdh).

G.   R. Simeon b. Eleazar (E omits: Simeon b.) says, "On the intermediate days of festivals one ties [the branch to the tree in order to graft it,]

H.   "but if one does so during the Sabbatical year, one cuts [the grafted branch off the tree]."

T. 1:9

Grafting branches on a tree (D-F) and applying mud to its trunk (A-C) are standard agricultural practices and so are forbidden during the Sabbatical year. Simeon's lemma is included here because it relates tangentially to D-F. Farmers may graft branches during the intermediate days of a festival, when cultivation is permitted, but not during the Sabbatical year, when all forms of planting are forbidden. One who violates this rule must cut off the grafted branch to rectify the transgression which he has committed (see M. 2:6B-C).[15]

A.   They (1) mark a tree with a red mark,[16]

B.   and they (2) weigh it down with stones,

C.   and they need not be concerned about [violating the laws of] the Sabbatical year

D.   or about [violating the prohibition against following] the ways of the Ammorites.

T. 1:10 (=T. Shab. 7:15)

The pericope augments T.'s discussion of ways in which people may tend trees during the Sabbatical year. The tree referred to at A-B bears fruit which will not ripen and fall off the branch. According to b. Shab. 67a,[17] marking the tree with red paint is a sign to passersby to pray for it. Weighing down the branches weakens the tree so that it yields its fruit. These practices do not constitute cultivating, nor are they deemed to be superstitious, pagan customs.

A.   They (1) remove stones, (2) remove thorns, (3) cut off [excess roots], (4) chip stones, (5) direct the vines and (6) suspend wild fig branches in fig trees,[18] (E omits: 1, 5 and 6)

B.   until the New Year [of the Sabbatical year =M. 2:3H-I].

C.   And one may (7) remove the nymph [i.e., insect larvae which would destroy the plant].

D.   R. Simeon b. Eleazar says, "Also: they (ed. princ. adds: do not) "blind" (smyn) the grapevines during the Sabbatical year [which prevents new branches from growing].[19]

T. 1:11

T. develops the rule of M. 2:3H-I. Each of the activities listed at A and C benefits plants immediately and so may be performed until the beginning of the Sabbatical year. Simeon's gloss, D, refers to spreading oil on the buds of a grapevine, which prevents new shoots from sprouting. This assures that the vine does not become so entangled that it prevents the proper ripening process of the grapes. Since this procedure is crucial to the healthy development of vines, Simeon rules that it is permissible during the Sabbatical year itself.[20]

2:6

A.   They do not (1) plant [a tree,] (2) sink [a vine into the ground so that it emerges nearby as an independent plant,] or (3) graft [one branch to another] during the year preceding the Sabbatical within thirty days of the New Year.[21] [Since these plants would take root after the beginning of the Sabbatical year, this would constitute forbidden cultivation of the Land].

B.   And if, [in violation of the rule at A,] one (1) planted [a tree,] (2) sank [a vine into the ground,] or (3) grafted [one branch to another, within thirty days of the beginning of the Sabbatical year,]

C.   one must uproot [that which was planted, sunk or grafted, so as to rectify the transgression which he has committed].

D.   R. Judah says, "All grafting that does not take root within three days will not take root. [Thus the time period specified at A should be three days, not thirty]."

E.   R. Yose and R. Simeon say, "Within two weeks."

M. 2:6 (A-E: b. R.H. 10b; b. Yeb. 83a; y. M.S. 1:2[52c]; y. Orl. 1:2[61a]; D: b. Pes. 55a)

Late in the sixth year, farmers may not plant or transplant trees, vines and branches. Since these plants would take root only after the seventh year has begun, this would violate Scripture's injunction against cultivating the Land during the Sabbatical year. This rule, predictable from all that has gone before, generates a secondary issue, raised by the gloss at C. People may not derive benefit from agricultural activities that they have performed in violation of the law. Accordingly, farmers who violate the rule of A-B must uproot that which they have planted.

Judah (E) and Yose and Simeon (F) disagree with A's claim that it takes up to thirty days for a new graft to take root. Though this discussion has not been cast as a dispute with the foregoing rule, its point in the present context is apparent. Judah would restrict farmers from planting only during the final three days of the sixth year, Yose and Simeon would extend this time period to two weeks.

A.   One who (1) plants [a tree], (2) sinks [a vine into the ground], or (3) grafts [one branch to another] thirty days before the New Year [of the Sabbatical year so that the new plants take root before the beginning of that year; cf. M. 1:7A]--

B. [the plant] is considered to be one year old (^{C}1th 3́nh) [at the New Year],

C. and one is permitted to allow it to grow (lqyymn) during the Sabbatical year.

D. Less than this [i.e., if the tree is planted or the vine sunk into the ground, or the branch grafted, within thirty days of the New Year],

E. it is not considered to be a one year old [at the New Year],

F. and one is forbidden to allow it to grow during the Sabbatical year, [rather one must uproot it].

G. The fruit of a sapling (so E; V, ed. princ. read: this sapling) is forbidden [for common consumption if it appears on the branch] before the fifteenth of Shebat [of the fourth or fifth year of the tree's growth, for this date is considered the New Year for trees; cf. M. R.H. 1:1].

H. [That is to say], if [fruit appears while the tree has the status of] orlah [i.e., before the fifteenth of Shebat of the tree's third year of growth, this fruit may not be consumed in accordance with the laws of] orlah.

I. [And] if [fruit appears while the tree has the status of] rb^{C}y [i.e., before the fifteenth of Shebat of the tree's fourth year of growth, this fruit must be redeemed, in accordance with the laws of] rb^{C}y.

> T. 2:3 (=T. R.H. 1:8; A-H: y. Orl. 1:2[61a];
> y. R.H. 1:2[57a]; A-J: b. R.H. 9b-10a)

T. paraphrases M. 2:7A-C (A-F), supplemented at B and E by rules for calculating the age of a tree. The central point is that a tree's age is not necessarily reckoned in full calendar years. Rather, the period of time between the date when a tree takes root and the beginning of a new calendar year is reckoned as a full year of growth. This is illustrated by the contrasting cases at A-C and D-F. That which a farmer plants thirty days or more before the beginning of the New Year takes root before the first of Tishre, as we learned at M. 2:7A. Such plants are considered a full year old on the New Year.

The supplementary material, at G+H-I, refers to the restrictions which apply to fruit during the first few years of a tree's growth. The fruit which a tree produces during its first three years has the status of orlah and may not be consumed (Lev. 19:23). During its fourth year of growth, the tree's fruit (termed rb^{C}y) must be brought to Jerusalem and consumed there. With this basic information in hand, we can make sense of the rule at G, expanded at H-I. When appying the restrictions of orlah and rb^{C}y, we do not calculate the age of a tree according to the calendar year, which begins and ends on the first of Tishre. Instead, fruit which appears on the branch after the first of Tishre, when a tree becomes four years old, but before the fifteenth of Shebat, is assigned to the preceding calendar year. Such fruit belongs to the tree's third year of growth and so is subject to the restrictions of orlah. This is because the growing season for fruit-bearing trees begins and ends on the fifteenth of Shebat, not the first of Tishre.

A.   They plow an irrigated field and irrigate them [i.e., the plants growing in an irrigated field],

B.   thirty days before the New Year [of the Sabbatical year].

C.   Rabbi says, "Until <u>thirty</u> (<u>ed. princ.</u> and E: three) <u>days before the New Year</u> [=B,]

D.   "so that one may plant and it will take root (<u>ed. princ.</u> omits:) and one may sow and it will take root [before the Sabbatical year begins]."

E.   They do not examine seeds [which are placed] in dung (<u>ed. princ.</u> and E add: and in a pot),[22]

F.   but they do examine those [which are placed] in earth and in a pot.

G.   And they allow [the seeds placed in a pot] to remain from the Sabbatical year to the year following the Sabbatical.

H.   And they allow the aloes[23] to grow [in pots] on the roof,

I.   but they do not irrigate them.

T. 1:12

Rabbi explains the rule of M. 2:6A-D. Plowing and irrigating thirty days before New Year assures that new plantings will take root before the Sabbatical year begins. The series of rules which follows, E-F+G and H-I, are autonomous both of Mishnah and of the foregoing. Seeds growing in the ground, or in a dung heap sitting on the ground, are subject to the restrictions of the Sabbatical year, while those growing in a pot are not. As a result, during the Sabbatical year one may not examine seeds growing in the ground to see if they have sprouted, for this is an act of cultivation (E). Those growing in a pot, however, are not subject to the law and so may be maintained throughout the Sabbatical year (F+G). Aloes are soft, frail plants grown for their fragrance and medicinal value.[24] Since they are grown in pots and used as house plants, they may be grown during the Sabbatical year. They may not be watered, however, for this violates the rule of M. 2:4N.[25]

2:7-9

A.   (1) Rice, (2) durra,[26] (3) millet[27] and (4) sesame,[28]

B.   that took root before New Year [of any year in the Sabbatical cycle, but continued to grow into the following year,]

C.   are tithed according to the [rules which apply to produce of the] previous year, [that is, the year during which they took root.]

D.   And, [in particular, if any of the plants mentioned at A] took root before New Year [of the Sabbatical year,] they are permitted during the Sabbatical year. [That is, they are not subject to the restrictions that apply to seventh-year produce; see M. 8:1ff. As at A-C, the year during which these grains take root determines their status with respect to the laws both of tithing and of the Sabbatical year.]

E.   And if not [that is, if they did not take root before the New Year, but rather, during the Sabbatical year itself,]

F. they are forbidden during the Sabbatical year [that is, subject to the restrictions that apply to seventh-year produce.]

G. And [if any of these types of produce took root during one of the other years of the Sabbatical cycle,] they are tithed according to the [rules that apply to produce of the] year following.

M. 2:7 (Sifra Behar 1:7; b. R.H. 13b)

H. R. Simeon Shezuri says, "Egyptian beans[29] that one originally sowed for the sake of their seed, [that is, not in order to eat the vegetable,]

I. "are analogous to them, [that is, the types of produce mentioned at M. 2:7A, and so are subject to the rule of C-G above.]

J. R. Simeon says, "Large beans,[30] [like Egyptian beans, also]

K. are analogous to them [and so likewise are subject to the rule of C-G above]."

L. R. Eleazar (S: Eliezer) says, "Large beans [are tithed according to the rule governing produce of the previous year, only] if they begin to form pods (mŝtrmlw) before New Year.

M. 2:8

M. (1) Shallots[31] and (2) Egyptian beans which one deprived of water (N, T[3] omit: water) thirty days before New Year

N. are tithed according to the [rules that apply to produce of the] previous year. [By depriving these plants of water, the farmer indicates that he does not wish to cultivate the vegetable, only its seed. Since this produce has been cultivated for its seed, alone, it has the status of rice and so is subject to the rule of M. 2:7A-D.]

O. And if, [in particular, shallots or Egyptian beans were deprived of water for the last thirty days of the sixth year,] they are permitted during the Sabbatical year.

P. And if not, [that is, if one did water them during the last thirty days of the sixth year,]

Q. they are forbidden during the Sabbatical year.

R. And [if the farmer planted them in one of the other years of the Sabbatical cycle,] they are tithed according to the [rules that apply to produce of the] following year.

S. "And [concerning] a naturally-watered field [that is, one which requires only periodic irrigation] [32]--

T. "[the rule at N-S applies provided that the farmer] has deprived [the shallots or beans] of water for two periods [of watering,]" the words of R. Meir.

U. But sages say, "[That rule applies only if the farmer has deprived the plants of water for] three [periods]."

M. 2:9 (M-S: b. R.H. 14a)

Rice and other grains pose a problem, for they generally are harvested over two successive calendar years. That is, we speak of produce that takes root and first becomes ripe in one year, but is harvested both during that year and well into the year following.[33] The problem is that the agricultural restrictions in effect during the first of the two years, when the farmer begins to gather his rice, may differ from those that apply during the following year, when he harvests the bulk of the crop. For example, during the first, second, fourth and fifth years of the Sabbatical cycle, farmers must dedicate a portion of their produce as second tithe. They bring this food, or its equivalent in coin, to Jerusalem and consume it there. During the third and sixth years, however, this same portion of produce is designated as poorman's tithe and given to needy Israelites. Moreover, the crop of the Sabbatical year, which is exempt from tithes altogether, is subject to other special restrictions, spelled out in detail in Chapters Eight and Nine. In the case at hand, then, a single crop of rice harvested over two years may be subject to two quite distinct sets of agricultural restrictions. In order to resolve the ambiguous status of this produce, Mishnah's authorities rule that the year during which the rice takes root determines the calendar year to which it belongs. This assures that the crop as a whole is subject to only one set of agricultural rules.

Some types of produce that are gathered over two years also pose an additional problem. At H-L, we consider types of plants, such as Egyptian beans, which can be cultivated either as seeds for planting or as food for eating. Since these beans sometimes are grown for their seeds, they may fall into the category of rice. They then would be governed by the restrictions of the year during whch they took root. Alternatively, since these beans, like all other vegetables, are raised for consumption, they might be subject to the tithes of the year during which they are harvested. Simeon Shezuri (H-I) and Simeon (J-K) both hold that the intention of the farmer resolves the issue. The purpose for which he cultivates this produce determines whether it has the status of rice or of vegetables. Eleazar, L, however, claims that certain beans are subject to the rules governing produce of the preceding year only if their pods, which contain the seeds, begin to form before New Year.[34]

The final unit of law, M-R, specifies that the farmer must indicate, through his actions, whether he cultivates a crop as vegetables or as seeds. In the case at hand, he withholds water from beans or onions during the last month of the calendar year. This prevents the vegetables from developing and indicates that he intends to gather the seeds alone. The point at which the plants take root, then, will determine the restrictions to which they are subject, in accordance with the rule at A-G. The dispute at S-T vs. U introduces a secondary consideration, the type of field in which these plants are growing. In fields that do not need frequent watering, the farmer can prevent his vegetables from developing only by depriving them of water for longer than a single month. I can find no significance to the specific spans of time proposed by Meir and sages.

A.   Egyptian beans
B.   which one deprived of water thirty days before the New Year (E omits: before the New Year)

C. are tithed according to the [rule which applies to produce of the] previous year,

D. and [if they were planted in the sixth year] one is permitted to allow them to grow during the Sabbatical year.

E. And if not [that is, if one did water them within thirty days of the New Year of the Sabbatical year,]

F. one is forbidden from allowing them to grow during the Sabbatical year,

G. and [if they were planted in any year of the Sabbatical cycle other than the sixth], they are tithed according to the [rule which applies to produce of the] following year [=M. 2:9A-G with slight variations].

H. Under what circumstances does this rule apply?

I. In an irrigated field.

J. "But with respect to a naturally watered field

K. "[this rule applies] if one has deprived it of water for two periods (mrw^{c}wt; ed. princ. reads: mrb^{c}wt)," the words of R. Meir.

L. And sages say, "[Which one deprived of water for] three [periods] [=M. 2:9T-V with slight variations].

T. 2:4

M. R. Yose b. Kiper said in the name of R. Simeon Shezuri, "Under what circumstances does this [rule, T. 2:4A-G,] apply?

N. "So long as one sowed [the crop intending to harvest] the vegetable, but [later] decided (wh$\check{s}$b) [to harvest it] for its seed [which he indicates by depriving the crop of water].

O. "However, if one originally sowed [the crop intending to harvest] the seed,

P. "and part of [the crop] took root before the New Year and part of it took root after the New Year,

Q. "they do not separate tithes from it on behalf of another batch [of produce],

R. "nor do they [separate tithes] from another batch on its behalf.

S. "Rather, one gathers this crop [which contains a mixture of produce of two separate years] into [a separate] threshing floor, and tithes from that batch [of produce] for that [same] batch."

T. As a result, he tithes from the new [crop, which took root in that year], on behalf of the new and from the old [crop, which took root during the preceding year] on behalf of the old.

U. [and so he designates] poorman's tithe and second tithe in due proportion.

V. [This is the manner of separating tithes for such a batch of produce]: He takes the tithed produce and designates it as poorman's tithe and [then designates this same produce again as] second tithe.

W. If he originally sowed the crop [intending to harvest it both] for its seed and for the vegetable,

X. or if he sowed [the crop intending to harvest it] for its seed and he [later] decided [to harvest it] as a vegetable [as well],

Y.   the seed is tithed according to [the rule applicable to produce of] the preceding year
        and the [crop's] vegetable [is tithed according to the rule in effect] at the time of
        its harvest.

T. 2:5 (M-U: b. R.H. 13b; b. Men. 30b)

The focus of the pericope, A-L, goes over the ground of M. 2:9. By withholding
water from a crop of Egyptian beans, the farmer indicates his intention to harvest only
the seed, not the vegetable. As with other seeds, these beans are subject to the
restrictions of the year in which they take root. Two glosses, at D and F, expand in a
minor way upon Mishnah's rule. Produce which is not subject to the restrictions of the
Sabbatical year may be maintained during that year. This allows farmers to gather the
seeds for planting in the year following.

This rule draws in its wake two further units of law, M-S+T-V and W-Y, which
present contrasting cases. A single crop of beans which a farmer cultivated for their seed
takes root both before and after the New Year. It follows that some of the beans are
subject to the tithes of the preceding year, some to the tithes of the subsequent year.
Since this crop contains a mixture of produce of two separate years, it must be tithed
separately from beans belonging entirely to one year or the other (Q-S). The proper
procedure in this case is spelled out at T-V. A single batch of produce is designated as
both second tithe and poorman's tithe, thus fulfilling the tithing requirements of both
years.[35]

In the final case, at W-Y, the farmer cultivates a crop both for its vegetable and for
its seed. Each type of produce is tithed in the proper year--the seeds, in the year in which
they formed, and the vegetables, in the year in which they were harvested.

A.   Said Rabban Simeon b. Gamaliel, "The House of Shammai and the House of Hillel did
        not differ [concerning the laws of tithing in the following two cases]:

B.   "Concerning (1) ripened produce [the Houses agreed that it is [tithed according to
        the rule] of the previous year,

C.   "and concerning (2) produce which has not sprouted buds [they agree] that it is
        [tithed according to the rule] of the following year.

D.   "Regarding what did they differ?

E.   "With respect to produce which is forming pods.

F.   "For the House of Shammai say, '[It is tithed] according to the [rule in effect in the]
        previous year.'

G.   "And the House of Hillel say, '[It is tithed] according to the [rule in effect in the]
        following year.'"

H.   It follows that there are three rules [which govern the tithing] of vegetables. [These
        rules, which may be inferred from the preceding unit of law, T. does not spell out
        explicitly].

I.   Egyptian beans which one sowed [intending to harvest them] as a vegetable, [not for their seed, as at M. 2:8H-I],

J.   even though they took root before New Year,

K.   and they were harvested after the [New] Year,

L.   are subject to [the separation of] tithes.

M.   And the year (šᶜh) in which they are harvested [determines the rules which govern] their tithing.

N.   And tithes are removed from seeds on behalf of vegetables and from vegetables on behalf of seeds [of the same crop].

O.   (E: And) if [an Egyptian bean plant] produced ripened pods (qswsym gmwrym) before the New Year,

P.   its seed is tithed according to the [rule applicable to the produce of] the previous year and its vegetable [is tithed according to the rule applicable] at the time of its harvest.

T. 2:6

Q.   (1) Dill³⁶ and (2) coriander³⁷ (E omits: coriander) which one sowed [intending to harvest them] for their vegetables (E: for their seed),

R.   even though they took root before the New Year,

S.   and they were harvested after the New Year,

T.   are subject to [the separation of] tithes [as a single crop].

U.   And the year (šᶜh) at which they are harvested [determines the rules which govern] their tithing.

V.   And the tithes are removed from seeds on behalf of vegetables and from vegetables on behalf of seeds (so E; ed. princ.; V reads: for vegetables) [of the same crop].

W.   (E: And) if [dill or coriander plants] reached one-third of their growth before the New Year,

X.   their seed is tithed according to the [rule applicable to produce of] the preceding year, and their vegetables [are tithed according to the rule applicable] at the time of their harvest.

Y.   Dill which one sowed [intending to harvest it] for its seed,

Z.   its seed is tithed and the pods and the vegetables are exempt [from the separation of tithes].

AA.   [If] he sows for pods (ed. princ. and E omit:) for vegetables

BB.   its seeds and pods are tithed and the vegetables are exempt [from the separation of tithes].

T. 2:7a

T. continues the discussion of rules for the separation of tithes, the topic of M. 2:7-9 and T. 2:3-5. The pericope is in three parts: the Houses-dispute at A-E+F, the two formally parallel units of law at G-M+N-O and P-V+W-X, and finally, the rules at Y-Z and AA-BB, which supplement the preceding discussion. Since each of these rules makes its own point, we shall take them up in turn.

The Houses dispute the ambiguous status of produce which has begun to form pods, but is not yet ripe at the beginning of the new calendar year. Such produce could belong to the preceding year (Shammaites) or to the following year (Hillelites). The Shammaites' view, it should be noted, supports Eleazar's rule about Egyptian beans, at M. 2:8L. F merely summarizes the rules for separating tithes from vegetables: produce which ripens before New Year clearly is subject to the tithes of the preceding year; that which has not yet begun to grow is subject to the tithes of the following year; and that which has only formed pods, about which the Houses disagree.

The rule of G-M complements the case considered by Simeon Shezuri at M. 2:8H-I. As we recall, he claims that Egyptian beans sowed for their seed are subject to the tithes of the year in which they take root, in accordance with the rule governing grains. Beans also might be sowed as vegetables. In this case, T. rules, the farmer separates the tithes due in the year in which they are harvested. The gloss at N-O qualifies this rule. If the pods, which contain the seeds of the bean, formed before New Year, the seeds are subject to tithes separately from the vegetable. Since they could have been harvested prior to the new calendar year, they are deemed produce of the preceding year. The parallel case at P-V+W-X merely reiterates the same point for the case of dill and coriander.

At Y-Z, the farmer sows dill in order to gather its seed, rather than for the vegetable, as at P-V. The result is predictable. Only that which the farmer gathers is subject to tithes. The final case, which clearly is meant to develop this point, is unintelligible. Lieberman, TK, p. 504, on the basis of y. Ma. 4:5 and Maimonides, Heave-offering, 2:5, emends the text as follows:

AA. If the farmer sows intending to harvest pods (reading: zr^c lzyryn),

BB. the seeds, vegetables and pods are tithed (eliminating the word, ptwr, "exempt").

The point now is clear. When the farmer collects the pods, the seeds and vegetables likewise are ready for harvest. All parts of the plant, therefore, are subject to tithing, even though he gathers only the pods.

I.   A.   All [plants which people generally grow as] vegetables, [but] which [a farmer] sowed [intending to harvest them] for their seed--

     B.   [the farmer's] intention is null.

     C.   [With the result that] the vegetables are liable [to the separation of tithes],

     D.   but the seeds are exempt [from the separation of tithes].

T. 2:7b

II. E.   (E omits: E-H) Wheat and legumes [which people generally grow for seed, but] which [a farmer] sowed [intending to harvest them] as vegetables (so Lieberman, TZ, p. 171; E,V, and ed. princ. read: for their seed)--

     F.   [the farmer's] intention is null.

G.　　[With the result that] their seeds are liable [to the separation of tithes]

H.　　but their vegetables are exempt [from the separation of tithes].

III.　I.　　Beans, barley, and fenugreek [which people generally grow for their seed but] which [a farmer] sowed [intending to harvest them] as vegetables--

J.　　[the farmer's] intention is null.

K.　　[With the result that] their seeds are liable [to the separation of tithes],

L.　　but their vegetables are exempt [from the separation of tithes].

T. 2:8 (I-L: y. Ma. 4:6[51c]; b. Erub. 28a)

T. presents a new theory regarding those crops which can be cultivated either as vegetables or for the sake of their seeds. Common practice, rather than the intention of the individual farmer, now is deemed decisive. This principle, clearly expressed in the triplet, directly contradicts that of M. 2:8-9 and T. 2:4-5.

A.　　Cress[38] and hedge-mustard[39] [normally cultivated as both seeds and vegetables]

B.　　which [a farmer] sowed [intending to harvest them] for their seed,

C.　　(ed. princ. omits: C-D) both the seeds and the vegetables are tithed.

D.　　If he sowed them [intending to harvest them] as vegetables,

E.　　both the vegetables and the seeds are tithed.

T. 2:9a (b. Erub. 28a)

This rule reinforces the point of T. 2:7b-2:8, that common practice supersedes the intention of the individual farmer. The point is made here with respect to cress and hedge mustard, types of plants normally cultivated both as seeds and as vegetables (see M. Ma. 4:5). Each part of the plant is subject to tithes at the appropriate time.

A.　　Rabban Simeon b. Gamaliel says, "Summer onions[40]

B.　　"[the stalks of which] one bent over [in order to gather the seeds which grow at the top] (following Lieberman, TK, p. 172, who reads: $\acute{s}$rknn; E: $\acute{s}$rqnn; V: $\acute{s}$rbsn) before the New Year,

C.　　[are subject to the same rule as produce grown for its seed cf. M. 2:8-9, and so] are tithed according to the rule which applies to produce of the previous year.

D.　　"and they are permitted during the Sabbatical year [that is, they are exempt from the restrictions governing seventh-year produce].

E.　　"And if not, [that is, if one bent over the heads of the onions after the New Year of the Sabbatical year],

F.　　"they are forbidden during the Sabbatical year,

G.　　"and [if one did so after the New Year in any other year of the Sabbatical cycle], they are tithed according to the [rule which applies to produce of the] following year."

T. 2:9b

We return to the principle, expressed at M. 2:9, that the farmer's intention to harvest produce for its seeds or as a vegetable, determines its status. In the present case, the farmer tramples the stalks of the onions, containing the seeds of the plant, which he then collects.[41] Since he is concerned to harvest only the seeds of the onions, the plant is subject to the tithes of the year in which it takes root. The details of the rule are a reprise of M. 2:9O-S.

A.   If [summer onions] had [begun growing in the] second [year of the Sabbatical cycle] and the third year arrives,

B.   they do not bend them and they do not deprive them of water [during the second year],

C.   in order that [the produce will be deemed part of the crop of the third year and so] will be [subject to] poorman's tithe (E omits D-F and reads: in order that it will be subject to second tithe).

D.   [If summer onions] had [begun growing during the] third [year of the Sabbatical cycle] and the fourth year arrives,

E.   they do bend them and they do deprive them of water [during the third year],

F.   in order that [the produce will be deemed part of the crop of the third year and so] will be [subject to] poorman's tithe (so Lieberman, TZ, p. 172; E, V, and ed. princ. read: second tithe).

G.   And one is permitted to bend over (so Lieberman, TZ, p. 172, who reads: lrkn; E,V, and ed. princ. read: ldkn) [the tops of the onions, as at E], by foot,

H.   for (w-) this is the way everyone is accustomed [to do it].

T. 2:10

The onions referred to at A and D could be subject to either second tithe (given in the second and fourth years of the Sabbatical cycle) or to poorman's tithe (given in the third year). The pericope's point, made by the contrasting rules at A-C and D-F, is that it is preferable to designate produce as poorman's tithe, for this benefits needy Israelites. Thus, the farmer cultivates the onions in a way which assures that they will be subject to poorman's tithe.

The formally distinct ruling, G-H, makes a secondary point. It is not necessary to bend over each onion stalk individually, thereby insuring that its seeds are prevented from further growth. The common practice, to trample them by foot, is less effective, but easier.

A.   (1) Grain and (2) legumes

B.   which reached one-third [of their growth] before the New Year,

C.   are tithed according to the [rules which apply to produce of the] previous year, [that is, the year in which they were planted].

D.   And [if they were planted in the sixth year], they are permitted during the Sabbatical year [that is, they are not subject to the restrictions which apply to seventh-year produce].

E.   And if not [that is, if they did not reach one-third of their growth before the New
     Year, but during the Sabbatical year itself],

F.   they are forbidden during the Sabbatical year [that is, they are subject to the
     restrictions applicable to seventh-year produce],

G.   and [if they were planted in any year of the Sabbatical cycle other than the sixth],
     they are tithed according to the [rule which applies to produce of the] year following
     [=M. 2:7A-G with slight variations].

H.   R. Simeon Shezuri says, "Egyptian beans that were originally sowed for [the sake of
     their] spikes [that is, for their greens],

I.   "and similarly, large beans, and all similar [crops when sown for their spikes, which
     reach one-third of their growth before the New Year],

J.   "are tithed according to the [rules which apply to produce of the] previous year,
     [that is, the year in which they were planted].

K.   "And [if they were planted in the sixth year], they are permitted during the
     Sabbatical year.

L.   "And if not, [that is, if they did not reach one-third of their growth before the New
     Year],

M.   "they are forbidden during the Sabbatical year,

N.   "and [if they were planted in any year of the Sabbatical cycle other than the sixth],
     they are tithed according to the [rule which applies to produce of the] year following
     [=M. 2:7C-D, cf. M. 2:8A-D]."

O.   Said Ben Azzai before R. Aqiba in the name of R. Joshua, "Also: [This rule applies
     if the beans merely] took root [prior to the New Year]."

P.   R. Aqiba retracted [his earlier opinion] in order to teach in accordance with the
     words of Ben Azzai.

T. 2:13

The by now familiar rule of M. 2:7 is applied to a new class of produce. Grain and
legumes become subject to tithes when they reach one-third of their full growth, for this
is the point at which these crops become valuable to the farmer (see M. 4:9 and M. Ma.
1:3). If this occurs before New Year, these crops are subject to the tithes of the
preceding calendar year (A-G). The same criterion is applicable to beans cultivated for
their greens, rather than for either their seeds or as a vegetable (H-N). Joshua, O, objects
to the notion that beans grown for their greens are subject to a different criterion from
those grown for their seeds. The point at which the beans take root determines the tithes
to which they are subject, regardless of the farmer's purpose in planting them.

2:10

A.   Gourds which one left [in a field during the sixth year] so that [they would dry out,
     at which time the farmer would break them open and collect their] seeds--

B.   if they became hard [and dry] before the New Year of the Sabbatical year,

C.   and [the gourds themselves] became unfit (<u>wnpslw</u>) (B, L omit:) for human food (G[4]
       adds: and animal food),

D.   one is permitted to leave them [in the field and to gather the seeds] during the
       Sabbatical year. [Since these gourds were no longer edible when the Sabbatical year
       began, they are exempt from the restrictions of the law; cf. M. 7:1-2. The farmer
       therefore may tend these gourds for their seeds alone and allow the vegetable to dry
       out.]

E.   And if not [that is, if the gourds do not harden before the New Year of the
       Sabbatical year, but rather remain edible,]

F.   one is forbidden to leave them [in the field and to gather the seeds] during the
       Sabbatical year. [Since these gourds still were edible at the beginning of the
       Sabbatical year, they are regarded as produce of that year. The farmer must use
       these gourds for food, in accordance with M. 8:1, and may not leave them to dry out
       in the field.]

G.   Their buds[42] [that is, those which sprout from these gourds during the Sabbatical
       year] are forbidden during the Sabbatical year.

H.   "And [during the Sabbatical year] they sprinkle water on a field of grain (lit., white
       dust)," the words of R. Simeon.

I.   R. Eliezer b. Jacob forbids [such sprinkling].

J.   "They flood (<u>mmrsyn</u>)[43] rice [paddies] during the Sabbatical year," (reading with nine
       MSS.:) the words of R. Simeon.

K.   (Omitting: R. Simeon says,) But they do not trim[44] [the rice plants].

M. 2:10

The farmer at A wishes to cultivate gourds only for their seeds, not as vegetables
for eating. He does this by leaving these gourds in the field to dry out. Once the gourds
become dry, the seeds inside are ripe and ready for harvesting. With these basic facts in
hand, we can understand the problem addressed by the contrasting rules at B-D and E-F.
If the gourds left in the field during the sixth year continue to grow into the seventh year,
they become subject to the restrictions that apply to all edible produce of the Sabbatical
year. In particular, they may be used only as food for eating, in accordance with the rule
of M. 8:1. The farmer therefore may not allow these gourds to go to seed, but rather
must eat them or sell them for other edibles, in accordance with the rules governing
sanctified produce of the Sabbatical year (see M. 8:1ff.). On the other hand, if the gourds
themselves become dry and inedible during the sixth year, and merely remain in the field
into the following year, they are exempt from these restrictions. The farmer then is free
to leave the vegetables to dry out so that he later may collect their seeds (A-D). The
point of G is that buds that sprout from these gourds during the Sabbatical year are
regarded as a separate entity. They are subject to the restrictions of that year, even if
the gourds themselves are not.

The quite separate unit of law at H-K addresses an entirely new issue, whether
irrigation is permitted during the Sabbatical year. Eliezer regards watering as an act of

cultivation, which clearly is forbidden (I). Simeon, however, recognizes that refraining from irrigation throughout the Sabbatical year would cause the soil to dry out and become unusable. In order to preserve the fertility of the soil, he permits farmers to water fields and rice paddies during the Sabbatical year (H, J). Trimming the rice plants, however, is forbidden. This promotes the ripening of the rice[45] and so constitutes forbidden cultivation (K).

A.   All (E omits: All) vegetables that hardened (so Lieberman, TZ, p. 172, who reads: šhwqšw; V, E read: šhwšqw) [before the beginning of the Sabbatical year]--

B.   one is permitted to tend them during the Sabbatical year [=M. 2:10D].

C.   If they were soft (so ed. princ. and E: rkyn; V: dkyn, "thin")

D.   one is forbidden (E omits:) from tending them during the Sabbatical year [=M. 2:10F],

E.   so as [to avoid] the appearance [of committing a transgression, that is, lest someone mistakenly think that the vegetables were planted during the Sabbatical year, in violation of the law].

F.   They do not obligate him [i.e., the farmer] to uproot arum.

G.   Rather, they leave it [i.e., arum] as it is.

H.   If [an arum tuber] sprouted in the year following the Sabbatical,

I.   it is permitted.

T. 2:11

J.   They do not obligate him [i.e., the farmer] to uproot artichokes,

K.   but he trims the leaves.

L.   If [an artichoke] sprouted in the year following the Sabbatical,

M.   it is permitted.

T. 2:12

T. offers a general rule based upon the case of M. 2:10A-E. Vegetables are deemed to belong to the crop of the year in which they sprout. Nonetheless, vegetables which begin growing in the sixth year may remain ripe and edible into the seventh year. A farmer may not cultivate such produce during the Sabbatical year, for it might appear that he was maintaining crops planted in violation of the law (C-E). Vegetables which become hard before the beginning of the New Year, by contrast, clearly are produce of the sixth year. Farmers are free to maintain this produce in the field during the Sabbatical year (A-B).

Arum (F-I) and artichokes (J-M) are subject to special restrictions, for they grow underground over a period of two or more years. Farmers who leave these types of produce in the ground throughout the Sabbatical year, therefore, are not suspected of cultivating crops of the Sabbatical year (F-G, J). Since only a portion of the tuber's growth occurs during the Sabbatical year, that which sprouts from it in the following year is exempt from the law (H-I, L-M). In the case of artichokes, however, one must trim away the new leaves which sprout from the tuber each year. This indicates that the farmer is not maintaining the artichokes for the sake of these new growths (K).

A. They sprinkle a field (ed. princ. and E add: during the) year preceding the Sabbatical,
B. so that vegetables will sprout during the Sabbatical year.
C. And not only that, but also during the Sabbatical year they sprinkle it [that is, a field,]
D. so that vegetables will sprout in the year following the Sabbatical.
E. Onions which began growing during the year preceding the Sabbatical and continued growing during the Sabbatical year--
F. they sprinkle water (E omits: water) on them,
G. so that they will be easy to uproot.

T. 2:1 (A-D: b. M.Q. 6b)

H. [As regards] an arum [tuber] which sprouted buds during the Sabbatical year--
I. one may not (E: they do not) remove [the buds] from it during the Sabbatical year (E omits: during the Sabbatical year)
J. so as [to avoid] the appearance [of committing a transgression].
K. (E omits: K-N) Onions which began growing during the year preceding the Sabbatical and continued growing during the Sabbatical year,
L. or onions that began growing during the Sabbatical year and continued growing during the year following--
M. they sprinkle water on them,
N. so that they will be easy to uproot.

T. 2:2

T. presents two separate explanations for the rule that watering is permitted during the Sabbatical year (M. 2:10H,J). First, this preserves the moisture level in the soil and so enables crops to grow during the following year (A-D). Moreover, tuberous plants, such as onions, may be sprinkled during the Sabbatical year. This is not part of the cultivation of the crop, but merely enables farmers to remove the tubers from the soil (E-G, K-N). This discussion is interrupted by the quite separate rule, H-K, concerning arum. The tuber referred to at H grows in the ground during the Sabbatical year. Nonetheless, it is harvested in the year following the Sabbatical and so belongs to the crop of that year. It follows that the tuber, as well as the buds which sprout from it during the Sabbatical year, are exempt from the law. These buds may not be harvested, however, for they appear to be produce of the Sabbatical year.

CHAPTER THREE

Shebiit Chapter Three

The chapter as a whole concerns the problem posed by a farmer who during the seventh year engages in activity that is permitted, but nonetheless appears to be committing a transgression. A person who gathers stones from a field for use in construction, for example, may look to others as though he is clearing the land for cultivation. Gathering stones is problematic because, though technically permitted, it may lead others to commit actual transgressions. Mishnah's authorities therefore rule that Israelites must avoid even the appearance of cultivating the land during the seventh year, in addition to observing the restrictions of the Sabbatical year in fact. Though this rule has a clear practical purpose, to prevent possible violations of the law, it also points toward a deeper principle. For Mishnah's framers, appearing to violate the laws of the seventh year is forbidden because this would undermine Israel's conception of itself as a community sanctified by God's laws. That is, an Israelite who appears flagrantly to transgress the restrictions of the seventh year acts as though those laws did not apply to him. In doing so, he separates himself in the eyes of others from the community of Israel, which is commanded by God to observe the law. Thus, in the view of Mishnah's framers, all Israelites have a responsibility to demonstrate to one another that they are not transgressors, as well as to uphold the law in fact. This single principle of law is developed in the chapter's two distinct thematic units, M. 3:1-4, on manuring fields, and M. 3:5-10, on removing stones from a field. Let us now briefly review the details of these laws.

We deal first with farmers who wish to store manure in their fields during the Sabbatical year for use as fertilizer during the eighth year. This is permitted provided that the farmer indicates that he does not intend to fertilize his field during the Sabbatical year itself. It must be apparent to all that he is only storing manure for later use. He shows this in one of three ways, by placing the dung in large storage heaps (M. 3:2, 3:3A-B,D,F), by piling the manure slightly above or below ground level (M. 3:3C,E,G), or by restricting the size of the area covered with dung (M. 3:4). This discussing of manuring fields is introduced at M. 3:1, a ruling that permits farmers to bring manure into their fields only late in the Sabbatical year, when the ground has dried out. This assures that the dung will not actually fertilize the soil during the seventh year.

The central point of M. 3:5-10 is that people who collect stones for use as building materials during the Sabbatical year must do so in a manner that indicates that they are not preparing the ground for cultivation. They may gather only large stones, which clearly will be used for construction (M. 3:5-7, 3:8E-3:9), or they must leave a layer of rubble on the ground (M. 3:7E-H). This shows that their intent is not to clear the field for planting. By the same token, a person who clears stones from land which ordinarily is not cultivated need not scruple about appearing to violate the law (M. 3:10A-B, 3:6G-N, 3:7I-J). One rule, M. 3:8A-D, though related topically to the present discussion, makes a separate point. Farmers may not repair damaged terraces during the sixth year, for in doing so they prepare the land for cultivation during the Sabbatical year. Fixing terraces during the seventh year itself, however, is permitted. This is done solely to make the land ready for planting during the eighth year. This ruling further illustrates the central principle of Chapters One and Two, that Israelites may not perform agricultural activities during the sixth year which benefit the land only during the Sabbatical year.

3:1

A.   From what time [during the Sabbatical year] do [Israelite farmers] bring manure out [to their fields to store it there] in dung heaps [for use as fertilizer, during the following year, not during the seventh year itself, which would be forbidden]?

B.   "From the time [during other years of the Sabbatical cycle] when workers (^{C}wbdy ^{C}bwdh; 3 MSS. read: ^{C}wbry ^{C}byrh, "transgressors of the laws of the Sabbatical year")[1] cease [spreading manure in their fields]," the words of R. Meir. [From this point on, the manure which the farmer places in heaps in the field will not have the effect of fertilizing the crops of the seventh year, which would be forbidden].

C.   R. Judah says, "From the time when the [ground] moisture (mtwq; lit., sweetness)[2] dries up." [Since at this point the ground no longer will absorb the nutrients from the manure, the farmer will not be engaged in fertilizing.]

D.   R. Yose says, "From the time when [the ground hardens] forming clumps (mšyqšr)."[3]

M. 3:1

A farmer during the Sabbatical year wishes to store manure in his field for use as fertilizer during the following year. This poses a problem, for even though storing the dung in itself is permitted, the farmer's action may have the secondary effect of fertilizing the crops of the seventh year. The question under dispute is when during the Sabbatical year farmers may begin to store up manure in their fields without thereby enriching the produce of that year. Meir, B, looks to the point during other years of the Sabbatical cycle when farmers ordinarily quit fertilizing their crops. In general, farmers stop spreading manure toward the end of the growing season, when the dung no longer would benefit the crops growing in the field.[4] At the corresponding point during the Sabbatical year, Meir assumes, manure may be stored in the field without improving the crops of that year. Judah and Yose, on the other hand, hold that the conditions in the field during the Sabbatical year itself are decisive. Once the ground has dried out, placing dung in the field no longer will have the effect of enriching the soil (C,D). The farmer then may begin to stockpile his manure. Judah and Yose, who both adopt this view, appear to differ from one another only in a matter of formulation.[5]

3:2

A. [In accordance with the rule of M. 3:1], how much manure [may they bring out to a field during the Sabbatical year]?

B. Up to three dung heaps per seah-space [of land],

C. each [dung heap containing no less than] ten baskets [of dung],

D. each [basket containing a volume of no less than] a letek [that is, fifteen seahs, of dung].[6]

E. They may add to the [number of] baskets [above 10 per dung heap],

F. but they may not add to the [number of] dung heaps [above three per seah-space].

G. R. Simeon (G[7], K: Judah) says, "Also: [They may add to the number] of dung heaps."

M. 3:2

During the Sabbatical year farmers must store manure in a manner that indicates that they do not intend to fertilize their fields, which would be forbidden. By piling substantial quantities of dung in a few large heaps, the farmer signifies that he is storing this manure for use during the following year. This is permitted, as we know from M. 3:1. A secondary dispute at E-F vs. G considers whether a farmer who wishes to store more than the specified quantity of manure (B-D) may make additional dung heaps in the field. Covering a larger portion of the field with dung might create the impression that the farmer was engaged in fertilizing. For this reason, E-F restricts the number of dung heaps that a farmer can make within each seah-space of land. By limiting the surface area covered with manure, the farmer shows that he is not using it as fertilizer. Simeon, G, on the other hand, argues that the number of heaps within the field is of no consequence. Piling dung in large mounds in itself indicates that the farmer is storing it for later use.

A. [During the Sabbatical year] they do not gather grass [which grows] on dung,

B. but they may gather [loose pieces of] straw [which have been mixed in with the dung].

C. They add straw or stubble [to a dung heap] in order to increase [its volume].

D. They add water [to a dung heap] so that it will decompose (so E, V: Šysrh; ed. princ.: Šyprh, "it will sprout").

E. And they hoe it so that it will swell.

F. "They do not add to [the number of] baskets or to [the number of] dung heaps [above the numbers specified in M. 3:2] (E omits: or to the dung heaps)," the words of R. Meir.

G.   R. Judah says, "They may add (E omits:) to the [number of] baskets but they may not
      add to the [number of] dung heaps."

H.   R. Simeon says, "Also: [They may add to the number] of dung heaps" [=M. 3:2E-G].

I.   [And, in the view of all authorities, piling manure in a field during the Sabbatical
      year is permitted] only if there are at least three dung heaps in a seah-space.

                                      T. 2:14

Manure which a farmer stores in his field during the Sabbatical year may contain
seeds that subsequently sprout greens. This grass, like that which grows from the ground,
is subject to the restrictions of the Sabbatical year and so may not be harvested. People
may collect straw from a dung heap, however, for this has not sprouted from the dung, but
merely was mixed in with it (A-B). The point of this rule is that a dung heap in certain
respects shares the status of the ground on which it sits. That which grows from it, like
that which grows from the ground itself, is governed by the laws of the Sabbatical year.
The rules which follow, C-E, qualify this principle. Unlike the ground, a dung heap may be
hoed and watered during the Sabbatical year. This is part of the process of preserving the
manure and is not done in order to cultivate the field.

At F-H+I, three Ushans dispute the rule of M. 3:2E-G. The positions of Judah
(equivalent to the anonymous rule of M. 3:2E-F) and Simeon are familiar from Mishnah
and need no further explanation. Only the view attributed to Meir (F) is new. He argues
that the quantity of dung specified in M. 3:2A-D constitutes the maximum which a farmer
may accumulate in his field. Increasing this amount, he assumes, might make it appear
that the farmer wishes to fertilize his field. The gloss at I makes the point that the
farmer must make at least three piles, in order to show that he is engaged in storing
manure.

                                      3:3

A.   [During the Sabbatical year] a man constructs within his field three dung heaps per
      seah-space, [as specified by M. 3:2B-D].

B.   "(G[7], S add: And) [if a farmer has too much manure to fit into three piles of the
      size specified at M. 3:2, then he may construct] more than that [number, that is,
      more than three heaps per seah-space]. (B, N read: mhsyb; "More than [three, he
      must form them in the manner of] quarried stone, [one basket on top of an-
      other]"),[8] the words of R. Simeon, [which correspond to his view at M. 3:2G].

C.   But sages forbid [the construction of more than three dung heaps per seah-space]
      unless the farmer either deepens [the ground where the manure is deposited by]
      three [handbreadths] or raises [the ground by] three [handbreadths. By piling the
      manure in this unusual manner, the farmer indicates that he is storing it, not using
      to fertilize his field].

D.   A person [who does not have enough dung to form three piles of the size specified at
      M. 3:2B-D] places [all] the manure in his possession in one large pile ('wsr).

E. R. Meir forbids [the farmer from doing this] unless he either deepens [the ground by] three [handbreadths] or raises [the ground by] three [handbreadths].

F. If one had a small amount [of manure, he forms a single pile and] continues to add to it.

G. R. Eleazar b. Azariah forbids the [farmer from doing this] unless he either deepens [the ground by] three [handbreadths] or raises [the ground by] three [handbreadths],

H. or unless he places [the manure] on rocky ground.

> M. 3:3 (D-H: b. M.Q. 4b; F-H: y. B.M.
> 5:6[10c]; G-H: y. M.Q. 1:2[80b])

The question, familiar from M. 3:2, is how a farmer can store manure in his field during the Sabbatical year without appearing to fertilize his land. Two opposing views on the matter are presented in three disputes at B vs. C, D vs. E and F vs. G-H. Simeon, in line with his position at M. 3:2G, claims that simply piling the dung in heaps, rather than spreading it around, indicates that it is in storage for use during the following year. On his view, reflected also in the anonymous rules at D and F, the number and size of these piles is of no importance. Sages (C), Meir (E) and Eleazar b. Azariah (G-H) hold that farmers must take further precautions to avoid the appearance of performing a transgression.[9] By piling the manure either slightly above or slightly below ground level, the farmer makes it clear that he is not fertilizing the topsoil. Eleazar adds that a farmer who piles dung on rocky soil, which is not arable, clearly would not be suspected of fertilizing the land.

3:4

A. One who uses his field as a fold [for his flock during the Sabbatical year, so that, as a result, the animals drop dung throughout the field] (hmdyr 't śdhw), makes an enclosure [that measures] two seah-spaces in area. [By limiting the surface area covered with dung, the farmer indicates that his intention is not to fertilize the land, in violation of the law].

B. [After the enclosed area is filled with manure he creates a second fold adjacent to the first. How so?] He removes three sides [of the original enclosure] and leaves the middle side [that is, the fourth side, in place. With the other three sides of the original fold he creates a second enclosure of the same size.]

C. The result is that he encloses within a fold [an area totaling] four seah-spaces.

D. Rabban Simeon b. Gamaliel says, "[He may continue to create enclosures in this manner and so enlarge the area until it measures a total of] eight seah-spaces."

E. [If] his entire field was four seah-spaces in area,

F. he sets aside a small section [of the field, which he does not enclose within the fold,]

G. so as [to avoid] the appearance [of committing the transgression of fertilizing his field during the Sabbatical year].

H.   And he removes [manure] from within the enclosure and places it in his field in the
      accepted manner of those who handle manure [during the Sabbatical year, that is, in
      accordance with the rule of M. 3:1-3].

                                        M. 3:4

      A farmer who, during the Sabbatical year, uses his field as a fold for livestock may
appear to be fertilizing the land. By allowing the flock to spread manure over only a
limited area, four seah-spaces in all, the farmer gives public evidence that he is not
engaged in the performance of this transgression. Gamaliel, D, disputes a matter of little
importance, the precise size of the area which may be included within the fold. At
E-G+H, a secondary unit of law, we consider the problem posed by a farmer whose entire
field measures only four seah-spaces. If he were to use this entire area as a fold, in line
with the rule at A-D, he would appear to be fertilizing. He therefore leaves a small
portion of his field outside the enclosure, to show that he is not engaged in manuring any
part of the field.

      At H, the discussion shifts from problems of appearing to violate the law, to the
matter of preventing actual transgressions. The farmer may not allow the dung which the
animals leave in the pens actually to fertilize the field. Rather, he must collect the
manure and store it in heaps, in accordance with the procedures spelled out at M. 3:1-3.

A.   One who uses his field as a fold,

B.   makes an enclosure two seahs in area [=M. 3:4A-B].

C.   [When the enclosure] is filled [with manure],

D.   he removes [manure] from within the enclosure and forms dung heaps in his field in
      the accepted manner of those who handle manure [=M. 3:4I with slight variations].

E.   And he proceeds to make another enclosure.

F.   Said R. Judah, "To what case does this rule apply?

G.   "To a case where his flock was small.

H.   "But if his flock was large,

I.   "even [an enclosure] one kor in area, or two kors in area is permitted."

J.   R. Simeon b. Eleazar says, "[One desiring to use his field as a fold] sinks a stake in
      the middle [of the field] and surrounds it with four enclosures in its four sides."

K.   "If his entire field was two seahs in area,

L.   "he should not enclose all of it.

M.   "Rather he sets aside a small section [of the field]

N.   "so as [to avoid] the appearance [of committing a transgression]," the words of R.
      Meir [=M. 3:4G-H].

O.   R. Yose (E: sages) permits [the farmer to use his entire field as a fold].

                                        T. 2:15

P. He removes [his flock] from one enclosure,

Q. and places [it] in another enclosure (E: this enclosure).

R. "[He may do so] only if he does not return them to the original enclosure," the words of R. Meir.

S. And sages permit [him to return them].

T. 2:16

T. (Ed. princ. omits 2:17) He removes [his flock] from one field,

U. and places [them] in another field.

V. [He may do so only if he does not return them to the original field," the words of R. Meir.

W. And sages permit [him to return them].

T. 2:17

X. He removes [his flock] from one enclosure,

Y. and places [them] in another enclosure.

Z. "[He may do so] only if there is not a space of [more than] eight seahs between [the first enclosure] and the other [enclosure]," the words of R. Dosethai b. R. Judah.

AA. R. Yose b. Kipper says in the name of R. Eleazar, "[There must not be a space of more than] two seahs [between them]."

BB. And within these two seahs he milks [his flock] and shears them,

CC. and he transfers [his flock from one enclosure to the other] (wmknys wmwsy'; lit., "he takes them out and brings them in) by way of a path (drk ^{c}lyyh) [which connects the two enclosures].

T. 2:18

T.'s version of M. 3:4 (A-E) is followed by a long series of rules for creating a fold during the Sabbatical year. Judah (F-I) rejects the rule of M. 3:4B-C, which limits the size of a fold that a farmer may make during the Sabbatical year. He is not concerned that a farmer who makes a large enclosure will appear to be using the animals to fertilize his field. Since the farmer's intention is solely to create a fold, he need not worry about appearing to commit a transgression. Simeon b. Eleazar (J) offers an alternative to Simeon b. Gamaliel's procedure (M. 3:4E) for creating four adjacent folds. At K-N vs. O, Meir and Yose dispute whether a farmer may convert his entire field into a fold during the Sabbatical year. Meir, in line with M. 3:4F-H, holds that this is forbidden, since it looks as though the farmer is fertilizing his field during the Sabbatical year. Yose, like Judah (F-I), regards the intention of the farmer, not the way his action appears to others, as probative. He may use his entire field as a fold so long as he does not intend to fertilize it.

The dispute between Meir and sages (P-R vs. S) concerns the procedure for using two adjacent folds. Meir prohibits the farmer from moving his flock back to the area occupied by the first enclosure after the second has filled with manure. By reconstructing this fold, he would appear to be creating a third enclosure, in violation of M. 3:4A-D, which permits him to make only two. Sages, however, are concerned only that the farmer does not create a third enclosure on new, previously unused land. Returning the flock to the first enclosure, then, is permitted, for in doing so no new land will be covered with manure.[10] T. 2:17 merely repeats this dispute and should be omitted, in accordance with ed. princ.

The point of the dispute at X-Z vs. AA is clear. The two enclosures need not be adjacent, but only in close proximity to one another. This prevents animals from spreading manure randomly over a large area as they are transferred from one to the other. I cannot account for the difference between the specific distances proposed by Dosethai and Yose. The gloss at BB-CC addresses the same concern. The farmer may milk and shear his flock outside of these folds, for the amount of manure left in the open field will be negligible.[11] Nonetheless, he transfers them between the two enclosures along a path, to prevent the animals from shitting all over the field.

A.   They construct enclosures using all [types of materials];
B.   with (1) stones, (2) matting, (3) straw, (4) reeds and (5) stalks.
C.   [They may make an enclosure] even with three ropes, one on top of another,
D.   so long as there is not a space of [more than] three handbreadths between [one] rope (E: reed) and another
E.   [that is, sufficient space] for a lamb to enter.

T. 2:19 (=T. Kil. 4:3)

Farmers may construct a fold in any manner which assures that livestock cannot escape from it.

A.   On Sabbaths, festivals or the intermediate days of festivals, they [that is, gentile workers] do not drive a flock into a fold [on behalf of Israelites,]
B.   even [if they do so] as a favor.
C.   [For example,] if they [that is, the flock,] came [into the fold] of their own accord,
D.   they [that is, the gentiles,] do not assist them.
E.   And it is not permitted to appoint a [gentile] guard [to keep the flock within the enclosure]
F.   or to move the flock [on Sabbaths or festivals from one place to another within the fold].
G.   (E omits: G-J) If they [that is, gentile workers] were driving a flock into a fold on Sabbaths or on festivals,
H.   it is permitted [for them to do so].
I.   And it [also] is permitted to appoint a guard

J.   and to move the flock [from one place to another within the fold].

K.   Rabbi says, "They drive a flock into a fold on the Sabbath as a favor, on a festival [in exchange] for his meals, and on the intermediate days of a festival [the gentile worker may do so] even if he receives his [regular] salary."

T. 2:20 (b. M.Q. 12a)

The question at hand is whether on Sabbaths and festivals a gentile may do work on behalf of Israelites that they themselves are forbidden from doing. Before we turn to the substance of the matter, however, we must distinguish the several units of law which comprise the discussion before us. The anonymous rule at A-B together with Rabbi's lemma at K present a dispute. This is apparent from the parallel language and structure of the two rules, each of which refers to Sabbaths, festivals and the intermediate days of festivals. The intervening materials at C-J break this pattern and so constitute a separate discussion. As we shall see, this block of material in fact is composed of several distinct rulings: C-D, which glosses A-B, and E-F+G-J, a matched pair of rules which directly contradict one another.

The rule at A-B claims that under no circumstances may gentiles perform forbidden labor for Israelites on Sabbaths and festivals. Since Israelites themselves may not tend their flocks on these days, they also may not benefit from the labor of gentiles. Rabbi, K, disagrees, for he holds that the law regulates only the conduct of Israelites on these holidays. Moreover, different rules govern the labor of gentiles on Sabbaths, on festivals and on the intermediate days of festivals, for these days possess varying degrees of sanctity. On the Sabbath, Israelites may ask a gentile to tend their flocks so long as they do not engage in an ordinary business transaction, while on the intermediate days of festivals, business is permitted in the usual manner.

Two separate glosses, C-D and E-F, provide further illustrations of the opening rule (A-B). An Israelite may not allow gentiles voluntarily to perform forbidden labor for him, even if the work itself is very minimal (C-D). Nor, clearly, may an Israelite engage gentiles to assist him in herding his animals on Sabbaths or festivals (E-F). G-J, as noted above, directly disputes E-F. I cannot account for this ruling, which probably should be omitted following the Erfurt manuscript. The pericope as a whole never mentions the laws of the Sabbatical year and has been placed here because it addresses the topic of M. 3:4 and T. 2:19, driving a flock into a fold.

3:5

A.   [During the Sabbatical year] a man may not begin to open a stone quarry in his field, [for in doing so he may appear to be clearing the land for cultivation,]

B.   unless the field contains [enough stones to construct] three piles [of hewn blocks,]

C.   each [pile] three [cubits long] by three [cubits wide] by three [cubits] high,

D.   [so that] their measure is [equivalent to] twenty-seven stones. [That is, each pile
would contain no less than twenty-seven blocks, each measuring one cubic cubit].

M. 3:5

This issue, as at M. 3:1-4, is how a person may perform a permitted activity during
the Sabbatical year without appearing to engage in forbidden cultivation. In the case at
hand, a farmer who removes stone from a field during the Sabbatical year may appear to
be cultivating the land in preparation for planting. This would be forbidden. By removing
substantial quantities of rock, however, the farmer indicates that his only intention is to
quarry, not to clear the land.[12]

A.   [During the Sabbatical year] a man may not begin to open a stone quarry in his field,
B.   unless it contains [enough stones to construct] three piles [of hewn blocks],
C.   each [pile] three [cubits long] by three [cubits wide] by three [cubits] high [=M.
3:5A-C].
D.   (E omits:) Said R. Judah,
E.   "To what case does this [rule, A-C], apply?
F.   "To the case where one intends to prepare [the land as] a field [that is, to prepare it
for cultivation].
G.   "But, in the case where one does not intend to prepare [the land as] a field,
H.   "even a major act of cultivation (dbr mrwbh)[13] is permitted."

T. 3:1

I.   Said Rabban Simeon b. Gamaliel, "To what case does this [rule, A-C], apply?
J.   "To the case where one does not (E reads: does) intend to prepare [the land as] a
field,
K.   "But, in the case where one intends (E reads: does not) to prepare [the land as] a
field,
L.   "even the most minor act of cultivation (klšhw) is forbidden."

T. 3:2

Judah and Simeon b. Gamaliel dispute the theory underlying the rule of M. 3:5A-C,
cited at A-C. Since Simeon endorses the view which I adopted in my comment to
Mishnah, I deal with his ruling first.[14] He maintains that Mishnah's rule refers to a person
who intends to quarry his field, not to cultivate it. The point of the law is that a farmer
may not quarry his field during the Sabbatical year in a manner which appears to violate
the law. On the other hand, if one intends to prepare the ground for cultivation, he may
not clear stones from a field at all. This would be a flagrant violation of the law (K-L).
On Judah's view, however, we deal with a farmer who wishes only to cultivate the
ground. The purpose of the law, then, is to prescribe a procedure by which a farmer may

clear his field of stones without in fact violating the law. He quarries a large quantity of stone, for this in itself is permitted even though it has the secondary effect of preparing the land for cultivation (F). It follows from this position that a farmer who wishes only to quarry his field need not scruple about violating the restrictions of the law. Since he is engaged in a permitted activity, he is free to work the field as he wishes (H).

A.   A rock which lies [partly buried] in the ground,

B.   and [its] tip (E: 'ygr; V: 'ygd) juts out from it [that is, through the earth]--

C.   if it [that is, the tip, considered by itself] is of this measure [that is, one cubic cubit; cf. M. 3:5],

D.   it is permitted [to remove it].

E.   And if not [that is, if the tip of the rock is smaller than this,]

F.   it is forbidden [to remove it].

T. 3:3

A farmer may remove a rock from his field during the Sabbatical year only if he knows for certain that it is one cubic cubit in measure, as required by M. 3:5. T. illustrates this point by taking up the case of a rock lodged in the ground only part of which is exposed. Only if the visible portion meets Mishnah's requirements may the farmer remove it from his field.

3:6

A.   [As regards] a wall consisting of ten stones, [each of which is so large that it can] be carried [only] by two men--

B.   lo, these [stones] may be removed [from the field] during the Sabbatical year. [The size of the stones indicates that the people are collecting them for use in con- struction, not clearing them away to prepare the land for cultivation].

C.   [The preceding rule applies only if] the height of the wall is ten handbreadths [or more].

D.   Less than this, [that is, if the wall is less than ten handbreadths high,]

E.   he may chisel[15] [stones from the wall]

F.   but he may level [the wall] only until it is one handbreadth from ground level, [but not raze it to the ground. This again indicates that he is not clearing the land under the wall for cultivation].

G.   To what does this [rule, A-F,] apply?

H.   [To a case of removing stones] from within one's own [field].

I.   But from that of his neighbor, he may remove any amount he wishes. [Since a person would not be suspected of cultivating his neighbor's field, in this case he will not appear to be engaged in a transgression.]

J.   To what case does this [rule, A-F,] apply?[16]

K.   To a case in which he did not begin [to remove the stones] during the year preceding the Sabbatical, [but rather during the Sabbatical year itself].

L.   But if he did begin [to remove stones] in the year preceding the Sabbatical, he may remove any amount he wishes [during the Sabbatical year].

M. 3:6

A person may tear down a stone fence during the Sabbatical year to use the stones for construction, provided that he does not appear to be clearing the field for cultivation. This principle, familiar from M. 3:5, is expressed through the two-part rule at A-C and D-F. Removing large numbers of sizable stones from a field during the Sabbatical year is permitted, for it is apparent that the farmer intends to use these stones for construction (A-C). If a person wishes to tear down a smaller wall, however, he must do so in a manner which indicates that he does not wish to clear the land, that is, by leaving a layer of stones behind.

Two formally parallel qualifications of this rule, G-I and J-K, make a single point. A person who clearly is not preparing his field for cultivation may remove any amount of stone, large or small. A man who tears down his neighbor's wall, for example, would not be suspected of violating the law, since one does not customarily cultivate his neighbor's land (H-I). Similarly, if one begins removing stones from a field during the sixth year, Mishnah's framers assume that his intent is to use the stones forthwith, not to clear the land for cultivating during the Sabbatical year.

A.   [During the Sabbatical year] they do not remove a fence which [stands] between two fields [in order to cultivate these two plots of land together,]

B.   whether it is a fence of wood or a fence of stone.

C.   To what does this [rule, A-B,] apply?

D.   [To the case of] one who intends to prepare a field [for cultivation].

E.   But [if he removes the fence] for the wood, it is permitted.

T. 3:16

People may not dismantle a fence during the Sabbatical year in order to cultivate the field. Gathering materials for construction, on the other hand, is permitted. This notion, that the intention of the farmer determines whether his action is permitted, contrasts sharply with the view of M. 3:6, that one must avoid even the appearance of committing a transgression.

3:7

A.   Stones which a plow moved,

B.   or that were covered [in the ground] and were uncovered [after plowing]--

C.   if there are among them two [stones so large that they are] capable of being carried [only] by two men,

D.   lo, these [stones] may be removed.

E.   One who clears stones from his field,

F.   removes the topmost ones and leaves those which are touching the ground.

G.   (O^2, Ca, M, Z omit: G-H) And so [in the case] of a heap of pebbles (P, K omit:) or a pile of stones--

H.   one removes the topmost ones and leaves those which are touching the ground.

I.   If there is beneath them [that is the pebbles or stones] a [large] rock (O^2 omits:) or straw,

J.   lo, these [stones also] may be removed.

M. 3:7

Principles familiar from the preceding rules are applied to a new case: a farmer who wishes to remove from his field stones that lie loose on the surface of the ground. The point, once again, is that he may do so only if the stones are large enough for him to use in construction (A-D). In this case, it is apparent that he is not clearing his field for cultivation.

The formally quite separate pair of rules at E-F and G-H reiterate the point of M. 3:6F. One who gathers stones from his field for use in construction must leave a small layer of rocks on the ground. This indicates that his intention is not to clear his field for cultivation. The qualification of this rule, at I-J, is obvious. A farmer may clear away stones that lie on a rock or on straw. Since he does not in fact prepare any land for planting, he will not appear to be violating the law.

A.   Stones [which have become] fixed [in the ground] (twšbwt) which a plow moved [=M. 3:7A]--

B.   if there are among them two stones which are capable of being carried [only] by two men,

C.   lo, these [stones] may be removed. (=M. 3:7C-D]

T. 3:4a

A spells out the fact implicit in Mishnah's rule. The stones referred to at M. 3:7 are lying on the surface and so are subject to a separate rule from those which comprise a wall (M. 3:6) or a quarry (M. 3:5).

3:8-9

A.   During the year preceding the Sabbatical, after the rains have ceased, they do not build terraces (mdrygwt)^{17} on the sides of ravines,

B.   for this prepares [the ravines for cultivation] during the Sabbatical year, [when working the land is forbidden].[18]

C.   However, during the Sabbatical year, after the rains have ceased, one may build [terraces,]

D.   for this prepares [the ravines for cultivation] during the year following the Sabbatical [when working the land is permitted].

E.   And [during the Sabbatical year when a farmer builds a retaining wall for a terrace,] he may not support [it] with dirt, [for in doing so he would appear to be engaged in an act of cultivation].

F.   But [rather one who wishes to build a retaining wall during the Sabbatical year] constructs a rough embankment (hys) [using only stones. Since the farmer does not move any dirt, he will not appear to be leveling the land, in violation of the laws of the seventh year].

G.   [As regards] any stone [which is near enough to a person building a wall, as at E-F,] that he can [merely] stretch out his hand and pick up [the stone]--

H.   lo, this [stone] may be picked up [from the field and placed in the wall. Since this person removes the stone from the field and adds it to the wall forthwith, it is apparent that he is not engaged in clearing the land for cultivation].

M. 3:8

I.   Stones [so large that they can be carried only on one's] shoulder ('bny ktp) may come from anywhere [for use in constructing a wall. That is, a farmer may remove such stones even from his own field and need not scruple about appearing to cultivate the land. From the size of these stones it is clear that they will be used in construction].

J.   And a contractor (kbln)[19] brings (K: them) [stones of any size] from anywhere. [Since he obviously has been hired to build a wall, he is not suspected of preparing this land for cultivation.]

K.   And what [size stones] are [considered] "stones [which must be carried on one's] shoulder?"

L.   "Any stone that cannot be picked up with one hand," the words of R. Meir.

M.   R. Yose (O[2]: Judah) says, "Stones [which must be carried on one's] shoulder are what their name implies,

N.   "[that is,] all [stones] that are picked up two [or] three [at a time and carried] on the shoulder."

M. 3:9

A farmer may not repair terraces if he thereby prepares the land for cultivation during the Sabbatical year. This principle of law, familiar from the discussion of Chapters One and Two, is illustrated by the contrasting rules at A-B/C-D. It follows that during the spring of the sixth year farmers may not repair terraces damaged during the rainy winter season. This would prepare the ground for planting during the Sabbatical year (A-B). They may, however, mend terraces during the seventh year itself. This activity, though performed during the Sabbatical year, prepares the ravines for cultivation during the eighth year alone, when working the land is permitted (C-D).

A secondary issue, addressed at E-F, concerns a farmer who repairs his terraces during the Sabbatical year, as permitted by the rule at C-D.[20] In doing so, he may appear to others to be clearing land, a forbidden activity. In order to avoid this problem, E-F permits the farmer only to bolster the retaining walls, by replacing stones that have washed away. He may not gather dirt from the vicinity to fill in spaces behind the wall, however, for he then would appear to be leveling the ground for cultivation (E-F).

The central point of G-H+I-N, familiar from all that has gone before, is that during the Sabbatical year a person may gather stones only if it is clear that he is not engaged in cultivation. Thus, picking up rocks and immediately placing them in a wall is permitted (G-H). Likewise, people may remove large stones from a field, and contractors may take stones of any size, for these materials clearly will be used for building (I,J).

Meir and Yose (K-L vs. M-N) dispute the precise size of the stones referred to at I. In Meir's view, "stones carried on one's shoulder" refers to any stone too heavy to be removed from the field with one hand. Yose interprets the phrase literally and so maintains that the law applies to a group of stones (Hebrew: 'bny, plural) which together can be transported only in this way.

A.   R. Nehemiah says, "[Contrary to M. 3:8A-B,] they build terraces on the side of (ed. princ.: on top of) ravines in (E: from) the year preceding the Sabbatical.
B.   "And during the Sabbatical year one may support them [i.e., the terraces] with dirt,
C.   "and he places it [i.e., the dirt] (so Lieberman, TZ, p. 175 who reads: nwtnw; E, V, and ed. princ. read: nwtnn, "he places them the terraces") on the side of (E, ed. princ.: on top of) ravines."

T. 3:4b

Nehemiah rejects the principles of law which underlie two of Mishnah's rulings, M. 3:8A-B and E-F. In his view, the law prohibits farmers from cultivating the land only during the Sabbatical year itself. During the sixth year, however, they may perform agricultural activities, such as the repair of terraces, which benefit the land during the seventh year (A). Moreover, Nehemiah holds that merely appearing to cultivate the land during the Sabbatical year does not in itself constitute a transgression. Farmers may bolster their terraces with dirt during the Sabbatical year, even though this may appear to be a forbidden act of cultivation. In fact, it is part of the process of repairing the terraces, which clearly is permitted (B-C).

3:10

A.   One who builds a fence [during the Sabbatical year] between his [property] and the public domain is permitted to dig down to rock level [in order to supply a firm foundation for the fence. Since this land ordinarily is not cultivated, a person who clears this area need not scruple about appearing to work the land].

B.   What should he do with the dirt?

C.   "He piles it up in the public domain and repairs it [that is, he uses the dirt to fill holes in the road,]" the words of R. Joshua.

D.   R. Aqiba says, "Just as one does not do damage in the public domain, so too one does not repair it."

E.   What should he do with the dirt?

F.   He piles it up in his own field in the manner of those who store manure [during the Sabbatical year; cf. M. 3:2].

G.   And likewise, [the rule of A^{21} applies to] one who digs a well, a trench, or a cave [during the Sabbatical year].

M. 3:10

Land adjacent to a public road generally is not suitable for cultivation. A householder who clears this area and builds a fence upon it during the Sabbatical year therefore will not appear to be engaged in forbidden cultivation. This rule sets the stage for the dispute at B-C vs. D-F, the focus of the pericope. A person who removes dirt in the process of building a fence may not deposit it in a field. This might create the impression that he was spreading new topsoil in order to enhance the field's fertility. Thus, Joshua and Aqiba agree that one must avoid the appearance of committing this transgression, though they differ in their views of how best to do so. Joshua (C) holds that people should use the dirt for a clearly non-agricultural purpose, to repair a public road. Aqiba, however, objects that an individual has no right either to disturb or to improve a public thoroughfare, since this property does not belong to him (E). An alternative manner of dealing with the dirt, spelled out in the anonymous rule at E-F, would be acceptable to Aqiba. By piling it in a few large heaps in his own field, in accordance with the procedure specified at M. 3:2 for storing dung, a farmer shows that his intent is not to improve his field, only to store the dirt there.

The gloss at H poses an exegetical problem, for it is not clear to which of the foregoing rules it applies. It may refer to the immediately preceding ruling, at E-F. In that case, its point is that one who digs a well or other hole, whether at the edge of public property or elsewhere, may pile the dirt in heaps in his own field. The fact that the formal pattern of G (present participle + direct object) matches that of A, however, has led me to translate the stich as referring back to the opening rule. On this reading, the gloss returns us to the rules that apply when digging at the edge of public property during the Sabbatical year. Since people generally do not cultivate these areas, one who digs a well, trench or cave on this land will not appear to be violating the law.

A.   "They clear stones [from a] road [in] the public domain," the words of R. Joshua.

B.   R. Aqiba says, "Just as one is not permitted to do damage [in the public domain] so too one may not clear stones [from the public domain; cf. M. 3:10E].

C.   "And if he did clear stones,

D.   "he should take them to the sea, the river or a dumping ground (lmqwm htrsyn)."

E.   They remove stones in order [to clear] a private road, and in order [to clear] a public road, and in order [to clear space for] a (ed. princ. adds: road [used for a]) funeral procession.[22]

T. 3:5 (A-D: T. B.Q. 2:12)

T. recapitulates Joshua and Aqiba's dispute of M. 3:10D vs. E, this time with respect to removing stones from a public road. Since their positions are identical to those presented in Mishnah, only the two new rules, C-D and E, require comment. Aqiba holds that one who does remove stones from a public road, in violation of the law, must deposit them in a remote place. His point, presumably, is that this prevents people from creating a public nuisance (C-D). The independent rule at E simply carries forward Joshua's position. The pericope as a whole has no bearing on the laws of the Sabbatical year and appears to be primary to the discussion of T. B.Q. It has been included here only to supplement the dispute in M. 3:10, which itself is tangential to Mishnah's central concern.

A.   And [during the Sabbatical year] they place pitcher-shaped vessels [containing dirt] (so Lieberman, TZ, p. 176, who reads: tphym; E, V, and ed. princ.: sphym, "after-growths")[23] on rooftops and maintain them,

B.   and they scruple about neither the [restrictions of the] Sabbatical year nor [the restrictions governing] the working of the Land [of Israel].

T. 3:6

The ruling before us is problematic, for the language at A is unclear. One's understanding of the rule depends upon the interpretation of tphym, which refers to pitcher-shaped vessels (A+). If these pots are unperforated, then the soil contained within them is not subject to the rules which govern cultivation of the Land. This would account for the rule that during the Sabbatical year farmers may grow plants in these vessels.[24] This reading creates a problem, however, for it does not explain the stipulation that these pots have been placed on rooftops. Lieberman offers an alternative interpretation of tphym which solves this problem, but assumes a still more complex set of facts. Birds, which use pots of this type as nests, may drop seeds in the dirt. This might cause plants to sprout during the Sabbatical year. The point, then, is that the farmer need not scruple about such matters, even though during the Sabbatical year it generally is forbidden to grow plants on one's roof. This reading, though supported by other rulings in T.,[25] appears to me more speculative. Since the pericope bears no relation either to Mishnah or to the surrounding materials in T., however, neither reading can be dismissed as entirely implausible.

A.   Olives [that began growing during the] year preceding the Sabbatical,

B.   and continued [growing] during the Sabbatical year--

C.   they (1) clear stones [from the ground surrounding the olive tree,] (2) remove thorns, (3) fill holes that are under them [the trees' roots, with] dirt, and (4) dig trenches from one [tree] to another.

D.   And moreover, even in the case of olives [that began growing during the] Sabbatical year

E.   and continued [growing] during the year following the Sabbatical,

F.   it is permitted to do so [that is, to perform the types of labor listed at C.]

T. 3:7 (D-F: Sifra Behar 1:4)

The agricultural activities under discussion are performed for the sake of the tree, not for the benefit of the fruit growing on the branch.[26] As we recall from M. 2:5Y-Z, work of this type is permitted even during the Sabbatical year itself, for any benefit to the fruit is deemed secondary and of no consequence. Farmers thus may tend trees at any time, whether the olives on the branch are from the crop of the sixth year (A-C) or of the Sabbatical year (D-F). This rule is only tangentially related to Mishnah, in that it refers to the activity of removing stones from a field (C1), the subject of M. 3:7-9 and T. 3:5.

CHAPTER FOUR

Shebiit Chapter Four

Mishnah's framers conclude their discussion of the prohibition against working the land during the seventh year by considering the consequences of violating the rules set forth in Chapters One through Three. Their discussion unfolds in three parts. First, they affirm that one may not become an accessory to a transgression, for example, by using a field cultivated by Israelites during the Sabbatical year. This basic principle, presented at M. 4:2A-E and 4:3, is the subject of a series of Houses-disputes at M. 4:2F-J. The Shammaites throughout take the position, consistent with the foregoing rules, that under no circumstances may people participate in the transgressions of others. They therefore may not eat produce that either grew in a field tilled during the seventh year or that was misappropriated by a farmer who deprived others of access to this food. The Hillelites, however, hold that people should not be penalized on account of another Israelite's transgression. Those who played no part in cultivating the field or in mishandling its produce should not be deprived of the land's yield, which during the Sabbatical year rightfully belongs to all.

The second main unit of the discussion, M. 4:4-6, takes up agricultural activities that have the effect of cultivating the land, but nonetheless are permitted. We speak, for instance, of a farmer who cuts off vines during the Sabbatical year in order to obtain material for weaving. This has the secondray effect of cultivating the vine's growth. At issue is how a farmer engaged in these permitted activities during the Sabbatical year can avoid committing this transgession. Two opposing views are presented in a series of disputes (M. 4:4A-B vs. C, M. 4:5A-D vs. E-F and M. 4:6A-B vs. C). We might hold that the farmer must indicate, by the way in which he performs his action, that he does not intend to cultivate his plants. He does this by altering the accepted procedure for pruning vines, cutting them either higher or lower than usual. Alternatively, since the intention of the farmer in fact is to engage in a permitted activity, we might rule that the secondary effects of his action are of no consequence. He therefore may proceed in the usual manner.

A final unit, M. 4:7-10, complements the foregoing discussion by considering activities that do not constitute cultivation of the land, yet are forbidden during the Sabbatical year. In particular, farmers may not cut down a fruitbearing tree or gather its yield before the fruit is ripe and ready to eat. This is forbidden, for God has designated all fruit that grows during the Sabbatical year as food for Israelites. Farmers thus must leave fruit on the branch until it is fully ripe and edible (see Chapter Eight). These rules form a fitting transition between all that has gone before, which deals with working the

Land and caring for trees during the Sabbatical year, and the remainder of the tractate, which explores the restrictions that apply to produce that grows during the seventh year.

One rule, M. 4:1, stands outside the framework of this entire discussion. It reiterates the central principle of M. 3:5-10 and in fact concludes the previous chapter's inquiry.

4:1

A.   At first they held:

B.   [During the Sabbatical year] a man gathers wood, stones (12 MSS. omit: stones)[1] and grass from his own [field] just as he [generally] would gather [them] from [the field] of his neighbor,[2]

C.   [that is, he gathers only] the large ones (hgs hgs). [Since he leaves the small pieces of wood, he indicates that he is not engaged in clearing the field for cultivation, but rather is collecting material for construction].

D.   ‹ When transgressors [that is, people who gathered both large and small stones from their own fields during the Sabbatical year in order to prepare the land for cultivation] increased in number, they ordained that:

E.   one should gather [stones] from the field of another (M, K omit:) and the other should gather [stones] from the first man's [field,]

F.   [so long as they do] not [do so] as a [mutual] favor. [That is, people may not agree to gather stones from one another's fields during the Sabbatical year in order to prepare the land for planting.]

G.   And, needless to say, one may [not] stipulate [to provide] others with meals [as payment for their labor of gathering stones from one's field. This would provide an incentive for the laborers to clear the field of stones entirely].

M. 4:1

This brief account of the law's history draws together two separate rules with respect to gathering stones and similar objects from fields during the Sabbatical year. According to the redactor,[3] the sages enacted the rules at B-C and D under separate historical circumstances and for distinct purposes. The first rule, which parallels M. 3:5-6, assures that people who gather stone and wood for construction during the Sabbatical year do not appear to be engaged in a transgression. By collecting from their fields only large pieces, while leaving the small items behind, the farmer indicates that he has no intention of preparing the field for cultivation. This rule, however, posed a problem, for it enabled transgressors actually to clear their own fields for cultivation, while claiming that they were acting within the law. To solve this problem, sages later ruled that people gathering stones and wood for construction must take these materials only from their neighbors' fields. This prevented transgressors from clearing their own fields, but continued to permit people to collect the building materials they wanted during the Sabbatical year.[4] The glosses at F and G both make a single point, that a person may not compensate his neighbors for removing wood and stones from his field. This assures that they will not go out of their way to clear the field entirely.

A.   At first they held:

B.   [During the Sabbatical year] a man may gather stones (so Lieberman, TZ, p. 176, who reads: 'bnym; E, V, and ed. princ. read: zytym, "olives") from his own [field] in the same manner as he gathers [them] from [the field] of his neighbor [in other years of the Sabbatical cycle]--

C.   that is, he gathers the large ones [= M. 4:1A-C with slight variations].

D.   It turned out [that farmers] would give each other [permission to clear one another's fields] as a favor [in violation of the law; cf. M. 4:1G-H].

E.   [So] it was ordained that [cf. M. 4:1D]

F.   they bring [stones only] from [a place which is] accessible [i.e., from ownerless property] and from [a place which is] nearby (E: from nearby and from the alleyway)."

G.   And in his own heart he will know (whlb ywd^C) whether [he gathers the stones] for a permitted purpose (l^{C}ql) [i.e., to use them for building] or out of perverseness (l^{C}qlqlwt) [i.e., to clear the land for cultivation].

T. 3:8 (G: b. Sanh. 26a; Lam. Rabbah 1:5)

H.   At first they held:

I.   A man may gather pebbles and shards from his own [field] in the same manner as he gathers [them] from [the field] of his neighbor--

J.   [that is, he gathers] the large ones,

K.   When the transgressors increased in number,

L.   they retracted and forbade [one from doing so]. [= M. 4:1A-D with variations].

T. 3:9

T. continues the story of M. 4:1, relating further transgressions and subsequent changes in the law. According to D, farmers began clearing each other's fields for cultivation during the Sabbatical year, despite the prohibition of M. 4:1G-H. In order to deter people from transgressing, the law was revised a second time to permit gathering materials during the Sabbatical year only from ownerless property. The concluding gloss, G, makes the point that ultimately the motives of the individual determine whether he acted in accordance with or in violation of the law. H-L, reiterates the rule of M. 4:1 for other types of materials.

4:2

A.   A field that was cleared of thorns [during the Sabbatical year]

B.   may be sown during the year following the Sabbatical. [Since removing thorns is not a forbidden act of cultivation, the farmer who sows this field during the eighth year does not derive benefit from the performance of a transgression].

C.   [But a field] that was improved, [that is, plowed during the Sabbatical year,]⁵

D.   or that was used as a fold [during the Sabbatical year for animals such that it was fertilized by the dung that the animals left on the ground, see M. 3:4,]

E.   may not be sown during the year following the Sabbatical. [Since plowing and fertilizing a field are forbidden during the Sabbatical year, the farmer may not derive benefit from this field during the eighth year].

F.   [As regards] a field that was improved [during the Sabbatical year]--

G.   the House of Shammai say, "They [that is, other Israelites] do not eat of its produce [that grows] during the Sabbatical year. [People may not derive benefit from produce that was cultivated illegally during the Sabbatical year]."

H.   But the House of Hillel say, "They do eat [produce of this field that grows during the Sabbatical year. Israelites who did not commit the transgression of cultivating the field should not be deprived of their right to eat produce of the Sabbatical year]."

I.   The House of Shammai say, "They do not eat produce of the Sabbatical year [which was given by the owner of a field] as a favor."

J.   But the House of Hillel say, "They eat [produce of the Sabbatical year] whether or not [it was given by the owner of the field] as a favor."

K.   R. Judah says, "The rulings [attributed to the Houses, I vs. J,] are reversed, [for] this is among the lenient rulings of the House of Shammai and the stringent rulings of the House of Hillel."

> M. 4:2 (A-B: b. M.Q. 13a; b. Git. 44b, b. Bek. 34b; C-E: y. Sanh. 3:5 [21b]; F-K: Sifra Behar 1:5; I-J: M. Ed. 5:1)

The central principle, expressed through the rules at A-B and C-E, is that people may not derive benefit from a field cultivated during the Sabbatical year. In doing so they would become accessories to this transgression. This point is illustrated through the contrast between agricultural activities that do not prepare the land for cultivation, which are permitted during the Sabbatical year, and those which make the field ready for planting, which are not. Clearing away the thorns that grow in a field during the Sabbatical year is necessary to prevent these plants from depleting the nutrients in the soil. Since engaging in this activity during the Sabbatical year entails no transgression, during the following year the farmer is free to work the field. Plowing a field or allowing the dung of one's animals to fertilize the soil during the Sabbatical year, by contrast, constitute forbidden cultivation. A farmer who improves his field in these ways may not benefit from his transgression by sowing the field during the eighth year.

The two Houses-disputes at F-G vs. H and I vs. J carry forward the discussion of benefiting from the transgressions of others. The issue at F-G vs. H focuses on the status of fruit that grows in a field worked during the Sabbatical year. The Shammaites claim that no one may eat this fruit, for people may derive no benefit from land which has been cultivated during the seventh year. The Hillelites, however, maintain that people who need food to eat during the Sabbatical year should not be penalized on account of someone else's transgression. Since they played no part in improving this field during the Sabbatical year, they should not be deprived of their right to eat the fruit that it produces.

The second Houses-dispute, at I vs. J-K, concerns a farmer who offers to give others as a gift produce of the seventh year that grows in his field. Since this fruit, in fact, is ownerless, however, the householder has no authority to give it away. May people accept this produce as a gift, thus implicitly affirming the farmer's ownership of it? According to the Shammaites, this would entail becoming a party to the farmer's transgression of misappropriation. In the view of the Hillelites, however, the farmer's claim to give this fruit away is null and void, since the produce does not belong to him in the first place. All may eat this food, notwithstanding the householder's misappropriation of it. Judah's reversal of the Houses' opinions (K) refers only to this second dispute, as evidenced by the parallel rule at M. Ed. 5:1.

A.   [As regards] a field which has been improved [during the Sabbatical year]--

B.   they may not sow it (E: maintain it) during the year following the Sabbatical (E: during the Sabbatical year) [= M. 4:2A-B with slight variations].

C.   What is [considered] a field which has been improved?

D.   Any (reading with E: kl; V, ed. princ. read: kl zmn, "anytime") [field which] people [normally] plow five [times during a season in other years of the Sabbatical cycle,] but which one plows six [times during the Sabbatical year,]

E.   or [a field which people normally plow] six [times during a season in other years of the Sabbatical cycle,] but which one plows seven [times during the Sabbatical year].

F.   Shammai the Elder says, "If the time were right I would decree concerning [such a field] that it may not be sown [during the year following the Sabbatical]."

G.   The court which succeeded him decreed concerning [such a field] that it may not be sown.

T. 3:10

T. claims that an improved field is one which has been plowed more times during the Sabbatical year than it usually is plowed during other years. This elucidation of M. 4:2C presupposes that during the Sabbatical year it is permitted to plow a field in the ordinary manner. Such a view, however, is found nowhere else in M.-T. and, in fact, contradicts M. 1:1 and 2:1, which make it clear that this is forbidden. Nor can I account for T.'s interpretation of this rule on the basis of surrounding materials in Mishnah, for M. 4:3 likewise assumes that plowing during the Sabbatical year is entirely forbidden. According to F-G, Shammai endorsed the rule presented at A-B, but some unspecified circumstances[6] prevented the enactment of this restriction until a later period.

4:3

A. During the Sabbatical year they [contract to] lease from gentiles newly-plowed fields. [The Israelite farmer may benefit from the gentile's cultivation of the land during the seventh year by leasing his field for sowing during the eighth year. Since gentiles are permitted to work the land during the seventh year, the Israelite does not thereby participate in the performance of a transgression].

B. But [they do] not [lease] from an Israelite [a field which he has plowed during the Sabbatical year, for one may not benefit from an Israelite's transgression].

C. And they assist[7] gentiles [in their agricultural labors] during the Sabbatical year,

D. but [they do] not [assist] an Israelite [who engages in such activities during the Sabbatical year].

E. And they greet [gentiles] in the interests of peace.

M. 4:3 (C-E: M. Sheb. 5:9J-K, b. Git. 61a;
E: b. Ber. 17a)

Gentile farmers are not obligated to observe the restrictions of the Sabbatical year. This is because, unlike Israelites, gentiles have been granted no special relationship to the Land of Israel. God has neither set aside this area as their exclusive possession nor commanded them to live in it.[8] Since the Land is sanctified for Israelites alone, gentiles are free to till their fields during the Sabbatical year. It follows that Israelites may help gentiles cultivate their fields or derive benefit from land that they till during the Sabbatical year, for this does not contribute to the performance of a transgression (A, C). The contrasting rules (B, D), which prohibit participating in the transgressions of Israelites, go over the ground of M. 4:2A-E. A quite separate rule, E, has been placed here merely because it concerns dealings between Israelites and gentiles.

A. [During the year following the Sabbatical][9] they do not lease a newly-plowed field from an Israelite suspected of transgressing the laws of the Sabbatical year. [Since this field clearly was plowed during the Sabbatical year, one may not lease it and so become an accessory to this transgression].

B. But [during the year following the Sabbatical] they may buy from him [that is, one who violates the law] a field sown [during that year. In this case, it is unclear whether the field was plowed during the seventh year, in violation of the law, or during the eighth year, when plowing is permitted].

C. [Sages permitted this] because they decreed only such rules as they could enforce (following Lieberman, TK, p. 518, who emends the text here to accord with the parallel stich at T. 3:13 G below).[10]

T. 3:11

D.   One who rents [a field] from a gentile stipulates with him [that he will rent only] on condition that the gentile sows [the field during the Sabbatical year].

T. 3:12

E.   [As regards] a gentile or Samaritan who plowed [a field and in the process uncovered a burial place]--

F.   [sages] do not declare them [such fields] to be grave-areas [and hence unclean, cf. M. Oh. 17:3,]

G.   because they decreed only such rules as they could enforce. [That is, such a ruling would have the effect of greatly multiplying the number of unclean fields and so would make it impossible for Israelites to live in the Land].[11]

H.   [Similarly, sages decreed] that Israelites may not raise small livestock [such as goats, for these animals destroy the crops of the Land,][12]

I.   but they may raise large livestock, [such as cows, for these animals, though destructive, are needed to plow the Land].[13]

J.   [Sages permitted this] because they built (E: decreed) only such a fence as could stand.

T. 3:13 (H-I: b. B.Q. 79b)

Sages did not decree excessively stringent rulings, for Israelites inevitably would violate them and thereby come to disregard the law. This central point draws together the rule concerning the Sabbatical year at A-C+D with rules concerning the uncleanness of graveyards (E-G) and the raising of livestock (H-J). Only the first of these is germane to our tractate and requires further clarification. One may not rent a field cultivated during the Sabbatical year, for one then becomes an accessory to this transgression (cf. M. 4:3B). This sets the stage for the more subtle issue addressed at B. We now wish to know whether during the year following the Sabbatical one may buy a field already sown with grain. Since this land could have been plowed during the Sabbatical year, we might hold that purchasing it is forbidden, in line with the rule at A. Prohibiting this transaction, however, would pose a serious problem, for any sown field which one wished to purchase during the eighth year might have been cultivated during the seventh year itself. This prohibition then would prevent farmers from buying fields during the eighth year altogether. Since people certainly would not abide by this rule, sages simply permitted such purchases.

The rule at D makes a quite separate point and has been inserted here to supplement the discussion of renting fields (A-C). During the Sabbatical year an Israelite may not work a field which he has rented from a gentile, a point which M. 4:3A-B takes for granted. The non-Israelite, who is exempt from the restictions of the law, must sow and tend the field for himself during this year.

4:4

A.   [As regards] one who thins out [the small shoots growing between] olive trees [during the Sabbatical year]--

B.   the House of Shammai say, "He may raze [these olive shoots, but he may not uproot them, for this would have the effect of preparing an area of land for cultivation]."

C.   But the House of Hillel say, "He may uproot [them completely. The farmer's intention is to prevent the proliferation of shoots from choking out the mature tree, which is permitted. The secondary effect of his labor therefore is of no consequence]."

D.   But they [that is, the Hillelites] concede with respect to one who clears away [a sizeable number of shoots, thus leveling a substantial area of the field, that he may not uproot these shoots, but only raze them. The farmer thereby demonstrates that he is not engaged in forbidden cultivation].

E.   Who is one that thins out?

F.   [One who uproots only] one or two [shoots at a time].

G.   [Who is] one that clears away [shoots from a substantial area of his field]?

H.   [One who removes] three [or more trees growing] side by side.

I.   To what case does this [rule, A-D+E-H,] apply?

J.   [It applies to one who removes trees] from his own field.

K.   But [if he does so] from the field of his neighbor,

L.   even one who clears away [shoots from a large area of the field] may uproot [the trees. Since no one would suspect the farmer of cultivating his neighbor's land, he need not scruple about appearing to violate the law].

M. 4:4

Removing new shoots from an area around the trunk of an olive tree assures that its branches have sufficient space to develop properly. This is permitted during the Sabbatical year since it is necessary to the healthy development of the tree. The problem is that removing these shoots also has the unintended effect of clearing some land for cultivation, which, of course, is forbidden. How can the farmer engage in this permitted activity without, in effect, transgressing? The Shammaites require the farmer to alter the usual procedure for removing the shoots. He cuts the shoots off at ground level, rather than uprooting them entirely, as he would if he were preparing to till the soil (A-B). The Hillelites, by contrast, permit the farmer to uproot the trees in the usual manner. On their view, since the farmer in fact is protecting his olive trees, a permitted activity, we take no account of the secondary effects of his labor (C). The Hillelites, at D, concede that a farmer who, in the process of thinning out trees, clears a sizeable area of land must refrain from uprooting the trees. This indicates that he is not preparing the land for cultivation.

This dispute draws in its wake two explanatory units of law. E-H clarifies the distinction, critical to the Hillelite position, between thinning out trees and clearing away an area around them. A qualification of the entire foregoing discussion, I-L, makes a point familiar from the parallel rule at M. 3:6G-J. One who removes wood from his neighbor's field will not be suspected of violating the law, since people generally do not cultivate the fields of others.

4:5

I. A. One who truncates an olive tree [during the Sabbatical year in order to obtain wood for building][14] should not cover [the stump] with dirt. [This would be the usual way of sealing the surface of the stump when one cuts back a tree in order to cultivate new branches].

B. Rather, he covers it with stones or with stubble. [Since this is not the usual manner of sealing the tree's stump, it indicates that the farmer is not engaged in cultivating the growth of new branches].[15]

II. C. [Likewise,] one who cuts down the branches of a sycamore [during the Sabbatical year in order to obtain wood for building] should not cover [the stump] with dirt.

D. Rather, he covers it with stones or with stubble.

E. [Contrary to the foregoing rules,] during the Sabbatical year they do not cut down a virgin sycamore [that is, a young tree which never before has been cut][16]

F. because it [that is, the cultivation of new branches which necessarily results from truncating the tree] is [forbidden] labor.

G. R. Judah says, "[Cutting] in the normal manner is forbidden.

H. "But he either [cuts the sycamore] high (mgbyh) [above the ground, that is,] ten handbreadths [or more from ground level,] or he razes it down to the ground."

M. 4:5 (E-H: b. B.B. 80b, E-F: b. Nid. 8b)

During the Sabbatical year farmers may truncate a tree in order to obtain wood for construction, just as they may gather wood from the ground for the same purpose (M. 4:1). Cutting back the tree has the secondary effect, however, of causing the trunk to generate new branches. The question, as at M. 4:4, is how to cut limbs off a tree for use as wood without engaging in the transgression of cultivating new boughs. According to the parallel rules at A-B and C-D, the farmer must alter the usual procedure for growing new branches. Ordinarily when farmers cut back a tree in order to generate new growth they immediately spread dirt on the surface of the stump. This protects the soft heart of the tree from bleeding excessively and so prevents the stock from dying. Once the stump has formed a new outer shell, shoots sprout and eventually develop into fully-grown branches. By protecting the stump with stones or stubble, rather than with dirt, the farmer thus indicates that he is simply harvesting wood, not cultivating new limbs.

The rule at E-F, which breaks with the formal pattern of the foregoing, presents a quite different theory of the law. Since truncating the sycamore tree necessarily has the effect of cultivating new branches, the farmer may not do so under any circumstances. Judah (G-H), who rejects this view, reiterates the point of the opening rules. The intention of the farmer is to engage in a permitted activity. The subsequent growth of new boughs therefore is of no consequence. As at A-D, the farmer indicates his intention by departing from the ordinary manner of cultivating new branches, that is, by truncating the tree either higher or lower than usual.[17]

A. One who cuts down the trunk of a sycamore [during the Sabbatical year, for the purpose of obtaining wood] [= M. 4:5C with slight variations]--

B. lo, he should neither smooth off [the surface of the stump] nor cut in a stepped manner (ydryg).

C. Rather, [when he makes his first cut,] he is careful (so E, V: mkwyn; ed. princ.: msyyn, "he marks") that the cut is even. [That is to say, after cutting off the trunk, one may not return and level off the stump, for this is the ordinary procedure for cultivating a tree].

D. R. Judah says, "In a place where they are accustomed to cut in a stepped manner, one may smooth off [the surface of the stump, and in a place where they are accustomed] to smooth off, one may cut in a stepped manner."

E. "Lo, (E omits: Lo) one raises [the point at which he cuts to] one handbreadth [above the ground] and cuts."

F. And so, [in accordance with his ruling at M. 4:5G-H,] did R. Judah say, "One who buys [the trunk of] a virgin sycamore from his neighbor during the first six years of the Sabbatical cycle [in order to obtain wood for construction]--

G. "lo, one [that is, the seller] raises [the point at which he cuts to] ten handbreadths [from the ground] and cuts."

H. It turns out that (nms't 'mr) there are three kinds of virgins:

T. 3:14

I. (1) A virgin woman, (2) virgin soil, and (3) a virgin tree (E: sycamore).

J. A virgin woman is any [woman] who has never had intercourse.

K. Virgin soil is any [soil] that has never been worked.

L. Rabban Simeon b. Gamaliel says, "Any [soil] that has no shards in it."

M. A virgin tree is any [tree] that has never been cut back.

T. 3:15 (H, I-M: y. Nid. 1:4 [49a], b. Nid. 8b;
L: T. Oh. 16:5)

Each of the several distinct rules before us (A-C, D-E, F-G, H-M) addresses the topic of M. 4:5C-D, the manner in which one may cut down a sycamore tree during the Sabbatical year. The central principle, familiar from M. 4:5A-D, is that the householder must indicate that he cuts the tree only to obtain wood, not to cultivate new branches. Thus, one may not smooth off the stump for this is part of the ordinary procedure for cultivating new boughs (A-C). Similarly, Judah (D) spells out a further way in which poeple during the Sabbatical year deviate from the usual manner of cutting down trees. E is problematic, for it refers neither to the procedure discussed by Judah at D, nor to his ruling which follows at F-G. I can make sense of this stich only by assuming, as Lieberman does, that it elucidates the meaning of Judah's lemma at M. 4:5H (which T., however, does not cite). Judah, as we recall, permits farmers to cut down a virgin sycamore during the Sabbatical year if they "raze it to the ground." The point of E, then, is that leaving no more than a single handbreadth of the trunk intact is equivalent to razing the tree. Judah's rule at G-H supports his position at M. 4:5H. One who buys a tree for its wood ordinarily cuts off the trunk ten handbreadths from the ground. Thus, during the Sabbatical year, people who truncate trees likewise should cut them at this height, for this indicates that they are not engaged in cultivating new boughs.

The independent unit of law at H-M has been placed here on account of M, which defines the term "virgin tree" mentioned at M. 4:5E.

A.   [As regards] one who uproots a carob tree or the trunk of a sycamore [and thereby overturns a large amount of soil]--

B.   [if he does so] for the [use of the] wood, it is permitted.

C.   But [if he does so] for the [benefit of the] field, it is forbidden.

T. 3:17

Unearthing carob or sycamore trees, which have extensive roots,[18] has the secondary effect of preparing a large area of land for cultivation. This might be deemed forbidden labor, in line with the principle of M. 4:5E-F. T., however, rules that the farmer's intentions, not the results of his action, are decisive. So long as he does not intend to cultivate his field, he may uproot these trees. This rule, it should be noted, does not invoke the central principle of Chapter Three, that during the Sabbatical year one must avoid even the appearance of violating the law.

A.   [As regards] holes [in the ground] formed when a tree was removed--

B.   lo, this hole one may not cover (V: yhph; ed. princ., E: yksh) with dirt.

C.   Rather, he covers [i.e., fills in the hole] with stones or stubble [= M. 4:5A-B, C-D with variations].

T. 3:18

The principle of M. 4:5 is applied to a new set of facts. A farmer wishes to fill a pit in his field, in order to prevent people or animals from falling in and injuring themselves.[19] By using stones or stubble, rather than dirt, he demonstrates that he is not engaged in cultivating his land.

4:6

A.   One who (1) snips off the ends of vines or (2) cuts reeds [during the Sabbatical year, in order to obtain materials for weaving or for use as wood][20]--

B.   R. Yose the Galilean says, "He should cut at a distance of one handbreadth [from the usual place where vines or reeds are trimmed for the purpose of cultivating them. In this way the farmer indicates that he is not engaged in forbidden labor]."

C.   R. Aqiba says, "He cuts in his usual manner,

D.   "with (1) an ax, (2) a sickle, (3) a saw, or with whatever (G[9], K add: kind) he wants [to use]."

E.   [As regards] a tree that was split in two--

F.   they may bind it during the Sabbatical year,

G.   not so that [the tree] will grow together [again] (l' $\underline{\text{šy}^{C}\text{lh}}$),

H.   but so that [the tree] will not [split] further ($\underline{\text{šl' ywsyp}}$).

M. 4:6 (E-G: Lam. Rabbah 3:4)

The farmer at A wishes to cut off segments of vines or reeds for use in building or weaving. The problem, familiar from M. 4:4 and 4:5, is that the farmer who engages in this permitted activity also cultivates the plants, by cutting away excess growth. The dispute at B vs. C goes over the ground of the Houses-dispute at M. 4:4A vs. C. Yose, in line with the Shammaite view, requires the farmer to cut back reeds in an unusual manner, thus indicating that he is not trimming them as an act of cultivation (B). Aqiba, consistent with the Hillelite position, claims that the secondary effect of the farmer's activity in unimportant. Since he engages in a permitted activity, he may proceed in the usual manner (C).

The gloss of Aqiba's rule at D poses a problem. On the one hand, it appears to clarify Aqiba's position that one may cut reeds "in the usual manner." Yet, the notion that the farmer may use any tool he wishes has no counterpart in Yose's lemma at B. The gloss thus stands outside the framework of the dispute,[21] which concerns the height at which the farmer cuts these reeds, not the tools that he employs to do so. It appears that the gloss, rather than clarifying Aqiba's position in the dispute, merely serves to inform us about the tools which farmers usually use when cutting reeds.

The quite separate unit of law at E-H carries forward the rule of M. 4:5A-D. One may care for trees during the Sabbatical year in order to prevent them from dying, but not in order to cultivate new growth.

A.   [As regards] one who cuts reeds [during the Sabbatical year; = M. 4:6A(2)]--

B.   lo, he raises [the point of his cut to] one handbreadth [above the ground] and cuts [cf. M. 4:6B].

C.   R. Judah says, (so Lieberman, TK, p. 522, on the basis of y. 4:5 [35b]; E,V, and ed. princ. read: Simeon b. Gamaliel),[22] "In a place where they are accustomed to cut, he plucks, [and in a place there they are accustomed] to pluck, he cuts.

D.   "Lo [when one cuts reeds] he raises [the point of his cut to] one handbreadth [above the ground] and cuts" [= B].

E.   They do not kindle reeds (so Lieberman, TZ, p. 178, who reads: mtylyn 'š bqnym; E,V, and ed. princ. read: mtylyn 't hqnym) in a reed thicket,

F.   because that is the usual labor [performed in reed thickets, in order to encourage future growth].[23]

G.   (E omits:) R. Simeon b. Gamaliel permits.

H.   And so, [in line with his position at G,] did R. Simeon b. Gamaliel say, "A man is permitted to plant a non-fruitbearing tree to make a fence during the Sabbatical year."

T. 3:19

T.'s discussion of cutting reeds during the Sabbatical year goes over the ground of M. 4:6A-B and T. 3:1D-E. By cutting reeds in an unusual manner, the householder indicates that he wishes to use the stalks for construction, which is permitted (A-B, C-D). These rules draw in their wake the dispute at E-F vs. G+H, which turns to a new procedure for cultivating reeds. Farmers set fire to reeds in order to thin out the excess growth and promote the development of the plants. This is a forbidden act of cultivation (E-F). Simeon, however, holds that reeds, together with all other non-fruitbearing trees, are exempt from the restrictions of the law. It follows that during the Sabbatical year farmers are free both to cultivate (G) and to plant (H) such vegetation.

A.   (Ed. princ. adds: During the Sabbatical year) they train a cow [to plow] only in a sandy area [which is unsuitable for cultivation].

B.   R. Simeon b. Gamaliel says, "Also: in the field of one's neighbor it is permitted [to train a cow to plow,]

C.   "so long as [the farmer] does not press the colter, [a small blade which makes cuts in the soil to facilitate the work of the plowshare. That is, the farmer may not leave marks in the field as he would if he were actually tilling the soil]."

D.   Abba Saul says (V omits: says), "He cuts down (so Lieberman, TZ, p. 178, who reads: mbrh; E: mkrk; V: mgrr; ed. princ.: mgdr) [reeds growing] in the thicket and razes [the undergrowth] to ground level,

E.   "so long as he does not cut through [the undergrowth] with a spade [which appears to be a forbidden act of cultivation]."

T. 3:20

Three distinct rules (A, B-C, and D-E) make the familiar point that during the Sabbatical year one must avoid the appearance of committing a transgression. A person may plow in a sandy area or in the field of his neighbor, for these are places where one ordinarily would not be suspected of cultivating the land (A, B-C). Abba Saul's lemma returns us to the topic of M. 4:6, cutting down reeds during the Sabbatical year. This is permitted so long as one does not use the tools ordinarily employed when cultivating the land (D-E).

4:7-9

	A.	After what time during the Sabbatical year do they [gather and] eat the fruit of trees? [Gathering fruit too early in the ripening process is prohibited. By doing so, the farmer would prevent fruit that grows during the Sabbatical year from being used as food, as M. 8:1,2 requires].
I.	B.	[As regards] (1) unripe figs:
	C.	From the time they begin to glisten [i.e., when they begin to mature and become shiny,]
	D.	[the farmer] may eat them [as a random snack together] with his bread in the field.
	E.	[And when] they have ripened (bhlw),
	F.	he may gather them into his house [and eat them.]
	G.	And similarly, [when the figs have ripened] during the other years of the Sabbatical cycle, they become liable to [the separation of] tithes.

M. 4:7

II.	H.	(M omits: H-M) [As regards] (2) unripe grapes:
	I.	From the time they produce liquid
	J.	[the farmer] may eat them with his bread in the field.
	K.	[And when] they have ripened (hb'yš)
	L.	he may gather them into his house [and eat them].
	M.	And similarly, [when the grapes have ripened] during the other years of the Sabbatical cycle, they become liable to [the separation of] tithes.

M. 4:8

III.	N.	[As regards] (3) olives:
	O.	From the time a seah [of olives] will yield a quarter [-log of oil,]
	P.	[the farmer] may crush them and eat [them] in the field.
	Q.	[When a seah of olives] yields a half [-log of oil,]
	R.	he may press [them] and anoint [himself] in the field.
	S.	[When a seah of olives] yields a third [of its total eventual output, that is, a full log of oil,]
	T.	he may press [the olives] in the field and gather them into his house.
	U.	And similarly, [when the olives have reached a third of their eventual yield] during the other years of the Sabbatical cycle, they become liable to [the separation of] tithes.

V.   And [as regards] the fruit of all other trees--

W.   the season [during other years when they become liable] to [the separation of]
     tithes is the season during the Sabbatical year [when they may be eaten].

M. 4:9 (Sifre Behar 1:10-12)

All edible produce that appears on the branch during the seventh year is designated
by God as food for Israelites living in the Land. People therefore may not gather fruit of
the Sabbatical year before it ripens, for this would prevent Israelites from using the
Land's yield in the proper way, as food (see M. 8:1,2). This single principle is spelled out
three times, for figs (B-G), grapes (H-M), and olives (N-U), three of the most common
crops of the Land of Israel. In each case, we distinguish two stages in the ripening
process. In the spring, people may make a random snack of the fruit which has become
just ripe enough to be edible. Later, when the crop as a whole is fully mature and ready
for harvest, farmers may gather the fruit into their homes and eat it. By fixing the times
when people may gather and consume this fruit, Mishnah's authorities assure that people
do not misuse the sanctified produce that grows during the seventh year.

In the case of olives, a third, intermediate stage in the ripening process is important. Before the crop is ready for consumption, olives can produce sufficient oil for
anointing. Farmers may gather them at this time, because olives, unlike figs and grapes,
may be used during the Sabbatical year as a source of oil for emoluments, as well as for
food (see M. 8:2C-D, T. 6:4Q-R, T. 6:8D-E).

A series of parallel glosses (G, M, U, V-W) relate the rules for collecting produce of
the Sabbatical year to those governing the separation of tithes. During the first six years
of the Sabbatical cycle, a crop becomes liable to the separation of tithes only after it is
ripe and edible. This is because, at the point when the farmer begins to take possession of
this produce, he also must satisfy God's claim against the fruit of the Land. He does this
by giving a portion to God's representatives, the priests and Levites.[24] So too, during the
Sabbatical year, when the Land's yield belongs to all Israelites and so is not liable to the
separation of tithes at all, fruit becomes available for Israelite householders to gather and
eat freely only when it is ripe and usable as food.

A.   [As regards] unripe figs [which began growing] during the year preceding the
     Sabbatical (so ed. princ. and E; V: during the Sabbatical year)--

B.   they do not boil them (reading with y. 4:6: 'yn šwlkyn; E, ed. princ.: 'yn hwlkyn; V:
     'yn twklyn) during the Sabbatical year.

C.   [As regards] late ripening figs [which are hard and remain inedible unless they are
     processed]--

D.   it is permitted to boil them during the Sabbatical year,

E.   because that is the normal manner [of preparing them].

F.   [As regards] hearts of palms[25] (reading with E: bqwr; V, ed. princ. read: bqyr) and
     the inflorescence of palms[26]--

G.   it is permitted [to boil them during the Sabbatical year].

T. 3:21

Produce of the Sabbatical year must be eaten in its natural unprocessed state. This assures that no edible part of the produce will be lost during the course of processing, in line with the rule that fruit of the Sabbatical year may not be wasted (M. 4:7-9; see also M. 8:1ff.) Thus figs, which are edible when raw, may not be boiled (A-B). Late-ripening figs and the hard portions of the palm, by contrast, may be cooked, for otherwise they are inedible (C-E, F-G).

4:10

A.   After what time during the Sabbatical year may they not cut down a [fruitbearing] tree [for by doing so one would prevent fruit that already is growing on the branch from ripening? This would waste edible produce of the Sabbatical year in violation of M. 8:1,2].

B.   The House of Shammai say, "[Regarding] all trees--after they have produced [recognizable] fruit."[27]

C.   The House of Hillel say, "(1) [Regarding] carob trees--after their [branches] begin to droop (mšyšlšlw);[28] (2) [regarding] vines--after they produce berries;[29] (3) [regarding] olive trees--after they blossom; and (4) [regarding] all other trees--after they produce [recognizable] fruit."

D.   And [concerning] every [fruitbearing] tree--

E.   after it has reached the point [when, in other years of the Sabbatical cycle, its fruit would be subject to the separation] of tithes, it [again] is permitted to cut it down. [At this point, the fruit is ready for harvest and so will not be lost when the tree is cut down].

F.   [During other years of the Sabbatical cycle] how much [fruit] need there be on an olive tree so that one may not cut it down [in accordance with the prohibition against razing fruitbearing trees?; cf. Dt. 20:19-20].[30]

G.   A quarter [-qab of fruit].

H.   R. Simeon b. Gamaliel says, "[The rule that applies to] each [tree] depends upon [the quality of the yield of] that olive tree."

M. 4:10 (A-C: b. Ber. 36b; b. Pes. 52b; F-H:
b. B.Q. 91b)

Cutting down a fruit bearing tree prevents any unripe produce on the branch from developing into mature, edible fruit. This is forbidden, because all fruit that grows during the Sabbatical year is designated as food and so must be allowed to ripen fully. This principle, familiar from M. 4:7-9, generates the question disputed by the Houses at A-B vs. C. When in the ripening process does fruit take on the status of food, with the result that the tree on which it grows may not be cut down? According to the Shammaites, the point at which the tree begins to produce recognizable fruit is decisive. Razing a tree at this time would prevent the newly formed fruit from developing into fully edible produce. The Hillelites, who agree in general with this criterion, make an exception for certain species of fruit. Since carobs, grapes and olives are not clearly visible when they first appear on the branch,[31] the Hillelites offer separate criteria by which a farmer can readily determine when this produce has begun to form. An independent rule, D-E, which considers the point at which the ripening process concludes, carries forward the discussion in a logical manner. Once fruit becomes fully ripe, the farmer is free to cut down the tree. By gathering the fruit on the branch before felling the tree, he can prevent this edible produce from being wasted.

The dispute at F-G vs. H, which does not concern the laws of the Sabbatical year, has been appended here because it too relates to cutting down fruitbearing trees. At issue is the amount of fruit that a tree must yield in order to be subject to the prohibition against destroying fruitbearing trees (Dt. 20:19-20). According to F-G, if the quantity of olives growing on a tree is negligible, less than a quarter qab, the tree may be razed.[32] Simeon, H, however, claims that one must take into account the quality and value of a tree's produce, as well as its quantity. Though the details of his position are not clearly spelled out, he apparently holds that olive trees bearing high quality fruit, even in small quanitities, may not be cut down.

A.   After what time [during the Sabbatical year] is one allowed to cut down a tree (so E; V, ed. princ.: during other years of the Sabbatical cycle) [without thereby preventing fruit of the Sabbatical year that grows on the branch from ripening fully, which would be a violation of the law]?

B.   After the point during other years of the Sabbatical cycle (reading with Lieberman, TZ, p. 179) when [its fruit] would become subject to [the separation of] tithes [cf. M. 4:10D-E].

T. 3:22

T. paraphrases the rule of M. 4:10D-E.

A.   They do not sell a field planted with trees to one suspected of transgressing [the laws of] the Sabbatical year, unless [the seller] stipulates (E: stipulated) with [the buyer] that [he sells on condition that the buyer] has no share in the trees, [but only purchases the soil in which they are planted] (so V, E, ed. princ.: [on condition that the buyer] will give him [his share of the fruit]).[33]

B.   R. Simeon permits [this sale even without such a condition,] for [the seller normally] tells [the buyer,] "I sold [you] what is mine, [that is, the field, but not the fruit of the trees, which is ownerless during the Sabbatical year,] you go out and claim what is yours [that is, the field together with a fair share of the land's yield]."

T. 3:23 (C-D: y. Ma. 5:3 [51d])

One who sells an orchard during the Sabbatical year must take precautions to prevent the buyer from violating the laws of the Sabbatical year. By specifying that he sells only the land, not its fruit, he notifies the buyer that that person has no right to cut down the trees and so prevent the fruit from ripening (cf. M. 4:10). Simeon (B) claims that the seller is not responsible for the buyer's actions. He need not specify that he sells only the land, for he does not own the land's yield during the Sabbatical year and so could not sell it in any event.

CHAPTER FIVE

Shebiit Chapter Five

Two separate thematic units comprise the chapter before us. The first, M. 5:1-5, addresses problems raised by types of produce that grow over a period of two or more calendar years. The second, M. 5:6-9, discusses the prohibition against assisting others during the Sabbatical year in the performance of transgressions. Since these units of law are both formally and substantively distinct, I discuss each of them in turn.

Produce that grows over two successive calendar years, from the sixth year into the seventh or from the seventh year into the eighth, poses a problem. How do we determine the status of this food? This question is critical, for the householder must know whether his crops are subject to the tithes that must be separated during the first six years of the Sabbatical cycle, or whether they are governed by the special restrictions that apply to sanctified produce of the Sabbatical year (see Chapters Eight and Nine). Two alternative views are put forward in the disputes at M. 5:1 and 5:5. We might hold that the year during which a crop of produce begins its extended growing season determines its status. Only fruit or vegetables that begin to develop during the Sabbatical year are subject to the restrictions of that year. It follows that the law does not govern crops that begin to grow during the sixth year, even though they continue to grow during the seventh year itself (M. 5:1A-D, 5:5A-B). Alternatively, the year during which the majority of a crop's growth occurs might be determinative. On this view, if half or more of a vegetable's development takes place during the seventh year, it is deemed subject to the restrictions governing crops of that year. (M. 5:1E, 5:5C).

One of the plants that grows over more than one calendar year, the arum tuber (cf. M. 5:5), also poses other problems, discussed at M. 5:2-4. These tubers commonly are stored underground for extended periods of time. If fully-grown tubers stored during the Sabbatical year sprout leaves, the farmer will have engaged in a forbidden act of planting. Precautions must be taken, therefore, to assure that tubers are stored during the Sabbatical year in a manner which prevents them from producing new leaves (M. 5:2). If tubers stored underground do sprout leaves during the Sabbatical year, yet another problem arises. The leaves of this plant, unlike the tuber, grow and die within a period of a few weeks. Since their entire growing season takes place within the Sabbatical year, it is not clear whether they are subject to the same restrictions as the tuber from which they grew (M. 5:3A-C vs. D-E). Finally, at M. 5:4, we consider the case of arum tubers that finished growing during the sixth year, but remained in the ground during the seventh. Farmers may uproot these tubers during the Sabbatical year, for they are part of the crop of the preceding year. Nonetheless, in doing so thay may appear to be engaged in forbidded cultivation. The Houses (M. 5:4C vs. D) thus dispute whether or not a farmer who uproots tubers during the Sabbatical year must do so in an unusual manner, to indicate that he is not performing a transgression.

At M. 5:6-9, we consider the circumstances under which one may sell or lend agricultural equipment to others during the Sabbatical year without thereby becoming an accessory to their transgressions. The central principle is presented at M. 5:6 and reiterated at M. 5:7. One may sell a person any tool which could be used in a permissible manner. We assume that the buyer will not use it in violation of the law. One may not, however, give a person a tool which he could use only in violation of the law, since this would be a clear act of complicity (M. 5:8B-E). M. 5:8F and 5:9 qualify this rule in an obvious way. People may not assist those who clearly are engaged in commiting transgressions or who have expressed their intention to do so. Only the Shammaites (M. 5:8A) dispute the underlying principle of these rules. On their view, one may not sell an animal during the Sabbatical year if there is any possibility at all that the buyer will use it to plow his field, in violation of the law.

5:1

A.   White figs[1] [which appear in the seventh year--the restrictions of the] Sabbatical year [apply] to them [in the] second [year of the new Sabbatical cycle, rather than in the seventh year itself,]

B.   because they [i.e., white figs] take three years to ripen fully (ᶜwŝwt lŝlŝ ŝnym).

C.   R. Judah says, "Persian figs[2] [which appear in the seventh year--the restrictions of the] Sabbatical year [apply] to them [in the] year following the Sabbatical [that is, in the first year of the new Sabbatical cycle, rather than in the seventh year itself,]

D.   "because they [i.e., Persian figs] take two years to ripen fully."

E.   [Sages] said to him, "They ruled ('mrw) [concerning] white figs alone."

M. 5:1 (Sifra Behar 1:1, b. R.H. 15b, Gen. Rabbah 10:4)

Certain types of fruit first appear on the branch during the Sabbatical year, but become fully ripe and edible only after that year has ended. Such produce poses a problem. It begins growing during the Sabbatical year and so, like all produce of that year, should be subject to the restrictions of the law. Yet, during the Sabbatical year this fruit still is immature and so cannot be subject to restrictions that govern fully ripened produce. We wish to know, first, whether this fruit is deemed part of the crop of the Sabbatical year, even though it is not fully ripe during that year, and second, if it is, when the restriction of the law take effect. The law governing such anomalous produce, presented in the parallel rules at A-B and C-D, answers both of these questions. This fruit is subject to the law only when it becomes ripe and ready for human consumption. That is to say, fruit that forms during the Sabbatical year is subject, even if it concludes the ripening process in subsequent years. This point, as we shall see, is important for our understanding of M. 5:3,5. Moreover, the year during which this produce becomes available for people to eat determines when the restrictions of the law apply. Prior to this time, the fruit is not ready to be picked and so in any case could not be subject to the law.

Sages, E, distinguish the case of Persian figs, which grow over two years, from white figs, which take three years to ripen. They hold that figs which complete half of their development during the seventh year are deemed fully ripe and so are subject to the law during that year.[3]

A. R. Judah says, "Persian figs [which appear in the seventh year--the restrictions of the] Sabbatical year [apply] to them [in the] year following the Sabbatical year [i.e., in the first year of the new Sabbatical cycle, rather than in the seventh year itself,]

B. "because they [i.e., Persian figs] take two years to ripen fully (ᶜwśwt lślś śnym) [=M. 5:1C-D]."

C. Sages said to him, "Lo, these [i.e., Persian figs,] grow near you in Tiberias, and they ripen (ᶜwśwt) within a single season (bnwt śntn)!"

T. 4:1

T. cites Judah's ruling of M. 5:1C-D and provides an explanation for the sages' rejection of this ruling. According to C, the sages' disagreement with Judah concerns the facts of the case. Persian figs ripen fully within the seventh year and so no problem of liability to the law after the seventh year arises. In T's view, sages do not dispute the principle of M. 5:1A-B.

5:2

A. One who stores arum[4] [for preservation, by covering it with earth] during the Sabbatical year [must do so in a manner which prevents the tubers from sprouting leaves]--

B. R. Meir says, "He [must] not [store] less than two seahs,

C. "[he must not make a pile less] than three handbreadths high,

D. "and [he must put no less than] a handbreadth of dirt above it."

E. But sages say, "He [must] not [store] less than four qabs,

F. "[he must not make a pile less] than a handbreadth high,

G. "and [he must put no less than] a handbreath of dirt above it,

H. "and he [must] store it in a thoroughfare (bmqwm dryst 'dm)."

M. 5:2

The farmer at A wishes to store arum tubers in the ground,[5] an activity that is permitted during the Sabbatical year. He must take precautions, however, to insure that the tubers stored in this way do not sprout leaves, for this would constitute a forbidden

act of planting.[6] How does he do this? Meir and sages agree that the best way to prevent
arum from sprouting is to store a large quantity in a single pile and cover it with some
dirt. I cannot account for the specific quantities of arum and dirt which they require.[7]
Sages, who allow the farmer to store smaller quantities of arum, also hold that he must
place it in a thoroughfare,[8] so that people trammpling on it will help prevent it from
sprouting.

A. One who stores arum [for preservation by covering it with earth] during the
    Sabbatical year [=M. 5:2A]--
B. R. Meir says, "It is customary [that he] store it in an earthen vessel, so that it will
    not sprout.
C. "Although there is no [explicit Scriptural] proof for this matter, there is an allusion
    to the matter, 'Put them in an earthen vessel, that they may last for many days'
    (Jer. 32:14)."

                                    T. 4:2

T. cites M. 5:2A, but at B, attributes to Meir a different ruling with respect to the
storing of arum during the Sabbatical year. Meir's solution to the problem that the arum
might sprout is to store it in an earthen vessel, rather than in the ground.

                                    5:3

A. An arum [tuber which was stored underground during the Sabbatical year (cf. M. 5:2)
    and remained stored in the ground] after the Sabbatical year had passed (šᶜbrh ᶜlyw
    šbyᶜyt)--
B. R. Eliezer says, "If the poor gathered its leaves, [which sprouted during the
    Sabbatical year,] it is well (lit., "they have gathered") [but the poor have no claim
    upon the tuber that grows underground].
C. "But if [the poor did] not [gather its leaves during the Sabbatical year, the owner of
    the arum] must settle accounts with the poor, [when the tuber is uprooted, by giving
    them a portion of the tuber itself]."[9]
D. R. Joshua says, "If the poor gathered its leaves [which sprouted during the Sabbati-
    cal year,] it is well.
E. "But if [the poor did] not [gather its leaves during the Sabbatical year,] the poor
    have no account with him. [That is, the owner of the arum owes them nothing after
    the Sabbatical year is over]."

                                    M. 5:3

The arum tubers referred to at A completed their growth during the sixth year. The
farmer then uprooted them and placed them in the ground for storage, a common way of
preserving tubers (cf. M. 5:2).[10] The problem arises if these tubers sprout leaves during
the Sabbatical year, for it is unclear whether or not these leaves are subject to the

restrictions of the law. On the one hand, they grew during the Sabbatical year, so that we might regard them as sanctified produce of that year. On the other hand, the leaves are a by-product of the stored tuber, which had finished growing during the sixth year. The leaves, like the tuber, then might be exempt from the restrictions of the law. The question is resolved at B and D. Eliezer and Joshua agree that leaves which sprout during the seventh year must be regarded as produce of that year. The poor therefore may collect and eat these greens.[11] A secondary problem, addressed at C vs. E, arises if during the Sabbatical year the poor do not collect the leaves to which they are entitled. Once the Sabbatical year has ended and the leaves have died, do the poor have a claim upon the tuber that remains in the ground? Eliezer's and Joshua's opposing answers to this question represent two distinct views concerning the relationship between the tuber and its leaves. For Eliezer, the whole constitutes a single plant. Since the poor were entitled to a portion of the arum, but did not collect the leaves, they must be given a part of the tuber instead. When the householder uproots his arum in the eighth year, he estimates the portion of the tuber that grew during the Sabbatical year and gives it to the poor (C). Joshua, however, considers the tuber and its leaves as separate entities, for indeed they have distinct growing seasons. The poor have a claim only against the leaves, not the tuber. When the householder harvests the tubers in the year following the Sabbatical, therefore, he owes no part of this produce to the poor (E).

A. Arum [which grew during the Sabbatical year and remained in the ground] after the Sabbatical year had passed [=M. 5:3A]--

B. R. Eliezer says, "If [the owner] delayed three years [before uprooting the arum] he gives the poor a fourth [of his arum.]

C. "If [the owner] delayed two years, he gives the poor a third [of his arum.]

D. "[If the owner delayed] one year, he gives the poor half [of his arum.]

T. 4:3

Eliezer here specifies the portion of arum which the poor are to receive (cf. M. 5:3 B-C) if they do not collect the arum leaves during the Sabbatical year. The poor receive that percentage of the total arum which is equal to the ratio of one year (the Sabbatical) to the total number of years during which the arum remained in the ground. The poor, therefore, receive only as much arum as grew during the period when they were entitled to gather its leaves.

5:4

A. Arum [which finished growing] during the sixth year [but] which remained [in the ground in storage] during the seventh year (šnkns lšbyᶜyt),

B. and also summer onions,[12] and madder[13] from good soil--

C. The House of Shammai say, "They uproot them [during the seventh year] with wooden rakes [so as to avoid the appearance of cultivating the Land]."

D.   But the House of Hillel say, "They uproot them with metal spades."

E.   And [the Shammaites] concur [with the Hillelite position] concerning madder from stony soil, that they uproot it with metal spades.

M. 5:4

The dispute concerns tuberous plants, such as arum, onions and madder, which finish growing during the sixth year,[14] but remain stored in the ground into the Sabbatical year. The farmer who uproots these tubers during the Sabbatical year may appear to be cultivating new produce, which is forbidden. In order to avoid the appearance of violating the law, the House of Shammai (C) require the farmer to uproot this produce with a wooden rake, an instrument not normally used for cultivating. The Hillelites, however, are not concerned with appearances, for the farmer in fact is engaged in uprooting tubers, a permitted activity. So long as he does not cultivate produce of the Sabbatical year, he may uproot tubers using the normal instrument, a metal spade. The Shammaites agree with the Hillelite position only in the case of uprooting madder from stony soil. Since the wooden rake is not strong enough to do this, they permit the use of a metal tool (E).[15]

5:5

A.   When is one permitted to buy (lkh)[16] arum in the year following the Sabatical [on the assumption that this produce is not subject to the restrictions of the law?]

B.   R. Judah says, "Immediately."

C.   And sages say "When the new [produce][17] becomes plentiful (mšyrbh hhdš) [in the marketplace, that is, in the spring of the year following the Sabbatical].

M. 5:5

Arum tubers present a problem, for they grow underground over a period of several years.[18] Thus a tuber harvested at the beginning of the eight year began to grow during the sixth year and continued to develop throughout the Sabbatical year. The problem is that it is unclear whether these tubers are subject to the restrictions governing produce of the sixth, seventh or the eighth year. The answer to this question is important to the householder who wishes during the eighth year to buy arum tubers that are exempt from the restrictions of the Sabbatical year (A). Judah (B) maintains that arum tubers are governed by the same principle that applies to other types of produce, such as figs, that grow over more than one calendar year. Fig trees sometimes produce buds in one calendar year, but yield ripened fruit only in the year following. Figs which grown over two successive years are subject to the restrictions of the year during which they began to grow, that is, when the buds first appeared (see T. 4:20). Likewise, arum tubers, according to Judah, which begin to grow during the Sabbatical year are subject only to the restrictions of that year. The year during which they ripen and are harvested is of no account (see M. 5:1A-D). Tubers in the market at the very beginning of the year following the Sabbatical, therefore are exempt from the law, since these began growing during the sixth year. Sages (C), by contrast, take account of a plant's entire growing season, not only the year during which it begins to grow. On their view, the year during which most of a tuber's growth occurs determines its status. At the beginning of the eighth year tubers in the market are subject to the restrictions of the preceding year, since half or more of their growth has taken place during that year. Arum uprooted later in the year, after the crops of the new season have been harvested, has a different status. This produce has grown more during the sixth and eighth years combined than during the seventh. It therefore is exempt from the restrictions of the Sabbatical year.

A. When is one permitted to buy (lkh) arum in the year following the Sabbatical under any circumstances (mkl mqwm)?[19] [i.e., even if the seller is suspected of not observing the laws of the Sabbatical year.]

B. R. Judah says, "Immediately" [=M. 5:5A-B].

C. R. Judah says, "An incident:

"We were in Ein Kusi and we ate arum at the conclusion of Tabernacles in the year following the Sabbatical (read with y. Sheb. 5:5: šlmws'y šby^{c}yt; E, V, ed. princ. read: in the Sabbatical year). [And this was] on the authority of R. Tarfon."

E. R. Yose said to him, "Is that the evidence (r'yh) [for your ruling]? I was with you, and it happened after Passover!"

T. 4:4

Yose rejects the precedent which Judah provides for his ruling at M. 5:5B. According to Yose, the incident to which Judah referred actually occurred after Passover, the official beginning of the new harvest (see Lev. 23:9ff.). This coincides with the point after which sages said that arum could be purchased (M. 5:5C).

5:6

A. These are tools which the artisan is not permitted to sell during the Sabbatical year:

B. (1) a plow and all its accessories, (2) a yoke, (3) a pitchfork,[20] (4) and a mattock.[21]

C. But he [i.e., the artisan] may sell:

D. (1) a hand sickle, (2) a reaping sickle,[22] (3) and a wagon and all its accessories.

E. This is the general rule:

F. [As regards] any [tool] the use of which [during the Sabbatical year] is limited exclusively to the performance of an act which is a transgression--it is forbidden [to sell such a tool during the Sabbatical year.]

G. [But, as for any tool which may be used both for work which is] forbidden and [for work which is] permitted [according to the laws of the Sabbatical year]--it is permissible [to sell such a tool during the Sabbatical year.]

M. 5:6 (b. A.Z. 15b)

During the Sabbatical year a person may not help his fellow to perform a transgression, by selling him tools that he will use in violation of the law.[23] This principle, illustrated by the contrasting rules at A-B and C-D, is spelled out in the general rule at E-G. We distinguish two types of tools. Those used exclusively for cultivating and winnowing, activities forbidden during the Sabbatical year, may not be sold. The seller can only assume that the buyer will use these tools for a forbidden purpose (B). Sickles and wagons, by contrast, are used for harvesting, an activity permitted during the Sabbatical year provided the farmer does not collect more than his fair share of the land's yield.[24] Since these tools could be used for a permitted purpose, the person who sells them may assume that he does not become an accessory to a transgression (D).

5:7

A. [During the Sabbatical year] a potter sells [to one person no more than] five oil containers and fifteen wine containers,

B. because it is usual (drkw) [for a person] to gather from ownerless produce [enough olives and grapes to produce this much wine and oil during the Sabbatical year].

C. But if [during the Sabbatical year a person] gathered more than this amount [of olives and grapes,] it is permitted [to sell that person more than this number of containers].

D. And [the potter] sells [an unlimited number of containers] to a gentile in the Land [of Israel] and to an Israelite outside of the Land [of Israel].

M. 5:7

During the Sabbatical year, people may gather and process only small quantities of food at one time. This is because that which grows during the seventh year is considered ownerless and must be shared by all. This principle (cf. M. 8:1ff.) generates the problem of the pericope, which carries forward M. 5:6's discussion of complicity. If a potter sold a large number of containers during the Sabbatical year, he might thereby assist people who wish to gather and store more than their fair share of produce. How can he avoid becoming an accessory to this transgression? The answer, presented at A-B, is that one may sell only a limited number of containers to a single buyer. Additional vessels may not be sold, for these would be used to store produce that the buyer gathered in violation of the law. C adds an obvious qualification. The potter may sell more containers to a person who has legitimately gathered a larger amount of produce than is usual.

D makes a separate point. Israelites who live outside the Land and gentiles are not bound by the restrictions of the law. Since they may gather and process unlimited quantities of produce, the potter is free to sell them any number of containers.

5:8

A. The House of Shammai say, "During the Sabbatical year a person may not sell to another a heifer suited for plowing."

B. But the House of Hillel permit [one to sell such a heifer,] because he [i.e., the buyer] may slaughter [and eat] it.

C. [During the Sabbatical year] a person may sell to another fruit [the seeds of which are used for sowing,] even during the planting season.

D. And a person may lend to another a seah-measure [used for measuring harvested produce,] even if one knows that he has a threshing floor.

E. And a person may make change for another, even if one knows that he employs (yš lw) laborers.

F. And regarding all of these [transactions--if the partner to the transaction] explicity [stated his intention to violate the law,] they are forbidden.

M. 5:8 (b. A.Z. 15b, y. Dem. 6:5 [25c])

The Houses dispute the principles established at M. 5:6E-G, presented here in a new form. We now wish to know whether one may sell an animal which the buyer could use during the Sabbatical year either in a permitted way, as food, or in a forbidden way, to cultivate the land. The Hillelites, consistent with M. 5:6, allow this transaction, for the buyer will not necessarily use the animal in violation of the law.[25] The Shammaites, however, wish to assure that the seller does not unwittingly become an accessory to the buyer's transgression. Since the seller does not know why the buyer wants the animal, he may not sell it.

Three anonymous rulings, C-E, carry forward the Hillelite view.[26] We assume that a person will use seeds (C), a seah-measure (D), or change (E) for a permitted purpose, even if there is a possibility that he intends to commit a transgression. F provides a self-evident qualification of this principle. One may not transact business with a person who states explicitly his intention to violate the law.

A. They may not sell produce of the Sabbatical year to one who is suspected of [violating the laws of] the Sabbatical year.

B. A single rule applies both to seeds which are edible and to seeds which are not edible [for either type of seed could be used for planting].

C. The House of Shammai say, "During the Sabbatical year one may not sell him [that is, one who is suspected of violating the law] a field."

D. But the House of Hillel permit [the sale of the field, for he may leave it fallow during the Sabbatical year].

T. 4:5 (C: b. A.Z. 15b)

T. rejects the rule of M. 5:8C (A+B). One may not sell fruit of the Sabbatical year to a person who might plant the seeds, in violation of the law. At C vs. D, the Houses continue the discussion of complicity, reiterating their positions at M. 5:8A vs. B. with respect to a new case.

5:9

I.   A.   A woman may lend to a neighbor (lhbrth) who is suspected [of not observing the laws] of the Sabbatical year:

      B.   (1) a sifter, (2) a sieve, (3) a millstone, (4) or an oven.

      C.   But she may not sift or grind [flour] with her [since we assume that this grain was planted in violation of the law].

II.   D.   The wife of a <u>haber</u> [that is, one who eats ordinary food in accordance with the rules of cultic purity] may lend to the wife of an ordinary Israelite (^{c}m h'rs) [who does not scruple about the laws of purity]:

      E.   (1) a sifter, (2) or a sieve,

      F.   and she may sift or grind or shake [dry flour] with her, [for in these cases the ordinary Israelite woman does not render the flour unclean and so commit a transgression].

      G.   But from the time that [the ordinary Israelite woman] pours water [over the flour and thereby renders the flour susceptible to the uncleanness, cf. Lev. 11:34, the wife of a <u>haber</u>] may not touch [the flour] next to her,

      H.   because one does not assist those who commit a transgression.

      I.   And all [of the allowances noted at A-B and D-F] were only made in the interests of peace.

      J.   And during the Sabbatical year one may assist gentiles [to do work which is forbidden to Israelites,] but one may not assist Israelites [to do such work during the Sabbatical year].

      K.   And they greet them [i.e., gentiles,] in the interests of peace.

> M. 5:9 (=M. Git. 5:9; G-H: y. A.Z. 4:10
> [44b]; H: y. Dem. 3:1 [23b]; J-K: M. 4:3C-E)

One may assist people who are suspected of violating the law, but not those whom one knows to be acting improperly. This principle, familiar from the foregoing rules, is reiterated at A-C and D-H. A woman may lend tools to a neighbor suspected of not observing the law (A-B, D-F), but may not help her when it is apparent that she is committing a transgression (C, G-H). The rule at D-H, which relates to the laws for preserving the cleanness of foods, has no bearing on the laws of the Sabbatical year. It has been placed here because it further illustrates the principle of A-C. A gloss, I, explains that these rulings promote peaceful relations among Israelites. This draws in its wake J-K, a separate rule which makes a parallel point, that assisting gentiles during the Sabbatical year helps to maintain cordial relations with them.

CHAPTER SIX

Shebiit Chapter Six

The laws of the Sabbatical year do not apply uniformly throughout the Land of Israel. This is because some regions of the Land are considered more sanctified than others. Mishnah's framers believe that the level of sanctity which inheres in each area of the Land depends upon the length of time during which the Israelites lived in that location. The longer the period of Israelite occupation, the greater is the sanctity which inheres in that region, and concomitantly, the more stringent are the restrictions that apply to the land and its produce. This central principle, spelled out at M. 6:1, generates a secondary discussion on the status of Syria, at M. 6:2, 5-6. This country poses a problem for the application of the law, because it is not within the boundaries of the Land, yet many Isrealites settled there in the period following the Babylonian exile. It thus is not clear whether Syria is subject to the same rules as the Land of Israel. Three distinct views are put forward in the chapter. Aqiba (M. 6:2C-E) and Simeon (M. 6:5B,D) hold that the extensive Israelite settlement within Syria has, in effect, made it part of the Land. Accordingly, all the restrictions that apply in the Land of Israel also are in force in Syria. At M. 6:2A-B, Mishnah's authorities claim that Syria is subject only to some of the restrictions of the Sabbatical year, for it was settled only relatively late in Israelite history. Finally, M. 6:5-6A, C treats Syria as a foreign country. Since it is outside the original borders of the Land, it is entirely exempt from the restrictions that apply there.

Two units of law, M. 6:3 and 6:4, stand outside the framework of this discussion. Both deal with problems posed by produce that grows over more than one calendar year, an issue familiar from M. 5:1 and 5:5. At M. 6:3, we wish to know how to determine whether onions that remain in the ground from the Sabbatical year into the year following are subject to the restrictions of the law. The presence of new leaves during the Sabbatical year indicates that the onions began to grow during that year. Such onions, therefore, are subject to the rules governing the use of sanctified produce of the seventh year (see Chapters Eight and Nine). M. 6:4 concerns a householder who, during the year following the Sabbatical, wishes to buy vegetables in the market. At the outset of the eighth year the produce for sale in the market clearly began growing during the seventh year and so is subject to the restrictions of the law. Only after the crop of the eighth year has ripened and been harvested may the householder assume that the food he buys no longer belongs to the crop of the seventh year. A qualification of this rule at M. 6:4C raises a geographical issue and may account for the inclusion of this law in the present chapter. A single type of produce ripens earlier in some regions of the Land than in others. In such cases, we do not differentiate produce grown in one region from that grown elsewhere. Once a vegetable has become ripe in one place, similar produce in markets throughout the Land also is assumed to be from the new crop.

6:1

A.   Three provinces ('rswt) [are delineated] with regard to [the laws of] the Sabbatical year:

B.   (1) [Regarding] all [of the land] which was occupied [by Joshua and again] by those who returned from Babylonia [after the exile]

C.   [that is, the area] from the Land of Israel[1] [in the south] to Kezib[2] [in the north]--

D.   [produce cultivated during the Sabbatical year in violation of the law,] may not be eaten[3] and [the land of this region] may not be worked [during the Sabbatical year].

E.   (2) [Regarding] all [of the land] which was occupied by those who came out of Egypt, [but was not re-conquered after the Babylonian exile,]

F.   [that is, the area] from Kezib to the river [i.e., the brook of Egypt[4], in the south,] and [from Kezib] to Amana [in the north]--

G.   [produce cultivated during the Sabbatical year in violation of the law,] may be eaten, but [the land of these regions] may not be cultivated [during the Sabbatical year].

H.   (3) [Regarding the land] from the river and from Amana and beyond (lpnym)[5] [that is, from the river southward and from Amana northward]--

I.   [produce cultivated during the Sabbatical year] may be eaten, and [the land of these regions] may be cultivated [during the Sabbatical year].

M. 6:1 (Sifre Dt. 51, M. Hal. 4:8)

The restrictions of the Sabbatical year do not apply uniformly throughout the Land of Israel. Some areas, inhabited by the Israelites for long periods of time, are subject during the Sabbatical year to stringent restrictions. Fewer restrictions, however, apply to regions occupied by the Israelites for shorter periods of time. Why is this so? Mishnah's authorities assume that Israelites sanctify the land which God gave them by dwelling in it. The degree of sanctity which inheres both in the Land and in the produce that grows from it, therefore, is determined by the length of time during which the Israelites inhabited it. The implications of this principle are spelled out in the three-part rule before us. The area occupied by the Israelites both before and after the Babylonian exile is subject to the full restrictions of the law. During the Sabbatical year one may neither cultivate the land within this region, nor eat produce that grew on land cultivated in violation of the law (B-C). A second region was occupied before the exile, but not afterward. Here only the prohibition against cultivation applies. The secondary prohibition against benefiting from produce cultivated by others in violation of the law is not in force (D-E). Places that Israelites never settled are not deemed part of the Land of Israel at all. They are entirely exempt from the restrictions of the Sabbatical year (F-G).

A.   What is [considered part of] the Land of Israel?

B.   From the river [which is] south of Kezib [in the north] and beyond [i.e., southward; see M. 6:1].

C.   [And the settlements] bordering on Ammon and Moab [and] Egypt are [divided into] two regions:

D.   In one region (so Lieberman, TZ, p. 180, TK, p. 531) [produce cultivated during the Sabbatical year in violation of the law,] may be eaten, and [the land] may be cultivated, but in the other [region, produce cultivated during the Sabbatical year] may not be eaten, and [the land] may not be cutlivated.

T. 4:6 (T. Hal. 2:6; y. Sheb. 6:1 [36d])

E.   [As regards] settlements in the Land of Isreal which are near the border--

F.   they appoint a guard so that the gentiles do not break across [the border, into the Land of Israel,] and steal produce of the Sabbatical year.

T. 4:7

G.   [These are] the cities in the vacinity of N'vay[6] [the fields of which were once] permitted [to be cultivated during the Sabbatical year,] but were [later] forbidden [when these cities became populated with Israelites]:

H.   Tyre,[7] Ts'yar,[8] Gashmay,[9] Zizyon,[10] Yagri Tab,[11] Danab Hurbatah,[12] and the fortified city of Beit Hereb.[13]

T. 4:8 (y. Dem. 2:1, [22d])

I.   These are the forbidden cities in the vicinity of Tyre[14] [that is, the fields of these cities may not be cultivated during the Sabbatical year]:

J.   Shetseth,[15] Betseth,[16] Pi-M'tsubah,[17] Upper Hanitha,[18] Lower Hanitha, Resh Maya,[19] Beit Karya,[20] 'Emek,[21] Mazi.[22]

T. 4:9 (y. Dem. 2:1 [22d])

K.   [These are] the cities in the vacinity of Susita,[23] [the produce of which] is subject to tithing:

L.   'Aynosh,[24] Ein Ter'a,[25] Ram Barin,[26] 'Iyon,[27] Yaadut,[28] Kfar Harub,[29] Nob,[30] Haspiah,[31] and Kfar Tsemah,[32]

M.   Rabbi exempted [the produce of] Kfar Tsemah [from tithes.]

T. 4:10 (y. Dem. 2:1 [22d])

N.   The region of the Land of Israel[33] [includes the following areas]:

O.   The Crossing of Ashkelon,[34] the Tower of Sher,[35] the Cliff of Dor,[36] the fortification wall[37] of Caesarea and the fortification wall of Acre, the source of the waters of Gaton,[38] Gaton itself, and Kabritha,[39] and Kaznita,[40] Fort of the Galilee,[41] Hollows of Aitha,[42] Fort of Khur and Great Khuray,[43] Tafnith, S'noftha, the cave region of Yattir,[44] Mamtsi of Abhata, and the source of the waters of Marhesheth, and the river of Yiphtsael and 'Ulshatha, Avlas, and the Tower of Harub, the Hollow of Iyon,[45] Mesha, Tukrath, the towns of Bar-Sanigora, Tarn'gola above Caesarea, Kenath,[46] Hagra,[47] Trachona in the area of Bozrah, Y'gar Sahadutha, Nimrin, Melah d'Zarvai, Yubka,[48] Heshbon, and the brook of Zered,[49] Raphia, Ammon, Moab, and R'kam Geah, and the gardens of Ashkelon, and the great road which leads to the desert.

T. 4:11 (y. Sheb. 6:1 [36c]; Sifre Eqeb 51)

The area of the Land of Israel is specified (N-O), as well as the border areas within which the restrictions of the Sabbatical year apply (G-J). E-F is included because it relates to border settlements. Some of the settlements bordering on Ammon, Moab, and Egypt are deemed to be fully part of the Land of Israel, and so are subject to all of the restrictions of the Sabbatical year (see M. 6:1C). Others are deemed to be outside the Land of Israel, and so, subject to none of these restrictions (C-D).

6:2

A.   In Syria, [farmers] may do work [during the Sabbatical year] involving harvested [produce] (btlwš), but [they] may not [do work] involving unharvested [produce] (bmhwbr).

B.   [That is,] 1) they may thresh, winnow, trample and bind [wheat into sheaves],
                    2) but they may not reap, harvest grapes, or cut olives.

C.   R. Aqiba stated a general rule:

D.   "Any [agricultural activity] of a type which is permitted (kl škyws' bw mtr) [during the Sabbatical year] in the Land of Israel--

E.   "they may do [such work] in Syria."

M. 6:2

We wish to know whether during the Sabbatical year Syria is subject to the same restrictions as the Land of Israel. Syria enjoys an ambiguous status[50] because many Israelites lived there during the period following the Babylonian exile,[51] though it was not within the boundaries of the Land of Israel (see M. 6:1). A-B claims that Syria is subject only to some of the restrictions of the law, for it was settled relatively late in Israelite history. During the Sabbatical year the farmer in Syria, like his counterpart in the Land of Israel, may not cultivate his field and harvest its yield as he does in other years (B2). Produce that grows in Syria during the Sabbatical year, however, is not subject to all of the restrictions that govern food grown in the Land of Israel. In Syria, grain may be processed in the usual manner (B1),[52] unlike produce that grows in the Land, which may be processed only in small quantities and in an abnormal way (cf. M. 8:6). Aqiba disagrees with this rule, though his lemma has not been cast as a dispute with the foregoing. He claims that the number of Israelites that inhabit the Land in the present, rather than in the past, determines its status with respect to the laws of the Sabbatical year. Since in Mishnaic times Syria had a large Israelite population, a single set of restrictions, on Aqiba's view, should be operative throughout both countries.

A.   R. Aqiba concedes that in Syria one may not sow, or plow, or weed [during the Sabbatical year],

B.   because none of these [agricultural activities] is of a type which is permitted in the Land of Israel.

C.   For any [agricultural activity] of a type which is permitted [during the Sabbatical year] in the Land of Israel--they may do [such work] in Syria [=M. 6:2D-E].

D.   In Syria, one may not engage in [an agricultrual activity][53] involving produce which is unharvested [=M. 6:2A with variations].

E.   but, [if gentiles] uproot [produce, the Israelite] may bind [the produce] for them.

F.   [And this ruling applies] provided that it is not he [the Israelite] who harvests [the produce] and they [the gentiles] who bind it for him.

G.   [If gentiles] harvest grapes, [an Israelite] may trample [the grapes] for them.

H.   [If gentiles] harvest olives, [an Israelite] may pack[54] [the olives for processing] for them.

I.   Under what circumstances does the ruling [that one may not process produce harvested by an Israelite] apply?

J.   To one who takes produce out of (read: mtwk with E, ed. princ.: V reads: btwk) [an Israelite's] home, [for he assumes that the Israelite harvested this produce].

K.   Or, to one whose friend [who is an Israelite] sent him produce [for he assumes that his friend harvested the produce].

L.   But [as for] one who buys [produce] in the marketplace--lo, this [gentile seller][55] harvests [the produce] with his own hand,

M.   So [the buyer] need not scruple. [He may process this produce, since he assumes that the gentile who sold it to him likewise harvested it.].

T. 4:12 (E-H: T. Hal. 2:5)

A-C notes the intersection between Aqiba's ruling of M. 6:2C-D and the anonymous ruling of M. 6:2A-B. According to T., Aqiba's view is that activities involving unharvested produce, such as sowing, plowing, and weeding, are not permitted during the seventh year in Syria. This is in agreement with the rule at M. 6:2A-B. Moreover, Aqiba prohibits farmers in Syria from engaging in activities involving harvested produce, since these are not permitted in the Land of Israel. This contrasts with M. 6:2A-B.

D-G qualify the ruling that in Syria the Israelite farmer is not permitted to harvest, but is permitted to process harvested produce (M. 6:2A-B). One may process only produce which has been harvested by gentiles (E). Such produce was not harvested in violation of the law, since neither gentiles nor their crops are bound by the restrictions of the Sabbatical year. I-M further qualify this ruling.[56] One is not permitted to process produce which may have been harvested by Israelites (I-K). This would constitute aiding an Israelite in the transgression of the law, which is forbidden. One may process produce bought from a gentile in the marketplace, however, since the seller is assumed to have harvested the produce himself (L-M).

6:3

A.   Onions [that were left in the ground from the sixth year into the Sabbatical year] upon which rain has fallen and which [subsequently] sprouted [leaves]--

B.   if the leaves are dark (s̲hwryn) [green in the Sabbatical year, the onions] are forbidden. [These onions are subject to the restrictions of the law, since they began growing during the Sabbatical year].

C.   [But,] if [the leaves] became light green (hwryqw), lo, these [onions] are permitted. [They are exempt from the restrictions of the law, for the color of their leaves indicate that they finished growing during the sixth year].

D.   R. Hanina ben Antigonos says, "If [onion bulbs] can be uprooted [during the Sabbatical year] by their leaves, [the onions] are forbidden.

E.   "But, in contrast to this [case,] during the year following the Sabbatical [onions that can be uprooted by their leaves] are permitted, [for we assume that they grew during the eighth year alone, not during the Sabbatical year]."

M. 6:3 (b. Ned. 58a; A-C: b. Ned. 59a-b)

A problem arises when onions remain in the ground from the sixth year into the year following. If this produce began to grow during the Sabbatical year, it is subject to the restrictions of the law. If, by contrast, they finished growing during the sixth year and simply remained unharvested during the following year, they are exempt. We determine whether these onions began to grow during the Sabbatical year by examining their leaves. At A-C, for example, the presence of young, dark-colored leaves during the Sabbatical year indicates that the onions began to grow during that year. The law applies (B). Pale, old leaves, on the other hand, signal to the farmer that no new growth has occurred recently. These onions are produce of the sixth year (C). Hanina examines leaves in a different way, by testing whether they still are strongly attached to the bulbs. If the onions can be uprooted by their leaves during the Sabbatical year, he concludes that they sprouted recently and so are produce of that year (D). The same test applies to onions that remain in the ground from the seventh year into the eighth year, with the opposite result. Produce that can be uprooted by its leaves during the year following the Sabbatical is exempt from the restrictions of the law (E).[57]

A. Onions which remained [in the ground] from the sixth year into the Sabbatical,

B. or which remained (šys'w) from the Sabbatical year into the year following--(see M. 7:3A,E)

C. If they have grown as much [in the sixth year, or in the eighth year,] as the produce which first appeared in that year has grown, they are permitted. But, if not, they are prohibited.

D. Said R. Yose, "An incident: They planted onions in an untilled vineyard (so Lieberman, TK, p. 539) in Sepphoris, In the year following the Sabbatical, they sowed it with barley, and the workers went down [to the fields] and weeded, and brought back vegetables [i.e., onions] in their baskets.

E. "The case come before R. Yohanan ben Nuri, who said, 'If they grew [in the eighth year] as much as the produce which began growing in that year, they are permitted, and if not, they are prohibited.'"

T. 4:13

T. provides a single, new criterion that applies both to onions which remain in the ground from the sixth year into the Sabbatical and to those which remain in the ground from the Sabbatical into the year following. The onions in question are permitted only if they have grown as much in either the sixth or the eighth year as onions which first sprouted in those years would normally grow. Such onions are not deemed produce of the seventh year, since most of their growth did not occur during that year. D-E provide a precedent for this ruling.

6:4

A. When in the year following the Sabbatical is one permitted to buy a [given type of] vegetable [on the assumption that this produce is from the new crop and so is exempt from the law]?

B. Once [the new crop of] that same type [of vegetable] has become ripe (msy^{c}sh kyws' bw).

C. Once the [portion of the crop which] ripens early [in the year, in one location] (hbkyr) has become ripe, the [portion of the crop which] ripens later [in the year, in another location] (h'pyl) [likewise] is permitted [that is, may be purchased.][58]

D. Rabbi permitted the purchase of vegetables immediately in the year following the Sabbatical.

M. 6:4 (D: y. Peah 7:3 [20b]; y. Dem. 2:1
[23c]; y. B.B. 9:5 [17a])

Vegetables for sale in the market at the beginning of the year following the Sabbatical belong to the crop of the preceding year. Since they began to grow and were harvested during the seventh year, they are subject to the restrictions of the law.[59]

Later in the eighth year, however, new crops of vegetables, exempt from the restrictions of the Sabbatical year, ripen and become available for purchase. At what point in this year may a householder assume that the vegetables he purchases are produce of the new year (A)? According to B, one must wait until the new crop of that species is ripe. Once farmers start to harvest the vegetables that began growing during the eighth year, householders can be sure that all similar produce in the market belongs to the new crop. A qualification of this ruling, C, addresses a secondary problem. The entire crop of a vegetable does not become ripe at the same time throughout the Land of Israel. We might imagine then that in each climatic region of the Land one must wait to puchase vegetable until the crop within that region has become available. C claims, however, that each species of produce becomes subject to the law at a single time throughout the Land. Once the new crop has become ripe in one place, and so may be purchased, all similar produce in other locations may be purchased as well.

Rabbi, D, clearly rejects the foregoing principle, though the basis for his ruling is not apparent. His position that produce may be purchased immediately may reflect the theory that the restrictions of the Sabbatical year are in force only for the duration of that year. Once the Sabbatical year has ended, produce that grew during that year loses its sanctity. The purchase of this food thus is not governed by the restrictions that apply to the purchase of sanctified produce of the Sabbatical year (see M. 8:3). This interpretation of Rabbi's lemma remains problematic, however, for it attributes to him an extreme position which contradicts the view assumed throughout the tractate.[60]

A. One may eat a vegetable which ripens late on [the basis of the permitted status of] that which ripens early [see M. 6:4C].

B. [One may eat a vegetable] from far away on [the basis of the permitted status of] that which grows nearby.

C. [When produce] is permitted in one place, [that produce] is permitted in all places.

D. [As regards] garlic, arum and onions--

E. Once the dry produce is permitted, the fresh produce is permitted.

F. [However, once the] fresh produce [is permitted], the dry produce is not permitted, until the time of threshing.

G. Each species [of produce] renders permissible [for purchase] only (so Lieberman, TK, p. 540, reading '!' for 't) [other produce of] its same species.

H. And they may only judge species [of produce] to be permissible on the authority of a sage.

I. And all [produce harvested] in the year following the Sabbatical is liable to tithes.

T. 4:14

The ruling of M. 6:4C applies to like produce from different geographical regions (A-C). D-F apply the principle of M. 6:4B to produce at successive stages of processing, rather than at successive stages of ripening. Once the produce which has already had time to dry is permitted (according to the criterion of M. 6:4B), the fresh produce is likewise permitted (E). One must wait to purchase the dried produce, however, until the new, fresh produce has been harvested and had time to dry (F). This is because, in the case of garlic, arum and onions, even after the new, fresh produce may be bought, the dried produce might be from the Sabbatical year. G restricts the ruling of A-C to produce of a single species. Since different species of produce become ripe at different times, even after the new crop of one species is permitted, produce of another species may yet be from the Sabbatical year. H glosses this ruling. I is separate and has been included here because it relates to produce harvested in the year following the Sabbatical. Although such produce has an ambiguous status with respect to the restrictions of the Sabbatical year, it is subject to the separation of tithes. This is because produce becomes liable to tithes when it is harvested.[61]

A.   A vegetable planted on the eve of the New Year of the Sabbatical year--

B.   lo, one may not gather it (so E; V, ed. princ., add: bšby^{C}yt) [but must wait to pick it] until the new crop [of the year following the Sabbatical] is permitted (so E, which reads: šytyr hhdš; V, ed. princ. read: šytry 't hhdš).

C.   R. Simeon b. Eleazer says, "At the beginning of the eighth year he may, however, gather its leaves (read with Lieberman, TZ, p. 185: ^{C}lyw; E, V, ed. princ. read: hymnw) and bring them into his house,

D.   "even at a time when produce which is similar to the vegetable (reading with E: bw; V, ed. princ. read: bhn) is not being sold in the market."

T. 4:15

The point of A-B is that a vegetable, planted on the day before the seventh year begins, is deemed produce of the Sabbatical year. This is because virtually all of the growth of this vegetable occurs during the Sabbatical year. Such a vegetable cannot be harvested and sold until the new crop of the year following the Sabbatical is permitted, in accordance with the ruling of M. 6:4D. Simeon (C) qualifies this ruling. Although the vegetable itself may not be harvested until this time, the leaves which grow from it are separate. They may be harvested even before the point at which the vegetable may be purchased.[62]

A.   At first they ruled, "[During the Sabbatical year] they may not pickle [vegetables], dry [fruit], nor import dried [fruit] or pickled [vegetables] from abroad into the Land [of Israel]."

B.   Our rabbis permitted one to pickle [vegetables], dry [fruit] and import dried [fruit] and pickled [vegetables] from abroad into the Land [of Israel].

C.   [At first they ruled, "During the Sabbatical year] they may not import vegetables from abroad into the Land [of Israel]."

D.   Our rabbis permitted one to import vegetables from abroad into the Land [of Israel].

E.   Just as they may import vegetables from abroad, so they may import legumes and
      grain from abroad into the Land [of Israel].

                                    T. 4:16

F.   Rabbi and his court permitted the purchase of vegetables immediately in the year
      following the Sabbatical [=M. 6:4D].

                                    T. 4:17

G.   [As regards] produce of the Sabbatical year which comes from abroad into the Land
      [of Israel]--
H.   They may not sell it by volume or by weight or by number.
I.   Lo, it is [handled] like the produce of the Land [of Israel].

                              T. 4:18 (A-E: b. Ned. 53b; b. Sanh. 12a; B:
                              y. Peah 5:1 [18d]; y. Ter. 6:6 [44b]; y. Sheq.
                              1:2 [46a]; y. Ned. 6:13 [39d]; y. Sanh. 1:2
                              [18d]; F: y. Peah 7:4 [20b]; y. Dem. 2:1
                              [22c]; y, B.B. 9:7 [17a])

        The form "our rabbis permitted" unites three rules concerning the proper manner of
handling produce of the Sabbatical year. The parallel rulings of A-B and C-D, however,
make a single point quite separate from that of F, which repeats M. 6:4D[63]. Produce
which is subject to the restrictions of the Sabbatical year must be kept separate from
similar produce which is not subject to these restrictions. This is to prevent people from
accidentally confusing lots of produce which are similar in their appearance, but
dissimilar in their status. Accordingly, one may not dry or press fresh produce of the
Sabbatical year, since such produce looks no different than similar produce of other years
(A). Likewise, one may not import produce to the Land of Israel during the Sabbatical
year, since such produce cannot be distinguished from similar produce which grew in the
Land of Israel (C). Later rabbis abolished these restrictions, since no transgression of the
law directly results from these activities (B,D). E glosses D and extends the ruling to
types of produce other than vegetables.
        The ruling of G-I is formally separate from the foregoing, but makes a similar
point. Produce imported from another country during the Sabbatical year is subjected to
the restrictions which apply to produce grown in the Land of Israel (I). The purpose of this
ruling is to insure that all produce bought and sold during the Sabbatical year is subject to
the same restrictions. Specifically, during the Sabbatical year produce may not be traded
according to standard measurements (H). This is because produce of the Sabbatical year
is sanctified and may not be traded like produce of other years (see M. 8:3).

A. [During the Sabbatical year] one may import plants or <u>karmulin</u>[64] from another country into the Land [of Israel],

B. but not from another country into the Land [of Israel in order] to eat their leaves in the Land [of Israel].

C. One may not import grapes from another country into the Land [of Israel] and trample them in the Land [of Isreal].

D. And [one may] not [import] olives from another country into the Land [of Israel] and pack them in the Land [of Israel].

E. And [one may] not [import] stalks of flax from another country into the Land [of Israel] and soak them in the Land [of Israel].

F. But one may import dried figs[65] and raisins and stalks of flax [which have been processed] from another country into the Land [of Israel].

G. but not from another country into the Land [of Israel] in order to process them in the Land [of Israel].

H. Rabbi permitted them to import these things for processing [during the Sabbatical year] into the Land of Israel [in the areas] near the borders (<u>smk lhwsh l'rs</u>).

T. 4:19

This pericope continues to explore the topic of T. 4:16, the importation of produce during the Sabbatical year into the Land of Israel. The point of these rulings is that produce of the Land of Israel must be kept separate from the imported produce. One may import plants during the Sabbatical year, since these are not edible and cannot be confused with produce of the Land of Israel (A). One may not import plants along with their leaves, however, since the leaves are edible and could be confused with native produce (B). The parallel rulings of C-E state that produce imported during the Sabbatical year may not be processed in the Land of Israel. This is to insure that the imported produce is not processed together with the produce of the Land of Israel. The ruling of F-G merely states the converse of these rulings. Rabbi (H) permitted the importation of produce for processsing during the Sabbatical year in the areas near the borders, since there the imported produce would not be mistaken for produce of the Land of Israel.

A. [Concerning] any tree the fruit of which begins to form prior to the fifteenth of Shebat [which is the new year for fruit-bearing trees cf. M. R.H. 1:1] --lo, [its fruit is deemed to be produce] of the preceding year (lš^cbrh) [i.e., of the calendar year which already ended].[66]

B. [Concerning a tree the fruit of which begins to form] after the fifteenth of Shebat--lo, [its fruit is deemed to be produce] of the current year (l^ctyd lbw') [i.e., of the calendar year which has not yet ended].

C. R. Nehemiah says, "To what [sort of tree] does this ruling apply?

D. "To a tree which bears new fruit twice a year (š^cwsh šty brykwt bšnh).

E. "But [as regards] a tree which bears new fruit only once a year--

F. "for example, olives, dates, and carobs--

G.   "even if [the tree's] fruit begins to form prior to the fifteenth of Shebat, [i.e.,
     between the first of Tishre and the fifteenth of Shebat], it is as if such fruit began
     to form after the fifteenth of Shebat."

H.   R. Simeon b. Gamaliel says, "[The period] from the appearance of the leaves [of the
     fig tree] until [the appearance of] the underdeveloped figs (hpgyn) is fifty days.

I.   "[The period] from [the appearance of] the underdeveloped figs until [the ripening of]
     inferior figs [which grow from buds of the preceding year and generally drop off the
     tree] (following Lieberman, TZ, p. 184, who reads: šytyn hnwblwt; V reads: šytyn
     wnwblwt, E. ed. princ. read: šyhyw nwblwt) is fifty days.

J.   "And from [the ripening of] inferior figs until [the ripening of well-developed] figs
     (t'nym) is fifty days."

K.   Rabbis says, "Each [of these intervals] is forty days (reading with E: 'rb^{C}ym; V, ed.
     princ. read: 'rb^{C}ym 'rb^{C}ym)."

L.   And all [figs which become ripe] prior to this time [i.e., the fifteenth of Shebat]--lo,
     they are [deemed to be produce] of the preceding year [=A],

M.   [and all figs which become ripe] after this time--lo, they are [deemed to be produce]
     of the current year [=B].

                         T. 4:20 (b. R.H. 15b; b. Bek. 8a)

        Produce of fruit-bearing trees is regulated by two distinct yearly cycles which do
not coincide. The calendar year, which begins on the first of Tishre, determines which
agricultural offerings are to be given from produce grown in that year. In the first,
second, fourth, and fifth years of the Sabbatical cycle, the farmer dedicates second tithe,
while in the third and sixth years, he dedicates poorman's tithe. The new growing season
for fruit trees, on the other hand, begins on the fifteenth of Shebat, three and a half
months after the start of the new calendar year. Fruit which appears after the fifteenth
of Shebat poses no problem for the system of agricultural offerings. Such fruit is subject
to the agricultural restrictions of the calendar year in which it appears. The problem is
how to determine which agricultural restrictions apply to fruit which appears after the
beginning of the new calendar year (i.e., the first of Tishre), but before the beginning of
the new growing season (i.e., the fifteenth of Shebat). Such fruit could be subject to the
restrictions of the preceding calendar year, since it appears before the fifteenth of
Shebat, while the old crop of fruit is still on the branch. Alternatively, such fruit may be
subject to the restrictions of the new calendar year, since this is the year in which it
appears. A-B's point is that the fifteenth of Shebat, rather than the first of Tishre,
determines the status of this fruit. Fruit which appears before the fifteenth of Shebat is
deemed part of the old crop and is subject to the restrictions of the preceding calendar
year.

        According to Nehemiah (C-G), the ruling of A-B applies only to trees which bear two
crops of fruit within the same calendar year. The first crop of fruit, which appears before
the fifteenth of Shebat, grows from buds which appeared on the branch during the
preceding calendar year. Such fruit, accordingly, is subject to the agricultural restric-

tions of the preceding calendar year. The crop of fruit which appears after the fifteenth of Shebat, on the other hand, grows from buds which appeared after the the beginning of the new calendar year. This crop is subject to the restrictions of that year. Nehemiah claims that trees which bear fruit only once a year are subject to a different rule. These trees both produce buds and yield fruit within the same calendar year. Such fruit clearly belongs to the calendar year during which the entire growth process occurs (G).

Simeon and Rabbi apply Nehemiah's ruling to the case of fig trees, which bear two crops of fruit within a single calendar year.[67] The first crop of figs appears prior to the fifteenth of Shebat, and so, belongs to the preceding calendar year. The crop of figs which appears after the fifteenth of Shebat, however, belongs to the current calendar year. This is the point made at L-M, which repeat A-B. The issue of the time interval separating the two crops of figs, disputed by Simeon and Rabbi at H-J vs. K, is a moot point. Both parties agree that fig trees bear two crops within a single calendar year and, therefore, are subject to the ruling as stated.

A. An incident: R. Aqiba picked a citron on the first of Shebat and dealt with it in accordance with the words of the House of Hillel [who hold that the new year for fruit-bearing trees begins on the fifteenth of Shebat] and in accordance with the words of the House of Shammai [who hold that the new year begins of the first of Shebat; see M. R.H. 1:1.]" [Aqiba separated both second tithe, as if the citron were fruit of the second (or fifth) year, and poorman's tithe, as if it were fruit of the third (or sixth) year.][68]

B. R. Yose in the name of R. Judah [said, "R. Aqiba dealt with the citron] in accordance with the words of R. Gamaliel [who holds that citrons, like vegetables, are subject to the separation of the tithes required in the year in which they are picked] and in accordance with the words of R. Eliezer [who holds that citrons, like other fruit trees, are subject to the separation of the tithes required in the year in which they become ripe; see M. Bik. 2:6.]" [Aqiba separated second tithe, required in the year in which the citron grew and poorman's tithe, required in the year in which it was picked].[69]

C. Said R. Yose, "R. Abtolemos affirmed in the name of five elders that a citron is subject to [the separation of the] tithes [required] in the year in which it is picked.

D. And in Usha our rabbis voted concerning [this matter] and ruled that a citron is subject to [the separation of] tithes and to [the law of] removal in the year in which it is picked." [This is explained below at F-G.]

E. R. Simeon said, "A citron which remained [on the tree] (šnkns) from the sixth year into the Sabbatical, or which remained [on the tree] (šys') from the Sabbatical into the year following, is exempt from [the separation of] tithes and exempt from [the law of] removal.

F. "The only [fruit] which is subject to [the separation of] tithes is that which grew under conditions of liability and was picked under conditions of liability.

G.   "The only [fruit] which is liable to [the law of] removal is that which grew during the
      Sabbatical year and was picked during the Sabbatical year."[70]

> T. 4:21 (y. Bik. 2:5 [65b]; y. R.H. 1:2 [57a];
> b. Erub. 7a; b. R.H. 14a; b. Yeb. 15a; C: b.
> Suk. 40a)

The pericope is related tangentially to M. 6:4A-B in that it concerns that status of
produce which grows in one year but is harvested in the following year. The issue is
whether a citron is subject to the tithes required in the year in which it becomes ripe, as
are fruit trees, or to the tithes required in the year in which it is harvested, as are
vegetables. According to the two versions of the incident at A-B, Aqiba took both
positions into account. Yose (C-D) cites precedents for the ruling that a citron is subject
to the tithes of the year in which it is picked. Simeon (E-G) rejects the whole issue as
phrased at A-B and C-D. He holds that the citron, like all produce, is subject to the
restrictions of a given year only if it both becomes ripe and is harvested in that year.

6:5-6

A.   They may not export oil [in the status of heave-offering which has become unclean
      and is fit only for] burning or produce of the Sabbatical year from the Land of Israel
      to [countries] outside the Land.
B.   Said R. Simeon, (L omits: Simeon) "I have heard [it stated] explicitly that they may
      export [these things] to Syria, but they may not export [them] to [countries] outside
      the Land."

M. 6:5 (Sifra Behar 1:9)

C.   They may not import produce designated as heave-offering from another country to
      the Land of Israel.
D.   Said R. Simeon, (L omits: Simeon) "I have heard [it stated] explicitly that they may
      import [such produce] from Syria, but they may not import [it] from [countries]
      outside the Land."

M. 6:6 (y. Hal. 4:5 [60b])

Two parallel disputes address the issue of Syria's ambiguous status, the topic of M.
6:2. Simeon (B,D), in line with the position attributed to Aqiba (M. 6:2C-E), holds that the
same agricultural restrictions apply both to produce grown in Syria and to that which
comes from the Land of Israel. Since a large number of Israelites live in Syria, it is
regarded in every way as part of the Land. The rules at A and C claim that all regions
outside the original borders of the Land (cf. M. 6:1), including Syria, are exempt from the
restrictions that apply within the Land. With the central point of the disputes in hand, let
us now turn to the details of the rule at A and C.

The principle underlying the rule at A is clear. Sanctified food must be used by Israelites living in the Land. People may not treat these edibles like ordinary produce, by exporting them to other countries where they will be used as common food. Mishnah's authorities characteristically express this point by focusing upon the liminal case, produce that is sanctified, yet is not subject to all of the restictions that generally apply to other sanctified agricultural offerings. We deal in the first instance with oil in the status of heave-offering that has become unclean. This oil no longer can be eaten by priests and so is not subject to the restrictions governing the use of clean heave-offering. In particular, this oil may be burned in a lamp to provide light for ordinary Israelites as well as for priests (see M. Ter. 11:10). Produce of the Sabbatical year likewise is sanctified. God has designated the yield of the Land during the seventh year as food, which must be shared equally by all Israelites. Nonetheless, this produce is exempt from many of the restrictions that apply to other agricultural offerings, for it is not eaten in a state of cleanness (like heave-offering), nor brought to Jerusalem (like second tithe), nor presented at the altar of the Temple (like first-fruits). Even though these types of produce, unclean heave-offering and produce of the Sabbatical year, do not possess the full sanctity of food given to the priests, they remain sanctified produce of the Land. People may not export this food, as if it were a common commodity.

The contrasting rule at C makes a complementary point. One may not import produce from other countries and treat it as though it enjoyed the status of sanctified food from the Land of Israel. A householder living outside the Land has designated some of his produce as heave-offering. The farmer's act of designation alone, however, cannot make this produce sanctified, for only that which grows in the Land of Israel is invested with this special status.

A.   "Produce of the Sabbatical year which was exported to another country--[the owners of the produce] remove it in the place [to which it has been exported]," the words of Rabbi.

B.   R. Simeon b. Eleazar says, "[The owners of the produce] bring it to the Land [of Israel] and remove it in the Land [of Israel].

C.   "As it is written [in Scripture], 'In your land [i.e., the Land of Israel] all its yield shall be for food (Lev. 25:7).'"

T. 5:1 (b. Pes. 52b)

At issue is how one continues to observe the law if, contrary to the ruling of M. 6:5A, he takes produce of the seventh year out of the Land of Israel. Rabbi (A) holds that the law of removal is observed in the place to which the produce has been exported. In other words, the law of removal applies to this produce even outside of the Land of Israel. Just as if it had never been exported, the produce is removed from the possession of 'its owner when similar produce is no longer available in the fields of the Land of Israel. Simeon (B) maintains that the law of removal does not apply outside of the Land of Israel. The previous violation must be rectified before further restrictions of the

Sabbatical year may be observed. The owner must first return the produce to its proper place, in the Land of Israel, and then observe the law of removal there. At C, Simeon offers a prooftext for his opinion.

A. Produce designated as heave-offering may not be imported from another country into the Land of Israel [=M. 6:5C].

B. Said Rabban Simeon b. Gamaliel, "In Acre, I once saw Simeon b. Kahana drinking wine in the status of heave-offering.

C. "When he said, 'This [wine] comes from (bydy m-) Cilicia,'[71] they required him to drink [the wine] in a boat [i.e., he was not permitted to bring the produce into the Land of Israel]."

T. 5:2 (y. Hal. 4:12 [72d])

Simeon b. Gamaliel describes an occasion on which the ruling of 6:5C was applied.

CHAPTER SEVEN

Shebiit Chapter Seven

The tractate begins a protracted essay, encompassing Chapters Seven through Nine, on a new topic: the restrictions that apply to produce which grows during the Sabbatical year. Mishnah's framers proceed logically, first delineating the types of produce subject to the restrictions of the law, then, in subsequent chapters, presenting these restrictions in detail. In order to understand the point of the criteria presented in the chapter before us, however, we must begin with an overview of the restrictions themselves. These are of two types, (1) restrictions governing the use and transfer of produce of the Sabbatical year, and (2) the law of removal. The restrictions of the Sabbatical year provide that edible produce which grows during that year belongs equally to all Israelites. For this reason, individuals may neither use this food for their own financial gain nor sell it in the usual manner, as they would produce which they owned. This sanctified produce has been designated by God as food for Israelites and may not be used for any other purpose. The law of removal prevents people from stockpiling produce meant to be shared by all. Once all edibles of a certain species have disappeared from the fields, people must remove food of that type which they have stored in their homes. By making this food accessible again for people to collect, the householder assures that all Israelites equally share in the food which grows during the Sabbatical year. With this summary of the law in hand, let us turn to the substance of our chapter, which specifies the criteria that determine the liability of produce to these two sets of restrictions.

The restrictions of the Sabbatical year apply only to produce used for human consumption, animal consumption, or as dyeing matter (M. 7:1-2). These types of produce are singled out because in other years of the Sabbatical cycle such produce generally is bought and sold in the market. During the Sabbatical year, however, the yield of the Land is treated as ownerless and so may not be used for the financial gain of individuals. Accordingly, those particular types of produce which Israelites ordinarily use for commercial purposes may not be used in this way during the Sabbatical year.

The law of removal applies only to annuals, not perennials. This is because, as I explained above, the law requires people to remove produce from their homes when similar produce disappears from the field. Accordingly, only those types of produce which die at the conclusion of each growing season and disappear from the field can be subject to this law. Perennials, by contrast, grow continuously for more than one season. Since they do not disappear from the field, there is no point at which they could be subject to the law.

On the basis of these criteria, the chapter defines two mutually exclusive categories of produce: (1) produce subject to the restrictions of the Sabbatical year, but not to the law of removal, and (2) produce subject both to the restrictions of the Sabbatical year and to the law of removal. These two categories of produce are defined in the two formally balanced general rules at M. 7:1B-D and M. 7:2R-T. The bulk of the chapter presents lists of produce which fall into one or the other of these categories (M. 7:1G-L, M. 7:2W-Z, M. 7:3A-C and M. 7:5-6). Only two of the chapter's units break with its central theme. M. 7:3D-7:4 consists of a series of rulings that address the issue of conducting business with sanctified and prohibited foods. It appears here because M. 7:3D-E, the first in this series of rulings, is related topically to the list of produce which precedes it. At M. 7:7, we consider whether produce of the Sabbatical year which has become mixed with produce of other years renders the common produce subject to the restrictions of the law. It is included here because the rose, which serves to exemplify the rule governing mixtures, appears in the list of produce at M. 7:6.

7:1-2

A.   They stated an important general rule concerning [the laws of] the Sabbatical year:
B.   All [produce] which is:
    1)   fit for human consumption, animal consumption, or is a species [of plant used for] dyeing,
    2)   and which does not continue to grow in the ground [for longer than one season, i.e., plants which are not perennials][1]
C.   is subject to [the restrictions of] the Sabbatical year,
D.   and the money [received when the produce is sold] is subject to [the restrictions of] the Sabbatical year.
E.   [This produce also] is subject to removal [i.e., the produce must be removed from one's possession when similar produce disappears from the fields,]
F.   and the money [received when the produce is sold] is subject to removal.
G.   Now what is [considered fit for human consumption]?
H.   The leaf of wild arum,[2] the leaf of miltwaste,[3] chicory,[4] leeks,[5] purslane,[6] and ornithogalum.[7]
I.   And [what is considered] fit for animal consumption?
J.   Thorns[8] and thistles.[9]
K.   And [what is considered] a species [of plant used for] dyeing?
L.   Aftergrowths of woad[10] and seed of safflower.[11]
M.   They are subject to [the restrictions of] the Sabbatical year,
N.   and the money [received when the produce is sold] is subject to [the restrictions of] the Sabbatical year.
O.   They are subject to removal,

P.   and the money [received when the produce is sold] is subject to removal.

M. 7:1 (A-B: b. Shab. 68a; y. Shab. 7:1[8d];
F: b. Nid. 51b; K-P: b. B.Q. 101b)

Q.   And they stated yet another general rule [concerning the laws of the Sabbatical
      year]:
R.   All [produce] which is (so K and nine other MSS; Albeck and others add: not)[12]
      1)   fit for human consumption, animal consumption, or is a species [of plant used
            for] dyeing,
      2)   but which [unlike the produce referred to at M. 7:1] continues to grow in the
            ground [from one season to the next, i.e., plants which are perennials]
S.   is subject to [the restrictions of] the Sabbatical year,
T.   and the money [received when the produce is sold] is subject to [the restrictions of]
      the Sabbatical year.
U.   [But such produce] is exempt from removal,
V.   and the money [received from the sale of the produce] is exempt from removal.
W.   What are [plants which are perennials]?
X.   The root of wild arum, the root of miltwaste, hart's-tongue,[13] bulb of ornitho-
      galum,[14] and hazelwort.[15]
Y.   And among dyeing matter [these are perennials]:
Z.   Rubia tinctorum[16] and round-leaved cyclamen.[17]
AA.   They are subject to [the restrictions of] the Sabbatical year,
BB.   and the money [received from the sale of this produce] is subject to [the restrictions
      of] the Sabbatical year.
CC.   [But] they are exempt from removal,
DD.   and the money [received from the sale of the produce] is exempt from removal.
EE.   R. Meir says, "The money [resulting from the sale of produce listed at X and Z] must
      be removed before the New Year [of the eighth year]."
FF.   They said to him, "[The plants themselves] are not subject to removal. [Thus by an
      argument a minori ad majus [it is clear that] the money [received from the sale of
      the produce likewise is not subject to removal]."

M. 7:2

Two general rules define the types of produce subject to two distinct sets of
restrictions: rules governing the proper use of produce of the Sabbatical year and the law
of removal. In order to understand the criteria for liability to these rules, however, we
must first briefly review their content, presented fully in Chapters Eight and Nine.
Produce of the Sabbatical year enjoys a special status. Unlike crops of other years, which
the householder cultivates and gathers for his own use, the yield of the Land during this
year has the status of ownerless property. Since this food belongs equally to all Israelites,

it may not be treated as a common commodity, like produce that grows in other years. In particular, individuals may not use it for their own financial gain, for example, as currency for the repayment of debts or for the purchase of other goods (cf. M. 8:4-5). People also must sell it or process it in an unusual manner, to indicate that the produce is not their own private property (cf. M. 8:3,6). A separate injunction, the law of removal, prevents Israelites from hoarding produce of the Sabbatical year. It prescribes that once all vegetables of a certain species either have been gathered from the field or have died, food of the same type that individuals have stored in their homes must be removed. At the appropriate time, the householder places the produce outside his house, making it accessible to all. This procedure assures that crops of the Sabbatical year remain available for everyone to collect and eat at all times.

With this review of the law in hand, we turn now to the point of the rules before us. At B and R, we learn the criteria for liability to the restrictions of the Sabbatical year and to the law of removal. Only types of produce crucial to the Israelite economy are governed by the restrictions of the Sabbatical year. Food, animal fodder, and dyeing matter are the agricultural products generally bought and sold in the market during other years of the Sabbatical cycle. During the seventh year, therefore, these types of produce alone are subject to the restrictions of the law (B1, R1). A separate criterion determines the liability of produce to the law of removal. Only annuals are subject to this law; perennials are exempt. This is because, as I have explained, the law of removal takes effect only when all produce of a given species disappears from the field. Perennials, which continue to grow from one season to the next, always are available for people to gather and eat. Since, in fact, they never disappear from the field, the householder need not remove them from his home (R2). Only annuals, which grow and die within a single season, are subject to this law (B2).

In addition to specifying the kinds of produce subject to these restrictions, Mishnah's framers also address a secondary issue, the status of money received when a householder sells such produce. This transaction is governed by rules similar to those that apply to the sale of produce in the status of second tithe (cf. M. M.S. 2:1-4:12). That is to say, money received in exchange for sanctified produce becomes subject to the restrictions governing the food itself. These funds, like the produce for which they were traded, cannot be used for the financial gain of individuals (cf. M. 8:8). Rather, the householder may use this money only to purchase other produce which, in turn, becomes subject to the restrictions of the law.[18] Similarly, Mishnah's authorities claim that money received from the sale of annuals is governed by the law of removal. I cannot explain the procedure for removing such money, however, for in Chapter Nine, where we find the rules for the removal of produce, there is no discussion of the money received from the sale of this produce.

The rules that I have just explained are presented in two parallel, tightly structured units of law. We deal first with types of produce governed by both sets of restrictions (M. 7:1), then with produce subject to the restrictions of the Sabbatical year, but not to the law of removal (M. 7:2). In each case, Mishnah first presents a general rule, which states the restrictions that apply to this type of produce and to the money received from its sale (A-F, Q-V). Then, the redactor of our pericope has provided us with examples of produce that meet these criteria (G-L, W-Z). Finally, the apodosis of the general rule is repeated (N-P, AA-DD), thus creating a carefully balanced composition.

A dispute, at EE vs. FF, upsets the formal balance of these rules. Meir and sages disagree about whether money received from the sale of perennials is subject to removal. Sages (FF), in line with DD, claim that money received from the sale of this produce is governed by the same rule as the produce itself. Since perennials are exempt from removal, so too is the money received from their sale. Meir (EE), however, recognizes that money received from the sale of perennials, which are exempt from the law, cannot be distinguished from money received in exchange for annuals, which are governed by this law. All money, in his view, must be subject to a single rule. This position generates a secondary problem. When do these coins become subject to the law? Ordinarily, money received from the sale of produce should be subject to removal when that type of produce itself becomes subject to the law. Since this rule cannot apply in the case of perennials, which are exempt from the law altogether, Meir stipulates that the householder must remove this money by the end of the Sabbatical year.

A.   1) Pepperwort,[19] 2) endive,[20] 3) rose petals,[21] and 4) oak-tree leaves,[22]

B.   are subject to [the restrictions of] the Sabbatical year,

C.   and the money [received when the produce is sold] is subject to [the restrictions of] the Sabbatical year.

D.   And they are subject to removal,

E.   and the money [received when the produce is sold] is subject to removal.

F.   1) Lesbian-fig root,[23] 2) rose root and 3) oak-tree root,

G.   are exempt from [the restrictions of] the Sabbatical year,

H.   and the money [received when the produce is sold] is exempt from [the restrictions of] the Sabbatical year.

I.   And they are exempt from removal,

J.   and the money [received when the produce is sold] is exempt from removal.

T. 5:3

T. provides examples of produce which meet the criteria specified at M. 7:1B. Pepperwort, endive, and rose petals (A) all are edible. Oak-tree leaves are used for making dye.[24] These types of produce, therefore, are subject both to the restrictions of the Sabbatical year and to removal. The types of produce listed at D, on the other hand, meet neither of the criteria stated at M. 7:1B. Such produce is subject neither to the restrictions of the Sabbatical year nor to the law of removal (E-F).

A.   R. Meir (E: Judah) says "The money [resulting from the sale of the produce listed at M. 7:2H, J] is removed anytime before the New Year [of the eighth year].

B.   They said to him, "[The plants] are not subject to removal. [Thus] by an argument a minori ad majus [it is clear that] the money [received from the sale of the produce likewise] is not [subject to removal]" [=M. 7:20-P].

C.   He said to them, "I adopt a more stringent position with regard to the money [resulting from the sale of such produce] than to the produce (^{C}yqr) itself."

D.   Oil [pressed from olives grown during] the Sabbatical year--they light [a lamp] with it.

E.   [However, if a householder] sold [this oil] and purchased [with the resulting money] different [oil]--they do not light [a lamp] with it [i.e., the new oil].

T. 5:4

T. cites the dispute between Meir and sages and supplies Meir's defense of his position. Meir holds that the argument a minori ad majus is inapplicable here, for reasons which I have explained in my comment to M. 7:2. D-E is separate, for it refers neither to perennials, nor to the question of removal. It has been placed here because it presents a case in which more stringent restrictions apply to produce purchased with produce of the seventh year than to this original produce. This unit appears again at T. 6:14, where it belongs, and I will explain it fully there.

A.   (1) Crozophora tinctoria,[25] (2) bulb of ornithogalum,[26] (3) yar^{C}anah [an alkaline plant used as soap],[27] (4) lixivium [a sort of soap],[28] and (5) 'ahal [another plant used as soap][29]

B.   are subject to [the restrictions of] the Sabbatical year

C.   and the money [resulting from the sale of this produce] is subject to [the restrictions of] the Sabbatical year.

D.   And they are subject to removal,

E.   and the money [received from the sale of this produce] is subject to removal (=M. 7:1C-F).

F.   (1) Carob root, (2) the root of thorns,[30] (3) sumac leaves,[31] (4) white blossom[32] and rice

G.   are exempt from removal,

H.   and the money [resulting from their sale of this produce] is exempt from removal (=M. 7:2U-V).

T. 5:5-6

T. provides further examples of produce which meet the criteria set forth at M. 7:1B and 7:2R. Crozophora tinctoria and bulb of ornithogalum (see M. 7:2H) are species of plants used for dyeing. The remaining produce listed at A, though normally used for soaps, are deemed to be types of dyeing matter.

A.   (1) Din [an unidentified plant], (2) basar [an unidentified plant], and (3) seed of woad[33] [which are neither edible nor used as a dyeing matter and so, are not subject to the restrictions of the law according to the rule of M. 7:1B]

B.   [may not be sown during the Sabbatical year], but are sown [instead] in the year
      following the Sabbatical,

C.   because it is their purpose [to yield produce which is a kind of dyeing matter].

T. 5:7

T. takes up an ambiguous case with respect to the rule of M. 7:1-2. Seed of woad,
which is neither edible nor a kind of dyeing matter, should not be subject to the restrictions of the Sabbatical year. This seed, however, produces woad, a kind of dyeing matter
which is subject to the restrictions of the law (see M. 7:1L). Accordingly, the seed may
not be planted during the Sabbatical year.

7:3-4

A.   The husk and blossom of pomegranates,[34] walnut shells,[35] and pits of fruit[36] [which
      are types of dyeing matter]

B.   are subject to [the restrictions of] the Sabbatical year,

C.   and the money [received from the sale of this produce] is subject to [the laws of] the
      Sabbatical year [cf. M. 7:1C-D].

D.   The dyer may dye [with produce of the Sabbatical year] only for himself,

E.   but [the dyer] may not dye for a fee.

F.   For they may not do business with: 1) produce of the Sabbatical year, 2) firstlings
      (Num. 18:15-18), 3) heave-offering (Num. 8:8-13), 4) carrion (Dt. 14:21), 5) terefah
      meat (Ex. 22:30), 6) abominations (Lev. 11:1-47), or 7) creeping things.

G.   And during the Sabbatical year one may not gather (reading lwqt for lwqh)[37]
      vegetables [growing in] the field and sell them in the market.

H.   But [if] one gathers (T[3] reads: buys) [vegetables], his son may sell [them] for him.

I.   If one buys [produce of the Sabbatical year] for his own use, and left [some of the
      produce unused]

J.   he is permitted to sell [the produce which remained].

M. 7:3

K.   If one bought a firstling [which is blemished and so, unfit for comsumption by
      priests, cf. M. Bek. 5:2] for his son's wedding feast or for a festival and did not need
      it

L.   he is permitted to sell [the firstling].

M.   Hunters of wild animals, fowl or fish who accidentally caught (šnzdmnw lhm)
      unclean animals [cf. Lev. 11:1ff.]

N.   are permitted to sell [such unclean animals] (S, b. Pes. 23a add: to gentiles).

O.   R. Judah says, "Even one who [is not a hunter and who] accidentally encountered
      (ntmnh lw lpy drkw) [an unclean animal] may buy and sell [it],

P.   "so long as he does not make his livelihood in this way."

Q.   But sages prohibit [acquiring an unclean animal for the purpose of selling it].

M. 7:4 (M-N: b. Pes. 23a)

The central point of the discussion is that people may not conduct business with sanctified or forbidden foods (F). Since people are not free to eat these foodstuffs, they also may not benefit from them in other ways, by deriving financial gain from their sale. This principle explains the prohibition against dyeing for a fee during the Sabbatical year which is introduced in turn by the list of dyeing materials (A-C)[38] that are subject to the restrictions of the law (cf. M. 7:1-2). The series of rulings that follows (G-H, I-J, K-L, M-N, O-P vs. Q) take up a critical question: What constitutes doing business? Four separate rules claim that a commercial transaction is defined as acquiring something for the purpose of selling it. At G, for example, a person gathers produce of the Sabbatical year in order to sell it in the market. This is forbidden. The householder at H, however, gathers produce for the use of the household alone. Since he picked these vegetables as food for his family, his son may sell them in the event that he gathered more than the family could consume.[39] Similarly, people may sell sanctified foods which they acquired solely for their own use (I-J, K-L) and hunters may sell forbidden foods which they caught accidentally (M-N).

At O-P vs. Q, Judah and sages dispute whether a person who finds an unclean animal may pick it up and sell it to others. Sages (Q) carry forward the position of the foregoing rules. People may not acquire an unclean animal for the purpose of selling it, because this constitutes trading in forbidden foods. Judah proposes a different definition of engaging in business. On his view, the way in which people earn their living is the critical consideration. One may trade in unclean animals occasionally, provided that this does not become one's primary source of income (O-P).

A.   (1) Dyers and (2) fatteners [of animals][40]
B.   may buy coarse bran (mwrsn) from any place and need not refrain [from doing so, even though the bran is produce of the Sabbatical year].
C.   (Ed. princ. omits:) [They may not do business with] carrion (=M. 7:3F4).
D.   And they do not sell it [i.e., carrion] on strings [in the manner of properly slaughtered meat],
E.   but they sell it limb by limb on top of boards (mtwt)

T. 5:8

T. provides two qualifications of Mishnah's rules. Coarse bran is considered refuse. Even though this produce is used by dyers and as feed for animals, therefore, it is not deemed subject to the restrictions of the law. C-E cites and qualifies M. 7:3F4. Mishnah's ruling prohibits one from selling carrion only if this meat could be mistaken for that of properly slaughtered animals. This meat may be sold, however, in a manner which indicates that it is carrion.

A.   One may not bring (1) village dogs,[41] (2) porcupines,[42] (3) cats or (4) apes (reading with E: wqwpwt; V, ed. princ. read: wqypwt)

B.   to sell them to a gentile and to make a profit (wlyśkr)[43] with them.

C.   However, [as regards] (1) fish-brine,[44] (2) cheese of Bithynien,[45] (3) bread and (4) oil of theirs [i.e., of gentiles]--

D.   it is permissible to sell them to a gentile and to make a profit with them.

T. 5:9

T. amplifies the rule of M. 7:3F6. The animals listed at A may not be eaten by Israelites. In accordance with the ruling of M. 7:3F, one may not trade in these animals. Foodstuffs produced by gentiles, however, may or may not contain substances which Israelites are prohibited from eating. For this reason, Iraelites may trade in such foods.

A.   [During the Sabbatical year] one may not gather vegetables which grow wild and sell [them] in the market.

B.   But [if] one gathers [vegetables], his son may sell [them] for him (=M. 7:3G-H).

C.   R. Simeon b. Eleazar says, "Also: one may hire workers who will bring [the vegetables] (reading with Lieberman, TZ, p. 187, wyknysw for wyknys) into [the farmer's] house."

D.   One who buys a firstling [which is blemished and so, unfit for consumption by priests, cf. M. Bek. 5:2] for his son's wedding feast or for a festival, and does not need it,

E.   it is permissible to sell [the firstling] (=M. 7:4I-K).

F.   Rabbi says, "I say that he may not sell it for a profit (šl' ymkrnw 'l' ldmyw)."

T. 5:10

T. takes up two questions concerning what constitutes doing business with produce of the Sabbatical year (cf. M. 7:3F). Simeon (C) holds that hiring workers to bring produce in from the fields does not constitute doing business with the produce. The householder has gathered these vegetables for his own use. On Rabbi's view (F), one may not sell an unneeded firstling for profit. A sale for profit constitutes a forbidden business trans-action.

7:5

A.   Young sprouts of the service tree[46] and of the carob tree

B.   are subject to [the restrictions of] the Sabbatical year,

C.   and the money [received from the sale of this produce] is subject to [the restrictions of] the Sabbatical year.

D.   (K and 7 MSS. lack: D-E)[47] They are subject to removal

E.   and the money [received from the sale of this produce] is subject to removal [cf. M. 7:1C-F].

F.   Young sprouts of the terebinth,[48] the pistachio tree,[49] and the white-thorn[50]

G.   are subject to [the restrictions of] the Sabbatical year,

H.   and the money [received from the sale of such produce] is subject to [the restrictions of] the Sabbatical year.

I.   [But they] are exempt from removal,

J.   and the money [received from the sale of this produce] is exempt from removal [cf. M. 7:2S-V].

K.   But the leaves [of the trees listed at A and F] are subject to removal,

L.   because they fall off of the stem (m'byhn).

M. 7:5

The types of edible produce listed at A and F fall into the category of perennials. They therefore are subject to the restrictions of the Sabbatical year but are exempt from the law of removal (cf. M. 7:2R-V).[51] K-L make a separate point. The leaves of these sprouts are annuals. They are subject to removal, in accordance with the rule at M. 7:1B-F.

A.   Young sprouts of the terebinth, the pistachio tree, the white-thorn and garden cress[52] [=M. 7:5D].

B.   R. Meir says, "[If one has gathered] sprouts with leaves [they] are exempt from (so V; E reads: subject to) removal."

C.   But Sages say, "Leaves with sprouts are subject to (so V; E reads: exempt from) removal."

D.   R. Simeon says, "The sprouts are exempt from removal, but the leaves are subject to removal.

E.   because [the leaves] fall off (šnšrw) of the stem" [=M. 7:5G-H with slight variation].

F.   And all [of the sprouts mentioned at A] which began growing during the sixth year and continued growing during the Sabbatical year,

G.   or which began growing during the Sabbatical year and continued growing during the year following the Sabbatical,

H.   are deemed as trees [and so, are subject to the laws of the year during which they began growing],

I.   except for garden cress, which is deemed as a vegetable [and so, is subject to the laws of the year during which it was picked].

T. 5:11

T. takes up an ambiguous case left open by Mishnah. Sprouts are gathered together with their leaves. Meir (B) holds that they are subject to the restrictions of the Sabbatical year, for they are governed by the rule regarding leaves (cf. M. 7:5G). Sages (C) maintain that they are governed by the rule regarding sprouts (cf. M. 7:5F) and so are exempt. Simeon (D-E) resolves the ambiguous status of this produce on the basis of Mishnah's own language. Since the leaves drop off the stem (i.e., the sprout), they are separate. They alone are subject to removal, the leaves are not.[53]

F-I refers to the ruling cited at A, but makes a separate point. Cress is a vegetable, unlike the other items listed at A, which are trees. As a vegetable, cress is subject to the laws of the Sabbatical year only if it is picked during that year.

B.   Olive leaves, leaves of reed, and carob leaves

C.   are exempt from removal,

D.   because they do not disappear from the field, [i.e., even though they may fall off the stem; (cf. M. 7:5K-L)].

T. 5:12b

The types of leaves listed at B occasionally fall off of the stem.[54] In general, however, these types of leaves grow and remain on the branch for more than one year. Since all of the leaves do not fall off at once, there is no point at which they all disappear from the field. Accordingly, they cannot be subject to removal.

T. 5:12a is discussed after M. 7:6, to which it is supplementary.

7:6

A.   Rose, henna,[55] balsam,[56] and lotus[57]

B.   are subject to [the laws of] the Sabbatical year,

C.   and the money [received from the sale of this produce] is subject to [the laws of] the Sabbatical year.

D.   R. Simeon says, "Balsam is exempt from the laws of the Sabbatical year,

E.   "because it is not [deemed to be] produce [but rather a resinous sap secreted by the plant]."

M. 7:6 (A-B: b. Nid. 8a; C-D: b. Nid. 8b;
y. Orl. 1:5 [61b])

Aromatic plants (A) are classified as dyeing matter[58] and so are subject to the laws of the Sabbatical year (M. 7:1-2). Simeon (D-E) disputes the rule concerning balsam. He claims that only plants and the fruit that they produce are subject to the restrictions of the law. Since balsam falls into neither category, it remains exempt.

A.   R. Judah b. Isaiah, the perfumer, testified before R. Aqiba, in the name of R. Tarfon, that balsam is subject to the laws of the Sabbatical year.

T. 5:12a (b. Nid. 8b)

Judah supports the position of M. 7:6A-B, against that of Simeon, M. 7:6C-D.

7:7

A.   [As regards] a fresh rose [of the Sabbatical year, which is subject to the law of removal and] which one preserved in old oil [of the sixth year which is exempt from removal]--

B.   [when the times for removal arrives], one takes the rose [out of the oil, and the oil remains exempt from removal. Since a fresh rose does not impart its flavor to the oil, the oil does not take on the status of the rose].

C.   But [as regards] an old [rose, of the Sabbatical year which is subject to the law of removal and which one has preserved] in new [oil, of the year following the Sabbatical]--

D.   [the oil] is subject to removal. [Since a dried rose does impart its flavor to the oil, the latter does take on the status of the rose].

E.   [As regards] fresh carobs [of the Sabbatical year which are subject to the law of removal and] which one preserved in old wine [of the sixth year],

F.   or old [carobs of the Sabbatical year which one preserved] in new [wine of the year following the Sabbatical]--

G.   [in both cases, the wine] is subject to removal, [since both fresh and dried carobs impart their flavor to wine].

H.   This is the general rule:

I.   [As regards] any [produce which is subject to removal and] which imparts its flavor [to other, exempt produce with which it is mixed]--

J.   one must remove [the mixture, in accordance with the law of removal].

K.   [This is the case only if the two lots of produce in the mixture are] of two separate species.

L.   [But if the two lots of produce are] of the same species--

M.   Even a minuscule amount [of produce subject to the law of removal renders the other produce with which it is mixed subject to removal. This is the case whether or not the forbidden produce would flavor the permitted produce].

N.   Even a minuscule amount of [produce subject to the restrictions of] the Sabbatical year renders subject [to these restrictions permitted produce] of the same species [with which it is mixed].

O.   But [if the two lots of produce are] not of the same species,

P.   [only produce of the Sabbatical year which] imparts its flavor [renders the other produce forbidden].

M. 7:7 (M-N: T. Ter. 5:15; b. Ned. 58a)

The problem arises when produce of the Sabbatical year becomes mixed with produce of other years. We wish to know whether the common produce becomes subject to the special restrictions that govern the handling of produce of the Sabbatical year (see

Chapters Eight and Nine), or whether it remains exempt from these restrictions. The answer is spelled out fully in the general rule at H-M, reiterated at N-P. Let us begin by explaining this general theory of mixtures and then turn to the formally separate rule at A-G, which exemplifies it.

Only if produce of the Sabbatical year becomes inextricably mixed with common produce does the mixture as a whole become subject to the restrictions of that year. That is to say, if even the smallest quantity of sanctified food is absorbed into the common produce, the latter takes on the status of produce of the seventh year. This rule assures that even minuscule amounts of sanctified produce never are neutralized in a mixture, but always remain subject to the restrictions of the law. If, on the other hand, it is possible to remove produce of the Sabbatical year from a mixture intact, the ordinary produce remains unaffected. This principal generates two separate rules, one governing mixtures composed of two distinct species of produce, and another governing homogeneous mixtures. We determine whether two separate species of produce have combined to form a single entity by examining the flavor of the resulting mixture. If the flavor of the forbidden produce has pervaded the formerly exempt food, we know that some produce of the Sabbatical year has been absorbed into the mixture. The entire mixture, therefore, becomes subject to the restrictions of the law (I-K, O-P). Mixtures containing only a single species of produce are another matter. These two batches of food immediately combine to form a single homogeneous mixture. Since both lots of produce in this case taste the same, it is impossible to remove the sanctified part intact. All such mixtures then are subject to the restrictions of the Sabbatical year (L-M, N-O).

The opening rule at A-G exemplifies the principle of I-K. Since a fresh rose does not flavor oil in which it is placed, it does not affect the status of that oil (A-B). A dried rose, on the other hand, does impart its flavor to oil and so renders it subject to the law of removal (C-D). Fresh and dried carobs, by contrast, are subject to a single rule. Since both impart their flavor to wine, they render the wine subject to the law of removal (E-G).[59]

A. A fresh rose [of the Sabbatical year] which has been preserved in old oil [of the sixth year]--

B. one removes the rose [from the oil], and the oil is then permitted [i.e., not subject to removal].

C. But an old [rose, of the Sabbatical year which has been preserved] in new [oil, of the year following the Sabbatical]--

D. [the oil] is subject to removal [=M. 7:7A-D with slight variations].

T. 5:13

E. Fresh carobs [of the Sabbatical year] which have been preserved in old wine [of the sixth year]-- [=M. 7:7E]

F. one removes the carobs, and the wine is permitted.

G.   But old [carobs of the Sabbatical year which have been preserved] in new [wine, of
      the year following the Sabbatical]--

H.   [the wine together with the carobs] are subject to removal [=M. 7:7F-G].

T. 5:14

T. reiterates much of M. 7:7, disputing only the rule regarding fresh carobs, M.
7:7E-G. According to T., fresh carobs and fresh roses are subject to a single rule, for
neither imparts its flavor to other produce with which it is mixed.

CHAPTER EIGHT

Shebiit Chapter Eight

Produce that grows during the Sabbatical year is sanctified, because during the seventh year ownership of the Land's yield reverts exclusively to God. Since God owns these crops, they are subject to special restrictions that do not apply to the harvest of other years. These restrictions are of two sorts. First, produce of the Sabbatical year must be used only as God intends. He specifically designates these crops as food for Israelites and their livestock (Lev. 16:6-7). Second, all Israelites must share equally the agricultural products which God has provided for them. Individuals thus may not treat that which grows during the Sabbatical year as if it were their own. With the theory of the chapter in hand, let us now turn to the details of the law, which spell out the restrictions that govern produce of the Sabbatical year (M. 8:1-6) and the penalties imposed for violating them (M. 8:7-11).

Israelites must use edible produce of the Sabbatical year for the purpose that it generally serves in other years of the Sabbatical cycle. That is to say, that which people ordinarily use only as food for human beings or as animal fodder may be used during the Sabbatical year only in these ways. Since, as Lev. 16:6-7 tells us, God sets aside these crops for the sustenance of Israelites, people may not waste this food by using it for any other purpose. This general rule, stated at M. 8:1 and reiterated at M. 8:2, forms the foundation of all that follows. Since this food is designated by God for a specific purpose, individuals may not treat crops of the Sabbatical year as they do ordinary produce of other years. M. 8:3-5 takes up the restrictions that apply to transactions involving produce of the Sabbatical year. Mishnah's authorities permit people to trade in these crops, so long as they do so in a manner that indicates that they do not own them. One may not sell this food as one does during other years, namely, using standard measurements. This prevents the seller from calculating the precise value of that which he sells, as he would in an ordinary business transaction (M. 8:3). Moreover, since individuals do not own edibles of the Sabbatical year, they may not use them to discharge personal financial obligations. Gifts are permitted, however, for these are not given to repay debts (M. 8:4-5). Finally, people must process this produce in an unusual place or with abnormal tools. This again indicates that this food is sanctified, unlike crops of other years (M. 8:6).

At M. 8:8-8:9C, we turn to the rules that apply when people violate the foregoing restrictions. People must rectify any misappropriations of this food by acquiring other edibles and treating them like the original sanctified produce. This assures that the sanctity which inheres in the agricultural products of the Sabbatical year never is lost

(M. 8:8, 8:9C). Eliezer, M. 8:9C, makes a separate point concerning the misuse of sanctified produce. People may not derive benefit from a transgression. Accordingly, if a person wastes oil of the Sabbatical year by rubbing it on a leather garment, the clothing must be burned to assure that no one wears it. These rules are both preceded and followed by supplementary materials. M. 8:7 presents two rules that introduce the discussion of misusing produce of the Sabbatical year. At M. 8:7A-C, we consider the extent to which a person is responsible to keep vegetables of the Sabbatical year from becoming inedible, which would prevent them from being used for their designated purpose. At M. 8:7D-E, Mishnah's authorities present the principle that produce of the Sabbatical year never loses its sanctity. This explains why the householder who misuses this food must substitute other produce and treat it in accordance with the restrictions of the Sabbatical year. A short appendix (M. 8:9D-8:10) to Eliezer's lemma has no bearing on the subject matter of the tractate. The chapter's closing rule, M. 8:11, disputes Eliezer's position that one may not benefit from produce of the Sabbatical year which others have handled improperly.

8:1

A. An important general rule they stated concerning [produce of] the Sabbatical year:
I. B. All [produce which during other years of the Sabbatical cycle] is used exclusively as food for human beings--
C. [during the Sabbatical year] they may not make of [such produce] an emollient for human beings,
D. and, it goes without saying, [they may not do so] for cattle.
II. E. And any [type of produce] which is not used exclusively as food for human beings [i.e., which is also used as emollients for people]--
F. they may make of [such produce] an emollient for human beings,
G. but [they may] not [do so] for cattle.
III. H. And any [type of produce] which is not used exclusively as food for human beings or for cattle [i.e., which might either be eaten or be used as fuel for burning]--
I. [if the one who gathered it] intended [to use] it [both] as food for human beings and as food for cattle,
J. they impose upon it the stringencies [which apply to food] for human beings, and the stringencies [which apply to food] for cattle.
K. [If the one who gathered such produce] intended [to use] it [only] for wood,
L. lo, it [this produce is deemed to be] like wood [and may be burned],
M. for example, savory,[1] marjoram[2] and thyme.[3]

M. 8:1 (y. Shab. 7:1[8d]; Sifra Behar 1:12)

To understand the pericope before us, we must first review Scripture's rules governing the use of produce of the Sabbatical year. God designates that which grows during the seventh year for the sustenance of Israelites and their livestock. This is stated explicitly in Lev. 25:6, "And the sabbath produce of the land shall provide food for you. . . . ." Mishnah's authorities express this principle in the rule that people may use edible produce of the seventh year only as they ordinarily use such produce during other years, namely, as food or medicine. The law thus assures that the Land's yield will be available to meet the basic needs of Israelites during the Sabbatical year, in accordance with Scripture's injunction. This central principle is worked out in a three-part construction. First, produce which generally is used exclusively as food for people may not be used during the Sabbatical year for any other purpose (B-D). Second, produce which people generally use either as food or as a lotion, may be used during the Sabbatical year only in these ways (E-G). Finally, at H-L+M, we turn to an ambiguous case, produce which during other years sometimes is used as food or fodder and sometimes as fuel. How are such plants to be used during the Sabbatical year? In this case, the intention of the farmer who gathers this produce resolves its ambiguous status. If he collects it as food or fodder, it is treated as such. Like food for people, this produce may not be used as a lotion, and, like animal fodder, it may not be used as wood for burning.[4] If, on the other hand, people gather this produce for use as fuel alone, it is not subject to these restrictions (K-L). As we recall from M. 7:1-2, wood is not governed by the restrictions of the Sabbatical year at all.

A. R. Eleazar says, "Bundles of savory (E lacks: savory), marjoram and thyme which one gathered for [use as] wood--

B. "they may (reading with Lieberman, TK, p. 558; E, V, and ed. princ. read: may not) burn them.

C. "[If they were gathered for use] as animal feed--

D. "they may not (reading with Lieberman, TK p. 558; E, V, and ed. princ. read: may) burn them."[5]

E. R. Simeon says, "Also: stalks [of savory, marjoram or thyme] which grew in an irrigated field (following E, ed. princ. which read: byt; V reads: byn) that has dried up--

F. "they may derive no benefit from them [after the time when the law of removal has taken effect]."

T. 5:15

G. Leeks[6] and wild herbs[7] that were gathered for their moisture [i.e., in order to moisten wheat; so Lieberman, TZ, p. 189]--

H. [the farmer] is entitled (reading with E, V, ed. princ. read: is not) to use them for their moisture.

I. [But if they were gathered for use] as animal feed--

J.   [the farmer] is not (reading with E; V, ed. princ. read: is) entitled to used them for their moisture.

T. 5:16

T. spells out the implications of the ruling at M. 8:1K-M. The permissible uses of savory, marjoram and thyme are determined by the purpose for which they were gathered. If gathered for use as wood, they are deemed to be wood and may be burned (A-B). If gathered as animal feed, however, they may be used only for this purpose (C-D). The parallel ruling at G-J makes the same point for produce which is used ordinarily either to moisten other produce or as animal feed. E-F makes a separate point. Stalks of savory, marjoram or thyme may not be used, even for wood, after the field in which they grew has dried up. This is because these edible types of produce are subject to the law of removal. Such produce may not be used after the field has dried up, when like produce is no longer available.

A.   Asphodelus[8] which was gathered for use as animal feed,
B.   lo, it is subject to removal.
C.   [If it was] placed under a mattress [in order to keep away snakes,][9]
D.   lo, it is as if it has been removed.

T. 5:17

E.   Straw of the Sabbatical year [a type of produce which is fit for animal consumption]--
F.   they do not place it in a mattress [as filling] or mix it with mud [for this produce must be used as animal feed; cf. M.8:1].
G.   If others placed it [in such places],
H.   lo, it is as if it has been removed.

T. 5:18

As at T. 5:15-16, we deal with the rules governing types of produce fit for animal consumption. Asphodelus and straw are perennials and so are subject to the law of removal (cf. M. 7:1-2). If people handle this produce improperly, however, by placing it in a mattress or mixing it with mud, it becomes impossible to carry out the procedure for removal. The point of C-D and G-H is that once produce has become irretrievable in this way, the householder bears no further responsibility for observing the law of removal. The produce is regarded as if it already had been removed.

A.   [As regards] wine [of the Sabbatical year] which fell into brine--
B.   one must remove it [i.e., the wine together with the brine] (E reads: it is forbidden to non-priests; see T. Ter. 9:6B-C).

C.   R. Eleazar b. R. Simeon says, "Lo, it is as if it has been removed (E reads: It is permitted to non-priests)."

T. 6:5 (T. Ter. 9:6)

T. reads together the issues of M. 7:7I-J and T. 5:17-18. Wine of the Sabbatical year imparts its flavor to brine with which it is mixed. In accordance with M. 7:7I-J, it renders the mixture as a whole subject to removal (A-B). Eleazar makes a different point. Like straw which has been mixed with mud (T. 5:18), wine which has fallen into brine cannot be retrieved. It is deemed to be removed.

A.   An oven that was fired with straw or with stubble of the Sabbatical year must be cooled down [i.e., one may not cook in it].
B.   They sell (omitting with E and ed. princ.: 'wklyn) food for human beings and animal feed [in order] to buy [with they money received from the sale] food for human beings.
C.   But, they may not sell animal feed [in order] to buy other animal feed.
D.   And it goes without saying that food for human beings [may not be sold in order] to buy animal feed.

T. 5:19

Since straw is generally used as animal feed, it may not be used to ignite an oven (A). This abnormal use of the produce violates the prohibition of M. 8:1. B-D is separate. Produce of the Sabbatical year which is exchanged for other produce of that year is not subject to the rule of M. 8:1. We might have thought that just as produce of the Sabbatical year may be used only as produce of its type is ordinarily used, so too, produce may be exchanged only for other produce of the same type. Money received from the sale of produce of the Sabbatical year, however, is invested with the sanctity of that produce. This money may be used only to purchase food for human consumption (B), and not to purchase animal feed (C-D). (See M. 7:1D and Chapter Seven, note 17.)

A.   Produce of the Sabbatical year [which is fit for human consumption]--
B.   they do not feed it to cattle, to wild animals or to fowl.
C.   If an animal walked on its own under a fig tree and ate figs,
D.   or under a carob tree and ate carobs,
E.   they do not require him [i.e., the farmer] (so Lieberman who reads: 'wtw; E, V, and ed. princ. read: 'wth) to chase the animal away (lhhzyrh).
F.   As it is written, "And your cattle and the beasts in your land may eat all its yield" (Lev. 25:7).

T. 5:20 (Sifra Behar 1:7)

T. refines the principle of M. 8:1 by distinguishing between the farmer's intentional misuse of produce and the misuse which results from the animal's eating. The farmer may not misuse food for people by feeding it to animals, in accordance with the rule of M. 8:1 (A-B). He is not responsible, however, if the animal on its own eats the wrong sort of produce. This is because the farmer is not held responsible for the misuse of this produce before he has gathered it. F provides the prooftext for this view.

8:2

A. [Produce of the] Sabbatical year is permitted for [purposes of] eating, drinking and anointing [i.e., as a salve].

B. [That is, one is permitted] to eat that which customarily is eaten, (S adds: to drink that which customarily is drunk) and to anoint [with] that which customarily is [used] for anointing.

C. One may not anoint with wine or vinegar,

D. but one may anoint with oil.

E. And the same [law applies] with respect to heave-offering and second tithe.

F. [The ruling regarding produce of] the Sabbatical year is more lenient than [the ruling regarding] them [i.e., heave-offering and second tithe,]

G. for [produce of the Sabbatical year] is [also] permitted for [purposes of] kindling a lamp. [Clean heave-offering and second tithe, however, may not be used for this purpose].

M. 8:2 (A-D: M. M.S. 2:1; Sifre Dt. 107;
F-G: Sifra Behar 1:10)

The point, as at M. 8:1, is that edible produce of the Sabbatical year may be used only as produce of its type ordinarily is used (A-B). C-D exemplify this rule. Since wine and vinegar generally are not used as a salve, during the Sabbatical year people may not use these sorts of produce for anointing (C). Oil, however, which generally is used as an emollient, may be used during the Sabbatical year for this purpose (D). The gloss at E-G extends this principle to other sanctified foods, produce in the status of heave-offering and to second tithe. I cannot explain why oil of the Sabbatical year may be used to kindle a lamp (G), for this directly contradicts the principle that edibles may be used only for eating. Perhaps they regarded lamps as a necessity, and so permitted the burning of oil for this purpose.[10]

A. [Produce of the] Sabbatical year is permitted for [purposes of] eating, drinking, and anointing.

B. To eat that which customarily is eaten, to drink that which customarily is drunk and to anoint with that which customarily is used for anointing [=M. 8:2A-B].

T. 6:1 (T. Ter. 9:10)

C.   To eat that which customarily is eaten. How so?

D.   They do not obligate one to eat the peel of a vegetable[11], bread which has become moldy, or a dish the appearance of which has changed (^cybrh swrtw).

T. 6:2 (T. Ter. 9:10)

E.   To drink that which customarily is drunk. How so?

F.   They do not obligate one to drink (gwm^c) a sauce of oil and garum[12] or a sauce of vinegar and garum[13], or to drink wine together with its lees.

G.   (E lacks: G-H) One who has a sore throat may not gargle[14] with oil [of the Sabbatical year].

H.   But he may add much oil to a sauce of oil and garum and swallow.

I.   One who has a toothache may not rinse them [i.e., his teeth] in vinegar [of the Sabbatical year] and [then] spit it out.

J.   But he may rinse [with vinegar] and [then] swallow.

K.   And one may dunk [his bread in any of the liquids mentioned above] in the usual manner and need not scruple [that, by eating such bread, he has improperly consumed produce of the Sabbatical year].

T. 6:3 (E-F: T. Ter. 9:10; G-H: T. Ter. 9:12; I-J: T. Ter. 9:11)

L.   To anoint with that which customarily is used for anointing. How so?

M.   A person may put oil [of the Sabbatical year] on a wound,

N.   provided that he does not take [the oil] with a rag (E adds: or patch of cloth) [which will absorb and thereby waste some of the oil] and put [the rag] on his wound.

O.   (E lacks: O-R) One who has a headache, or anyone on whom sores[15] appeared (^clw), may anoint with oil [of the Sabbatical year].

P.   But he may not anoint with wine or vinegar.

Q.   For [as regards] oil--its normal use is for anointing.

R.   But [as regards] wine and vinegar--their normal use is not for anointing [cf. M. 8:2C-D].

T. 6:4 (T. Ter. 9:13-14)

T., at C-D, E-K and L-R, elucidates in sequence the three parts of M. 8:2's rule. Only food need be eaten (C-D+E-F vs. G-H+I-J). K is obvious. Solids and liquids need not be consumed separately if ordinarily they are eaten together. O-R repeats M. 8:2B-D. Oil, unlike wine and vinegar, may be used for anointing. Still, one may not anoint in a way which wastes some of the oil (M-N).

A.   One may put a cake of pressed figs or dried figs [of the Sabbatical year] in fish-brine (E, ed. princ., lack: hmwryŝ) [or in a] cooked dish [in order to flavor them] in the manner in which he adds spices.

B. But he may not [later remove them and] press them to squeeze out their juices
    [since this ruins the figs for subsequent consumption].

C. But [in the case of] spices [of the Sabbatical year] this is permitted (E reads:
    forbidden)

D. since this is their normal use.

T. 6:6 (T. Ter. 9:7)

E. One who ties in a bundle spices [of the Sabbatical year] and places them in a cooked
    dish--

F. if they lose their flavor (btl t^{c}mn), they are permitted [i.e., exempt from the
    restrictions of the Sabbatical year].[16]

G. But if [they do] not [lose their flavor], they are forbidden, [i.e., subject to the
    restrictions of the law].

T. 6:7 (T. Ter. 9:7; T. M.S. 2:2)

The discussion of the permitted uses of produce of the Sabbatical year continues.
Figs are added to other foods for flavor. Figs of the Sabbatical year may be used in this
way, provided that one does not spoil them for later consumption (A-B). Spices, on the
other hand, normally are not eaten. In line with M. 8:2's rule, one who uses them need not
save them for consumption (C-D). E-G follows logically from Mishnah's rule. Since spices
are not eaten, once they have lost their potency, they no longer serve any purpose. When
this happens, they are no longer subject to the restrictions of the law.

A. They may not make wine [from grapes of the Sabbatical year] into an unguent,[17]

B. nor oil [from olives of the Sabbatical year] into spiced oil.[18]

C. But if one made the wine into an unguent, or the oil into spiced oil, he may anoint
    [himself] with the oil, but may not anoint [himself] with the wine or vinegar.

D. For [as regards] oil--its normal use is for anointing.

E. But [as regards] wine or vinegar--its normal use is not for anointing.

T. 6:8 (T. M.S. 2:3)

The point, stated explicitly at D-E, is obvious from what has preceded (cf.
M. 8:2C-D, T. 6:4Q-R). People may not turn edible produce into ointments. If one
violates this rule, one must use the resulting ointment in accordance with the permissible
use of the original produce.

A. A person may not put oil of the Sabbatical year on a slab of marble in order to roll
    on it [and anoint himself, for the oil which remains on the slab is wasted].

B. Rabban Simeon b. Gamaliel (E reads: Rabbi) permits [since marble is not porous, no
    oil will be wasted].

C. (E lacks: C-D) [As regards] oil of the Sabbatical year--they do not anoint with it with unclean hands.

D. [But if] it fell on his skin, he may rub in it, even with unclean hands.

T. 6:9 (T. Ter. 10:10-11)

E. [As regards] oil of the Sabbatical year--

F. they may not glaze an oven or stove with it [for this is not its primary use].

G. And they may not soften (lit.: anoint) shoes or sandals with it.

T. 6:10 (T. Ter. 10:11)

H. A man may not anoint his foot with oil [of the Sabbatical year] while [the foot] is in a shoe or sandal.

I. But he may anoint his foot and [then] put on a shoe.

J. (E lacks:) or anoint his foot and [then] put on a sandal.

T. 6:11 (T. Ter. 10:11)

K. A man may anoint himself with oil of the Sabbatical year and [then] roll around on a new leather spread[19]

L. and need not scruple. [Once produce of the Sabbatical year has been used, it is no longer subject to the restrictions of the law].

T. 6:12 (T. Ter. 10:11)

M. They may not spice oil of the Sabbatical year [since this will be used for anointing instead of for eating].

N. But [during the Sabbatical year] they may purchase in any place spiced oil for anointing [on the assumption that it is not produce of the Sabbatical year].

T. 6:13

O. (Ed. princ. lacks: O-P) [As regards] oil of the Sabbatical year--

P. they may kindle [a lamp] with it [cf. M. 8:2G].

Q. If one sold it [i.e., oil of the Sabbatical year] and purchased [with the proceeds] other oil--

R. they may not kindle [a lamp] with it [i.e., with the oil which was bought].

T. 6:14 (=T. 5:4D-E)

S. [As regards] oil of the Sabbatical year--

T. they may not put it into a fire [in order to generate heat].[20]

U.   R. Yose says, "They may soak (swb^C) a bundle of flax stalks (reading with V: ^{C}nys; E
     reads: ^{C}syw; ed. princ. reads: ^{C}sys) with it, and [then] put it [i.e., the bundle] in a
     fire [in order to kindle the stalks, for this is like using it to kindle a lamp].

T. 6:15

T. continues the catalog of materials, begun at T. 6:2, which supplement the rule of
M. 8:2. Only Q-R and S-U require explication. Money received from the sale of oil of the
Sabbatical year may not be used to purchase other oil to be used for kindling. This is
because money received from the sale of produce of the Sabbatical year may be used only
to purchase food for human consumption (cf. T. 5:19). The point of S-T is that since oil is
not generally used for purposes of heating, it may not be used in this way during the
Sabbatical year. One may use this oil, however, to kindle bundles of flax, for this is like
kindling a lamp, which is permitted (O-P).

A.   They may fuel (msykyn) a fire with olive peels[21] or with the husks of grapes[22] of
     the Sabbatical year.
B.   But they may not kindle a fire with nuts ('gwzyn) [of the Sabbatical year].
C.   and they may not fuel [a fire] with olives [of the Sabbatical year].

T. 6:16

The point is clear from the material which has preceded. Food may not be burned
(B-C), while produce not ordinarily eaten may be used as fuel (A).

8:3

A.   They do not sell produce of the Sabbatical year by volume, weight, or quantity [i.e.,
     number of pieces].
B.   And (7 MSS. omit: and) [they may] not [even sell] figs by quantity and [they may]
     not [even sell] vegetables by weight.
C.   The House of Shammai say, ["With respect to the rule at A,] Also: [One may] not
     [sell produce of the Sabbatical year] in bunches."
D.   But the House of Hillel say, "That which one is accustomed to bind [into bunches] in
     the home (5 MSS.: for the home) [that is, produce not generally sold in bunches in
     the market]--
E.   ["during the Sabbatical year] they bind [and sell] it [i.e., such produce] in the market
     (6 MSS.: for the market),
F.   for example, leeks and ornithogalum."

M. 8:3

People may not sell produce of the Sabbatical year in standard measurements. This would constitute conducting business with sanctified produce of the seventh year, which is forbidden (see M. 7:3F). By trading produce only in a casual way, the seller indicates that he is not attempting to receive fair value in exchange for the food that he sells, as he would in an ordinary commercial transaction. With the point of the opening rule in hand, let us turn to the secondary developments found at B and in the Houses-dispute at C vs. D-F.

The rule at B poses an exegetical problem. On the one hand, it clearly is not an independent rule, but rather serves as a gloss to A. In light of the prohibition against selling produce in any standard measurements (A), however, this rule concerning figs and vegetables appears to add nothing to the discussion. How then did the redactor of our pericope understand this rule and why has he placed it here? I can make sense of B only by assuming, as Albeck[23] does, that it serves as a subtle amplification of the foregoing rule. According to the opening ruling, during the Sabbatical year people must alter the usual procedure for selling produce. B's point then is that people may not sell a particular type of produce in any standard measurement whatsoever, even if they do so in an abnormal manner. That is to say, figs, which ordinarily are sold by volume (cf. M. Ma. 2:4), may not be sold even by number. Likewise, vegetables, which people generally sell in bunches (cf. M. Dem. 6:12), may not be sold by weight. The seller may trade produce of the Sabbatical year only in an entirely random manner, thereby indicating that he is not engaged in an ordinary business transaction.

The Houses (C vs. D-E+F) dispute whether people may sell produce of the Sabbatical year in bunches. The Shammaites (C) consider a bunch to be a standard measurement. By selling produce in this way, the farmer attempts to receive fair value for his greens, which is forbidden. According to the Hillelites (D-F), however, a bunch constitutes a standard measurement only for types of produce which usually are sold in that form. That which ordinarily is sold by volume or weight, however, may be sold in bunches during the Sabbatical year. By altering the usual procedure, the seller indicated that he is not engaged in a usual business transaction.[24] The Hillelites thus disagree with the principle expressed at A-B. They permit people to sell produce of the Sabbatical year in at least one standard measure, the bunch, provided that they do not ordinarily sell produce in that way.

A. They may not sell produce of the Sabbatical year by volume, weight, or quantity [=M. 8:3A].

B. And one may not fill a jug [with wine or oil of the Sabbatical year] and sell it as is (kmwt shw') [for it appears that he is selling produce by a fixed measure],

C. nor [fill] a basket [with produce of the Sabbatical year] and sell it as is.

D. Rather [one who wishes to sell produce of the Sabbatical year] says to him [i.e., to the prospective buyer] (E lacks: lw), "This jug I sell to you for a dinar," or "This basket I sell to you for a tressit."[25]

E.   One may not fill a basket [with produce of the Sabbatical year] and go and sell it in the marketplace [for he thereby sells a fixed quantity of produce].

F.   Even (reading with E and ed. princ.: 'p; V reads: 'bl) in the other years of the Sabbatical cycle this is prohibited,

G.   for this is a method of deception [since the seller alone knows the quantity of produce in the basket].

T. 6:18

T. supplements Mishnah's list of ways in which produce of the Sabbatical year may not be sold. Jugs and baskets hold specific quantities of produce and so may not be used for selling produce (B-C). Sellers are permitted to sell in jugs or baskets, however, if they tell buyers that they are selling by the container without referring to the specific quantity of produce (D). E-G disagrees with C-D. Under no circumstances may people sell by the basket for this is a deceptive manner of selling.

A.   The House of Shammai say, "They may not sell produce of the Sabbatical year for coins.

B.   "Rather [they only exchange it] for [other] produce,

C.   "so that [the seller] does not (reading with V, ed. princ.; E omits: not) purchase with the produce (bhn) inedibles (lit., a spade)."[26]

D.   But the House of Hillel (Lieberman supplies from E., ed. princ.: permits).

T. 6:19

The Houses dispute the unstated premise of M. 8:3A, that produce of the Sabbatical year may be exchanged for money. Contrary to M. 8:3, the Shammaites prohibit such transactions. Since produce of the Sabbatical year is intended to be used only as food, it may not be converted into any inedible commodity. The Hillelites permit such transactions. They assume that people will use the money to purchase other produce (D). This is the position assumed by M. 8:3A, as well as by several of Mishnah's other rules (M. 8:4I, M. 8:8, and the general rule at M. 7:1-2).

A.   They may not sell produce of the Sabbatical year to [an Israelite] who is suspected [of violating the restrictions] of the Sabbatical year,

B.   except [sufficient] food for three meals.

C.   In what case does [the rule of A] apply?

D.   [It applies] in the case of produce which keeps [without spoiling] (dbr šmtqym). [This produce remains edible after the time for removing it and so we do not give the buyer an opportunity to violate the law].

E.   But [as regards] that which spoils quickly (dbr š'yn mtqym)--[selling sufficient produce] for even a hundred meals is permitted. [Since this produce will spoil before the time for its removal, we are not concerned that the buyer will neglect to remove it].

F.   They may not sell to, nor from, a gentile or a Samaritan produce of the Sabbatical
      year.

G.   Others (E reads: sages) say, "They may sell to a Samaritan as much as four _issars_
      [worth of produce of the Sabbatical year]."

                                    T. 6:20 (A-B: b. Suk. 49a; y. Suk. 3:12[54a])

      T. continues M. 8:3's discussion of forbidden sales of produce of the Sabbatical
year. One may not sell produce of the Sabbatical year to people suspected of not
observing the law of removal. This prevents one from becoming an accessory to their
transgression. The two separate qualifications, B and C-E, are obvious. People may sell a
person suspected of violating the law small amounts of produce, for the buyer will
consume these before the time for removal.[27] Moreover, they may not sell such a person
food which keeps without spoiling for a long time, since this creates an opportunity for
him to violate the law.

      F vs. G raises a separate issue with regard to transfering produce of the Sabbatical
year. F's point is that all produce which grows during the Sabbatical year is designated
for the consumption of Israelites. Accordingly, non-Israelites may not derive benefit from
this produce or from the money received from its sale (F). G disputes the status of
Samaritans. Samaritans share the status of Israelites suspected of violating the law. In
line with the rule of A-B, therefore, people may sell them small amounts of produce.

                                            8:4

A.   One who says to his worker, "Here is an _issar_ for you [as a gift]" and "Gather
      vegetables of the Sabbatical year for me today"--

B.   his wage is permitted, [that is, this money is exempt from the restrictions of the
      Sabbatical year. Since he gave this _issar_ to the worker as a gift and did not
      explicitly exchange it for the produce, the money does not take on the status of the
      produce].

C.   [If, however, he said,] "In return for this [_issar_,] gather vegetables for me today"--

D.   his wage is forbidden, [that is, this money is subject to the restrictions of the
      Sabbatical year. Since he specified that this money was payment for the produce,
      the coin is regarded as money received from the sale of produce of the Sabbatical
      year].

E.   [As regards] one who took a loaf of bread [worth] a _dupondion_[28] from the baker [and
      said,] "When I gather vegetables [of the Sabbatical year] from the field I will bring
      you some'--

F.   [this exchange of produce] is permitted. [Since the customer did not specify that
      this produce constitutes payment of the _dupondion_ that he owes the baker, he has
      not used produce of the Sabbatical year to discharge a debt].

G.   [But if] he simply bought [the loaf of bread on credit, thereby incurring a debt to the
      baker,]

H.   he may not [later] pay [the baker] with money [received from the sale of produce] of the Sabbatical year.

I.   For they do not discharge a debt with money [received from the sale of produce] of the Sabbatical year.

M. 8:4 (A-D: b. A.Z. 62a; y. M.S. 3:1[54a];
I: y. Dem. 3:1[23b]; y. M.S. 1:1[52b];
y. M.S. 3:1[54a])

The pericope highlights the contrast between giving produce of the Sabbatical year to others as a gift, which is permitted, and using it for a commercial transaction, which is forbidden (see M. 7:3F). The two formally separate pairs of rules (A-B/C-D, E-F/G-H+I), however, raise quite distinct issues with respect to trading this produce. These must be explained separately. The first case, at A-D, relies upon the rule of M. 7:1-2, that money received from the sale of sanctified produce itself becomes subject to the restrictions of the seventh year. This money, like the produce itself, may be used only to acquire food, not to discharge a financial obligation. The point of the contrasting cases at A-B and C-D is to establish a legal fiction by which a person can acquire produce of the Sabbatical year without buying it outright. If the householder gives his worker an _issar_ as a gift, and the worker, in turn, gives him some produce as a gift, technically no sale has occurred. The money which the worker receives, therefore, does not become subject to the restrictions of the Sabbatical year (A-B). But if the householder explicitly buys produce from the worker, the money does become subject to these restrictions, for it was received from the sale of produce of the Sabbatical year (C-D).[29]

The second set of rules (E-I) considers a householder who wishes to trade produce of the Sabbatical year, or money he has received from selling it, for other goods. He may barter his vegetables for a baker's bread. As long as they exchange their goods as gifts, this is not regarded as a business transaction (E-F). At G-H+I, the customer owes the baker for a loaf of bread. In this case, he may not repay the dept using money he received by selling produce of the Sabbatical year. This is not a gift, but the payment of a financial obligation.

A.   They feed (reading with V, ed. princ.; E reads: do not feed) boarders produce of the Sabbatical year.

B.   But they do not feed either a gentile or a hired [day] laborer produce of the Sabbatical year.

C.   But if he was a worker hired for the week, the month, the year [or] for seven years (śbwᶜ),

D.   or [if the employer] has obligated himself [to provide the laborer's board]--

E.   they feed him produce of the Sabbatical year.

T. 5:21 (A-E: Sifra Behar 1:7; y. Dem.
3:1[23b])

F.   A court may not grant support to a woman [who lives apart from her husband] from produce of the Sabbatical year.

G.   Rather, she is sustained with [produce] belonging to her husband.

T. 5:22 (y. Ma. 3:1[50b]; y. Ket. 7:1[31b]; y. Ket. 13:1[35d])

T. exemplifies the rule of M. 8:4I. One may not use produce of the Sabbatical year to discharge a financial obligation. Accordingly, people may not feed this produce to a hired laborer in place of his wage (B). Likewise, a court may not assign produce of the Sabbatical year to a woman in fulfillment of her husband's obligation to sustain her (F). One may, however, feed such produce to boarders (A) or to long-term laborers (C-D). They are fed as members of the household, not in fulfillment of a financial obligation.

One may not feed a gentile (B) produce of the Sabbatical year for a quite separate reason. The yield of the Land during the seventh year has been designated by God for the sustenance of Israelites alone.

A.   [As regards] one who buys a loaf of bread [worth] a dupondion from the baker (ed. princ. adds: and says) "When I pick vegetables [of the Sabbatical year] I will bring you some [in exchange for the bread],"

B.   [this exchange of produce] is permitted [=M. 8:4E-F with slight variations].

C.   R. Judah and R. Nehemiah prohibit (reading with V, ed. princ.; E reads: say).

D.   [As regards] five people who were picking vegetables [of the Sabbatical year]--

E.   one [of the five] may not sell [that which they pick] on behalf of all of them [at once].

F.   Rather he [first] sells that which he picked (šlw) and [then sells] that which the others picked (šlhn) [so Sens, cited by Lieberman, TZ. p. 193].

T. 6:21

G.   [As regards] five brothers who were picking vegetables--

H.   one may sell [what they pick] on behalf of all of them,

I.   provided that they do not (E lacks: šl')[30] designate him as a permanent dis- tributor (pltr; lit.: shopkeeper).

J.   An innkeeper[31] who was cooking produce of the Sabbatical year [to serve in the tavern] may not calculate in the price [which he charges for the dish the value] of the produce.

K.   But he may calculate [in the price] the value of the wine and the oil [of other years of the Sabbatical cycle, which he used] and the value of his time (reading with Lieberman, TZ, p. 193: wškr btlh); ed. princ. and MSS. read: škr btlh).

T. 6:22

The pericope's three units (A-C, D-I, J-K) are held together by their common theme--doing business with produce of the Sabbatical year. Since the pericope as a whole makes no single point, I deal in turn with each rule. Judah and Nehemiah, A-C, dispute the ruling of M. 8:4E-F. They hold that the buyer may not give produce of the Sabbatical year to pay the baker for bread which he bought on credit. Since the buyer did not have the produce in hand at the time of the transaction, he incurred a temporary debt. In accordance with M. 8:4I, he may not use produce of the Sabbatical year to discharge this debt.[32] D-F and G-I raise a new question with respect to gathering and selling produce of the Sabbatical year.[33] At issue is whether selling produce on behalf of other is considered doing business. The answer is that groups of people are engaged in business only when they form a cooperative. Accordingly, a group may not appoint one of its members as its agent (D-E), nor may several brothers designate one brother as their permanent distributer (I). By doing so, they act as a cooperative engaged in a business venture. One member of a group may, however, act as the agent for each individual separately. This procedure indicates that each member of the group gathers and sells the produce in his own behalf (F).

J-K is independent of Mishnah. An innkeeper may not covertly sell produce of the Sabbatical year by including the value of that produce in the price he charges customers. He may, of course, charge them for other produce which he uses and for the time which he spends preparing the food.

A. A person may not say to his fellow, "Take this produce [of the Sabbatical year] up to Jerusalem (E adds: for me) that [we may] divide it [between us there]." [That is, he may not give produce of the Sabbatical year to another as payment for helping to carry the produce to Jerusalem].

B. Rather he says to him, "Take it up so that [together] you and I may eat and drink it (E and ed. princ. add: in Jerusalem)." [This produce is simply shared, not given as a payment for services rendered].

T. 6:23 (M. M.S. 3:1; b. A.Z. 62a)

C. And likewise, one may not say to a poor person, "Take this sela and [in return] bring me the gleanings [which you collect] today," (Lev. 19:9), or "Bring me the forgotten sheaves [which you collect] today" (Dt. 14:19), or "Bring me the produce left in the corner of the field [which you collect] today (Lev. 19:9).

D. Rather, he says to him, "[I exchange this sela] for the gleanings which you will collect today," [or] "for the forgotten sheaves which you will collect today," [or] "for the produce of the corner of the field which you will collect today."

T. 6:24

E.   And likewise [in the case of] a Levite (reading with E, V; ed. princ. lacks: a Levite).
      [That is an ordinary Israelite may not pay a Levite to collect tithes for him, but the
      Levite and the Israelite may exchange tithes and money as gifts].

T. 6:25a[34]

      T. provides further illustrations of M. 8:4's rule that one may neither acquire nor
dispose of santified produce by means of a business transaction. In accordance with
M. 8:4I, one may not give produce of the Sabbatical year to someone as payment for
carrying the produce to Jerusalem.[35] This constitutes discharging a debt (A). One may,
however, invite a person to come to Jerusalem and share produce of the Sabbatical year.
This produce is given as a gift, not as payment for carrying the produce (B). At C-D+E,
we turn to the acquisition of sanctified produce. Since a householder is not entitled to
gather poor-offerings, he may not contract with the poor to obtain them (C). The two
parties, however, may exchange gifts of poor-offerings and money (D). E glosses and
merely extends the same principle to the Levites and the produce which they receive as
tithes.

F.   [One] who had a sela [received from the sale of produce] of the Sabbatical year
      wished to purchase with it a cloak. He goes to a storekeeper and says to him, "Give
      me produce for this [sela]." [The storekeeper] gives him produce. [By means of this
      exchange, the unsanctified produce becomes subject to the restrictions of the
      Sabbatical year and the money becomes exempt from these restrictions]. And then
      this one [i.e., the customer] says to him [i.e., the storekeeper], "Lo, this produce is
      given to you as a gift." And he [i.e., the storekeeper] says to him, "Lo, this sela is
      given to you as a gift." [The person thereby reacquires the sela and purchases a
      cloak with it].
G.   [As regards] produce of the Sabbatical year--
H.   they may purchase with it neither water nor salt.
I.   R. Yose says, "They may purchase with it either water or salt."
J.   [As regards] produce of the Sabbatical year--
K.   they may not use it in an infusion (mšrh)[36] [that is, in a bleach-solution] or in
      lye-water (kbwsh)[37] [i.e., it may not be used to make substances for laundering].
L.   R. Yose says, "They may use it in (E adds: an infusion or) lye-water."

T. 6:25b (B: b. Suk. 41a; F-H: b. Suk. 40a;
b. B.Q. 102a)

      The theory at B is that of M. 8:4. Money received from the sale of produce of the
Sabbatical year may be exchanged for other commodities as gifts, but not used in a
business transaction. C-D and F-G accord with the principle of M. 8:1, 2. They maintain
that produce of the Sabbatical year may be used only as food. Accordingly, such produce
may not be used to purchase water and salt, which are not deemed foods (C-D),[38] or to

produce inedible substances, such as laundering solutions (F-G). Yose disputes both rules for the same reason. He maintains that produce of the Sabbatical year may be used for these purposes, since they are considered necessities (E, H).[39]

8:5

A. They do not give [produce of the Sabbatical year or money received from its sale as payment of wages[40]] to a well-digger, a bathhouse attendant, a barber or a sailor.

B. But one does give [such produce or money] to a well-digger [in exchange for water] to drink.

C. And to any of those [persons referred to at A,] one gives [produce of the Sabbatical year or money received from its sale] as a gift.

M. 8:5

People may not use produce of the Sabbatical year to pay the wages of a hired laborer (A), for this constitutes discharging a debt (see M. 8:4I). Exchanging such produce for water, however, is permitted. Since, according to M. 8:2, produce of the Sabbatical year is designated for eating and drinking, it also may be used to purchase other liquids for consumption (B). Gifts of this produce clearly are permitted, for these are not payments of financial obligations (C).

A. [As regards] ass-drivers, camel-drivers, and sailors, who performed their trade (s̆hyw ᶜwsyn) with produce of the Sabbatical year [that is, who transported such produce]--

B. their wages are [subject to the restrictions of] produce of the Sabbatical year (so E; V, ed. princ. read: their wages are [paid] with produce of the Sabbatical year).[41]

T. 6:26 (b. A.Z. 62a)

T. supplements M. 8:5 with a separate rule concerning the payment of wages during the Sabbatical year. T's point is that any money received from handling produce of the Sabbatical year is subject to the restrictions of that year. Thus, money received in exchange for transporting produce of the Sabbatical year is treated like money received from the sale of this produce.[42] It may be used only to purchase other produce which, in turn, becomes subject to the restrictions of the law.

8:6

A. Figs of the Sabbatical year--

B. they do not dry (qwzyn)[43] them in the [ordinary] drying place (bmqzh),[44]

C. but one does dry them in a deserted place[45] [where one ordinarily does not process figs].

D.   They do not trample grapes [of the Sabbatical year] in a vat,

E.   but one does trample [them] in a trough.

F.   And they do not prepare olives [of the Sabbatical year] in an olive-press or with an olive-crusher,[46]

G.   but one does crush them and place [them] in a small press.

H.   R. Simeon says, "He even grinds them in an olive press and places [them] in a small press [in order to complete the processing of the olives]."

M. 8:6 (Sifra Behar 1:3)

Produce of the Sabbatical year must be processed in an unusual manner, unlike produce of other years. The underlying principle is the same as the of M. 8:3 which, we recall, rules that people may sell this food only in a random fashion. By handling produce in an abnormal manner, people indicate that they do not own this sanctified food and thus are not free to treat it as they would ordinary produce of other years. This point is made three times in the parallel rules at A-C, D-E and F-G. Simeon, in his gloss at H, claims that not every step in the processing of olives must be altered. One may use the usual olive press for crushing the fruit, provided that one uses a small press, which is not the usual tool, to finish squeezing out the oil.

A.   [As regards] olives of the Sabbatical year--

B.   they may not press (^{c}wšyn) them with an olive crusher (so Lieberman, TZ, p. 195, who reads with ed. princ.: qtby; V reads: qtky; E reads: gynby) [see M. 8:6F].

C.   Rabban Simeon b. Gamaliel permits.

D.   Rabban Gamaliel and his court (so V, ed. princ.; E reads C and D together: Rabban Simeon b. Gamaliel and his court) ordained that they may press them [i.e., olives of the Sabbatical year] with an olive crusher.

E.   R. Judah says, "They may grind [olives of the Sabbatical year] with a millstone with which [olives] had not been ground in the other [previous] years of the Sabbatical cycle."

F.   R. Simeon says, "One crushes [olives of the Sabbatical year] and skims off [the oil which floats to the top] in a trough."

T. 6:27 (A-B: Sifra Behar 1:3)

Simeon b. Gamaliel (C) and Rabban Gamaliel (D) independently dispute M. 8:6's rule that one must process olives of the Sabbatical year in an abnormal manner. They hold that the prohibition against using produce of the Sabbatical year in an abnormal way applies only to the purpose for which it is used (see M. 8:1-2), not to the way in which it is processed. Judah (E) and Simeon (F) supplement M. 8:6G by proposing other abnormal ways of processing olives.

A.   [As regards] grapes of the Sabbatical year--

B.   they may not trample them in a vat.

C.   Rather, they trample them in a trough [=M. 8:6D-E with slight variations].

D.   R. Judah says, "One presses (reading with V, E; ed. princ. reads: they trample) them in a jug with his finger."

T. 6:28 (A-C: Sifra Behar 1:3)

Judah suggests another way in which to change the procedure for processing olives of the Sabbatical year.

A.   [As regards] figs of the Sabbatical year--

B.   They may (reading with Lieberman, TK, p. 570; V, E, and ed. princ. read: may not)[47] make them into dried figs,

C.   but they may not (so Lieberman; V, E, and ed. princ. read: may) make them into a cake of pressed figs.

D.   R. Judah says, "One [may make fresh figs into a cake of pressed figs so long as he] manually presses [them] (mm^{c}yk) and wipes off (mngyb) [the juice which exudes from them]."

E.   They may break apart pomegranates to make them into split, dried pomegranates.[48]

F.   And they may press (swhtyn) grapes to make them into raisins.

T. 6:29a

T. presents a new principle governing the processing of produce of the Sabbatical year. People may not convert produce of the Sabbatical year into man-made foods (C). Rather, this produce must remain as it is found in nature. Since both fresh and dried figs are found in nature, people may turn fresh figs into dried ones (A-B). Similarly, people may dry pomegranates (E) and make grapes into raisins (F). The notion that produce of the Sabbatical year must be eaten in one of its natural states carries forward the principle of M. 8:1,2. Since produce of the Sabbatical year is sanctified, people may not use it for any purpose they wish, as they would food of other years. Just as Israelites may not exercise control over these edibles by turning them into inedible products, so too they may not convert natural fruits and vegetables into processed foodstuffs.

Judah (D), who disputes the rule concerning pressed figs, accepts the principle of M. 8:6 (cf. also Judah's rule at T. 6:2E). Produce of the Sabbatical year may be processed into any form so long as this is done in an abnormal manner. Accordingly, people may turn fresh figs into pressed ones only if they do so by hand, not with the help of a press, as they do in other years.

8:7

A.   They do not cook a vegetable of the Sabbatical year in oil in the status of heave-
      offering,
B.   lest [the oil] cause it [i.e., the vegetable] to become invalid. [That is, the vegetable
      of the Sabbatical year, when cooked in this oil, takes on the status of heave-
      offering. It thus might be wasted, in violation of M. 8:1,2's rule, in the event that it
      became unclean and had to be burned].[49]
C.   R. Simeon permits [the cooking of vegetables of the Sabbatical year in oil in the
      status of heave-offering].
D.   [In the case of one who sold produce of the Sabbatical year, used the money received
      to purchase some other produce, and then exchanged this produce, in turn, for still
      other produce,] the very last [produce obtained in this manner] (wh'hrwn h'hrwn) is
      subjected to [the laws of] the Sabbatical year (ntps bśby^cyt),
E.   and the produce itself [i.e., the original produce of the Sabbatical year remains]
      forbidden [that is, subject to the restrictions of the Sabbatical year].

                              M. 8:7 (A-C: b. Zeb. 76b; D-E: Sifra Behar
                              3:3; b. Suk. 40b; b. Qid. 58a; b. A.Z. 54b; b.
                              Bek. 9b)

         The proper handling of produce of the Sabbatical year is addressed by two formally
and substantively distinct units of law. Let us first explain the dispute at A-B vs. C, and
then turn to the separate rule of D-E. As we know from the preceding rules, edible
produce of the Sabbatical year may be used only as food. The issue at A-B vs. C is the
extent to which people are responsible to insure that this food in fact will be consumed
and not wasted. The case at hand concerns a householder who cooks a vegetable of the
Sabbatical year in oil in the status of heave-offering. As a result, this vegetable, which
retains the status of produce of the Sabbatical year, also becomes subject to the
restrictions that govern produce designated as heave-offering. Like all food in the status
of heave-offering, if it becomes unclean, it may not be eaten. In order to assure that
produce of the Sabbatical year is not wasted, A-B rules that people may not cook such
produce in oil in the status of heave-offering. Simeon (C), by contrast, is concerned only
with actual, not possible, violations of the law. Cooking a vegetable of the Sabbatical
year in this way will not necessarily cause it to be wasted, for it might never in fact
become unclean. The act of cooking, therefore, is permitted.[50]
         The rule at D-E claims that produce of the Sabbatical year both transfers its status
to that for which it is exchanged and itself remains subject to the restrictions of the law.
How does this happen? If one exchanges produce of the Sabbatical year for money or for
other edibles, that which one acquires becomes subject to the restrictions of the law. If
this money or produce, in turn, is exchanged for still other produce, the newly acquired
item likewise becomes subject to the restrictions of the Sabbatical year. Moreover, the
original produce of the Sabbatical year never loses its sanctity. The underlying theory of

this rule is that the Land's yield during the Sabbatical year belongs to God. For this reason, people may not treat this sanctified food as a commodity to be used for acquiring ordinary, unconsecrated produce. To prevent this, the law stipulates that whatever one acquires in exchange for produce of the Sabbatical year immediately takes on the status of the sanctified food for which it was exchanged. Such a transaction, however, can never alter the status of the original produce. This is because, in the view of Mishnah's authorities, that which grows during the seventh year is inherently sanctified. No action of the householder can convert it into ordinary food.[51]

G. They may not purchase [produce in the status of] heave-offering with money [received from the sale of produce] of the Sabbatical year,

H. so that they will not cause it [i.e., the produce purchased, which is subject both to the rules governing heave-offering and to the restrictions of the Sabbatical year] to become invalid. [That is, the produce will be wasted in the event that it becomes unclean and cannot be eaten].[52]

I. But R. Simeon permits [=M. 8:7B-C with slight variations].

T. 6:29b

T. draws together the two separate units of M. 8:7 by reading M. 8:7A-B vs. C in light of the rule at M. 8:7D-E. The issue is whether produce in the status of heave-offering may be purchased with money received from the sale of the Sabbatical year. According to the rule of M. 8:7D, produce in the status of heave-offering purchased in this way would also become subject to the restrictions of the Sabbatical year. The positions are the same as at M. 8:7. G-H prohibits the purchase in order to prevent the produce from being used improperly. Simeon (I) permits the purchase, since it will not necessarily result in the misuse of the produce.

A. They do not deconsecrate [coins] (so Lieberman, TK, p. 572, on the basis of y. M.S. 3:2 [54a]; E, V, and ed. princ. read: produce) in the status of second tithe (so E, V, ed. princ. lacks: šyny) [by exchanging it in Jerusalem] for produce of the Sabbatical year. [That is, one may not restrict the opportunities for consuming produce of the Sabbatical year by subjecting it to the restrctions governing second tithe].

B. But if one deconsecrated [coins in the status of second tithe in this manner], he must eat it, [i.e., the produce of the Sabbatical year for which the coins were exchanged] in accordance with the restrictions [which apply] to both of them [i.e., both those restrictions which apply to produce in the status of second tithe and those which apply to produce of the Sabbatical year].

C. [As regards] produce of the Sabbatical year and produce in the status of second tithe (so V, E; ed. princ. reads: poorman's tithe) which were mixed together--

D. one must eat it [i.e., the mixture] in accordance with the restrictions which apply to both of them.

E. [As regards] produce of the Sabbatical year in exchange for which one purchased
    other [consecrated; so Lieberman, TZ, p. 195] foods--

F. one must eat it [the other consecrated produce] in accordance with the restrictions
    [which apply] to both kinds of produce.

G. [As regards] produce in the status of second tithe in exchange for which one
    purchased other [consecrated] foods--

H. one must eat it [the other consecrated produce] in accordance with the restrictions
    [which apply] to both [kinds of produce].

T. 7:1

I. There is a strict rule which applies to produce of the Sabbatical year which does not
    apply to produce in the status of second tithe,

J. and a strict rule which applies to produce in the status of second tithe which does
    not apply to produce of the Sabbatical year.

K. For [the restrictions of] the Sabbatical year apply ($^{C}\acute{s}h$): (1) to ownerless produce as
    well as to that which is owned; (2) to refuse from food as well as to food; (3) to food
    for human beings as well as to food for cattle; (4) to nutshells and peels of
    pomegranates as well as to that which they resemble [i.e., nuts and pomegranates.
    Since these are dyeing matters, they are subject to the restrictions of the Sabbatical
    year; M. Sheb. 7:3A-C].

L. This is not the case regarding produce in the status of second tithe.

T. 7:2

M. Produce of the Sabbatical year may be exchanged (lit., deconsecrated)[53] for
    anything, [that is, either for coins or for other produce].

N. But produce in the status of second tithe may be deconsecrated only [through
    exchange] for coins (so V, E, ed. princ. reads: for its same kind [of produce]) (Dt.
    14:24-25).

T. 7:3

O. Produce of the Sabbatical year is removed one species at a time (mkl myn wmyn).
    [That is, each species of produce is removed from one's home when that species
    disappears from the field] (M. Sheb. 9:5D-E).

P. But produce in the status of second tithe is removed all at the same time (following
    Lieberman, TZ, p. 195; V, E, and ed. princ. read: only from [its] same species
    (M. M.S. 5:6).

T. 7:4

Q.   [Regarding] produce of the Sabbatical year, both [the produce] itself and the coins
      [received in exchange for the produce] are forbidden [i.e., subject to the restrictions
      of the Sabbatical year] (M. Sheb. 8:7D-E).

R.   But [regarding] produce in the status of second tithe, either [the produce] itself or
      the coins [for which it is exchanged] is forbidden [but not both. That is, once the
      produce has been exchanged for coins, it is no longer subject to the restrictions
      which apply to produce in the status of second tithe].

T. 7:5

S.   [As regards] produce of the Sabbatical year (so E and ed. princ.; V omits S)--

T.   they may not use it to purchase peace-offerings [since one may not restrict the
      opportunity for non-priests to eat produce of the Sabbatical year].

U.   This is not the case for produce in the status of second tithe (M. M.S. 1:3).

T. 7:6

V.   There is a strict rule which applies to produce in the status of second tithe [which
      does not apply to produce of the Sabbatical year].

W.   For (1) the status of second tithe applies to the jug [which holds produce purchased
      with coins in the status of second tithe; M. M.S. 3:12]; and (2) [produce in the status
      of second tithe] renders forbidden [for common use] the money for which it is
      exchanged, [as well as] mixtures [with unconsecrated produce] about which there is a
      doubt [whether or not they actually contain produce in the status of second tithe, as
      well as] mixtures [of produce in the status of second tithe with unconsecrated
      produce] no matter how small the quantity [of produce in the status of second tithe
      which they contain; see T. Bik. 1:6] and (supply w-with E and ed. princ.) (3) [one
      who improperly eats produce in the status of second tithe] is obligated [to pay] the
      added fifth (Lev. 27:31) and (4) [produce in the status of second tithe] obligates [one
      who removes it from his domain] to recitation of the confession (see Dt. 26:12-15);
      and (5) [produce in the status of second tithe] is forbidden for consumption by one
      who is in mourning for a close relative (Dt. 26:14); and (6) [produce in the status of
      second tithe] is not permitted for consumption [outside of Jerusalem; so Lieberman,
      TZ, p. 196, unless it is deconsecrated; and (7) [oil in the status of second tithe] may
      not be used to kindle a lamp [since this produce must be consumed].

X.   This is not the case for produce of the Sabbatical year.

T. 7:7

Y.   Produce of the Sabbatical year and produce in the status of second tithe are the
      same [with respect to the following rule]:

Z.   They deconsecrate it[54] [through exchange] for an animal or fowl,

AA.   or for a beast which is blemished (M. M.S. 1:6).

BB. "This applies whether these are alive or slaughtered," the words of Rabbi.

CC. But sages say, "They referred only to a case in which they [already] are slaughtered." [This prevents people from doing business with produce of the Sabbatical year by using the animals acquired to raise flocks].[55]

T. 7:8

DD. Produce of the Sabbatical year and produce in the status of second tithe are the same [with respect to the following rules]:

EE. (1) They may not discharge a loan or debt with [either of] them.

FF. (2) They may not repay favors with [either of] them.

GG. (3) They may not redeem captives with [the funds received from the sale of either of] them.

HH. (4) They may not use [either of] them as groomsman's gifts.

II. (5) And they may not appropriate [either of] them for charity.

JJ. But (2) they may give them as a voluntary charitable gift.

KK. (2) and they must notify [the recipient that that which is given is produce in the status of second tithe or of the Sabbatical year],

LL. (3) and they may give them to an official of the city (hbr ^{c}yr)[56] as a favor.

T. 7:9

The opening series of rules (A-B, C-D, E-F, G-H) exemplify the principle of M. 8:7A-C. Produce in the status of second tithe which is either exchanged for or mixed with produce of the Sabbatical year is subject to the restrictions governing both types of produce. The pericopae which follow, explained in my translation, detail these restrictions. W(2) requires further explanation, for it contradicts both T. 7:5Q and M. 8:7D. These rulings state that produce of the Sabbatical year, like produce in the status of second tithe, does transfer its status to the money for which it is exchanged. Lieberman, TK, p. 573 argues that this rule has been included here by mistake, on the basis of the parallel text at T. Bik. 1:6.

8:8

I. A. They do not buy (1) slaves, (2) parcels of real estate, or (3) an unclean animal with money [received from the sale of produce] of the Sabbatical year.

B. But if one [used money received in this way and] purchased [one of the items listed at A,] he must [purchase and] eat [produce] of equal value (kngdn) [to replace the money of the Sabbatical year which he misused].

II. C. They do not bring bird-offerings [required] of men who have suffered a flux, women who have suffered a flux, or women after childbirth [if these are bought] with money [received from the sale of produce] of the Sabbatical year.

D.   But if one brought [an offering purchased with such money,] he must [purchase and] eat [produce] of equal value [to replace the money of the Sabbatical year which he misused].

III.   E.   They do not rub leather garments[57] with oil of the Sabbatical year.

F.   But if one rubbed [a garment with such oil,] he must [purchase and] eat [produce] of equal value [to replace the oil which he misused].

M. 8:8 (A-B: y. M.S. 1:1[52b]; y. M.S.
1:3[52d])

People who misuse produce of the Sabbatical year, in violation of the law, must purchase new food of equal value to replace it. These edibles take on the status of the produce which was handled improperly and must be consumed in accordance with the restrictions of the Sabbatical year. This penalty for misusing crops of the Sabbatical year, presented in the repeated apodosis at B, D and F, assures that this sanctified produce is not wasted. When a person misuses some of this food, thereby depriving others of the opportunity to consume it, he must restore an amount of produce equal to that which he has misapporpriated. On a secondary level of interpretation, this rule carries forward the principle of M. 8:7D-E. Mishnah's authorities regard the sanctity which inheres in produce of the Sabbatical year as a kind of physical substance which can never be destroyed. If the produce is misused, thereby preventing its sanctity from being discharged in the proper manner, the holiness must be transferred to other produce, which takes its place.

Only the rules prohibiting the misuse of this produce, and of the money received from its sale (A, C, E), remain to be explained. Since crops of the Sabbatical year may be used only as food or as an ointment, people may not waste this food by using it either to purchase inedibles (A) or to treat a leather garment (E). Moreover, that which grows during the Sabbatical year belongs equally to all Israelites and must be available for all to eat. People may not use this food to purchase foodstuffs designated for the consumption of the priests alone (C).

8:9-10

A.   A hide which one rubbed with oil of the Sabbatical year--

B.   R. Eliezer says, "[The hide] must be burned."

C.   But sages say, "[The one who smeared it with oil] must [purchase and] eat [produce] of equal value [to replace that which he misused].

D.   They said before R. Aqiba, "R. Eliezer used to say, 'A hide which one rubbed with oil of the Sabbatical year must be burned.'"

E.   He said to them, "Shut up! I will not tell you what R. Eliezer meant by this."

M. 8:9

F.   And they also said before [R. Aqiba], "R. Eliezer used to say, 'One who eats bread
     [baked by] Samaritans is like one who eats pork.'"

G.   He said to them, "Shut up! I will not tell you what R. Eliezer meant by this."

M. 8:10

Eliezer and sages disagree about the penalty imposed for using oil of the Sabbatical
year to treat leather, an act that violates the rule of M. 8:8E. Sages (C), in line with the
anonymous ruling of M. 8:8F, hold that one who deprives others of edible produce must
replace that which he misused. He does this by purchasing new oil and treating it in
accordance with restrictions of the Sabbatical year. This assures that the amount of food
available for consumption during the Sabbatical year is not depleted through the misuse of
these edibles. Eliezer (B) imposes a quite different penalty upon the person who
misappropriates oil of the Sabbatical year. He rules that the garment must be destroyed,
thereby insuring that no one benefits from the performance of this transgression. These
two rules, B and C, have been cast in the form of a dispute, as opposing responses to a
common superscription. The redactor of our pericope thus has made Eliezer appear to
reject the rule attributed to sages, that people must replace produce of the Sabbatical
year which they have misused. Yet the substance of Eliezer's position, taken by itself, is
not necessarily inconsistent with sages' view. That is to say, Eliezer could hold both that
the garment must be burned and, in addition, that the individual must replace the produce
that he misused. Thus, Eliezer's and sages' lemma both address a common issue but,
unlike must disputes, do not present diametrically opposed views on the matter at hand.[58]

The formally separate story at D-E serves as an appendix to the foregoing. We can
deduce only three pieces of information from the exchange: that Aqiba claims to know
the true meaning of Eliezer's rule concerning the penalty for misusing oil of the
Sabbatical year, that Eliezer's real views were not apparent to the students who repeated
his lemma, and that Aqiba will not reveal what Eliezer actually meant. As to how Aqiba
understood Eliezer's lemma and why he refused to reveal its meaning to others, the
pericope provides us with no information. We might speculate that Aqiba maintained that
Eliezer's statement was not to be understood as a legal ruling, but only as a comment
which would discourage people from violating the law.[59] The parallel narrative at F-G,
which again concerns Aqiba's interpretation of a ruling attributed to Eliezer, is unrelated
to the laws of the Sabbatical year.

8:11

A.   A bath which was heated by straw or stubble of the Sabbatical year, [in violation of
     the law]--

B.   one is permitted to bathe in it.

B.   But if one is highly regarded ('m mthšb hw'),

D.   lo, this [person] will not bathe [in such a bath].

M. 8:11

Straw and stubble of the Sabbatical year, which are fit for animal consumption, may not be used as fuel for burning (see M. 7:1-2, 8:1). Using a bath heated with such produce, however, is permitted (A-B). The bather, who is not responsible for mishandling the produce, may benefit from a transgression which has already been committed by others. This ruling clearly rejects Eliezer's position (M. 8:9B), that one may not derive benefit from sanctified produce which has been mishandled. According to C-D, a well-respected person may not use a bath heated in a manner that violates the law. Other people relying on his example, might incorrectly conclude that burning straw and stubble is permissible to begin with.[60]

CHAPTER NINE

Shebiit Chapter Nine

A discussion of the law of removal concludes the tractate's treatment of restrictions governing produce of the Sabbatical year. Let me begin by spelling out the substance of this law, for this is presupposed throughout Mishnah's discussion, yet never explicitly stated. The law requires people to remove produce of the Sabbatical year from their homes when edibles of the same species no longer are available for people to gather from the field. That is to say, once all vegetables of a certain type have been gathered or have died, people may no longer retain similar vegetables in their homes. Rather, they must take that which they have stored in their houses and place it outside. All Israelites may then collect and eat this food. This procedure prevents people from hoarding edibles and so assures that everyone has food to eat during the Sabbatical year. The law thus illustrates the principle of Chapter Eight, that crops of the Sabbatical year belong equally to everyone. For this reason, people must share with one another that which they have already gathered when similar produce is gone from the fields.

With this summary of the law in hand, we turn to the central problem of the chapter, addressed at M. 9:2-6. Under certain circumstances, it is unclear when the law of removal should take effect. We deal with cases in which an entire species of produce might not be subject to removal at a single time. How so? First, farmers in distinct regions of the Land of Israel harvest a single crop at different times. They complete the harvest of onions, for example, earlier in warm regions than they do in cool areas. Thus, we need to know whether onions become subject to the law at a single time, when onions no longer are growing anywhere in the Land, or whether the law takes effect at various times within distinct regions, as people finish harvesting the onions in that area. A similar issue arises under quite different circumstances. Sometimes part of a crop has disappeared from the field, while some portion of it has not yet been gathered, either because it is growing in a private courtyard or because it is not yet ready for harvest. On the one hand, since part of the crop remains to be harvested, we might rule that the law of removal does not yet take effect. On the other hand, the law might apply in such cases, for the species of the produce in question is not available for all Israelites to gather and eat. Through this discussion of ambiguous cases, Mishnah's authorities address a deeper issue. The underlying question is whether the inability of certain Israelite householders to gather and eat produce can affect the point at which the law of removal takes effect. Alternatively, the law might not be invoked until the last vegetable disappears from the field, irrespective of the ability of particular householders to gather the food. As we shall see, Mishnah consistently presents these two opposing views of the matter, which we now will briefly examine.

The first theory is that man through his actions and capacities determines when the law of removal takes effect. If Israelite farmers harvest a single species of produce in two or more separate lots, each crop is deemed a separate entity (M. 9:2-3, M. 9:6A-D). Similarly, the ability of Israelites to harvest and use crops of the Sabbatical year is decisive. As soon as produce of a given species no longer is available for all Israelites to gather, the householder must remove similar edibles from his home (M. 9:4A-B, D-G). Finally, the way in which man stores produce after he has harvested it likewise is probative. That is, if a householder stores several distinct species of produce in a single jar, the whole is treated as a single entity. It is subject to removal all at the same time (M. 9:5B, C). The principle underlying these rules is that man is the center of his world. Through their actions of harvesting and storing produce, Israelite farmers and house-holders order the world in accordance with their wishes. The manner in which ordinary Israelites treat crops of the Sabbatical year thus determines the point at which these edibles become subject to the law.

The opposing theory is that the law applies separately to each species of produce, no matter how Israelite farmers may handle them. Each type of produce is subject to the law of removal at only one time, when all edibles of that species have disappeared from the field (M. 9:4C, M. 9:6E). Similarly, the householder's act of mixing together several types of vegetables has no effect. Each species of produce in the householder's home becomes subject to removal only when edibles of that type disappear from the field (M. 9:5D). These rules express the notion that it is God's action, not man's, which determines the point at which the law takes effect. Each type of produce is a separate entity, for the natural distinctions between one species and another are fixed and immutable. Each species of produce, then, must be subject to the law of removal all at once, for this is how God has ordered the world.

The single unit of law which we have been discussing, M. 9:2-6, is flanked on both sides by secondary materials. M. 9:1, a dispute, concerns the circumstances under which one may assume that a crop has not been cultivated during the Sabbatical year. This belongs at the end of Chapter Eight, which likewise concerns transgressions involving crops of the seventh year. M. 9:7 is included only as a supplement to M. 9:6, for both refer to the time of the second rainfall. M. 9:8-9 conclude in a logical fashion the chapter's discussion of the proper time for removal of crops. We turn first to the actual procedure for removal, M. 9:8, and afterwards consider the consequences of not removing produce at the proper time, M. 9:9.

9:1

A.   1) Rue,[1]   2) goosefoot,[2] (K: asparagus and fenugreek),   3) purslane,[3] 4) hill coriander,[4]   5) water-parsley,[5] and 6) meadow-eruca[6] are exempt from [the separation of] tithes and may be bought during the Sabbatical year from anyone [even one suspected of violating the laws of the Sabbatical year,]

B.   because produce of their type is not cultivated, [but grows wild].[7]

C.   R. Judah says, "Aftergrowths of mustard [i.e., all mustard that grows uncultivated during the Sabbatical year,][8] are permitted [that is, this produce may be bought from a person suspected of violating the laws of the Sabbatical year,]

D.   "because transgressors are not suspect concerning them. [Since mustard grows uncultivated in abundance, people are not suspected of secretly cultivating it and then claiming that it grew by itself]."[9]

E.   R. Simeon says, "All aftergrowths are permitted [i.e., may be bought from one suspected of violating the law,] except aftergrowths of cabbage,

F.   "because produce of this type [that is, cabbage] does not [grow uncultivated] among wild vegetables."

G.   But sages say, "All aftergrowths are forbidden [that is, may not be bought from one suspected of violating the law]."[10]

> M. 9:1 (A-B: b. Suk. 39b; E-G: b. Pes. 51b; y. Ber. 1:1[3a]; y. Kil. 1:9[27b]; y. Orl. 2:8[62c]; y. Shab. 3:3[6a]; Gen. R. 79:6; Ecc. R. 10:8; G: Sifra Behar 1:3, 4:5; b. Men. 5b)

Types of produce that grow wild (A) enjoy a special status. During the first six years of the Sabbatical cycle, these edibles are exempt from the separation of tithes. Only cultivated crops are subject to the designation of this agricultural offering (M. Ma. 1:1). Moreover, these crops also are exempt from certain restrictions that apply during the Sabbatical year. Ordinarily a person who buys produce of the Sabbatical year must take precautions to insure that the food he acquires has not been cultivated during that year in violation of the law.[11] People thus may not buy edibles from individuals suspected of violating the laws of the Sabbatical year. Wild crops, such as purslane and coriander, however, pose no such problem. Since these weeds never are cultivated, the buyer knows that he does not become an accessory to a transgression. This rule, at A-B, sets the stage for the three-part dispute at C-G. We wish to know what species of produce a person may buy during the Sabbatical year on the assumption that they have not been cultivated in violation of the law. Judah (C-D) holds that spices which grow both wild and cultivated may be purchased during the Sabbatical year, even from a person suspected of transgressing the law. Since mustard, for example, grows wild in abundance, the buyer need not be concerned that the seller has cultivated it. Simeon (E-F) permits the purchase of all types of produce except cabbage, which never grows wild. Since this vegetable clearly has been cultivated during the Sabbatical year, people may not buy it. Sages (G), finally, wish to insure that people do not inadvertently purchase any produce of the Sabbatical year that has been handled in violation of the law. They thus prohibit people from buying any crops whatsoever from those suspected of committing transgressions.

A.   Aftergrowths of the Sabbatical year [i.e., produce which sprouts uncultivated in the year following the Sabbatical]--

B.   they do not gather them by hand.

C.   Rather, one plows them under in the usual manner.

D.   And [during the year following the Sabbatical] cattle graze in their usual manner [i.e., animals are permitted to eat these aftergrowths, for they are not subject to the restrictions of the law].

T. 5:23

Grain that grows uncultivated during the year following the Sabbatical is not regarded as sanctified, as is similar produce that sprouts during the Sabbatical year (see M. 9:1). One need not scruple, therefore, about the manner in which one harvests it (B-C) or about feeding this edible produce to animals (D). The farmer is free to plow this produce under, which fertilizes the ground and improves the crop of the new year.[12]

9:2-3

A.   Three regions ('rswt) [are delineated with respect to the laws] of removal:

B.   Judea, Transjordan, and Galilee.

C.   And each of these three [regions is divided into] three areas ('rzwt).

D.   [Galilee is divided into]: the upper Galilee, the lower Galilee, and the valley.

E.   From Kfar Hananiah and northward, [i.e.], all places in which sycamores do not grow, [are regarded as] upper Galilee.

F.   And from Kfar Hananiah and southward, [i.e.], all places in which sycamores do grow, [are regarded as] lower Galilee.

G.   And the vicinity of Tiberias [is regarded as] the valley.

H.   And within Judea [the three areas are]: the mountains [surrounding Jerusalem], the lowlands [near the coast of the Mediterranean Sea], and the valley [of the Jordan River extending southward to the Dead Sea].

I.   And the lowlands of Lod are [subject to the same rule] as the southern lowlands.[13]

J.   And its mountains [i.e., those near the lowlands of Lod] are [subject to the same rule] as the kings' hill-country.

K.   From Beit-Horon to the sea [is deemed to be] a single district (mdynh).

M. 9:2(A-C: b. Pes. 52b)

L. · And why have they stated [that the three regions are each divided into] three areas?

M.   Because they may eat [produce of the Sabbatical year which they have stored in their homes] in each [area] until the last [produce] of that area (h'hrwn šbh) is gone [at which time the law of removal takes effect. This applies without regard to whether or not such produce has already disappeared from the fields of the other areas within that region].

N.   R. Simeon says, "They stated [that there are] three areas only within Judea,

O.   "and the remainder of the regions [i.e., Galilee and Transjordan] are [subject to the same rule] as the king's hill-country. [That is, produce throughout Galilee and Transjordan becomes subject to the law of removal when all produce of that species has disappeared from the Judean mountains]."

P.   And all the regions [within the Land of Israel] are [considered] a single [area] with respect to [the removal of] olives and dates.

M. 9:3 (L-M: b. Pes. 52b)

To understand the specific issue addressed by the pericope before us, which opens the tractate's discussion of the law of removal (M. 9:2-9), we must first summarize the substance of the law. The purpose of this rule is to prevent people from hoarding produce of the Sabbatical year, which should be shared by all, as we know from the rules of Chapter Eight. The law of removal thus prohibits people from retaining edibles in their homes after crops of the same species have disappeared from the fields. When that which grows in the field either has been completely harvested or has died, people must remove produce of that species from their homes and place it outside. This food then is available for everyone to collect and eat. Thus, at the very point when crops no longer are available for people to gather from the fields, that which they have in their homes must again be made accessible to all. This assures that all Israelites share equally the produce that grows during the Sabbatical year.[14]

The tractate opens its exposition of the law of removal by addressing a fundamental problem. A single species of produce does not disappear from the field at the same time throughout the Land of Israel. For example, even after all the onions have been gathered from the fields in the Galilee, others may still be growing near Jerusalem. Under these circumstances, it is not clear whether or not householders throughout the Land must remove onions from their homes. There are two possibilities. All produce of a single species might become subject to removal at the same time. Since the law applies equally to all that grows during the Sabbatical year in the Land of Israel, we do not differentiate between that which grows in Galilee and other crops of the same species growing in Judea. In this case, people must remove food from their homes only when produce of that species no longer is available anywhere in the Land of Israel. Alternatively, we might take account of the fact that the Land's yield is divided into distinct crops which ripen and are harvested separately. On this view, the Land is composed of distinct regions delineated by their climates, which, in turn, determine the growing season of produce in that region. Thus, the law of removal might take effect at different times within distinct region of the country, as the vegetables of that region disappear from the fields. With the central issue of the pericope in hand, let us turn to the details of its discussion, which unfolds in a logical manner. The general rule (A-C), is first elaborated (D-G, H, I-K), then explained (L-M), and finally disputed (N-O, P).

The Land of Israel is divided into nine distinct areas for purposes of removal (A-C). This is because people harvest produce of a single species at different times within different regions.[15] The law of removal, therefore, applies separately within each area. People must remove food from their homes only when all similar produce has disappeared from the fields within that climatic region. This is the case whether or not similar crops still are growing in other areas of the Land. D-G and H present a list of the sub-areas comprising two of the major regions, Galilee and Judea. The sub-areas within Transjordan, which are not spelled out here, are supplied by T. 7:11P-R.[16]

A secondary issue, addressed at I-K, concerns the status of the region surrounding Lod. This area poses a problem, for it is located on the border between the coastal lowlands and the Judean mountains. We wish to know when produce growing in this area becomes subject to removal. I-J resolves this problem by dividing the area near Lod between these two climatic regions. The contrasting rule at K states that the entire area from Beit Horon to the coast of the Mediterranean Sea, including Lod and vicinity, is considered part of the lowlands of Judea.[17] The climate throughout this region apparently is sufficiently uniform that most crops growing there are harvested at the same time.

L-M clarifies the meaning of the rule at A-C, that each of the three distinct regions of the Land is sub-divided into three areas. As I explained above, this rule assures that as soon as each crop has been harvested in a particular area, householders living there must take that which they have in their homes and make it available for all to gather.[18]

Simeon (N-O) and the anonymous rule at P independently dispute A-C. Simeon claims that only Judea is divided into climatic regions for purposes of the law of removal (N). Produce growing throughout Galilee and Transjordan is subject to removal when similar crops disappear from the Judean mountains (O). The point of this rule is not apparent to me. Bert., for his part, suggests that this is because farmers finish harvesting crops in the Judean mountains later in the year than in any other part of the Land. This, however, is not an adequate explanation of Simeon's view. It does not account for Simeon's ruling that Judea, unlike Galilee and Transjordan, is divided into distinct areas for purposes of removal. P claims that olives and dates growing throughout the Land become subject to removal all at once, not region by region, as other produce does. Presumably this is because these crops ripen and are harvested at nearly the same time in all geographical regions.

A.   Three regions [are delineated with respect to the laws] of removal:

B.   Judea, Transjordan and Galilee.

C.   And each of these [regions] is [divided] into three [areas] [=M. 9:2A-C with slight variations].

D.   Why did they refer [specifically] to the mountains, the valley and the lowlands [of Judea; see M. 9:2H]?

E.   For they do not (reading with ed. princ.; E and V read: they do) eat [produce grown] in the mountains [which no longer is available in the fields] by virtue of the fact that [the same species of produce is still available] in the valley,

F.   nor [do they eat produce grown] in the valley [which no longer is available in the fields] by virtue of the fact that [the same species of produce is still available in] the mountains.

G. Rather, the mountains are the mountains, the valley is the valley and the lowlands are the lowlands. [That is, each is deemed a distinct area for purposes of removal; see M. 9:3L-M.]

H. And in reference to Syria they did not mention three [distinct] areas.

I. Rather, [in Syria] they may eat [produce of the Sabbatical year] from the [time when produce] first [appears in the field] until the last [produce of that species] has disappeared [from the fields in all parts of Syria].

J. R. Simeon says, "They stated that there are three areas only within Judea [=M. 9:3N]

K. But [as regards] the other [two] regions, they may continue to eat [produce of the Sabbatical year] until no more of that [species of produce] is left in Bethel and in Gidrah of Kisrin."

L. What area [of Judea] is designated as its mountains? This is the king's hill-country.

M. Its lowlands? These are the lowlands of Lod.

N. Its valley? [This is the area] between Ein Gedi and Jericho.

T. 7:10

O. Which area in the Galilee is [designated as] its valley? [An area] such as Gennesar and places near it (hbrwtyh).

P. R. Simeon b. Eleazar (so E, V: ed. princ. reads: Eliezer) says, "What area is [designated as] the mountains of Transjordan? [An area] such as the mountains of Mikhvar and Gedor (so Lieberman, TK, p. 576, on the basis of y. Sheb. 9:2 and T. R.H. 1:17) and places near it."

Q. [Which area is designated as] its [i.e., Transjordan's] lowlands? Heshbon and all of its towns which are in the tableland, Dibon and Ba'moth-ba'al and Beth-ba'al- me^{c}on (Josh. 13:17).

R. Its valley? [An area] such as Beth Nimra (so Lieberman, TK, p. 576, on the basis of Josh. 13:27; E, V, and ed. princ. add: Ramata) and places near it.

S. Rabban Simeon b. Gamaliel says, "A mark of mountains is [the growth of] pine trees, a mark of valleys is [the growth of] palm trees; a mark of river-beds is [the growth of] reeds; and a mark of lowlands is [the growth of] sycamores."

T. Even though there is no explicit reference to this matter, there is a [scriptural] allusion: And he [i.e., Solomon] made cedar as plentiful as the sycamore of the lowlands (I Kings 10:27)."

T. 7:11 (S-T: b. Pes. 53a)

U. They may eat produce in Beit-Melek until [produce of the same species] no longer remains in [the fields of] Beth-El.

V. Even though there is no explicit reference to this matter, there is a [scriptural] allusion: Benjamin is a wolf which pounces (Gen. 49:27). This refers to the land [of Benjamin, the area of Beth-El] which jumps [to produce crops early in the growing season].

W.   In the morning devouring the prey (ibid.) This refers to Jericho, where [all produce is gone from the fields] early [in the Sabbatical year] (šmwqdmt).

X.   And in the evening dividing the spoil (ibid.) This refers to Beth-el (E reads: Jericho) where [produce remains in the fields until] late [in the Sabbatical year] (šm'hrt).

T. 7:12

T. cites M. 9:2-3 and supplies further details concerning the division of the Land of Israel into distinct climatic regions.

J.   And all (so Lieberman, TZ, p. 198 on the basis of ed. princ.; E, V read: wš'r)[19] [three] areas [of the Land of Israel, that is, Judea, Transjordan and Galilee; see M. 9:3] are [deemed] one [as regards the removal of] olives and dates [=M. 9:3P].

K.   They may [continue to] eat olives [anywhere in the Land of Israel, which they have brought into their homes] until the last [olives] disappear [from the fields of] Tekoa[20] (so E, ed. princ.; V omits: tqw^c).

L.   R. Eliezer b. Jacob says, "[They may continue to eat olives which they have brought into their homes until olives disappear from the fields] of Gush Halab;"[21] (reading with b. Pes. 53a; E, V and ed. princ. read: even until...).

M.   [That is], until (kdy š) a poor person goes out and is not (E lacks: l') able to pick a quarter qab [of olives],

N.   either [by picking the olives which grow] at its top [i.e., at the top of the tree] or [by picking those which grow] below it [i.e., on the lower branches of the tree].[22]

O.   They may eat dates [anywhere in the Land of Israel which they have brought into their homes] until the last [date] is gone from [the fields of] Soar.[23]

T. 7:15b (K-O: b. Pes. 53a)

T. illustrates the rule of M. 9:3P. Olives and dates are subject to removal at the same time everywhere, when this produce no longer is available anywhere in the Land of Israel. Eliezer (L) and K simply dispute the place where olives disappear last. M-N glosses this dispute, presenting the criteria for determining that olives have disappeared from the field.

9:4

A.   They may [continue to retain in their homes and] eat [produce of the Sabbatical year which they have stored in their homes] by virtue of the fact that (^cl) ownerless produce [of the same species is growing in the fields],

B.   but [they may] not [retain such produce] by virtue of the fact that [produce of the same species is growing only] in privately-owned places,[24] [such as courtyards, where it is not available for all to gather. That is, produce must be removed from one's home when similar produce no longer is growing in the fields, even if such produce still is growing in courtyards].

C.   [In contrast to A-B:] R. Yose permits [people to retain produce of the Sabbatical
      year, which they have stored in their homes] by virtue of the fact that [produce of
      the same species is growing only] in privately-owned places. [That is, one removes
      produce from one's home when all produce of the same species has disappeared, both
      from the field and from private courtyards].

D.   They may [continue to retain in their homes and] eat [choice grain or the early crop
      of figs which they have stored in their homes] by virtue of the fact that late-
      ripening grain[25] or the second crop of figs[26] [which ripens during the Sabbatical
      year still is growing in the fields],

E.   but [they may] not [retain fruit which they have stored in their homes] by virtue of
      the fact that winter fruit,[27] [which generally ripens and becomes edible after the
      Sabbatical year has ended, is growing in the fields].

F.   R. Judah permits [people to eat fruit of the Sabbatical year which they have stored
      in their homes by virtue of the fact that winter fruit is growing in the field],

G.   provided that (kl zmn š) [this winter fruit] began to ripen before the end of the
      summer [of the Sabbatical year].

M. 9:4 (y. Pes. 4:2[30d])

Under certain circumstances it is unclear whether the law of removal should take
effect within a particular region of the Land. The problem arises when produce of a
certain species is growing, but is not available for all to gather and eat. Let me begin by
explaining how this situation can come about, for only then can we fully understand the
problem at hand. At A-B, all produce of a certain type growing in the open fields has
been harvested, but some still remains in private courtyards. In this case, a crop still is
growing, but in a place where it is inaccessible to most Israelites. A similar situation
arises at D-E. Toward the end of the Sabbatical year, when most produce already has
been harvested, certain late-ripening crops still are growing in the field. These crops,
however, may become ripe and ready for harvest only after the Sabbatical year has
ended. Here again, we have a situation in which produce is growing during the Sabbatical
year, but is not available for people to harvest and eat. The problem posed by both cases
is the same. Does the law of removal take effect when crops of the Sabbatical year no
longer are growing at all, or when produce no longer is available for everyone to collect as
food? Let me spell out these alternatives in greater detail. We might hold that the law
of removal takes effect only when all vegetables of a certain species have disappeared
from the field. If crops still are growing, even in private courtyards, the householder may
retain similar edibles in his home. On the other hand, the law might take effect as soon
as produce of a certain species no longer is available for everyone to gather and eat.
Thus, the householder may keep edibles in his home only as long as there is food for all to
harvest. The bulk of the pericope takes the latter position. People may not hoard edibles
in their homes when similar produce is not available for everyone. This would deprive
others of food meant to be shared by all. That which is not available for consumption
during the Sabbatical year, either because it grows in courtyards (A-B) or because it is not

yet ripe (D-E), is of no account. Judah's gloss, at F-G, reinforces this main principle for the case of late-ripening fruit. People may retain an early crop of fruit which they have stored in their homes provided that the second crop of that same species can, in fact, be harvested and eaten during the Sabbatical year.

Only Yose, C, adopts the alternative position. The law of removal takes effect only when all produce has disappeared, both from the field and from private courtyards. This is because, by definition, crops of the Sabbatical year belong to all Israelites. The fact that some produce grows in private courtyards is inconsequential. Householders may retain edibles in their homes until all produce of that type has been harvested.

A.	They may [continue to] eat figs [of the Sabbatical year which they have brought into their homes] until the undeveloped figs disappear [from the fields of] Beit Oni[28] (so V; E which reads: byty'ny; ed. princ. reads: bny byt pgy).

B.	Said R. Judah, "They stated [a rule concerning] the undeveloped figs of Beit Oni only as regards [the separation of] tithes [and not, as at A, concerning the removal of produce of the Sabbatical year].

C.	"[The proper ruling concerning this produce is]: The undeveloped figs of Beit Oni and the inferior dates ('hymy) of Tobaniah[29] are subject to [the separation of] tithes, [even though they are of poor quality and so scarcely edible]."

T. 7:14 (b. Pes. 53a)

A draws together the rule of M. 9:3P and M. 9:4D. Figs are subject to removal only when all figs have disappeared from Beit Oni, where they continue to grow longer than anywhere else in the Land of Israel. Judah, B-C, who rejects this ruling, offers a quite separate rule concerning the figs of Beit Oni.

A.	They may not eat [grain of the Sabbatical year which they have stored in their homes] by virtue of the fact that late-ripening grain (so Lieberman, TZ, p. 198, who reads: tpyhyn; V, E read: rpyhyn; ed. princ. reads: spyhyn) [still is growing in the fields] of Acre (E omits: of Acre).

B.	R. Yose says, "They may eat [grain of the Sabbatical year which they have stored in their homes] by virtue of the fact that late-ripening grain [still is growing in the fields] of Acre,

C.	"and [they may eat figs] by virtue of the fact that the second crop of figs [still is growing in the fields],

D.	"but [they may] not [eat fruit] by virtue of the fact that winter fruit [is growing in the fields]" [=M. 9:4D-E with slight variations].

E.	(E lacks:) R. Judah says, "[They may] even [eat fruit] by virtue of the fact that winter fruit [is growing in the fields; cf. M. 9:4F].

F.	R. Yose says (reading with ed. princ.; E, V omit: 'wmr), "[Concerning] the second crop of figs which ripened before the conclusion of the summer [of the Sabbatical year]--

G.   "they may eat [from the early crop of figs which they have stored in their homes] by virtue of the fact that it [i.e., the second crop of figs still is growing in the fields]."

H.   They may eat grapes [of the Sabbatical year] until the hanging grapes of Abel[30] (so Lieberman, TZ, p. 198, who reads: šb'bl; ed. princ.: šb'škwl; V: šb'kl) disappear [from the vineyards].

I.   If late-ripening clusters ('pylwt) [of these hanging grapes] remain, they may eat [other grapes] by virtue of them.

T. 7:15a (H-I: b. Pes. 53a)

T.'s main unit (B-D vs. E+F-G) presents its own versions of M. 9:4D-E and F-G. In Mishnah, as we recall, the anonymous rule at M. 9:4D-E and Judah's qualification of it at M. 9:4F-G express a single principle. People must remove crops from their homes if similar produce growing in the field will not become ripe and edible during the Sabbatical year. T. recasts these rulings as a dispute, thus bringing this unit of law in line with the dispute at M. 9:4A-B vs. C. That is, M. 9:4E's rule concerning winter fruit (which T. assigns to Yose) is now disputed by Judah's ruling, rather than qualified by it, as in Mishnah. T. thus drops the qualifying phrase, "provided that they ripened before the conclusion of the summer of the Sabbatical year" from its version of Judah's lemma, E. This phrase appears instead in Yose's rule concerning the second crop of figs, F-G.[31] The result is that Yose's ruling at B-D, qualified at F-G, expresses the very position of M. 9:4D-E. Only if produce growing in the field is edible during the Sabbatical year may people retain similar foodstuffs in their homes. Judah (E) disagrees. People may eat of the crop which they have stored in their homes even if the new crop growing in the field is not yet edible.

T. supplements this dispute with two further rulings. A, which disputes Yose's rule at B, and H-I, which applies Yose's rule to the case of grapes. In both cases, T. brings together the principle of M. 9:3P and that of M. 9:4D-E. The law of removal takes effect only when produce no longer is available anywhere in the Land of Israel.

9:5

A.   One who pickles three types of vegetables [of the Sabbatical year together] in a single jar--

B.   R. Eliezer says, "They may [continue to] eat [these vegetables] by virtue of the fact that the [vegetable which ordinarily is the] first [of the three to disappear from the field is still growing. That is, once the first of these vegetables disappears from the field, all the vegetables in the jar are subject to removal]."

C.   R. Joshua says, "[They may eat any of these vegetables] even by virtue of the fact that the [vegetable which ordinarily is the] last [to disappear from the field still is growing. That is, only when the last of these vegetables has disappeared from the field are the contents of the jar as a whole subject to removal]."

D.   Rabban Gamaliel says, "[As] each type [of vegetable] disappears from the field, one
      must remove that type [of vegetable] from the jar."

E.   (0^2, L, M, S, P and Z omit:) And the law is according to [Rabban Gamaliel's] words.

F.   R. Simeon says, "All vegetables [are regarded as] a single [species of produce] with
      respect to [the laws of] removal."

G.   The may eat purslane [of the Sabbatical year anywhere in the Land of Israel] until
      all types of vegetables[32] disappear from the valley of Beit Netofah.[33]

                                        M. 9:5 (A-E: b. Pes. 52a; Sifra Behar 3:5)

      The problem arises because three different types of vegetables have been pickled
together in a single jar (A). We wish to know when the contents of the jar becomes
subject to removal. On the one hand, each of the vegetables is of a different species.
Each, then, might be subject to the law of removal as produce of that type disappears
from the field. On the other hand, the householder has pickled these various types of
vegetables together in order to form a single relish. They therefore should be subject to
the law all at once. In the three-part dispute at B-D, Eliezer and Joshua take the latter
position. Since the householder has treated the vegetables as a single entity, they become
subject to the law of removal at only one time. Eliezer and Joshua disagree only about a
secondary point, whether the contents of the jar should be subject to removal when the
first of the vegetables has disappeared from the field (B), or alternatively, whether the
law takes effect only when the last of the vegetables no longer grows in the field (C).
Gamaliel (D) rejects the notion that the vegetables are to be treated as a single entity.
On his view, each separate species of produce becomes subject to the law only when that
type of vegetable has disappeared from the field.

      The two concluding rules, F and G, though formally not part of this dispute, respond
directly to it. Simeon (F) holds that all vegetables are subject to removal at the same
time. So long as any type of vegetable still is growing in the field, where people can
gather it freely, the householder need not remove that which he has stored in his home.
Simeon thus rejects the entire problem under dispute at A-E. All types of vegetables,
whether they have been pickled together or not, are removed only when the very last type
of vegetable disappears from the field. The formally quite separate rule at G has been
placed here to illustrate Simeon's position. People may continue to eat purslane, a
common salad vegetable, until all types of vegetables have disappeared from the fields of
Beit Netofah, where the growing season ends very late in the year. Underlying this rule is
the view that the law of removal does not apply at separate times within distinct regions
of the Land. This represents a significant extension of the principle at M. 9:3P, that the
entire Land is deemed a single region only with respect to the removal of dates and olives.

A.   They may eat purslane [of the Sabbatical year which they have brought it into their
      homes] until 'agotri [an unidentified plant] disappears [from the fields; see M. 9:5G].

B.   And inhabitants (so E, ed. princ. which read: bny; V reads: bgy) in the upper Galilee
      [may eat purslane] until lopsa [an unidentified plant] disappears [from the fields] of
      Beth Dagon[34] and the places near it.

C.   [As regards] the lower Galilee, [they may eat purslane] until 'uzniot (Aristolochia
      maurorium; so Lieberman, TK, p. 577)[35] disappear [from the fields] of Shimron (so
      Lieberman, TZ, p. 197, who reads šmᶜwnyy'; E, V read: šmᶜwn 'n').[36]

T. 7:13 (Sifra Behar 2:5)

T. claims that purslane is removed in different regions of the Land of Israel at
different times, contrary to M. 9:5G. The specifics of these rules, however, are unclear,
for the identity of the plants and places referred to is uncertain.

9:6-7

A.   One who picks fresh herbs [of the Sabbatical year does not have to remove this
      produce] until the moisture [in the ground] (lit., sweetness)[37] dries up [in the late
      summer at which time no more fresh herbs are available. At this time people must
      remove fresh herbs from their homes].[38]

B.   One who gathers dried plants [of the Sabbatical year does not have to remove this
      produce] until the second rainfall[39] [in the autumn of the year following the
      Sabbatical, at which time the dried herbs in the field rot and are no longer
      available. At this time, people must remove dried herbs from their homes].

C.   [One who picks fresh] leaves of reeds or leaves of vines [of the Sabbatical year does
      not have to remove this produce] until [the leaves in the field] fall off their stems.

D.   And one who gathers dried [leaves of reeds or vines during the Sabbatical year does
      not have to remove this produce] until the second rainfall [of the year following the
      Sabbatical].

E.   R. Aqiba (K: Judah) says, "With respect to all [produce referred to above, that is,
      both fresh and dried herbs and leaves, one does not have to remove them] until the
      second rainfall."

M. 9:6

F.   And likewise [the time of the second rainfall is determinative with respect to the
      following cases]:

G.   One who leases a house to his fellow, "Until the rains"--

H.   [the lessee retains possession of the house] until the second rainfall.

I.   One who has vowed [not to] benefit from his fellow, "Until the rains"--

J.   [the vow remains in force] until the second rainfall.[40]

K.   Until when may the poor enter the orchards [to collect the peah, gleanings, and
      forgotten sheaves left for them]?

L.   Until the second rainfall.[41]

M.   After what time may they derive benefit from or burn straw and stubble of the Sabbatical year?

N.   After the second rainfall [in the autumn of the year following the Sabbatical].

> M. 9:7 (I-J: M. Ned. 8:5; b. Ta. 6b; M-N: b. Ta. 6b)

Herbs and leaves are gathered from the field in two differnt forms, both fresh and dried. In the spring, people gather fresh foliage as food. Later in the year, they collect dried herbs and leaves for use as animal fodder. This poses a problem for the law of removal. At what point during the year must the householder remove herbs and leaves that he has stored in his home? We might view the fresh and dried forms of a single species of produce as two distinct entities, since they are harvested separately and used for different purposes. In this case, the law of removal would apply at one time to fresh leaves and later in the year to dried produce of the same species. Alternatively, we might regard both fresh and dried foliage as a single entity. Since both belong to a single species, they are subject to the law of removal at the same time. The dispute at A-B/C-D vs. E addresses this issue. The formally parallel rules, A-B and C-D, claim that people may retain each type of produce in their homes only so long as it still is growing in the field. When the ground moisture dries up, so that green herbs begin to die (A) or when fresh leaves wither and fall off their stems (C), people must remove these types of produce from their homes. The law of removal applies separately, however, to dried herbs and leaves. These become subject to removal only when the autumn rains cause the dry foliage in the field to rot. When that which remains in the field no longer can be used as animal fodder, people must remove similar produce from their homes (B, D). Aqiba (E) presents the opposing view. Fresh and dried produce of a single species is subject to removal at a single time. After the second rainfall, when the last of the dried herbs no longer is available in the fields, both fresh and dry herbs must be removed from people's homes.

A separate unit of law, G-N, has been included here because it concerns the time of the second rainfall. G-H and I-J make a single point. The phrase "until the rains" is ambiguous, for there are three distinct periods of rain in the autumn months. Mishnah's authorities resolve this ambiguity by ruling that "until the rains" refers to the second rainfall, midway through the rainy season (G-H, I-J). The poor may collect peah, gleanings and forgotten sheaves only until the second rainfall, for after this time their footsteps will cause damage to the field (K-L).[42] Straw and stubble of the Sabbatical year are fit for animal consumption and therefore must be used for this purpose (see M. 8:1). After the second rainfall, however, straw and stubble that remains in the field rots. Since this produce can no longer be used for its designated purpose, people are permitted to use it as they wish (M-N).[43]

A.   Rabban Simeon b. Gamaliel (E lacks: b. Gamaliel) says, "They may [continue to] eat [dates which they have in their homes] by virtue of [the dates] which [have fallen from their stems and are lodged] in upper branches (šbkypyn)[44] [of the date palms]."

B. "But they may not [continue to] eat [dates which they have stored in their homes] by virtue of [the dates] which [are lodged] in the [lower] prickly branches (šbšysyn)[45] [of the date palm, for in this case they are not accessible for people to gather]."

C. And [concerning] all other fruit of trees,

D. such as, (1) pears,[46] (2) crustumenian pears,[47] (3) quince[48] and (4) crab apples[49]--

E. they may eat [the fruit which grows in] the hill country by virtue of the fact that [fruit of the same kind still is growing in the fields] of the valley and they may eat [fruit which grows in] the valley by virtue of the fact that [fruit of the same kind still is growing in the fields] of the hill country.

T. 7:16 (A-B: b. Pes. 53a)

F. R. Simeon b. Eleazar says, (so E, ed. princ.; V omits: 'wmr), "All [of the types of produce listed at T. 7:16D] are like carobs [concerning which no distinction is made between the three regions of the Land of Israel; cf. M. 9:3. So Lieberman, TK, p. 580, on the basis of y. Sheb. 9:3 [38d]].

G. They may [continue to] eat the leaves [of all types of produce which they have stored in their homes] until the second rainfall, [when the leaves in the field rot].

H. They may [continue to] eat [produce of the Sabbatical year which they have stored in their homes] by virtue of the fact that [produce of the same kind remains available] in an irrigated field [which has dried up],[50]

I. for [produce growing in an irrigated field] does not disappear [from the fields].

J. The roots of cabbage stalks (ed. princ. lacks: roots) which have dried up [still] may not [be used] for the benefit [of Israelites. That is, people may not burn such produce [for fuel] for it is fit for animal fodder and accordingly must be used for this purpose].

K. R. Simeon says, "[As regards] the roots of cabbage stalks,

L. "even though they have dried up,

M. "they eat [fresh roots which people have in their homes] by virtue of them, [that is, by virtue of the fact that these dried roots remain in the field]."

N. Likewise, one who gathers (reading with M. 9:6B, D: hmgbb bybš; V, ed. princ. read: mgbyb wybyš; E reads: mgbb dbš) dried [roots of cabbage stalks for use as animal fodder] is liable to remove them [from his home when all similar produce is gone from the fields].

T. 7:17

T. supplements Mishnah's discussion of the law of removal with its own catalogue of rules. Since each unit of law makes its own point, we explain each in turn. Simeon b. Gamaliel (A-B) applies the principle of M. 9:4A-B to a case in which dates have fallen off the palm tree and become lodged in its branches. People may not retain edibles in their homes when others are not accessible for people to gather from the field. Accordingly, one may not continue to eat dates stored in one's home if those in the field are lodged among the prickly branches of the palm tree, where people cannot readily gather them (B). C-E, reiterated by Simeon at F, extends M. 9:3P's rule concerning olives and dates to all species of fruit. Fruit throughout the Land of Israel is subject to removal at the same time, without respect to diverse topographical regions. G, a singleton, applies the rule of M. 9:6B, D to all types of fruit.

H-I and K-M spell out the implications of M. 9:6E. We might think that when produce in the field dries out and no longer is edible, similar edibles in people's homes becomes subject to removal. This, however, is not the case. Dried produce, which no longer is fit for human consumption, still may be used as animal fodder. Produce fit for this purpose likewise is subject to the law of removal (see M. 7:1B1, E-F). So long as dried roots, which are used as animal fodder, remain in the field, people may retain fresh roots in their homes (H-I, K-M). J and N supply further rules regarding the removal of dried produce. People must use this dried produce for its designated purpose, as animal feed, and so may not waste it (J). N is obvious. People who gather dried produce must remove it from their homes when no more of it is available in the field.

A.   When [in the first six years of the Sabbatical cycle] must they keep off paths in the fields of others?

B.   After (reading with E, ed. princ.; V reads: until) the second rainfall [see M. 9:7K-L].

C.   R. Yose says, "When does this [rule] apply?

D.   "When the years proceed in their established order (tqnn). [That is, at the time when the rains fell in the proper manner].

E.   "Now that the years have become cursed (So V, ed. princ. which read: ntqnsw; E reads: ntqyymw) [such that the rains come as a curse, rather than as a blessing],

F.   "even though it has rained only once,

G.   "they must ask permission (so Lieberman, TZ, p. 199, who reads: lhmlk; E, V, and ed. princ. read: lhlk) [from the owner of the field before walking across it. The first rain might make the field wet enough that their footsteps would damage it]."

H.   Rabban Simeon b. Gamaliel says, "Rains which fall continually for seven days without stopping are considered (yš bhn) the second rainfall." [That is, this is equivalent to the amount of rain which falls during the second rainfall].

T. 7:18 (A-B: y. B.B. 5:1[15a]; b. Ta. 6b; b. B.Q. 81a, b)

Yose (C-G) and Simeon b. Gamaliel (H) each gloss the rule of M. 9:7K-L. Yose's claim is that since rains no longer fall in a regular manner, even a single rainfall is sufficient to make a field soggy. People who walked across such a field might damage it. Simeon b. Gamaliel provides a criterion by which people may determine whether the time of the second rainfall has come (H).

9:8

A. One who possesses produce of the Sabbatical year when the time for the removal [of that produce] arrives,

B. sets aside [sufficient] food for three meals for each [member of his household and then removes any remaining produce].

C. "And the poor may eat [this produce] after it has been removed, but not the rich," the words of R. Judah.

D. R. Yose says, "Poor and rich alike eat (B, C and N read: do not eat)[51] [of this produce] after it has been removed."

M. 9:8 (Sifra Behar 1:6)

When the law of removal takes effect, the householder places produce outside his home for all to gather, retaining a minimal amount as food for his family. This rule, at A-B, sets the stage for the focus of the pericope, the independent dispute at C-D. At issue is the status of these vegetables after the householder has removed them. On the one hand, the yield of the Sabbatical year is ownerless. Everyone, therefore, is equally entitled to eat it. Yet, Scripture specifies that these edibles are given by God "that the poor of thy people may eat" (Ex. 23:11). Do we distribute this food to all Israelites or to the poor alone? The answer turns on how one construes the purpose of the law of removal. According to Judah, C, the point of the law is to assure that needy Israelites have food to eat during the Sabbatical year. In accordance with Scripture's injunction, these agricultural products should not be given to the rich, for they have the means to purchase the food they need during the Sabbatical year. Yose, D, holds that the purpose of removing food from people's homes at a specified time is to maintain its equal distribution among all Israelites. Just as all gather and eat this produce while it grows in the fields, so too both rich and poor must share it after the time of removal.

A. In the past, agents of the court would sit near the gates of the city.

B. [From] each person [who harvested produce of the Sabbatical year and] who carried it [to them, these agents] would take it from him and return (reading with E: nwtnyn; V, ed. princ. read: nwtn) to that person [enough] food for three meals and the remainder they would deposit in the city's storehouse.

C. When the time for [the harvesting of] figs arrived, the agents of the court would hire workers [to harvest them], harvest [the figs], press them into cakes of pressed figs, place them in jars and deposit [these jars] in the city's storehouse.

D. When the time for [the harvesting of] grapes arrived, the agents of the court would hire workers [to harvest them], harvest the grapes, press them in presses, place the wine in jars and deposit [these jars] in the city's storehouse.

E. When the time for [the harvesting of] olives arrived, the agents of the court would hire workers [to harvest them], harvest the olives, pack them in a vat, place them in jars and deposit [these jars] in the city's storehouse.

F.   And they would distribute [portions] of this [stored up produce] on the eve of the Sabbath [and] each person [would receive an amount of produce] in accordance with [the size of] his household.

G.   When the time for removal came [that is, when all produce had been gathered from the field and placed in the city's storehouse]--

H.   "And the poor may eat this produce after it has been removed, but not the rich," the words of R. Judah.

I.   R. Yose says, "Poor and rich alike eat of this produce after it has been removed." [=M. 9:8C-D].

J.   R. Simeon says, "The rich eat produce from the storehouse after the time of removal."

T. 8:1 (H-I: Sifra Behar 1:6)

K.   [Before the time of removal], one who has produce [of the Sabbatical year] to distribute, [that is, one who has more produce than he can use],

L.   distributes it to the poor [but not to the rich].

M.   One who has produce of the Sabbatical year when the time of removal arrives,

N.   distributes it to his neighbors, relatives and acquaintances, takes it out of his house, places it on the door-step (reading with E: pth bytw; V, ed. princ. lack: pth), and says, "Fellow Israelites! All who need to take [this produce] may come and take!

O.   He then brings [the produce] back into his own home and continues to eat it until it is gone.

T. 8:2

T. claims that in the past courts regulated the harvest and distribution of produce of the Sabbatical year. Since they gave out only small amounts of produce at a time, individuals were not required to remove produce in their possession. Simeon's gloss (J) of the dispute at M. 9:8C vs. D rephrases Yose's position in terms of this earlier procedure. K-L and M-O spell out the implications of Yose's rule. One who has excess produce of the Sabbatical year prior to the time for its removal should give it to the poor alone. This is an act of charity to the poor, for after its removal this procedure will be available to the rich as well. M-O requires no further explanation.

9:9

A.   One who possesses produce of the Sabbatical year which he received through an inheritance or which was given to him as a gift [after the time for the removal of that produce had passed][52]--

B.   R. Eliezer says, "[Such produce] is given to those who eat it, [that is, to those who received the inheritance or gift.[53] They need not make these vegetables available for all to take as otherwise required by the law of removal]."

C.   But sages say, "The sinner may not benefit from his transgression. [That is, the recipients of this gift or inheritance may not benefit from the produce, for it never was handled in accordance with the law of removal].

D.   "Rather, [such produce] must be sold to those who eat it [that is, to the people who received this food as a gift or inheritance] and the money [received from this sale] must be divided among everyone. [This procedure assures that all benefit from the produce, not only those who originally received it as a gift or inheritance]."

E.   One who eats dough [made from produce] of the Sabbatical year before its dough offering has been removed is subject to the death [penalty, in the form of extirpation; see Lev. 22:9, M. Hal. 1:9].

M. 9:9 (C: M. Hal. 2:7; b. Yeb. 92b; b. Ket. 11a, 36b, 39b; b. Git. 55b; b. Sot. 15a; b. B.K. 38a, 39a; b. A.Z. 2b; b. Men. 6a; b. Nid 4b)

The problem addressed by the dispute at A-B vs. C-D arises when people mishandle crops of the Sabbatical year. In the case at hand, vegetables of the Sabbatical year were not removed at the proper time, in violation of the law. Subsequently, these edibles were given to others, either as a gift or as an inheritance. The question is whether the individuals who received these crops may benefit from the transgression of others.[54] In Eliezer's view, the recipients of these crops are not accessories to the transgression. They bear no responsibility either for mishandling the produce or for acquiring it. He thus allows those who received this food to treat it as their own. It is not subject to removal (B). Sages disagree. The people who inherited these crops may not deprive others of food which rightfully belongs to all. Sages therefore require the recipients to pay for the produce and to distribute the money to everyone. In this way, all share the value of the food, just as if the produce had been handled in accordance with the law of removal in the first place (C-D).

The formally distinct rule at E makes the point that produce of the Sabbatical year is liable to the separation of dough-offering. All dough, even that which is ownerless, is subject to this offering, in accord with the rule of M. Hal. 1:3. The penalty for violating this rule derives directly from Lev. 22:9. This rule, which has no bearing on the law of removal, apparently has been placed here because, like the foregoing, it deals with the penalties for mishandling produce of the Sabbatical year.

CHAPTER TEN

Shebiit Chapter Ten

The tractate's final chapter concerns an entirely new topic: the cancellation of debts by the Sabbatical year. The foundation of Mishnah's law is the injunction of Dt. 15:1-6, that every seventh year creditors must release debtors from their monetary obligations. This prevents poor Israelites from becoming destitute if they accumulate debts which they cannot repay. The primary interest of Mishnah's discussion is to define the circumstances to which Scripture's rule applies. This is worked out in two formally distinct units of law, M. 10:1-2 and 10:3-7, which together comprise the bulk of the chapter.

The several rules presented at M. 10:1-2 delimit the types of financial obligations subject to cancellation by the Sabbatical year. First, only loans, that is, simple advances of money, are cancelled. In keeping with Scripture's injunction, this assures that Israelites who are unable to repay their loans do not become indigent. Other types of debts, such as commercial credit, fines and damages, however, are not cancelled by the Sabbatical year. Releasing debtors from these sorts of payments would prevent shop-keepers from conducting their business or preclude injured parties from receiving just compensation. Moreover, not all types of loans are subject to cancellation (M. 10:3H-I). Secured loans remain collectable even after the Sabbatical year. This is because Mishnah's authorities regard the collateral as a temporary repayment of the loan until the borrower actually repays the money he owes. Since these loans are deemed not to be outstanding, they cannot be cancelled by the Sabbatical year. Finally, loans turned over to a court for collection are not cancelled. Scripture prohibits only the lender himself, not the court, from demanding payment of the loan (see Dt. 15:2). At M. 10:1I-L and 10:2A-E, Mishnah's authors present a separate criterion regarding the types of financial obligations cancelled by the Sabbatical year. The main point of these rules is to illustrate the principle of Dt. 15:1, "At the end of seven years thou shalt make a release. . . ." It follows from the formulation of Scripture's injunction that all debts incurred before or during the seventh year are subject to cancellation, while those created even one day after that year has ended remain collectable. These rules also specify that commercial credit owed to shopkeepers and laborers is cancelled by the Sabbatical year, contrary to the rule of M. 10:1, discussed above. The purpose of the Sabbatical year, according to these rules, is to prevent Israelites from becoming burdened with any long-term debts, whether in the form of loans or of commercial credit.

An extended discussion of the prozbul, a legal fiction by which a lender may prevent his loans from being cancelled by the Sabbatical year, occupies M. 10:3-7. The prozbul is a document that authorizes a court to collect outstanding loans on the lender's behalf. Since the court, rather than the lender himself, demands payment of the loan, this procedure technically does not violate Scripture's injunction (see M. 10:2H-I above). The institution of the prozbul, introduced at M. 10:3-4, is subject to several further qualifications, at M. 10:5-6. First, a lender may not write a prozbul in a manner which would infringe upon the rights of the borrower. Specifically, he may not post-date the document, by writing it on August 1, but dating it October 1, for example. This would permit him to collect loans he had not yet made when the prozbul was written and delivered to the court (M. 10:5A). Second, since a prozbul is written by a lender to protect his own financial interests, each lender must write a separate document (M. 10:5E-F). Finally, a prozbul may be written only if the borrower owns real estate. This property is regarded as a temporary repayment of the loan for the duration of the Sabbatical year. Since the loan is deemed not to be outstanding during that year, it is not cancelled. This enables the creditor, after the Sabbatical year has ended, to collect through the court the money owed him (see M. 10:2H-I above). An appendix to this rule, M. 10:6B-10:7, specifies what constitutes real estate for purposes of writing a prozbul.

The chapter's two closing rules, M. 10:8 and 10:9, form a fitting conclusion to the entire foregoing discussion. As we have seen, the chapter delineates ways in which creditors may collect the money owed them after the Sabbatical year, despite Scripture's injunction to the contrary. This has the effect of promoting stable and equitable monetary relationships among all Israelites. For the same reason, M. 10:8 and 10:9 claim that borrowers should honor their financial obligations, even if the Sabbatical year has released them from the legal duty to do so.

10:1

A. The Sabbatical year cancels a loan [whether recorded] in a document or not.[1]

B. A debt [owed to a] shopkeeper [that is, commercial credit] is not cancelled [by the Sabbatical year].

C. But if [the shopkeeper] converted it [that is, the debt] into a loan,

D. lo, this [loan] is cancelled [by the Sabbatical year].

E. R. Judah says, "[Each time a customer makes a purchase on credit from a shopkeeper] the preceding (hr'šwn hr'šwn) [debt which he owed that shopkeeper] is cancelled [by the Sabbatical year. That is, when a new debt is incurred by the buyer, his former debt automatically becomes a loan. The Sabbatical year cancels this loan]."

F. The [unpaid] wage of a hired laborer is not cancelled [by the Sabbatical year].

G. But, if [the laborer] converted it [the amount of his wage] into a loan,

H. lo, this [loan] is cancelled [by the Sabbatical year].

I. R. Yose says "[As regards] any work which ends during the Sabbatical year--

J. "[the unpaid wage for such work] is cancelled [by the Sabbatical year].

K. "But [as regards work] which does not end during the Sabbatical year [but rather after the Sabbatical year has ended,]--

L.   "[the unpaid wage for such work] is not cancelled [by the Sabbatical year. Since the
      obligation to pay this money was incurred only after the Sabbatical year ended, this
      obligation is not cancelled.]

M. 10:1 (A: b. Git. 37a)

Mishnah's discussion of the remission of debts during the Sabbatical year is based on
Deut. 15:1-2: "At the end of every seven years thou shalt make a release. . .Every
creditor shall release that which he hath lent unto his neighbor." The pericope before us
claims that only certain financial obligations are cancelled by the Sabbatical year.
Mishnah's authorities distinguish loans, which are cancelled by the Sabbatical year, from
commercial credit, which is not. Loans, whether written or oral, are simply advances of
money given for the benefit of a needy borrower. The lender gains no financial benefit
from the loan, for he may not charge interest to the borrower (Lev. 25:37; M. B.M. 5:1).
Debts incurred when people buy and sell goods (B) or services (F) on credit are another
matter. These transactions benefit the creditor as well as the debtor, for shopkeepers and
laborers must extend credit in order to conduct their businesses successfully. In light of
this distinction between loans and commercial credit, we can understand the point of the
rule at hand. Mishnah's authorities wish to protect the interests of the ordinary Israelite
householder. They therefore permit the cancellation of loans, for this prevents people
from becoming destitute if they repeatedly borrow money which they are unable to
repay. Commercial credit, however, is not cancelled by the Sabbatical year. This permits
Israelite shopkeepers and laborers to collect outstanding accounts, which is necessary for
them to earn their livelihood. With the central point of the pericope in hand, let us now
turn to the secondary materials at C-D+E, G-H, and I-L.

Two parallel units of law, C-D and G-H, qualify the foregoing rule by indicating that
a debtor and creditor may agree to convert an outstanding debt into a long-term loan.
This loan then is cancelled by the Sabbatical year. At E, Judah explains one way in which
commercial credit is converted into a loan. Each time a shopkeeper extends additional
credit to a single customer, he forgoes his right to demand immediate payment of the
previous debt. By doing so, he indicates that he regards this outstanding debt as an
advance. It therefore is cancelled by the Sabbatical year, in accordance with the rule
governing loans (A). As we shall see, T. 8:3 suggests another way in which people convert
commercial credit into loans, by recording the amount of money owed.

Yose (I-L), contrary to the principle explained above, claims that the Sabbatical
year cancels the obligation to repay commercial credit.[2] This assures that Israelites do
not become burdened with long-term debts which they cannot repay. His point, made
through the contrast between I-J and K-L, is that only commercial credit owed before or
during the Sabbatical year is cancelled. If an employer becomes obligated to pay his
laborer's wages before the Sabbatical year ends, he need not pay them. Wages owed to a
worker after the Sabbatical year has ended, on the other hand, still are collectable.

A. A debt [owed to a] shopkeeper is not cancelled [by the Sabbatical year] [=M10:1B].[3]

B. Said Rabbi, "Obviously the words of R. Judah [that when a new debt is incurred by
    the buyer the former debt becomes a loan, M. 10:1E, refers to a case in which the
    shopkeeper] records the monetary value [of the purchase] (so V, ed. princ.; E reads:
    the quantity of produce; cf. C below). [Since the shopkeeper recorded this debt as if
    it were a loan, it is treated as such. Accordingly, the Sabbatical year cancels it].

C. "The words of sages [that a debt owed to a shopkeeper is not cancelled by the
    Sabbatical year (cf. A above) refers to a case in which the shopkeeper] records the
    [quantity of] produce [which the customer purchased but not the amount of money
    owed] (so V, ed. princ.; E reads: the amount of the purchase; cf. B above). [Since in
    this case the shopkeeper did not treat the debt as a loan, but as a purchase on
    credit, it is regarded as a debt. It thus is not cancelled even if the same customer
    makes a new purchase on credit. Therefore, M. 10:1B and E are not contradictory,
    but refer to two different situations]."

T. 8:3

T. reconciles the anonymous rule of M. 10:1B with Judah's ruling, M. 10:1E. As we
recall, M. 10:1B rules that debts to shopkeepers are not cancelled by the Sabbatical year,
while Judah (M. 10:1E) claims that under certain circumstances they are. T.'s point is
that the way in which the debt is recorded is the decisive factor. Recording the value of
a debt makes it into a loan. This is cancelled by the Sabbatical year, in line with Judah's
ruling (B). If, on the other hand, the shopkeeper records only the amount of produce
purchased, but not its monetary value, the rule of M. 10:1B applies (C).

A. A woman's marriage document [which stipulates the amount of money which her
    husband owes her if he either divorces her or dies]--

B. [if] she accepted partial payment [of this sum of money from her husband before the
    Sabbatical year] and converted to a loan [to him the remaining amount, that is,
    converted the rest of the amount owed her into a loan to her husband,]

C. lo, the Sabbatical year cancels [this loan].

D. [But if] she accepted partial payment and did not loan [the remaining amount to her
    husband, or if] she loaned [to her husband the full amount specified in her marriage
    document] and did not accept partial payment [of this sum,]

E. lo, the Sabbatical year does not cancel [this loan].

T. 8:4 (b. Git. 18a)

T. exemplifies M. 10:1's principle that monetary obligations are not cancelled by the
Sabbatical year if this would leave the creditor with no means of financial support. This
principle applies to loans which a woman makes to her husband for the value of her
marriage document. This is because the marriage document is meant to assure a woman's

financial security in the event that her husband divorces her or dies. This point is made by the contrasting rules at A-C and D-E. The Sabbatical year does not cancel a woman's loan for the full value of her marriage document. Likewise, if a woman makes no loan to her husband at all, the Sabbatical year does not cancel his obligation to pay her. This would deprive her of the means to sustain herself (D-E). If, on the other hand, she has received part of the sum to which she is entitled, it is assumed that she can support herself. Accordingly, her loan for the remaining amount is cancelled by the Sabbatical year, as are ordinary loans (A-C).

10:2

A. One who slaughters a heifer and divides it [among purchasers] on the New year [of the year following the Sabbatical]--

B. if the month was intercalated [i.e., if the last month of the Sabbatical year had an extra day,[4] so that the debt which the purchaser owed to the butcher in fact was incurred during the Sabbatical year],

C. [this debt] is cancelled [by the Sabbatical year].

D. But if [the month was] not [intercalated],

E. [this debt] is not cancelled, [because the debt was incurred after the Sabatical year had ended].

F. [The monetary penalties owed by] a rapist, seducer (cf. Ex. 22:15-16), one who defames [an Israelite virgin] (cf. Deut. 22:13-19) or any [payment enjoined by an] act of a court,

G. are not cancelled [by the Sabbatical year].

H. One who loans [money in exchange] for security and one who hands over his bonds to a court [for collection]--

I. [these loans] are not cancelled [by the Sabatical year].

> M. 10:2 (A-E: b. Shab. 148b; y. Mak.
> 1:2[31a]; B-E: y. R.H. 3:1[48c]; y. Ned.
> 6:8[40a]; y. Sanh. 1:2[18d]; H-I: Sifre Deut.,
> 113; b. Git. 37a; b. Mak. 3b)

Under certain circumstances, it is unclear whether or not the Sabbatical year cancels monetary obligations. This problem arises in three different cases, A-E, F-G and H-I, which I explain in turn.

The last month of the Sabbatical year sometimes is intercalated. When this happens, the first day of the eighth year also is the last day of the Sabbatical year itself. Since this day both is and is not part of the seventh year, it is unclear whether or not the debt at A was incurred before the end of that year, and so, should be cancelled. The answer is expressed in the contrasting rules at B-C and D-E. The intercalated day is regarded as part of the seventh year. A debt created on this day therefore is cancelled. Financial obligations incurred even one day after the Sabbatical year has ended, by

contrast, remain collectable (D-E). This unit of law, consistent with the position of Yose
(M. 10:1I-L), clearly contradicts M. 10:1A-B. Debts owed to a merchant, as well as loans,
are subject to cancellation by the Sabbatical year.[5]

Monetary penalties and damages (F) serve to compensate people for some wrong-
doing which they have suffered. Since they are neither loans nor payments of business
obligations, it is not clear whether or not they are cancelled by the Sabbatical year. F-G
states that they are not. This assures that the Sabbatical year does not prevent injured
parties from collecting the compensation to which they are entitled.

The secured loan (H-I), presents a further case of ambiguity. Unlike simple
advances of money, a secured loan entails no risk to the lender. If the borrower defaults,
the lender has the right to retain the collateral which was given to him. For this reason,
Mishnah's authorities regard this security as a temporary repayment of the loan until the
borrower actually pays back the money he owes. Secured loans thus are never actually
outstanding with the result that they cannot be cancelled by the Sabbatical year.

Loans turned over to a court are not cancelled for a quite separate reason. Dt. 15:2
states that creditors are prohibited from collecting debts after the Sabbatical year.
Mishnah's authorities permit a court to collect the money on the lender's behalf, however,
for this procedure technically does not violate Scripture's injunction. This legal fiction
introduces the discussion of the prozbul, taken up in the pericopae that follow.

A. One who loans his fellow [money in exchange] for security, even if the debt is
    greater than [the value of] the security,
B. lo, [this loan] is not cancelled [by the Sabbatical year] [=M. 10:2H-I with slight
    variations].

T. 8:5

C. One who loans his fellow [money in exchange] for security or [who accepts] a note
    which contains a mortgage clause[6] [i.e., whether the security consists of chattels or
    real-estate],
D. lo, [this loan] is not cancelled [by the Sabbatical year] [=M. 10:2H-I with slight
    variations].
E. Just as the Sabbatical year cancels a loan, so too it cancels an oath [with respect to
    a loan. That is, ordinarily if a borrower claims that he has repaid part of his loan
    and the lender claims that he has not, the former must take an oath to this effect.
    The Sabbatical year, however, cancels the obligation to take such an oath].
F. Those [financial obligations] which the Sabbatical year cancels--the Sabbatical year
    [likewise] cancels an oath [concerning them].
G. And those [financial obligations] which the Sabbatical year does not cancel--the
    Sabbatical year [likewise] does not cancel an oath [concerning them].
H. R. Simeon says, "He [the creditor] cancels it, but his heirs do not cancel it,

I.   "As it is written, 'Every creditor shall release that which he hath lent unto his neighbor (Deut. 15:2)'" [implying that the creditor may not collect a loan, but his heirs may].

T. 8:6

T. presents a catalog of rules which supplement Mishnah's discussion of financial obligations cancelled by the Sabbatical year. Two glosses of M. 10:2H-I, at A and C, make a single point. Mishnah's rule applies uniformly to all types of secured loans. The value or nature of the property used as security does not alter the status of the loan. E-G is obvious. Since the Sabbatical year cancels loans, the oaths serve no purpose. H-I carries forward the point of M. 10:2H(2). The creditor himself is forbidden from demanding payment of a loan after the Sabbatical year. The creditor's heirs, like his agents, are not bound by this rule.

10:3-4

A.   [A loan against which] a prozbul [has been written, thereby authorizing a court to collect the loan on the lender's behalf,] is not cancelled [by the Sabbatical year].

B.   This is one of the things which Hillel the Elder instituted.

C.   When he saw that [shortly before the Sabbatical year began] people refrained from lending one another money [because they knew that their loans would be cancelled and they would lose their money,]

D.   [with the result that] they transgressed that which is written in the Torah, "Beware lest you harbor the base thought . . . [and so you are mean to your kinsman and give him nothing" (Dt. 15:9),]

E.   Hillel instituted the prozbul. [By allowing courts to collect outstanding loans on behalf of the creditor, this document enabled lenders prior to the Sabbatical year to grant loans that would not be cancelled.]

M. 10:3 (A-E: b. Git. 36a; B-D: Sifre Deut., 113)

F.   This is the text of the prozbul:

G.   "I transfer (mwsr) to you, Messrs. X and Y, judges in such-and-such a place, every debt (reading with Sifre Deut., 113: kl: all MSS read: škl)[7] which I have [i.e., which is owed to me] so that I may collect [the money owed me] anytime I wish."

H.   And the judges or the witnesses sign below.

M. 10:4 (A-C: b. Git. 36a; B-C: b. Git. 32b-33a; Sifre Deut., 113; y. Sanh. 5:5[23a])

A prozbul creates a legal fiction whereby creditors may collect outstanding loans which otherwise would be cancelled by the Sabbatical year. The creditor drafts a document designating a court as his agent to collect money owed by his debtors. This procedure is permitted, for Scripture prohibits only the creditor himself from collecting loans after the Sabbatical year begins. The court, however, may demand payment of the money and then turn it over to the lender (see M. 10:2H-I). This rule regarding the prozbul at A brings in its wake supplementary materials which explains the origin and purpose of this institution (B-E) and provides the basic text of the document (F-H).

A.   R. Judah says, "[Regarding] a prozbul which is [witnessed beneath each line of text, and then] folded [that is, the text is written on alternate lines leaving spaces for the witnesses to sign beneath each line of the text. The document is then folded so that the text reads continuously, while the signatures of the witnesses are on the lines which are folded back][8]--

B.   the judges sign inside [that is, at the bottom of the text] and the witnesses sign outside, [that is, on the lines which are folded back]."

C.   They said to him, "Acts of the court [such as the prozbul] do not require validation [by witnesses]."

T. 8:7

T. takes up the topic of M. 10:4H, the witnessing of a prozbul, but raises a new issue. What is the proper procedure for witnessing a folded prozbul? As a folded document, it must be signed by witnesses beneath each line of the text (cf. M. B.B. 10:1). M. 10:4H, however, specifies that a prozbul must be signed at the bottom of the entire text. Judah concludes that a folded prozbul must be witnessed in accordance with both procedures. The witnesses sign beneath each line and the judges at the bottom of the page (A-B). C rejects the position that a prozbul, folded or otherwise, requires the signatures of witnesses. As an act of the court, it is signed by the judges alone.

10:5

A.   An ante-dated prozbul is valid. [By placing an earlier date on the prozbul the creditor limits his own right to collect loans outstanding between the date recorded on the document and the date on which it actually was written].

B.   But a post-dated prozbul is invalid. [By placing a later date on the prozbul, the creditor would gain the right, to which he is not entitled, to collect loans which he had not yet made at the time the document was written].

C.   Ante-dated bonds are invalid. [By ante-dating the document, the creditor gains rights, to which he is not entitled, against the property of his debtor].

D.   But post-dated bonds are valid. [By post-dating the document, the creditor voluntarily restricts his own legal rights against his debtor's property].

E.   [If] one person borrows money from five persons, he writes a [separate] prozbul for each [of the creditors].

F.   [But if] five persons borrow money from one [creditor], he writes a single prozbul for all [of the debtors].

M. 10:5 (A: y. B.B. 10:10 [17d]; B: b. R.H. 2a, 8a; b. B.M. 17a, 72a; b. B.B. 157b, 171b; b. Sanh. 32a)

Two separate units of law, A-D and E-F, address a single topic, the proper procedure for writing a prozbul. Since these rules make quite distinct points, however, I explain them separately. The central principle of the opening unit (A-B/C-D) is that a creditor may not date either a prozbul or a bond in a way that would allow him to collect money to which he is not entitled. In the case of the prozbul, this means that a creditor may not post-date the document, for example, by drafting it on August 1, but dating it October 1. This is because, as we know from M. 10:3-4, a prozbul gives a creditor the right to collect only loans that he made before the date on which the document in fact was written and delivered to the court, in this case, on August 1. Dating the prozbul October 1, therefore, would allow the creditor to collect loans that he made after the time that he wrote the document. This is prohibited. A creditor may, however, ante-date a prozbul. If he writes the document on August 1, but dates it as of June 1, for example, he has merely restricted his own rights to collect outstanding loans. That is to say, by dating the document June 1, he forfeits his own right to collect any loans he may have made between June 1 and August 1.

The principle spelled out above for the case of the prozbul likewise determines the proper manner of dating other financial instruments, such as a bond. This document gives a creditor a lien against the property of his debtor, including property which the debtor sells to a third party after the date of the bond. If the debtor defaults, the creditor may foreclose on any property he owned at the time when the bond was executed, even if the debtor subsequently sold this property to others. A creditor thus may not pre-date a bond, by writing it on August 1, but dating it, for example, on June 1. Pre-dating would give the creditor the power to foreclose on property which the debtor sold before August 1, the date when the bond actually was written. This would be unfair to the person who bought property from the debtor on the assumption that there were no liens against it. If a creditor post-dates his bond, however, by writing the document on August 1, but dating it October 1, he merely forgoes certain of his rights against the debtor's property. Now, if the debtor defaults on the loan, the creditor may not foreclose on any property which the debtor sold between August 1 and October 1, as he would otherwise be entitled to do.

The point of E-F is clear in light of M. 10:3-4's discussion of the purpose of the prozbul. Since a creditor writes a prozbul to secure his loans from being cancelled, each lender must draft a separate document. This rule is implicit in the very wording of the prozbul, given above at M. 10:4G.

10:6

A.   They write a prozbul only on [condition that the borrower owns] real estate. [The
      borrower's land is regarded as a temporary repayment of the loan for the period of
      the Sabbatical year. This renders the loan exempt from cancellation (see M.
      10:2H-I) and enables the lender, by means of the prozbul, to collect the money owed
      him.][9]

B.   If [the borrower] has no [land,]

C.   he [the lender] transfers [to the borrower] some [minuscule] amount [of property]
      from his field [which enables the lender to write a prozbul].

D.   If [the borrower] had a field in the locale (b^c yr) [which he was holding] as security
      [for another loan, which was owed him,]

E.   they write a prozbul relying upon [such property].

F.   F. Huspit says, "They write [a prozbul] (1) concerning a man [who has borrowed
      money] relying upon his wife's property and (2) concerning orphans [who have
      borrowed money] relying upon the property of [their] guardians."

M. 10:6 (A-C: b. Git. 37a)

        The pericope spells out conditions under which a prozbul may be written, thereby
enabling a lender to collect loans which otherwise would be cancelled by the Sabbatical
year. To understand the central point, expressed at A, we must begin by explaining the
role of the borrower's land in achieving the purpose of the prozbul. The importance of
land, in the view of Mishnah's framers, is that, unlike other forms of property, it has
indeterminate value.[10] Even the smallest piece of real estate is potentially equal in value
to any outstanding loan. Thus, a minuscule quantity of the borrower's land would suffice
to serve as security against any loan, regardless of the amount. To understand the
importance in the present context of securing a loan, let us return briefly to the rule at
M. 10:2H-I. That pericope specifies that secured loans are not cancelled by the Sabbatical
year. The borrower's collateral serves as a temporary repayment of the loan until he
actually returns the money he owes. Since a loan which has been secured is not regarded
as outstanding, it cannot be cancelled by the Sabbatical year. Similarly, in the rule at A,
a small piece of the borrower's land functions like security. It is regarded as a temporary
repayment of the loan for the duration of the Sabbatical year, and so prevents the loan
from being cancelled. This legal fiction is formalized through the writing of a prozbul.
This document enables the lender, through the court, to collect the money owed him, as
provided by the rule at M. 10:3-4.

        With the main point of the pericope in hand, we turn now to the secondary
developments, at B-C, D-E and F. These rules provide that, even if the borrower in fact
owns no real estate, a prozbul may be written. At B-C, the lender simply gives the
borrower a small share of his own land. Since, as I said, even a minuscule quantity of land
is deemed to have immeasurable value, the creditor may then write a prozbul against the
loan. This rule underscores the function of the borrower's land, as I explained it above.

This small piece of real estate does not actually serve as security, for, if this were so, the borrower could not use the lender's land to secure his loan. Rather, the notion that even a sliver of land can take the place of the loan for the duration of the Sabbatical year is a legal fiction which enables lenders, by means of the prozbul, to collect outstanding loans.

The point of D-E is that having a claim against land belonging to another party is equivalent to actual ownership for purposes of writing a prozbul. If a debtor has a lien against real estate belonging to a third party, his creditor may write a prozbul against his loan. Huspit's lemma, F, builds upon this principle. A prozbul may be written against a borrower who derives benefit from the real estate of others, even if he has no legal claim upon it. This applies equally to a husband, who enjoys the usufruct of his wife's property, and to orphans, who derive financial support from the property belonging to their guardians.

A. Five persons who [each] borrowed money [for themselves from a single lender and recorded their loans] in a single document,[11]

B. for each [of the borrowers] who owns real estate, they write a prozbul,

C. but for each [of the borrowers] who does not own real estate, they do not write a prozbul.

D. R. Simeon b. Gamaliel says, "Even if only one [of the borrowers] owns real estate, they write a prozbul [for all five of the borrowers together]."

T. 8:8

Five people take out separate loans, but agree to simplify their transactions by borrowing simultaneously from a single lender. At issue is whether their activity constitutes a joint venture. B-C's point is that it does not. In accordance with the rule of M. 10:6, therefore, prozbuls may be written only for those borrowers who secure their loans with real estate. Simeon b. Gamaliel, D, disagrees. Since the five borrowers act together, one piece of land may be used as security for all of the loans together.

A. If the borrower owns real estate, but the lender does not,[12]

B. they write a prozbul against [such a loan].

C. [But] if the lender owns real estate, but the borrower does not,

D. they do not write a prozbul against [such a loan].

E. [If] he [i.e., the borrower] does not own real estate,

F. but his bondsmen or his debtors do own real estate,

G. they write a prozbul against [such a loan].

T. 8:9 (E-G: b. Git. 37a)

H. [The soil within] a perforated pot [sitting on the ground has the same status as real estate and so] they write a prozbul against it.

I.   [But a pot which is] not perforated, [even though it sits on the ground], they do not write a prozbul against it.

J.   R. Simeon says, "Even [a pot which is] not perforated, they write a prozbul against it."[13]

K.   R. Huspit says, "They write a prozbul for a woman against her husband's property."[14] [cf. M. 10:6F]

L.   At what time [of year] do they write a prozbul?

M.   Shortly before the New Year of the Sabbatical year (so V, ed. princ.; E reads: shortly before the New Year of the year following the Sabbatical).

N.   [If] they wrote [a prozbul] shortly before the New Year of the year following the Sabbatical,

O.   even if he [i.e., the lender] afterwards goes and tears up [the document],

P.   the [lender] may continue to collect [the loan] at any time [in the future] (lzmn mrwbh).

Q.   Rabban Simeon b. Gamaliel says, "Every loan made after the writing of a prozbul,

R.   "lo, it is not cancelled [by the Sabbatical year]."

T. 8:10 (H-I: b. Git. 37a)

T.'s catalog of rules concerns the circumstances under which a prozbul may be written, the topic of M. 10:6. Each of these rulings makes its own point, and so must be explained separately.

A-D simply spells out what M. 10:6A assumes. Since the borrower, not the lender, owes money, he is the party who must have real estate with which to secure the loan. E-G reiterates the point of M. 10:6D-E. The lender may write a prozbul if the borrower has a lien against the property of others.

The dispute of H-I vs. J concerns whether soil contained within a non-perforated pot has the status of real estate. If so, a prozbul may be written against it, in accordance with the rule of M. 10:6A. H-I's point is that soil is deemed to be land only if it physically is attached to the ground. Lenders may write a prozbul only against a perforated pot, for the soil within a non-perforated pot does not touch the ground. Simeon, J, rejects this distinction. All soil has the same status as the ground from which it was taken. Soil in any type of pot therefore is equivalent to real estate against which a prozbul may be written.

K transposes the wording of the lemma attributed to Huspit at M. 10:6F, that a prozbul may be written "for a man against his wife's property." Both rules, however, make the same point, carrying forward the principle of M. 10:6D-E and T. 8:9E-G above. If a borrower has a lien against the property of others, the lender may write a prozbul to protect his loan from being cancelled by the Sabbatical year. Thus, a prozbul may be written for a woman borrower whose husband owns real estate, for she has a claim against this property. If the husband dies, she may sell his property to raise money for her maintenance and for the value of her marriage contract (see M. Ket. 11:2).

The question at L is answered in two parts, M and N-P. A <u>prozbul</u> may be written either before the Sabbatical year begins or before it ends. The point of the rule as a whole is to distinguish that which is proper <u>de jure</u> from that which is permitted <u>de facto</u>. A <u>prozbul</u> should be written prior to the Sabbatical year, before loans are cancelled (M). Nonetheless, if the lender wrote the document during the Sabbatical year itself, it is deemed valid <u>de facto</u> (N-P). O's point is that a <u>prozbul</u> serves its purpose only during the Sabbatical year. After that year is over, the loan no longer is subject to cancellation and so the lender has no further need for the document.

Simeon, Q-R, rules that a <u>prozbul</u> works prospectively as well as retroactively. That is, he holds that it secures all the lender's loans from cancellation, those made after the writing of the document as well as those made beforehand. This contrasts sharply with the anonymous rule at M. 10:5A, that a <u>prozbul</u> protects only loans made before the document is written.

10:7

A.   [As regards] a bee hive [which sits on the ground but is not attached to it]^{15}--

B.   R. Eliezer says, "Lo, it [has the same status] as real estate, and [therefore],

   (1)   "they write a <u>prozbul</u> against it [cf. M. 10:4,]

   (2)   "it is not susceptible to uncleanness [so long as it remains] in its place,

   (3)   "and one who removes [honey] from it on the Sabbath is liable [for violating the prohibition against reaping; cf. M. Shab. 7:2]."

C.   But sages say, "It does not [have the same status] as real estate, and [therefore],

   (1)   "they do not write a <u>prozbul</u> against it,

   (2)   "it is susceptible to uncleanness [even if it remains] in its place,

   (3)   "and one who removes [honey] from it on the Sabbath is exempt [from violating the prohibition against reaping]."

M. 10:7 (=M. Uqs. 3:10; b. B.B. 65b, 80b; T. Uqs. 3:16)

The dispute concerns whether a bee hive that sits on the ground has the status of real estate. On the one hand, it should fall into the category of chattels, for it is not actually attached to the ground. Nonetheless, bee hives remain stationary for long periods of time and so might have the same status as the ground on which they sit. Eliezer, B, takes the latter position. Since a bee hive constitutes real estate, a <u>prozbul</u> may be written against a borrower who owns a hive, in accordance with M. 10:6A (B1). The rule at B2 relies on the notion that only movable objects, such as vessels, can become unclean. So long as the hive remains stationary then, it is not susceptible to uncleanness. Finally, since Eliezer regards a bee hive as land, gathering its fruit constitutes reaping (B3). This is forbidden on the Sabbath according to M. Shab. 7:2. Sages, by contrast, view a bee hive as movable property and all the rest follows (C). The entire dispute appears here because it refers to the conditions under which a <u>prozbul</u> may be written, the topic of the preceding pericope.

10:8

A.   One who repays a debt during[16] the Sabbatical year [even though he has no legal
      obligation to do so]--

B.   [the lender] must [refuse to accept payment and] say to him, "I cancel [the debt]."

C.   [If the borrower then] said to him, "Even so [I will repay it],"

D.   he may accept it from him.

E.   As it is written, "And this is the word of remission" (Deut. 15:2). [This verse
      provides a basis for the rule at A-D, that the lender must verbally notify the
      borrower that the latter is not obligated to repay the loan].

F.   Likewise [the same rule applies in the following case]:

G.   A murderer who went into exile in a city of refuge (cf. Num. 35:9-24),

H.   and whom the inhabitants of the city wished to honor,

I.   must [refuse to accept the honor and] say to them, "I am a murderer."

J.   [If then] they said to him, "Even so [we wish to honor you],"

K.   he may accept [the honor] from them.

L.   As it is written, "And this is the word of the murderer." (Deut. 19:4). [This verse
      provides a basis for the rule at G-K that the person must verbally notify the
      residents of the city that he is a murderer and so not entitled to receive the honor].

M.   10:8 (A-E: Sifre Deut., 112; b. Shab.
      148b; b. Git. 37b; F-L: M. Mak. 2:8; Sifre
      Deut., 181; b. Mak. 12b; T. Mak. 3:8)

A borrower may choose to repay a loan even though the Sabbatical year has released
him from the responsibility to do so. His creditor, however, has no right to this payment
and may accept the money offered to him only after he apprises the borrower of this
fact.[17] This assures that the borrower understands that his payment is strictly voluntary
(A-D). The formally parallel rule at G-K makes a similar point. A murderer may accept
the honor offered him provided he first informs people that he is not entitled to it. E and
L provide two similarly-worded Scriptural verses as prooftexts for these rules.[18]

10:9

A.   [As regards] one who repays a debt during the Sabbatical year [even though he has no
      legal obligation to do so]--

B.   the sages are pleased with him.

C.   One who borrows [money] from a convert whose children converted with him need
      not repay [the money owed the father] to his children [if the father dies before the
      loan comes due. Upon conversion, the father and his children are regarded as born
      again, with the result that their prior familial ties are not recognized by the law.

The children thus do not share in his estate and so are not legally entitled to receive the money owed to their father.][19]

D. But if [the debtor] repaid [the children, for a debt owed to their father, even though he was not legally obligated to do so,]

E. the sages are pleased with him.

F. All chattels are acquired through drawing [them into one's possession.[20] That is, only when the buyer draws the item that he purchases toward him is the transaction formally concluded.]

G. But [as regards] anyone who stands by his word [and does not withdraw from a sales agreement before the buyer has drawn the item toward him, even though either party to the transaction has the legal right to do so]--

H. the sages are pleased with him.

M. 10:9 (C-E: b. Kid. 17b)

People should conduct commercial transactions in a manner which goes above and beyond their minimum legal obligations. This point, exemplified in three parallel cases, is expressed by the repeated apodosis at B, F and H, "the sages are pleased with him." Responsible people repay their debts, even if they have no legal duty to do so (A-B, C-E). Likewise, parties to a sales agreement should conduct their transactions honorably. Each party should stand by the terms of the initial agreement, even if fluctuations in the market would make it more profitable for him to withdraw from the transaction (F-H). The pericope as a whole is included here on account of the rule at A-B concerning the repayment of debts during the Sabbatical year.

A. [As regards] (1) a thief, (2) one who lends money at interest [in violation of the law] or (3) [robbers] who repented and returned that which they improperly had acquired--

B. anyone [among the original owners] who accepts [such money or goods] from them [any of the people listed at A]--

C. the sages are not pleased with him.

T. 8:11 (b. B.Q. 94b)

A criminal offers to return stolen goods or money to the original owners. Although they legally are permitted to accept this offer, they should not do so. This would minimize the gravity of the transgressions and consequently encourage the criminal to continue his illegal activity.[21] This rule supplements M. 10:9, further exploring the relationship between legal and moral responsibilities.

NOTES TO INTRODUCTION

[1]I have not cited the only other Scriptural law concerning the Sabbatical year, at Ex. 23:10-11, for several reasons. First, it presents the principle that the land must rest every seven years in only a very cursory manner, while Lev. 25:1-7 spells this out in much greater detail. Second, the Covenant Code stipulates only that the land is to lie fallow every seventh year. It does not specify that a single year is designated for this purpose throughout the Land of Israel and so leaves open the possibility that farmers fallowed their fields on a rotating basis. Lev. 25:1-7, by contrast, is explicit that a single year is to be observed as "a Sabbath of the Lord," which accords with the assumption of Mishnah's entire discussion. Finally, in the one detail where the two Pentateuchal codes explicitly diverge, namely, with respect to who is entitled to eat produce that the land yields during the seventh year, Mishnah's framers adopt the view of the priestly writer. That is, Mishnah asserts throughout (with the single exception of Judah's view at Mishnah 9:8C) that produce of the seventh year is eaten by all Israelites, as specified by Lev. 25:6, not that it is reserved for the poor alone, as at Ex. 23:11. In all, it is clear that Leviticus serves as the basis for our tractate's discussion.

[2]For an extended explanation of the significance of the number seven in the agricultural calendar of ancient Israel, see J. Morgenstern, "Sabbath," IDB (4:135-137).

[3]The personification of the land is a common theme of the priestly writer. See, for example, Lev. 18:24-30 and 20:22-26, where the land itself is conceived of as ejecting those who defile it.

[4]The institution of the Sabbatical year, of course, is only one part of the system of agricultural restrictions established by Scripture and discussed by Mishnah's framers. Throughout the other years of the Sabbatical cycle, the Israelite farmer also must acknowledge God's ownership of the land, by paying agricultural taxes to the priests when they reap the land's produce. For a more extended discussion of the theology underlying Mishnah's system of agriculture, see Sarason, "Mishnah and Scripture," and Jaffee, Tithing, pp. 1-6.

[5]See W.D. Davies' discussion of the Biblical view that the Land belongs ultimately to God and that Israelites, by virtue of the relationship to God, must respect the sanctity of the land through observing God's commandments (The Territorial Dimension of Judaism, pp. 15, 17-19).

[6]Some Biblical scholars argue that the injunctions to leave the land fallow and to cancel debts in fact are closely related. D. Hoffman (Sefer Devarim, I, pp. 232-248) and Driver (Deuteronomy, p. 178), for example, contend that debtors are released from their financial obligations precisely because they have no income from the land during the seventh year. See also W. Brueggemann's theological discussion of the significance of the Sabbatical year as a time when Israelites affirm their covenantal relationship to God by relinquishing their claims both against the Land and against fellow Israelites (The Land, pp. 63-64).

[7]For general discussions of the institution of the Sabbatical year in the Biblical period, see R. de Vaux, Ancient Israel, pp. 173-175, and J. Morgenstern, "Sabbatical Year," IDB (4:141-144).

[8]In this respect it is interesting to note that the injunctions concerning the Sabbatical year spelled out at Lev. 25:1-6 and Ex. 23:10-11 appear amidst discussions of festivals and other sacred times (see Lev. 23:1ff., Ex. 23:12ff.). In Mishnah, however, the

- 215 -

tractate devoted to the Sabbatical year appears in the Order of Agriculture, not in the Order of Appointed Times.

[9]This conclusion accords well with that of Jacob Neusner, who summarizes the message of Mishnah as a whole in the following terms:

> The Mishnah's principal message, which makes the Judaism of this document and of its social components distinctive and cogent, is that man is at the center of creation, the head of all creatures upon earth, corresponding to God in heaven, in whose image man is made. The way in which Mishnah makes this simple and fundamental statement is to impute power to man to inaugurate and initiate those corresponding processes, sanctification and uncleanness, which play so critical a role in the Mishnah's account of reality. The will of man, expressed through the deed of man, is the active power in the world (Judaism, p. 270).

[10]The Sabbatical year is scarcely referred to in Scripture, apart from the passages already cited and discussed; see Neh. 10:32 and II Chron. 36:21. The only evidence we have that the Sabbatical year was observed at a later period derives from I Macc. 6:49, 53, and from Josephus (Antiquities, 13:228-235). These passing references are in no way comparable to the sort of sustained intellectual reflection on the topic which characterizes the tractate before us.

[11]For a complete description and discussion of the five syntactic patterns that characterize all of Mishnah's rules, see Neusner, Purities, XXI, pp. 164-234.

[12]In the analysis that follows I am indebted to the discussions of Jaffee, Tithing, pp. 15-19, and Peck, Priestly Gift, pp. 23-5, who clearly articulate how the exegete of Mishnah can utilize its literary forms for the interpretation of its meaning. My explanation of the reason for undertaking form-analytical exegesis of Mishnah's rules, however, differs from that suggested by Jaffee and Peck. They both argue that we must use form-analysis to understand the original meaning of Mishnah's rules because both the formulation and organization of these rules can be attributed to a single generation of rabbinic authorities. The meaning of these rules in their present context, therefore, is a function of the linguistic and literary forms into which they have been cast. But this fact, established by Jacob Neusner (Purities, XXI, pp. 245-6), should not be invoked to explain the purpose of the form-analytical approach to the text. Formal analysis is a critical tool for understanding the meaning of Mishnah's rules simply because the text is so highly formulaic in character. Whether these formal traits were imposed on Mishnah's rules by their final redactors or whether they were created at some earlier point in the transmission of these materials is a quite separate matter. In short, the justification for engaging in this sort of analysis depends solely upon the fact that the text displays certain formal traits, not upon a theory of how the text came to have these traits.

[13]My translation is based on the text provided by Albeck, though I have consistently made reference to the textual variants presented in Sacks-Hutner. Earlier English translations, by Danby and Blackman, also have been of value, particularly in the translation of plant names and other technical terms.

[14]These manuscripts are coded to Latin letters, which appear on the abbreviations and bibliography list at the front of this book.

[15]The vast majority of manuscript variants, which concern the precise spelling of a word or the use of definite articles and conjunctions, have no bearing on the interpretation of Mishnah's rules.

[16]Following each translation I also have provided a partial list in parentheses of other rabbinic documents which cite verbatim the passage at hand. This list of parallels is based on that which appears in the critical apparatus of Sacks-Hutner. It should be noted that I do not list parallels in y. Sheb., which cites every pericope of M.

[17]The beginning of these thematic units often are also demarcated by a shift in literary form or syntactic pattern. For a full discussion of the ways in which formal traits and theme define the intermediate units of a tractate, see Neusner, Purities, XII, pp. 113-163.

[18]I also have made use of modern, critical commentaries; Albeck and Correns, for Mishnah, and Freimark, for Tosefta. Most often these have been helpful in elucidating the meaning of difficult words or phrases. Methodologically, however, they neither address the form-analytical questions which lie at the center of my study nor contribute significantly to rabbinic modes of exegesis, which they generally merely summarize.

[19]My translation of Tosefta is based on the critical text provided in Lieberman's TZ.

NOTES TO CHAPTER ONE

[1]As we shall see, Chapter Two continues the discussion of work prohibited during the sixth year by turning to the rules that apply to grain fields.

[2]See note 4 below, which explains the dimensions of a seah-space.

[3]Throughout the discussion that follows, I have referred to the Pentecost as the date after which farmers may no longer plow their orchards. I have adopted the Hillelite formulation of this rule (M. 1:1C) purely for ease of exposition.

[4]A byt s'h, which I have translated as "seah-space," refers to an area of 2,500 square cubits (50 x 50 cubits long). Measuring a cubit as 56 cm, a seah-space equals 784 square meters. See Felix, Sabbatical, p. 28.

[5]Felix (Sabbatical, p. 29) offers several alternative estimates of this measure- ment including that of Maim. (Comm.) (that the loaf weighs 29 kg.) and another based on Josephus (Antiquities, 14, 7, 1) (49 kg.). For our purpose, which is to understand the principles underlying the law, the exact amount clearly is of no consequence.

[6]See M. Kil. 6:5, where this definition of 'yln srq is disputed.

[7]I follow Maim. (Comm.) and Bert. who interpret L to refer to the same distance from the tree as the place "where the gatherer stands with his basket behind him" (F). The parallelism of C-F and I-L indicates that this is the correct reading. Presumably F was not repeated verbatim at L because this measurement is applicable only to fruit-bearing trees.

[8]Felix (Sabbatical, p. 18) notes that the purposes of plowing a field of trees are "to ventilate the soil and provide the roots and its micro-organisms with oxygen, to remove excess carbon-dioxide, and to eradicate the weeds which compete with the roots of the trees for water and nutrient solutions. Similarly, plowing aids the retention of moisture in the soil, as it breaks up the capillaries through which the water rises to the surface and evaporates."

[9]This point is not explicitly made in the text. Yet, as TYY, Bert., and MR point out, Mishnah's authors clearly assume that Ex. 34:21 does not refer to the prohibition against working the land on the Sabbath, for at I-J they reject an even more forced interpretation of the verse.

[10]See Lieberman (TK, p. 483) who offers this interpretation of the way in which the trees are arranged within the seah-space.

[11]Lieberman (TK, pp. 482-3) cites y. and other sources which discuss whether this Gamaliel is the Yavnean or the son of R. Judah the Prince. The issue, of course, has no bearing on our understanding of the law.

[12]So Maimonides (Comm.), as well as MS. Sens, followed by TYY, interprets mwqpwt Ctrh as meaning "surrounded by a fence." The phrase which immediately precedes, "formed in a line," however, strongly suggests that the rule refers to the arrangement of the trees with the seah-space, as Maimonides proposes.

[13]Jastrow, p. 311, s.v., dlCt, translates, "bottle-shaped gourd, a general name for cucumbers, pumpkins, etc." See also Felix (Sabbatical, p. 75), who identifies this plant as Lagenaria vulgaris commonly known as the calabash gourd.

[14]See Felix (Sabbatical, p. 62), who explains that young trees, which do not have extensive root systems, need to be plowed during the summer in order to survive.

[15]TYY and Bert., on the basis of y. Sheb. 1:6, interpret E in light of Simeon b. Gamaliel's lemma at F-G. On this reading, E's rule applies only if the number of saplings is greater than the number of gourds, a qualification which Simeon then disputes. The two rulings, however, are formally separate and nothing in the language of E suggests that this is its point.

[16]I assume that there is no significance to the proportions, specified at A, of chate-melons to gourds to saplings.

[17]Maim. (Comm.) correctly notes that Eleazar's ruling could refer either to the fourth year of a tree's growth, when its fruit is redeemed and then eaten, or to the fifth year, when the fruit may be eaten forthwith. See y. Sheb. 1:6 which considers this question and determines that the fifth year is intended.

[18]See MR's comment on Eleazar's lemma, that the laws of Lev. 19:23-25 have nothing to do with the question at hand. He suggests tentatively that Eleazar's definition of a sapling is based on an interpretation of Lev. 19:23, "when you plant any tree for food." That is, only when the fruit of a tree is available for food, after five years, is it called a "tree."

[19]See T. 1:3 below, which offers this interpretation of Joshua's lemma. See also Felix (Sabbatical, p. 78) who cites T. and suggests that it is botanically accurate.

[20]Maim. (Comm.) and Lieberman (TK, p. 484) suggest that A-D refers to a tree stump which sprouts shoots, the case of M. 1:8E-G. I have rejected this interpretation, for T. neither refers to this rule in Mishnah nor depends on it for its sense.

NOTES TO CHAPTER TWO

[1] This unit of law, as we shall see, encompasses produce that grows over any two successive years, not only from the sixth into the seventh year. Nonetheless, the rule clearly has been placed here because it has special bearing on the laws of the Sabbatical year.

[2] These rules are found in Chapters Eight and Nine.

[3] Jastrow (p. 690, s.v., lbn) following TYT, TYY interprets the origin of the expression śdh lbn to be that a grain field, unlike an orchard, is "a bright, shadeless field." Sens in his comment to M. Peah 3:1 suggests that the term refers to the fact that vegetables become pale when they ripen.

[4] Bert. interprets mqs'wt and mdlᶜwt as referring to the chate-melons and gourds themselves. TYY objects that the words must refer to the fields in which these plants grow. This issue, so far as I can tell, has no bearing on the point of the rule at C.

[5] This parallelism indicates that the redactor of these rules has carefully phrased the unit of law before us as the beginning of a new stage in the unfolding of the tractate's discussion.

[6] My understanding of these and all other agricultural activities referred to below relies upon Felix (Sabbatical, pp. 90-118) who offers a detailed discussion of the purpose of each type of activity.

[7] See the extended discussion of manuring in White, Roman Farming, Chapter Five.

[8] White explains the importance of pruning vines as follows:

> The natural habit of the vine, if left to itself, is to grow prolifically in all directions from the stock, running to wood or leaf or both, the precious fruit-bearing shoots being choked, twisted or otherwise impeded by rank and useless growth . . . This means regular attention at different seasons of the year [is necessary], pruning in autumn or spring according to the climate, root-pruning and stock-cleaning in winter, moulding, shaping and tying, trimming of the leaves, and many other operations before the final stage of the vintage is reached in autumn.
>
> (pp. 237-238)

[9] Albeck, in line with Maimonides' (Comm.) reading of L, suggests that Joshua claims that the length of time during which the farmer may prune fruit of the sixth year must correspond to the length of time during which he pruned fruit of the preceding season. If, for example, he finished pruning the fruit of the fifth year before New Year of the sixth year, he likewise must stop pruning the crop of the sixth year before New Year of the seventh. See also Felix, Sabbatical, p. 102. Neither Albeck nor Felix, however, explains the rationale that underlies the position that they attribute to Joshua. My interpretation of the rule, based on y. 2:2[33d], is followed by Sens, Bert. and TYY. On this reading, Joshua permits pruning fruit during the Sabbatical year itself so long as the farmer merely continues an agricultural activity that he began during the sixth year. See also M. 3:6K-N, which makes the same point with respect to removing stones from a field during the seventh year.

[10]My interpretation follows Correns, (p. 45, note 23) who notes that Simeon at M. 2:5Y-Z and 2:10H, J also is assigned lenient rulings regarding agricultural activities permitted during the Sabbatical year. Maimonides (Comm.), Sens, TYY and Bert., following y. 2:2[33d], claim that Simeon allows pruning only until Pentecost of the sixth year, the point at which plowing must cease (see M. 1:1). This interpretation, however, ignores the fact that the purposes of these two activities are quite different. Plowing serves to improve the fruit of the seventh year, which is forbidden. By contrast, caring for a tree during the seventh year will prevent damage to the tree, and so is permissible. It should also be noted, in support of my interpretation, that Simeon explicitly permits farmers during the Sabbatical year to remove dead leaves from vines (see M. 2:2G), which serves the same function as pruning trees.

[11]So Lieberman (TK, p. 488) who notes that the citation of Mishnah at A-B strongly suggests that the dispute which follows likewise refers to watering saplings during the sixth year. The Shammaite position is also attributed to Eleazar b. Sadoq at M. 2:4P, where the rule explicitly refers to watering trees during the Sabbatical year itself.

[12]In this connection, see y. Sheb. 2:3, cited by Lieberman (TK, p. 488) which claims that the Eliezer mentioned at C is Eliezer b. Shammua, an Ushan.

[13]See y. Git. 3:5, which claims that in Galilee vines were generally pruned during or after Tabernacles, and in Judah, before Tabernacles.

[14]So Theophrastus, IV, 16, 5, cited by Lieberman, TK, p. 491. Lieberman appears to reject this interpretation in favor of the view expressed at b. A.Z. 40b, that the procedure is intended to benefit the tree. This interpretation, however, does not seem to make sense of T.'s rule that spreading resin on roots is prohibited, but doing so on leaves is permitted. My reading of the rule resolves this problem and seems to accord with the botanical information provided by Theophrastus.

[15]So Lieberman, TK, p. 492. This interpretation poses a slight problem, for the parallel construction of G and H suggests that the force of the participle in both clauses is the same. On Lieberman's reading, however, G rules that one is allowed to graft branches while H's point is that one is required to cut off a branch which has been grafted. I have adopted Lieberman's view, nonetheless, for I can find no other way of making sense of the rule.

[16]See Loew (Flora, I, p. 235), cited by Lieberman (TK, p. 492), who claims that this was a common practice in the ancient world.

[17]See also y. Sheb. 4:4 and b. Hul. 77b-78a. This interpretation of the pericope also is adopted by MB. See Lieberman, TK, p. 492, for a discussion of these sources.

[18]See Jastrow (p. 252, s.v., gmz) who notes that this process is called "caprification." See also T. 1:9D and Lieberman's comment, TK, p. 491. Caprification is "intended to hasten the ripening of cultivated figs and to improve the quality of the fruit, by suspending above the tree branches of the caprifig containing a species of wasps, which spread themselves over the whole tree, distributing the pollen of the male flowers." Webster's Twentieth Century Dictionary (1978:270).

[19]So Lieberman (TK, pp. 493-4) who cites Theophrastus (I, 8, 5), who explains that "the eye of a vine" is the point on the stem from which new branches sprout.

[20]Lieberman (TK, p. 494) interprets D as a continuation of the rule at T. 1:10, that blinding a vine weakens it and thus helps it to yield its fruit. But T. 1:10 speaks of a tree, while this rule concerns vines. Moreover, as Lieberman himself notes, blinding a vine does not weaken, but strengthens it, for this procedure prevents it from sending forth new shoots.

[21]Bert., on the basis of b. R.H. 10b, claims that the thirty days referred to at A (as well as the time periods mentioned at D and E) do not include a separate period of thirty days prior to New Year when all agricultural activity must cease. The language of the rule before us, however, does not support this reading.

[22]See Lieberman (TK, p. 495) for an extended discussion of these and other variant readings of this rule.

[23]So Lieberman (TZ, p. 168) who notes that the Biblical name for this plant is 'hl.

[24]So Freimark, p. 157, and Loew, Flora, II, pp. 149ff.

[25]Lieberman (TK, p. 495) attempts to explain this rule in light of T. 2:11 which requires people to uproot soft-stemmed plants during the Sabbatical year, for they appear to have been planted recently, in violation of the law. It is not clear to me, however, why aloes should be an exception to this rule, as Lieberman claims, nor does he account for the prohibition against watering these plants during the Sabbatical year (I). My interpretation relies on the immediately preceding rule (F-G) that potted plants (such as aloes) are exempt from the restrictions of the Sabbatical year.

[26]So Klein to Maimonides, Sabbatical, 4:11, and Danby. Jastrow, p. 254, s.v., dwhn translates "a species of millet."

[27]So Klein to Maimonides, Sabbatical, 4:11. Danby translates "panic."

[28]So Danby and Jastrow, p. 1537 s.v., šwmšwm.

[29]Jastrow, p. 1141, s.v., pwl translates "the Egyptian bean (Colocasia)."

[30]Jastrow, p. 100, s.v., 'pwn.

[31]So Danby. Jastrow, p. 184, s.v., bsl translates "onions which produce no seeds." In the context of the present rule, however, it is apparent that these onions are being raised for their seeds.

[32]Jastrow, p. 182, s.v., bᶜl translates "a field sufficiently watered by rain and requiring no artificial irrigation." The dispute which follows this dispute, however, clearly indicates that periodic watering in such a field is necessary.

[33]See M. Peah 3:2 which discusses the gradual harvesting of grain over an extended period of time. The same point is made with respect to the present rule in Rashi's comments on b. R.H. 13b.

[34]So Cahati (p. 353) who explains Eleazar's position in this way.

[35]So Lieberman, TK, p. 501, who explains the procedure in this way.

[36]So Jastrow, p. 1519, s.v., šbt. Lieberman, on the basis of Loew (Flora, III, p. 466) identifies this plant as anethum.

[37]So Jastrow, p. 623, s.v., kwsbr and Lieberman who cites Loew, Flora, III, pp. 441ff.

[38]Jastrow, p. 1548, s.v., šhlyym translates "a kind of cress or pepperwort (Lepidium sativum)."

[39]See Lieberman (TK, p. 504) and Jastrow (p. 264, s.v., grgyr) who translates "the stimulating plant garden-rocket, Eruca."

[40]See Lieberman (TK, p. 505) who identifies this plant with the shallots referred to at M. 2:9.

[41]Lieberman (TK, pp. 505-6) suggests that trampling the tops of the onions prevents seeds from further growth and so allows the bulbs of the onions to grow larger. The point of the rule, however, would appear to be that the farmer intends to grow onions for seeds and so I assume that this is the manner in which he harvests them.

[42]Felix (Sabbatical, p. 162) explains tmrwt as "the soft shoots at the ends of stalks, which are edible as a vegetable."

[43]Jastrow, p. 845, s.v., mrs translates "stir (mix) the ground of a rice field with water (so as to make it dough-like)."

[44]See Correns, who interprets mkshyn as weeding, not trimming. The point in either case, however, is the same. This is part of the process of cultivation and so is prohibited during the Sabbatical year.

[45]See Felix (Sabbatical, pp. 162 and 165) who explains the purpose of trimming rice plants in this way.

NOTES TO CHAPTER THREE

[1]See Bert., who adopts this reading. The difference between the two readings is of little importance, for in either case, Meir's lemma refers to the point at which manuring no longer is assumed to benefit crops.

[2]So Felix, Sabbatical, p. 170 and TYY. This interpretation of mtwq accords with its meaning in M. 9:6. Bert., Sens and Correns, however, claim that the word refers to the moisture in the dung itself. Albeck offers yet another reading and claims that a certain species of "sweet" grass is under discussion. For a complete account of the possible meanings of mtwq and the justifications for each, see Correns, pp. 59-60.

[3]See Felix, Sabbatical, p. 170. Alternatively, the subject of Yose's ruling might be dung; see note 2 above.

[4]For a full account of the process of manuring, see Felix, Agriculture, pp. 102-6.

[5]See y. Sheb. 3:1[34c], which notes that the two views are nearly identical.

[6]So Albeck, p. 144. See also Blackman, p. 249, who claims that the total amount of dung in each pile is equivalent to 47 gallons.

[7]My understanding of Simeon follows Bert., TYY and Sens. Alternatively, Simeon's point might be that so long as the farmer does not intend to fertilize the field, the fact that he may appear to be transgressing is of no importance. This position, as we shall see, is taken by Judah and Yose in T. 2:15. Nothing in the wording of Simeon's lemma permits us to determine definitively which principle underlies his ruling.

[8]The bulk of the MSS evidence indicates that the word mhsyb should not be here. See TYT, who suggest that the word has been added here by mistake on the basis of a similar phrase at M. 3:6, which reads: wphwt mkn mhsyb. It should be noted that, without the word in question, Simeon's rule reiterates the position attributed to him at M. 3:2G. For an explanation of the meaning of this rule if the word mhsyb is retained, see Felix, Agriculture, pp. 110-11.

[9]The position attributed to sages, Meir and Eleazar also lends itself to another interpretation, that the point of raising or lowering the dung heap is to prevent the manure from actually fertilizing the field. My reading, which follows the view of all the traditional commentators, takes into account the place of this pericope in the chapter's discussion. The point of the rule which immediately precedes, at M. 3:2, clearly is that by piling the manure in large heaps the farmer avoids the appearance of manuring the field. Moreover, at M. 3:4G the issue of avoiding the appearance of a transgression is stated explicitly. In their present context, therefore, the rules before us should be interpreted as addressing this same issue.

[10]So Lieberman, TK, p. 510

[11]Lieberman, TK, p. 510 suggests that the farmer's action of milking or shearing indicates that he has not brought the animals into the field in order to manure it. He also notes that milking and shearing are difficult to do within a fold, both because it is crowded and on account of the stench caused by the manure.

[12]My reading follows Maimonides, Comm. and Sabbatical, 2:6. Bert., Sens, MS and TYY interpret the rule to refer to a field in which stones are covered by dirt so that

plowing is necessary to remove them. The problem, in their view, is that the farmer who plows to remove stones will appear to be cultivating land during the Sabbatical year. The pericope, however, does not refer explicitly to plowing (compare M. 3:7), nor is it necessary to infer this fact in order to make sense of the ruling.

[13]So Lieberman (TK, p. 512), who suggests that the phrase dbr mrwbh may refer to other agricultural activities, such as watering the field in order to facilitate removing the stones.

[14]My decision to read M. 3:5 in this way is supported by the fact that the rulings which precede and follow (M. 3:1-4, 6-7) clearly are concerned with avoiding the appearance of committing a transgression.

[15]My reading follows Maim., Comm., and Bert. Sens understands the word mhsb to mean "quarry" and interprets E to mean that in the case at hand, the rules of M. 3:5, which govern quarries, apply. He thus ignores the fact that both B-C and the contrasting rule at D-F respond to the superscription at A. There are thus no grounds for reading this rule in light of the facts stipulated in the preceding pericope.

[16]Sens, Bert. and TYY read M. 3:5-6 as a single unit of law and so assume that the question at K refers to the entire preceding discussion. The parallel construction of G-J and K-N makes it clear that both questions refer to the immediately preceding rule, A-F.

[17]Alternatively, mdrygwt may refer to steps which are built to enable the farmer to descend into the ravine and draw the water which collects there; see Jastrow, p. 233, s.v., mdrygh and Danby. I reject this reading, however, for the only other occurrence of the word in Mishnah is at Kil. 6:2, where it clearly refers to a terrace on which vines are planted (see Danby, p. 35). See also Felix (Sabbatical, pp. 204-5), who adopts this understanding of the word and claims that it refers to terraces of the type which are commonly seen in Israel today. For more information on the cultivation of terraces, see Felix, Agriculture, pp. 50-51.

[18]Sens, Bert. and TYY, adopting the alternative understanding of mdrygwt (see note 1), claim that the issue is that the farmer who builds these steps will appear to be preparing the land for cultivation. The language at B and D, however, is unambiguous and indicates that the issue is whether the farmer will in fact prepare the ground for cultivation by building terraces. See also Felix (Sabbatical, pp. 204-5), who argues that during the sixth year the farmer may not repair terraces since he might appear to be violating the law. He may do so during the Sabbatical year itself, however, for otherwise the terraces might suffer severe damage and be destroyed by erosion entirely. This interpretation, however, rejects Mishnah's own exegesis at B and D and, furthermore, ignores the formally unitary construction of this unit of law which indicates that a single issue is under discussion throughout.

[19]So Jastrow, p. 1310, s.v., kbln. The word may also mean a tenant-farmer who rents the land at a fixed rate; see Jastrow, ibid., and Maim., Comm.. The point of the rule in either case remains substantially the same.

[20]TYY, Bert. and Sens, on the basis of y. Sheb. 3:7, read the phrase mkl mqwm as referring back to the rule of M. 3:6, that one may remove only large stones from one's own field, while stones of any size may be removed from one's neighbor's field. It is more likely, however, that the antecedent of the phrase is to be found in the immediately preceding rule, at M. 3:8. This reading also is adopted by Correns, Albeck and MR.

[21]Bert. and TYY assume that G refers to an activity performed during other years of the Sabbatical cycle. There is nothing, however, in the language or context of the rule to support this view. These commentators, as well as MS and Maimonides (Comm. and Sabbatical, 2:14), assume that G refers to the immediately preceding dispute at B-C vs. D-F, and so maintain that Joshua and Aqiba disputed the question of what to do with the dirt in this case as well. They thus ignore the fact that the dispute is formally separate from A-B and raises a quite secondary concern. G then should be read as a gloss of A, whose formal pattern it repeats, as I have noted in my comment.

[22]Lieberman (TK, p. 515) rejects ed. princ.'s inclusion of the word drk which would make the final clause of E formally parallel to those which precede it. Citing M. Men. 10:9, he claims that hspd at E refers to a house of mourning, not a road used for a funeral procession. The point of the rule on either reading would appear to be the same.

[23]Lieberman, ibid., adduces support for this emendation by citing T. 7:15 and y. Sheb. 39a, where the same word, tphym, again is mistakenly changed to sphym.

[24]See Lieberman, p. 515.

[25]Lieberman, ibid., cites T. Shab. 12:4 and 17:23, both of which refer to birds nesting in vessels which have been placed in the rafters of a house. He also draws on M. 9:4 and T. 7:15 which refer to eating produce of tpyhym during the Sabbatical year, in an attempt to interpret this rule. The context of those rulings, however, makes it apparent that the word there refers to late-ripening produce and so has no bearing on the rule before us. See my comments to those pericopae and Jastrow, p. 547, s.v., tpyh.

[26]Lieberman (TK, p. 515), relying on Sifra Behar 1:4, offers an alternative explanation of the rule. At A-C, the farmers are working for the benefit of the crop of the sixth year which remains on the branch. This is permitted. At D-G, the labor is performed for the benefit of the tree itself, which is permitted despite the fact that it may aid the produce of the Sabbatical year which still is growing. This interpretation is problematic, however, for nothing in the language of the rule suggests that the agricultural activity in question would not be performed for the same purpose in the sixth year as in the seventh.

NOTES TO CHAPTER FOUR

[1]The inclusion of the word, "stones," at A poses a problem, for the rules before us are not consistent with those at M. 3:6-7, which address the question of removing stones from a field during the Sabbatical year. This may account for the omission of the word from 12 MSS; see Sachs-Hutner, p. 31, note 2. See also Epstein (Mabo, pp. 395, 951) (followed by Lieberman, TK, p. 516) who suggests that the word "stone" entered the text by mistake on the basis of a beraita cited in y. 4:1. In the absence of any legal principle which requires distinct rules for the removal of stones as against other sorts of materials, however, I can find no compelling reason to omit the word from our text.

[2]R. Jonah, cited in y. 4:1, reads this rule together with M. 3:6H-I, which states that people may remove stones of any size from the fields of neighbors. On his reading, then, the rule at B-C establishes that one may remove only large stones from one's own field, but stones of all sizes from the fields of others. While the language of C could support this interpretation, such harmonization of these two rules is not necessary to make sense of the text before us, as my translation and comment indicate.

[3]We, of course, have no independent means of verifying whether or not this account of the law's history has any basis in reality.

[4]Alternatively, the point of E could be to prevent people from appearing to violate the law. On this reading, E is merely an extension of the rule at B-C, which serves the same purpose. Yet, in its present redactional setting, E should be read as a response to the increase in transgressions referred to at D. I therefore interpret it as a rule designed to prevent people from actually clearing their fields for cultivation, not merely from appearing to do so.

[5]The precise meaning of ntybh, "improved," (C, F) is not apparent, for the word does not appear elsewhere in Mishnah with reference to agriculture (Kasovsky, Mishnah, pp. 764-5). The idea that it refers to a field plowed during the Sabbatical year is based on T. 3:10 and is adopted by all the traditional commentators. Though T.'s interpretation is itself problematic, as I indicate below, I can find no compelling reason to reject the view that the word refers to plowing, rather than to some other agricultural activity.

[6]See Lieberman (TK, p. 517,), who claims that in the time of Shammai plowing during the Sabbatical year was permitted since this was necessary to pay the agricultural tax imposed by the Roman authorities. He then concludes that M. 4:2G, which assumes that such plowing is prohibited, derives from a later period. See, however, Neusner (Pharisees, I, p. 196), who notes that the economic necessity of working the land during the Sabbatical year should have increased, rather than lessened, in the generations after 70.

[7]The phrase mhzyq yd may mean either to encourage (verbally) or to assist (physically). See Jastrow (p. 444, s.v., hzq,), who adopts the former reading with respect to the rule before us. My reading accords with the translations of Correns and Danby. It should be noted that both readings are supported by the context of the rule, for A-B refers to working the gentile's land, while E refers to communicating with gentiles. The same interpretive problem arises with respect to the parallel rule at M. 5:9J-K.

[8]For extended discussions of the sanctity of the Land of Israel in Biblical and rabbinic sources see Breuggemann, The Land (esp. pp. 47-53) and W.D. Davies, The Territorial Dimension of Judaism (esp. pp. 1-52).

[9]As Lieberman (TK, p. 518) notes, this rule refers to the year following the Sabbatical, rather than to the Sabbatical year itself (cf. M. 4:3). This is apparent from the fact that B refers to fields which have been sown, an action which of course is forbidden during that year.

[10]Lieberman, ibid., cites y. 4:2 [35b], which supports this reading.

[11]See Lieberman, ibid., who also offers another interpretation of this rule, namely, that the sages recognized that they had no authority over the actions of non-Israelites.

[12]See M. B.Q. 7:7 where this rule is stated and b. B.Q. 79b which provides this explanation of it.

[13]So Rashi, Commentary, on b. B.Q. 79b. Though his interpretation is found neither in M. B.Q. 7:7 nor in the Talmud, I can find no more satisfactory explanation of this rule consistent with the point of the pericope as a whole.

[14]Olive trees also are truncated when they get old and cease bearing fruit. By cutting back the tree, one generates new branches which eventually will yield new olives. The parallelism of the rules at A-B and C-D, however, suggests that the purpose of both actions is the same, to obtain wood for building.

[15]Bert. and TYY, relying on y. Sheb. 2:3, maintain that covering the stump with dirt benefits the tree, which is forbidden (A, C), while covering it with stones or straw merely preserves the tree, which is permitted (B, D). See also Felix, Sabbatical, pp. 259-60. This interpretation, however, ignores the fact that both procedures protect the tree and moreover, the act of truncating in both cases serves the same purpose (to obtain wood) and has the same effect (to generate the growth of new branches). My interpre- tation follows Maimonides (Sabbatical, 1:19, 21) who notes that the operative distinction is between following the ordinary procedure and deviating from it.

[16]See T. 3:15M, which explains the term "virgin tree" in this way.

[17]It is interesting to note that Bert. and TYY fail to recognize the contradiction between A-D and E-F. They simply assume that under all circumstances one who truncates a virgin tree cultivates new growth. This act, like covering the stump of a tree with dirt, benefits the tree and so is forbidden. This interpretation is unacceptable, however, for it falsely assumes that in some cases cutting back a tree generates new branches and so is forbidden (A, D, E-F), but under other circumstances it will not have this effect (B, D) and so is permitted (see note 15 above). I am indebted to William M. ("Scotty") Ansell, curator of the Brown University greenhouse, for his detailed explana- tions of the procedures for truncating trees and of the ways in which this promotes the cultivation of new branches.

[18]See M. Peah 2:7-8, where the fact that carob trees have extensive root systems determines the way in which one designates peah from groves of such trees.

[19]Following Lieberman, TK, p. 521.

[20]My interpretation of the farmer's activity at A follows that offered by Felix, Sabbatical, pp. 265-6. He notes that the verb mznyb is a technical term for cutting the ends of vines for the purpose of using the stalks. I have rejected the view of Bert. that the farmer's purpose in cutting back reeds and vines is to make the main stems thicker and stronger. If this were the case, the activity would clearly be an act of cultivation and hence forbidden.

[21]TYY, realizing that D does not respond to Yose's lemma at B, suggests that it is an independent rule which represents the view of both authorities. D, however, cannot be an independent stich, for without the context supplied by C it is unintelligible.

[22]See the parallel rule attributed to Judah at T. 3:14D-E.

[23]See Lieberman (TK, p. 523), who argues that burning reeds also may be regarded as working the land, since it has the effect of clearing an area for planting.

[24]See Jaffee, Tithing, pp. 1-6, 25-6.

[25]So Jastrow, pp. 1340-41, s.v., qwr.

[26]So Jastrow, pp. 660-1, s.v., kpnyt.

[27]I follow Maimonides (Sabbatical, 5:17-18,), Sens, MS, and GRA, who interpret hwsy' to mean producing unripe fruit. Maim., Comm., TYY, and Bert. claim that it refers to the point at which the tree produces leaves. See Felix, Sabbatical, p. 290, who notes the various usages of this verb and discusses each at length.

[28]My interpretation follows Maim. (Comm.), and Danby. See also Sens, Bert. and Felix (Sabbatical, p. 288), who claim that mšyšlw refers to the point at which the fruit itself droops.

[29]See also y. Sheb. 4:8, [35c] which claims that this is when the fruit becomes moist.

[30]My reading accords with that of b. B.Q. 91b and is adopted by Maim. (Comm., and Kings, 6:9) as well as Sens, Bert., and Correns. Contrary to the discussion of y. Sheb. 4:8[35c], it is clear that this rule does not refer to cutting down a fruitbearing tree during the Sabbatical year. The preceding rules, together with the discussion which occupies Chapter Eight of the tractate, make it clear that produce of the Sabbatical year is sanctified so that even small quantities of this fruit could not be wasted.

[31]So Correns, p. 91.

[32]See b. B.Q. 91b, which claims that if the value of the wood exceeds that of the fruit, the tree may be chopped down. This principle clearly is found nowhere in the language of the rule before us.

[33]My interpretation is confirmed by M. Ma. 5:3, where this same rule appears and clearly makes the point that one should not give transgressors the opportunity to violate the law. See also Maimonides, Sabbatical, 8:6. Lieberman (TK, p. 526), however, claims that the point of the rule is that the seller does not own this fruit and so cannot sell it. While this surely is the case, as Simeon notes at B, it cannot explain the rule at A, for this would not account for the fact that the rule refers specifically to selling an orchard to one suspected of violating the law.

[1]See Jastrow, p. 1530, s.v., šwh, II. See also M. Dem. 1:1 which classifies white figs together with varieties of wild produce. The translation "white figs" relies on the explanation found at b. Ber. 40b, that bnwt šwh are t'ny hwwrt'.

[2]So Danby, p. 44. Loew (Flora, III, pp. 347f., 517; I, p. 240), cited by Lieberman, TK, p. 527, identifies this fruit as Mimusops Schimperi.

[3]T. 4:1 claims that sages (E) reject Judah's opinion (C-D) because in fact Persian figs conclude the ripening process in a single year. This reading of E, however, assumes that Judah was ignorant of the facts concerning Persian figs. I accept the information which Mishnah provides with respect to the growing seasons of these figs, and so interpret E in accordance with the one characteristic that distinguishes Persian figs from white figs.

[4]See y. 5:2 [35d], which classifies this plant together with onions, as does M. Peah 6:10. Loew, (Flora, I, p. 214f.), identifies it as arum. Felix, (Sabbatical, p. 389), likewise identifies it as arum paleastinum specifically Black Calla or Solomon's Lily.

[5]Theophrastus, (Enquiry, I, vi, 10), refers to the practice of inverting tubers so that they do not sprout, thus causing the tuber to become larger. See also Lieberman, TK, p. 527, note 4.

[6]Maim., (Comm.), Bert. and TYY all claim that the point of A-G is to avoid the appearance of planting. These same commentators, however, assume that the point of H is to prevent the arum from sprouting new leaves. While A-G could be read in either way, I can find no compelling reason not to interpret the pericope as addressing a single issue throughout.

[7]The measurements required by sages at E and F are one third the size of those required by Meir at B and C. See the table of dry measurements in Blackman, I, p. 18.

[8]H may be read as belonging to B-D as well as to E-G. Reading the stich as I have, however, gives it some significance in the dispute between sages and Meir.

[9]The appropriate manner of making accounts with the poor, not elucidated by this rule, is spelled out in T. 4:3. See Green, Joshua, pp. 45-7, who claims that the poor are given a portion of the leaves themselves. His interpretation, however, assumes that the leaves, like the tuber, grow over a period of more than one year, which is not the case. I have relied on Felix, (Sabbatical, pp. 318-20), who explains the growing process both of arum tubers and of their leaves.

[10]See Theophrastus, (Enquiry, 1,6,10), cited by Lieberman, TK, p. 527, note 4.

[11]The view, assumed by this rule, that produce of the Sabbatical year is reserved for the poor alone, is consistent with Ex. 23:10-11. Throughout the remainder of the tractate, however, Mishnah's authorities assume that all are entitled to gather this produce, in accord with Lev. 25:1-7. This difficulty probably stands behind y. 5:3's attempt to interpret this rule in light of M. 9:8, the only other rule in our tractate that refers to the poor. In that pericope, Judah claims that only the poor, not the rich, may eat produce of the Sabbatical year after the time of removal, while Yose claims that all may do so. All the commentaries, following the Talmud, thus attempt to explain the dispute before us in terms of this dispute between Judah and Yose. These interpretations

are untenable, however, for the rule at hand refers to the right of the poor to harvest the leaves, while the law of removal comes into play only after all produce in the fields has been gathered and brought into the people's homes. (See M. 9:2ff.)

[12]Jastrow (p. 184, s.v., bsl) translates "summer onions." According to Felix, (Sabbatical, p. 336), these onions are so called because they become ripe in the summer. He also identifies these with the onions referred to at M. 2:9A.

[13]Jastrow (p. 1138, s.v., pw'h) translates "Rubia Tinctorum, dyer's madder." According to Felix, (Sabbatical, p. 337), red dye is extracted from the root of this plant.

[14]Bert. comments that "arum of the sixth year" refers to tubers that have not yet produced leaves during the Sabbatical year. Though Mishnah never spells this out, his view is plausible, for a farmer can determine whether the tubers are growing only by observing whether or not they produce new leaves.

[15]My interpretation here follows Sens. Bert. and TYY claim that since rocky soil is not generally cultivated, no issue of appearing to violate the law arises. Maim., (Comm.), arrives at the same conclusion but supports his interpretation in a different way. He understands pw'h šlšlᶜwt as "madder with spikes" that is, with roots that dig deep into the soil making them difficult to remove. Felix, (Sabbatical, p. 337), rejects this interpretation on the grounds that we know of only one type of madder.

[16]Danby here translates lqh as "to gather." I have followed the translation offered by Correns and assumed by all the traditional commentaries. See also Danby's rendering of this word as it appears in the parallel rule at M. 6:4.

[17]For this meaning of hhdš, see Jastrow, p. 427, s.v., hdš.

[18]Mishnah assumes that the arum tuber has a growing season of three years.

[19]T's addition of the phrase "under any circumstances (A) does not seem to me to change the issue of Mishnah's dispute. Lieberman, TK, p. 180, interprets the phrase mkl mqwm literally. "In all places," he claims, means even in places in which farmers are suspected of not observing the law. But this phrase does not necessarily have this locative sense and there is no reason to assume, from the substance of the ruling, that geographical location plays a role.

[20]Danby and Jastrow (p. 756, s.vv., mzrh) translate "winnowing fan." I have followed the translation of BDB (p. 280, s.v., zrh). See the discussion of this agricultural tool in Felix, (Agriculture, pp. 258-60).

[21]Jastrow (p. 320, s.v., dqr) translates "a pronged tool, mattock."

[22]Danby here translates "scythe." I have followed his translations of mgl yd and mgl qsyr found at M. Hul. 1:2 which reflect the distinction between these two tools. See Felix, (Agriculture, pp. 204-8).

[23]According to Maim. (Comm.), followed by Bert., and Albeck, the ruling against selling instruments applies only to a buyer who is suspected of not observing the laws of the Sabbatical year. This distinction is unknown to the pericope before us.

[24]The principle that Israelites may gather only a limited quantity of produce at one time never is stated explicitly by M.-T. It may be inferred from this rule and, even more clearly, from that which follows, at M. 5:7. Moreover, this principle follows logically from the notion that produce of the Sabbatical year is ownerless, a theory worked out in detail in Chapters Eight and Nine.

[25]The notion developed here, that in doubtful cases we assume that a desirable rather than an undesirable situation will come about, is common in Mishnah. For another example of this principle in the context of agricultural law, see T. Ter. 6:13-17.

[26]Sens and TYY claim that the Shammaites would agree with the rulings at C-E and make an exception only in the case of selling a heifer, for people rarely slaughter an

animal which they could use to work the land. While this issue has no bearing on our understanding of the substance of these rules, it appears preferable to assign to the Houses consistent positions with regard to all transactions that could lead to transgressions.

NOTES TO CHAPTER SIX

[1]There is no explicit mention in Scripture of the boundaries of the Land of Israel during the period after the Babylonian exile. For reconstructions of the approximate boundaries of the Land at this time see EJ, 9:119 and The Westminster Historical Atlas to the Bible (Philadelphia, 1956), p. 51.

[2]Kezib is the city known in Scripture as Akzib, located north of Acre. See Jastrow, p. 62, s.v., 'kzyb.

[3]My reading of the phrase l' n'kl follows Maim., Comm. This interpretation is consistent with the rule at M. 4:21, the only other place in the tractate which prescribes circumstances under which produce of the Sabbatical year may not be eaten. There the Hillelites rule that one may not eat produce which others have handled in violation of the law, for one thereby becomes an accessory to their transgression. The phrase, however, lends itself to other interpretations. Maimonides, Sabbatical 4:26, claims that this rule prohibits eating produce that grows uncultivated from the seeds that dropped during the previous year's harvest (spyh). Sens, for his part, suggests that the rule prohibits people from eating produce after the Sabbatical year has ended unless it has been handled in accordance with the laws of removal (see Chapter Nine).

[4]Many commentators hold that hnhr refers to the Euphrates. This meaning of the word, although attested in Scripture (see BDB, p. 625, s.v., nhr), must be rejected. First, the Euphrates, like the mountains of Amana, is north of Kezib. If "the river" referred to the Euphrates, the rule at D would determine two separate northern borders while leaving the southern border unspecified. Moreover, the brook of Egypt is mentioned in Scripture as the southern border of the country during this period (Num. 34:5, Joshua 15:4, I Kings 8:65). Finally, T. Ter. 2:12 and T. Hal. 2:11 likewise establish this river as the Land's southern border.

[5]The geographical boundaries only make sense if we read wlhws in place of wlpnym. See Sachs-Hutner, p. 51, note 13 and Sifre Dt., 51. The same textual problem occurs at T. Ter. 2:12. Compare, however, the parallel ruling at T. Hal. 2:11 which has lhln where the former reads lpnym.

[6]For the sake of consistency, I have followed Jastrow in my transliterations of the place names occuring in the following material. As a result, my translations at L and O follow the test of y. Sheb. 6:1 [36d]. Where possible, I have cited other sources which provide more positive identification of the sites. According to Avi-Yonah (Geography, p. 155) N'vay was the capitol of Bashan; see also his map of this and surrounding regions, Avi-Yonah, p. 151.

[7]Jastrow, p. 1271. Trye, however, was not in this region. Klein (Transjordan, p. 42) identifies this as Tsaria, east of N'vay. See Avi-Yonah, p. 151.

[8]Jastrow, p. 1276. Perhaps Taryia, south of Tsaria; Klein, p. 42.

[9]Identified as Jasim, north of N'vay by Klein, p. 42. See Avi-Yonah, p. 151.

[10]Jastrow, p. 393. Also Zazun, southwest of N'vay. See Avi-Yonah, p. 151, 3.

[11]Jastrow, p. 563. Identified as Atmon, east of Zazun; Klein, p. 42.

[12]Jastrow, p. 315. Also Danibah, east of N'vay. See Avi-Yonah, p. 151, 3.

[13]Not identified by any of the sources available to me.

[14]The places on the following list were in the vicinity of Tyre.

[15]Jastrow, p. 1620, s.v., ṣ̌st

[16]Jastrow, p. 185. See Avi-Yonah, p. 149.

[17]Jastrow, p. 823. See Avi-Yonah, p. 149.

[18]Jastrow, P. 483. See Avi-Yonah, p. 149.

[19]Jastrow, p. 1478, s.v., ryṣ̌

[20]Jastrow, p. 666. Apparently a derogatory reference to Beit Badya, so Lieberman (TK, p. 533) on the basis of b. A.Z. 46a.

[21]Jastrow, p. 1090. Lieberman (TK, p. 533) reads Amon, following y. Dem. 2:1 [22d]. Perhaps the ruins of Hamon near Ein Hamel, north of Mazi.

[22]Jastrow, p. 754. Identified with ruins of Mazi, near Sulma of Tyre. See Lieberman, TK, p. 533.

[23]Jastrow, p. 967. Opposite Tiberias, above the Sea of Galilee.

[24]Jastrow, p. 1069. Identified as El-Unish north of Susita by Klein, p. 37. See Avi-Yonah, p. 151.

[25]Not identified.

[26]Jastrow, p. 194. Also Ram-Berek; see Avi-Yonah, p. 151.

[27]Jastrow, p. 1068. See Avi-Yonah, pp. 151, 3.

[28]Jastrow, p. 584. Also Harbat-al-Arayis; see Avi-Yonah, p. 151, 8. In ed. princ., this place name appears conjoined with the preceding as ᶜyn yᶜryt.

[29]Following y. Dem. 2:1 [22d]. The place name which appears in V, kpr yᶜrym cannot be identified.

[30]Jastrow, p. 883. Northeast of Susita; see Avi-Yonah, pp. 151, 8.

[31]Jastrow, p. 489. Northeast of Susita; see Avi-Yonah, pp. 151, 8.

[32]Jastrow, p. 1287. Southwest of Susita; see Avi-Yonah, pp. 151, 8.

[33]For a comparison of the parallels and manuscript versions of this text, see S. Klein, The Boundaries of Eretz Israel According to the Tannaim, in Studies in the Geography of Eretz Israel (Jerusalem: Mossad Harav Kook, 1965, Hebrew translated from original German by H. Bar-Daroma). In the following list I have footnoted only those places which can be tentatively identified.

[34]Jastrow, p. 1244. Road from Ashkelon to Sidon. See Lieberman, TK, p. 534.

[35]Jastrow, 1626. Also, Tower of Sharshon, identified as Tower of Satraton by Lieberman, TK, p. 534.

[36]Jastrow, p. 1603. On the Mediterranean coast, north of Kisrin; so Lieberman, TK, p. 534. See also, Avi-Yonah, pp. 129-30.

[37]Jastrow, p. 1541.

[38]Jastrow, p. 262. On Maphshuah River, 10 km. southeast of Achzib; so Lieberman, TK, p. 534.

[39]Jastrow, p. 610. Kabrath-al-kabri, 5 km. southeast of Achzib; so Lieberman, TK, p. 534.

[40]Identified as Kabrath Zawinita, 1 km. northeast of Kabritha; so Lieberman, TK, p. 535.

[41]Jastrow, p. 1409. Located 13 km. northeast of Achzib; so Lieberman, TK, p. 535.

[42]Jastrow, p. 1324. According to Lieberman, "the wells of Aitha" (TK, p. 535).

[43]Jastrow, p. 625. Identified as Karbath-al-Kura, 8 km. northeast of Aitha by Lieberman, TK, p. 535.

[44]Jastrow, p. 764. North of Khurah; so Lieberman, TK, p. 535.

[45]Jastrow, p. 933. Identified as Marj Iyun, Lieberman, TK, p. 536.

[46]Jastrow, p. 1395. Identified as Al-Kanoth, northwest of the mountains of Horan; so Lieberman, TK, p. 537.

[47]Jastrow, p. 425. Located south of Kenath, so Lieberman, TK, p. 537.

[48]Jastrow, p. 567. The River of Yabok; see Avi-Yonah, p. 162.

[49]Jastrow, p. 411. See Avi-Yonah, p. 171.

[50]According to y. 6:2 [36d] the purpose of this rule is two fold. It assures that people will not emigrate to Syria in order to avoid being subject to the restrictions of the Sabbatical year. Moreover, it enables those for whom these restrictions are excessively burdensome to find relief in Syria, so that they will not move to other countries. This interpretation, however, is suspect, for Syria's abiguous status is not limited to the law of the Sabbatical year and so should not be explained in these terms. I have chosen to read this rule in light of the immediately proceding pericope, M. 6:1, which specifically links the Israelites' occupation of geographical regions to the restrictions that apply within them. See also M. Hal. 4:7, 11; T. Kel. BK 1:5; T. Ter. 2:9-13; T. A.Z. 2:8; T. Peah 4:6.

[51]For a discussion of the extent of Jewish settlement in Syria, see Tcherikover, Hellenistic Civilization and the Jews, pp. 188-9 and EJ, 15:636-9.

[52]The rule at B does not explicitly state that one may perform these activities in Syria during the Sabbatical year without deviating from the usual practice, as one is required to do in the Land. This understanding of B1, however, is proposed by all the traditional commentators, who recognize that the point of A-B clearly is to contrast the restrictions applicable in Syria with those that govern produce grown in the Land.

[53]Lieberman (TZ, p. 181) reads 'tw "with him (i.e., the gentile)" in place of 'wtw "it (i.e., the agricultural activity)." Lieberman's reading, however, requires that both the singular 'tw and the subsequent plural hn refer to the gentile(s), while Cwsyn and 'wgd refer to the Israelite(s). Reading 'wtw as I have, avoids this confusion. Furthermore, 'wtw is used in exactly this sense in M. 6:2D.

[54]Reading Cwtm for 'wtm, following Lieberman (TZ, p. 182). See Jastrow, p. 1063, s.v., Ctn.

[55]I have followed the interpretation of HD for this lemma.

[56]Lieberman reads I-M as referring to the question of when in the year following the Sabbatical one is permitted to buy vegetables (see M. 6:4). His reading requires the emendation of the text from mlkt byd to lwkh myd, which is not necessary in the light of my interpretation. See Lieberman, TZ, p. 182; TK, p. 539.

[57]I have followed the interpretation of Sens and Bert. for A-C. See, however, Maimonides, Comm. and Sabbatical 4:20. On his view, the onions bulbs were uprooted in

the sixth year and lay on the ground during the Sabbatical year at which time they sprouted leaves. This produce is not subject to the restrictions of the seventh year. The issue relates only to the leaves. So long as they are green, they are deemed to be part of the exempt bulb. Once they have darkened, however, they are considered to be growing in the ground and are forbidden. While this is a plausible interpretation of A-C, Maimonides interprets D-E to refer to the bulbs of the onions. A unitary reading of the pericope is preferable, for D-E, which refers to uprooting onions that grow underground, is intelligible only in light of the rule at A-C. See also Sens and Bert., who interpret E as a continuation of A-C, rather than of D. On their view, the onions referred to at E finished growing in the sixth year and were uprotted during that year. They were subsequently planted in the Sabbatical year, grew for a time, and were uprooted (a second time) during the Sabbatical year. Finally, they were planted for a third time in the year following the Sabbatical. These onions are permitted, since the portions that grew during the sixth and eighth years exceed the portion that grew during the seventh. This interpretation clearly assumes a situation far too complex to be a plausible reading of E. My reading of the pericope both avoids such unnecessary complexities and makes sense of all the rulings with reference to a single issue.

[58]The ruling at C does not refer specifically to produce from more than one place and could be referring to portions of a crop which ripen separately in the same place. Interpreted in this way, however, the ruling merely states what is obvious. The interpretation followed here is preferable and is supported by T. 4:1A-C.

[59]The underlying assumption of this rule is that most vegetables, which begin to grow and ripen within a single calendar year, are subject to the restrictions of that year. This contrasts sharply with the rule governing produce that grows over more than one year, the status of which is a matter of dispute (see M. 5:1, 5).

[60]This interpretation, though problematic, is preferable to those offered by the Talmud, which explain Rabbi's rule with reference to special circumstances not mentioned in our text. At y. 6:4, the Talmud suggests that Rabbi's rule is consistent with his veiw that during the Sabbatical year he permitted the importation of produce from outside the Land of Israel (see T. 4:16-18). He assumes, therefore, that produce for sale at the beginning of the eighth year grew outside the Land and so is exempt from the restrictons of the law. This interpretation may be rejected, however, for it renders the question at A unnecessary. Even during the Sabbatical year itself one could buy vegetables that had grown outside of the Land. A second interpretation, presented at y. Peah 7:3, claims that Rabbi made his rule in response to a specific incident. People once came to him during the year following the Sabbatical with vegetables that they claimed had sprouted and ripened in the space of only a few days. This story, which first appears in a document redacted two centuries after Rabbi's death, is not plausible as an explanation of his rule.

[61]See Jaffee, Tithing, p. 1.

[62]Lieberman (TK, p. 540) suggests that the vegetable referred to may be the garlic, arum or onions mentioned at T. 4:14D.

[63]The redactor of T. changed the grammatical subject of Rabbi's ruling of M. 6:4D from singular to plural so that the verb "permitted" (htyrw) would be identical in all three rulings.

[64]A kind of gourd, the leaves of which are edible; so Jastrow, pp. 1421-2.

[65]So Jastrow, p. 266.

[66]See M. R.H. 1:1. For Scripture, the beginning of the new calendar year is in Tishre. See Lev. 25:9.

[67]See Encyclopedia Britannica, Eleventh Edition, vol. 10, pp. 332-3: "Fig trees usually bear two crops--one in the early summer from buds of the last year, the other in autumn from those on the spring growth; the latter forms the chief harvest. Many of the immature receptacles drop off from imperfect fertilization . . ."

[68]This assumes that Aqiba accepted Gamaliel's view (see M. Bik. 2:6 and T. Sheb. 4:21B) that citrons are liable to the tithes of the year in which they are picked.

[69]This assumes that Aqiba accepted the Shammaite view (see M. R.H. 1:1 and T. Sheb. 4:21) that the first of Shebat begins the new year for fruit-bearing trees.

[70]See Neusner, Pharisees, II, pp. 80-81. See also Liberman, TK, pp. 545-6 for a discussion of the many sources relevant to this pericope.

[71]A district in S.E. Asia Minor; so Jastrow, p. 1361.

NOTES TO CHAPTER SEVEN

[1]This is the only occurrence of this verb used in the present sense in Mishnah-Tosefta. See Jastrow, p. 1331, s.v., qwn.

[2]Jastrow, p. 700, s.v., lwp.

[3]So Danby. Jastrow, p. 315, s.v., dndn', translates "mint," following Maim. (Comm.)

[4]So Danby. Jastrow, p. 1052, s.v., ᶜwlšyn, translates "endives."

[5]Jastrow, p. 667, s.v., kryw'.

[6]Jastrow, p. 1448, s.v., rgylh.

[7]Jastrow, p. 464, s.v., hlb translates "ornithogalum, Star of Bethlehem, a bulbous plant." Danby translates "asphodel."

[8]Jastrow, pp. 430-1, s.v., hwh'.

[9]Jastrow, p. 321, s.v., drdr.

[10]Jastrow, p. 55, s.v., 'ystys. The plant itself is a perennial (see New Columbia Encyclopedia, p. 2997). The aftergrowths referred to here, however, are not perennial and so, meet the criteria of M. 7:1B2.

[11]So Danby. Likewise, Correns (Sabbatical, p. 115, note 16) who cites Loew (Flora, I, 394ff.) and Dalman (Arbeit, II, p. 300) in support of this translation. Jastrow, p. 1340, s.v., qwsh, translates "madder, a plant used in dyeing red."

[12]The reading followed here creates the proper contrast with M. 7:1. It is the change in the defining characteristics listed at B2 which accounts for the change in the ruling regarding removal (E-F). Also, reading the rule as I have accords with the lists of produce at G-J.

[13]So Danby, Jastrow, p. 1123, s.v., ᶜrqblyn, translates "Palm-ivy." See Loew, Flora, IV, p. 72.

[14]See Jastrow, p. 464, s.v., hlbsyn. Danby translates "Bethlehem-star."

[15]Jastrow, p. 145, s.v., bwkry', translates "an aromatic plant supposed to be hazelwort or spike-nard." See also Correns, Sabbatical, p. 116, note 21.

[16]Jastrow, p. 1138, s.v., pw'h, translates "puah, Rubia Tinctorum, dyer's madder."

[17]So Danby. Jastrow, p. 1480, s.v., rkp', translates "a tuberous-rooted plant used for dyeing (cyclaminus)."

[18]Mishnah does not say explicitly that this money may be used only for the purchase of other produce. This conclusion follows logically from the ruling of M. 8:7D-E and appears in Maimonides' codification of these laws; see Sabbatical, 7:1.

[19]So Danby to M. Pes. 2:6. See the New Columbia Encyclopedia, p. 2103, which notes that "most species of pepperwort are weedy, but one--the garden cress (Lapidium sativum)--is sometimes cultivated as an annual salad plant."

[20]Jastrow, p. 501, s.v., hrhbyn', translates "creeper on palm trees." See New Columbia Encyclopedia, p. 529, which notes that true endive has been used as a salad vegetable since antiquity.

[21]Jastrow, p. 375, s.v., wrd.

[22]Jastrow, p. 773, s.v., myl', translates "a species of oak from which the gallnut is collected (quercus infectoria) or the acorns of which are used as tanning material (quercus aegilops or Oak of Bashan)."

[23]So Jastrow, p. 640, s.v., klwpsyn translates "Lesbians, a species of figs."

[24]It seems that the insects which live on the leaves, rather than the leaves themselves, are the source of the dye. See New Columbia Encyclopedia, p. 1982: "The Mediterranean Kermes oak (Quercus coccifera) is host to the kermes insect, source of the world's oldest dyestuff." See also the entry, "Kermes," ibid., p. 1470.

[25]A plant used for dyeing; so Lieberman (TK, p. 549) on the basis of Loew (Flora, I, p. 595). Jastrow (p. 720, s.v., lšyšyt) translates "juice of a plant used for drying" (presumably should be "dyeing").

[26]See footnote 20 above. This plant appears at M. 7:2Z as a perennial which is not subject to removal. See Lieberman's extended discussion of the sources related to the identity of this plant, TK, p. 550. See also, Loew, Flora, I, p. 598.

[27]So Jastrow, p. 597, s.v., yr^cnh. See also Loew, Flora, I, p. 359.

[28]So Jastrow, p. 150, s.v., bwryt. See also Loew, Flora, I, p. 642ff.

[29]So Jastrow, p. 20, s.v., 'hl. See also Loew, Flora, ibid.

[30]So Jastrow, p. 11, s.v., 'gh.

[31]Jastrow, p. 21, s.v., 'wg, translates "red berry of the Venus summachtree." On this and on the preceeding plant name, see Lieberman, TK, p. 551. Sumac leaves are high in tannin, used as mordant in dyeing.

[32]Jastrow, p. 1223, s.v., prh translates "White Blossom, name of an aromatic shrub."

[33]See footnote 10 above. See also Lieberman, TK, p. 551 and Loew, Flora, I, pp. 494ff.

[34]Husks of pomegranates have medicinal value as vermifuge.

[35]Walnut shells are used as a dye. See New Columbia Encyclopedia, p. 2923.

[36]Jastrow, p. 271, s.v., gr^cyn translates "globule, especially the stone or kernel of a stone fruit, nut, etc." See Bert., who says they are edible. According to Correns, Sabbatical, p. 117, note 29, they are used in making dye.

[37]This reading is supported by T. 5:10, Nachmanides' Commentary to Lev. 25:5 and Tosafot to b. A.Z. 62a among others. See the lengthy note in Sachs-Hutner, pp. 60-1.

[38]So Correns, Sabbatical, p. 117, note 31.

[39]Bert. and TYY claim that the point of H, that the son may sell produce that the father has gathered, is that this avoids the appearance of engaging in business. The rule which follows at I-J, however, strongly suggests that we are dealing with a householder who has bought produce for his household, as indicated by the fact that his son takes the

excess food to the market. Moreover, the entire discussion clearly concerns the definition of a business transaction, while the issue of avoiding the appearance of committing a transgression is not raised.

[40]So Jastrow, p. 1156. s.v., ptm.

[41]Jastrow, p. 624, s.v., kwpry translates "Village dog, ferocious dog." Likewise Freimark, Schebiit, p. 224. See, however, Lieberman, TK, p. 552, note 27.

[42]So Jastrow, p. 443, s.v., hwldh.

[43]Reading with Lieberman, TZ, p. 187, note 22.

[44]Jastrow, p. 750, s.v., mwryys translates "brine, pickle containing fish-hash and sometimes wine."

[45]So Jastrow, p. 206, s.v., gbynh; see also p. 29, s.v., 'wnyyqy.

[46]So Jastrow (p. 411, s.v., zrd), who also notes that the interior portion of these sprouts was eaten as a relish.

[47]I can find no botanical evidence which confirms or denies that these types of produce meet the criterion of produce subject to removal.

[48]Jastrow, p. 66, s.v., 'lh.

[49]Jastrow, p. 145, s.v., bwtn'.

[50]So Danby; Jastrow, p. 42, s.v., 'td, translates simply "thorn."

[51]This is assumed by Mishnah's ruling. I can find no botanical information to confirm this, however.

[52]Jastrow, p. 16, s.v., 'dl, translates "garden-cress, summer-savory." See Loew (Flora, I, 505) who identifies this as lepidium latiforum.

[53]Lieberman, TK, pp. 555-6, following y. Sheb. 7:6 [37c], interprets the dispute here between Meir and sages in line with the dispute of M. 9:5. On Lieberman's view, Meir follows the opinion of Eliezer (M. 9:5B). He holds that when several sorts of produce have been stored together, they must all be removed together, as soon as the first of them disappears from the field. Sages, like Joshua (M. 9:5C), hold that they must be removed only when the last of them disappears from the field. This interpretation, however, is forced. T.'s language bears no resemblance to that of M. 9:5. Moreover, the issue raised by M. 9:5 has no place here, since T.'s problem is that only the leaves (and not the sprouts) are subject to removal. These difficulties can be avoided by interpreting the pericope in light of M. 7:5 alone.

[54]Even evergreens, such as the plants listed at B, lose some of their leaves. See New Columbia Encyclopedia, p. 2105, s.v., "perennial."

[55]So Danby; Jastrow, p. 624, s.v., kwpr, translates "cyprus flower."

[56]Jastrow, p. 1352, s.v., qtp, translates "resin gained by tapping, balsam."

[57]So Danby; Jastrow, p. 705, s.v., ltwm, translates "gum-mastich, a resin used as perfume." Jastrow also cites the interpretation of Maim. (Comm.) that lwtm is a chestnut, but correctly notes that this does not suit the context.

[58]So MR. This appears to be the correct understanding of the ruling inasmuch as henna is both a dye and the source of a perfume. See Encyclopedia Britannica, vol. 11, p. 356.

[59]Maim. (Comm.) interprets A-G in this way. In Sabbatical 7:21-22, however, he claims that at A-B the oil is exempt from removal because the rose is not yet subject to

removal, while at C-D the rose is already subject to removal and so renders the oil subject as well. He interprets E-G in line with the general rule regarding flavoring. This interpretation is unacceptable, however, for it severs A-D from E-G, while the formal contrast between them makes it clear that they are to be read as a single unit.

NOTES TO CHAPTER EIGHT

[1]So Danby; Jastrow, p. 974, s.v., sy'h, translates "a plant classified with hyssop, Satureia thymbra (savory)."

[2]So Danby; Jastrow, p. 37, s.v., 'zwb, translates "hyssop."

[3]Jastrow, p. 1343, s.v., kwrnyt, translates "thyme or origanum."

[4]Maimonides (Sabbatical, 5:11), Bert., TYT, and TYY, following y. Sheb. 8:1, interpret M. 8:1J to mean that this produce, like produce used exclusively as food for animals, may not be cooked, but must be eaten raw. Our pericope, however, knows no such distinction. Moreover, T. 5:15C-D makes it clear that the issue is using this produce as wood, rather than as animal feed.

[5]The logic of the rulings at A-B and C-D demands that this is the correct reading despite manuscript evidence to the contrary.

[6]Jastrow, p. 495, s.v., hsyr.

[7]Jastrow, p. 1524, s.v., śdh, translates "vegetable growing in the field (in the Sabbatical year)."

[8]So Lieberman (TK, p. 558), on the authority of Loew, Flora, II, p. 153ff. Jastrow, p. 1976, translates "a plant with wooly leaves, mullein."

[9]So Lieberman (TK, p. 558), who cites Pliny, book 22, ch. 22, par. 32.

[10]TYT, MS, Maimonides (Comm. and Sabbatical 5:1) cite Sifre 107 or Sifra Behar 1:10 which derive this ruling from the word thyh ("it shall be . . .") in Lev. 25:7.

[11]See Jastrow, p. 1392, s.v., qnybh, who translates "those parts of a vegetable which are stripped off, refuse."

[12]So Jastrow, p. 84, s.v., 'nygrwn.

[13]So Jastrow, p. 64, s.v., 'ksygrwn.

[14]Jastrow, p. 1122, s.v., crcr, translates "to keep a liquid in the throat for the sake of lubrication."

[15]Jastrow, p. 448, s.v., htt, translates "scab, scurf, sores."

[16]Haas, Second Tithe, pp. 41-42, translates "if their flavor is dissipated, they are permitted [to be used in this way]." While this is a plausible reading, the point of the rule seems to be not whether the spices may be used, but their status after they have been used. See also, Peck, Priestly Gift, pp. 308-9.

[17]So Jastrow, p. 68, s.v., 'lwntyt. Jastrow notes two other definitions of the term, "an aromatic water," and "a wine (vinum oenonthinum) used especially after bathing."

[18]So Jastrow, pp. 1110-1111, s.v., crb.

[19]So Jastrow, p. 1416, s.v., qrtwbl'.

[20]So Lieberman, TK, p. 563.

[21]See Jastrow, P. 263, s.v., gpt, who translates "peat made of olive peels."

[22]See Jastrow, p. 379, s.v., zg, who translates "pomace of grapes, husks, or kernels and flesh."

[23]Albeck's reading appears to be based on the interpretation offered by TYT, though in his note on p. 380, he explicitly claims to have rejected it. Most other traditional commentators make no effort to explain why B repeats what is obvious in light of A.

[24]My reading of the Hillelite view follows that of TYY and Cahati. Maimonides (Sabbatical, 6:4) suggests that the manner in which the vegetables are bound is decisive. That is, one may bind vegetables for sale in the market so long as one does so in an unusual manner, by tying them as people do in their homes. This reading presupposes, however, that there are two quite distinct ways of binding vegetables, a claim which is not supported by the language at D-E and for which Maimonides offers no other textual evidence.

[25]A coin worth three issars, Lieberman, TZ, p. 192.

[26]I have followed Lieberman's translation of qwrdwm as "inedibles." TZ, p. 192. I have not found this definition in any Hebrew dictionary nor have I found this term used this way elsewhere in M.-T. See Kasovsky, Mishnah, vol. 4, p. 1613; Tosefta, vol. 6, p. 170.

[27]This is the reason offered by Freimark, Sabbatical, p. 239. Lieberman (TK, p. 564), following Maimonides (Sabbatical 8:12), presents another plausible explanation of the rule, that one sells small ammounts of produce to people suspected of violating the law in order to sustain them.

[28]A Roman coin worth two issars, see Jastrow, p. 1143, s.v., pwndywn.

[29]Maimonides (Comm. and Sabbatical 6:12), Bert., MS, TYT, and Albeck all interpret A-D on the basis of y. Sheb. 8:4[38a]. On this reading, at A-B, the money is not subject to the restrictions of the Sabbatical year, since it was exchanged for the worker's labor, not for the produce. At C-D, by contrast, the householder buys produce of the Sabbatical year, with the result that this money does become subject to the restrictions of the law. The language at A and C, however, indiciates neither that A is a payment of wages, nor that C is a sale of produce. As I have explained the contrast between the language at A and C, it parallels the pair of rules that follows at E-F/G-H. In the first case (A-B, E-F), the two parties exchange gifts, while in the second case (C-D, G-H), they engage in a commercial transaction.

[30]See Lieberman (TK, p. 567), who notes that the rule has the same meaning with or without the negative, 'l'.

[31]This translation of hnwny (see Jastrow, p. 481) suits the present context better than the more common translation, "shopkeeper."

[32]I follow here the interpretation of y. 8:4[38a], cited by Lieberman, TK, p. 566.

[33]Both of these rulings contradict M. 7:3G. We recall that that rule prohibits gathering vegetables for the purpose of selling them altogether.

[34]E may be read either as an independent rule or as the beginning of the rule which follows, at T. 6:25F. That stich, however, is not a reapplication of the principle exemplified at C-D. We would not expect it to be introduced, therefore, by wkn (at E). Moreover, F has nothing to do with the Levite who is the subject of E. Finally, my reading is supported by b. Suk. 41a. See Lieberman's discussion, TK, pp. 567-8.

[35]This rule clearly is better suited to the case of second tithe (cf. M. M.S. 3:1) which must be eaten in Jerusalem.

[36]Jastrow, p. 858, s.v., mšrh, translates "infusion, steeping."

[37]Jastrow, p. 608, s.v., kbyšh, translates "water mixed with alkaline substanes, lye-water."

[38]The same principle is expressed at M. Erub. 3:1, M. M.S. 1:5.

[39]Following the interpretation of Lieberman, TK, p. 194, on the basis of y. 7:3[37b].

[40]Bert. and Albeck, who comment that these rules refer to money received from the sale of produce of the Sabbatical year, make no mention of using the produce itself in these ways. Their reading appears to rely on the immediately preceding rule at M. 8:4I, which refers to using money of the Sabbatical year to repay debts. This pericope, however, should not be read in light of that rule, which formally is quite separate. In any event, as we know from M. 7:1-2, the same rules apply to produce of the Sabbatical year and to money received when it is sold.

[41]Both readings of B are represented in disputes in b. A.Z. 62a and in y. 8:6[38b]. See Rashi to b. A.Z. 62a, who claims that transporters of produce may be paid with produce of the Sabbatical year, since this payment is given in the manner of a gift. This is permitted, in accordance with the rule of M. 8:5C. Nothing in the language of the rule, however, suggests that these wages were given as a gift.

[42]See Maimonides (Sabbatical 6:13) who offers a quite different reason for the rule that this money is subject to the restrictions of the Sabbatical year. He claims that these transporters of produce have violated the law by transporting more produce than they needed for their own use. They are penalized for their transgression by having their wages subject to the restrictions of the law. This interpretation, however, is unfounded, for it is neither supported by the language of T., nor necessary for making sense of the rule.

[43]Jastrow, p. 1405, s.v., qsh indicates that the verb could refer either to cutting figs or to storing them.

[44]Jastrow, p. 747, s.v., mwqsh translates both "the tool specially intended (for cutting figs)" and "the shed where figs are spread for drying."

[45]As indicated by Jastrow's translations (see notes 43 and 44 above), B-C may be read in two quite different ways. Danby translates "Seventh year figs may not be cut off with the fig-knife, but they may be cut off by a different knife;" so also Correns, Sabbatical, p. 131. This reading is also supported by TYY, and Bert. on the basis of Rashi's comment to b. Men. 54b. My interpretation follows that of Maimonides (Comm. and Sabbatical, 4:23), MS and Albeck. This interpretation is also supported by the meaning of mqsh at M. Ma. 3:2 and M. Par. 7:12. This reading fits the pericope best since the formally parallel rules at D-E and F-G refer to a change in the location of processing, rather than to a change in the manner of harvesting.

[46]So Danby. Jastrow, p. 1326, s.v., kwtby, translates "small wine or olive press with cylindrical beam."

[47]Lieberman follows the emendation of GRA, against all manuscript evidence. While neither Lieberman nor GRA provides a reason for this emendation, their reading makes sense of the pericope as a whole, for it brings the rule at B in line with those at E and F. See also Lieberman's comment to T. 8:1, TK, pp. 583-4.

[48]So Jastrow, p. 1215, s.v., prd.

[49]Following the interpretation of Maimonides (Comm. and Sabbatical 5:4) and also Bert. So also Correns, Sabbatical, pp. 131-2. Alternatively, the concern may be that the produce will be unavailable as heave-offering once it is removed, in accordance with the

restriction governing produce of the Sabbatical year (so Rashi to b. Zeb. 76a and Sens). The redactional context of the rule dictates the preferable reading. M. 8:8 deals explicitly with rendering inedible produce of the Sabbatical year. The issues of removal and of invalidation of produce for use as heave-offering, on the other hand, play no part in the chapter (see M. 8:8 and comment).

[50]See M. 5:8, where the Houses engage in a similar dispute concerning whether a heifer used for plowing may be sold during the Sabbatical year. The Hillelites, M. 5:8B, hold that an action is permissible even though it may result in a transgression.

[51]The paradigm for this rule is Scripture's injunction concerning the substitution of one animal for another which has been designated as an offering. See Lev. 27:33, which states that both the originally designated animal and the animal which has been substituted for it are regarded as sanctified. This rule is developed in detail in Mishnah-tractate Temurah.

[52]Lieberman, TK, p. 571, suggests that the rule is to prevent produce subject to the restrictions of the Sabbatical year from being prohibited for consumption by non-priests. While this interpretation is plausible, I have inerpreted T. in line with Mishnah's concern, as T.'s repetition of Mishnah's language suggests that it should be.

[53]Produce of the Sabbatical year is never deconsecrated, see M. 8:7E and the rule which follows at T. 7:5Q. The verb mthll has been used here in reference to produce of the Sabbatical year on account of its correct use in the rule governing produce in the status of the second tithe, which follows immediately at T. 7:3N. Although Lieberman, TK, p. 572, does not state this explicitly, his exegesis assumes that this is the proper understanding of the rule. See also the lengthy dispute over this rule at b. Suk. 40b-41a.

[54]See footnote 53 above.

[55]See Maimonides, Sabbatical, 6:9.

[56]Levy, vol. 2, p. 9, defines hbr ʿyr as the general community council or organization, which appears to be the meaning intended at M. Ber. 4:7. See Freimark, Sabbatical, pp. 250-1, note 53, for a bibliography dealing with the meaning of this term.

[57]Alternatively, klym may be translated "vessels," see Danby and Correns, Sabbatical, p. 133. Either translation is acceptable, since using oil for either purpose would be forbidden. Note that the rule which follows, M. 8:9A, takes up the question of treating a leather garment with oil.

[58]This is not technically an artificial dispute, for each of the opposing lemmas does in fact respond to a single issue, the penalty imposed for misusing produce of the Sabbatical year. See Porton, "Dispute."

[59]See y. Sheb. 8:8[38b], where later authorities dispute whether Eliezer's view was more strict or more lenient than this statements imply. See also Neusner, Eliezer, I, pp. 41-3, who suggests that Eliezer's view probably was more lenient than his lemma suggests, for there could be no more strigent position than requiring the owner of the garment to burn it.

[60]This understanding of C-D is based on y. 8:8[38d] and is reflected in the interpretations of Sens and Bert. Maimonides (Comm. and Sabbatical 6:20), holds that the highly respected person may not bathe, since others may honor him by burning fragrant species of edible produce, in violation of the law. MR proposes a different reading for the entire pericope. A-B's rule refers to a place where trees are not found in abundance. In such areas, people are permitted to use straw and stubble for purposes of heating. C-D refers to places in which straw and stubble generally are not used for this purpose, but are "highly valued" (mthšb hw'). In this case, clearly, one may not bathe in a bath heated with these materials, in violation of the law. Both of these interpretations, however, are unnecessarily complicated and have no basis in the language of the pericope.

NOTES TO CHAPTER NINE

[1]So Danby; see also Jastrow, p. 1159, s.v., pgm.

[2]So Danby. Jastrow, p. 593, s.v., yrbwz translates "strawberry-blite."

[3]So Danby; see also Jastrow, p. 464, s.v., hlglwg.

[4]So Jastrow, p. 623, s.v., kwsbr. Danby translates "hill-coriander."

[5]So Jastrow, p. 673, s.v., krps. Danby translates "celery."

[6]So Danby. Jastrow, p. 265, s.v., grgr translates "berry, grain."

[7]The verb nšmr may also be translated "privately-owned." See Jaffee's transla- tion of M. Ma. 1:1; Jaffee, Tithing, p. 28. See also note 4, p. 169.

[8]See Maimonides (Sabbatical, 4:1) who defines the meaning of spyh ("after-growth"), which Mishnah never spells out explicitly.

> Whatever the land produces in the Sabbatical year, whether from seed that has dropped into it before that year, or from roots whose produce has been harvested before and which yield new produce--both are called aftergrowth, whether it be grass or vegetables that have grown spontaneously without planting . . . (Klein, p. 359)

[9]See Columbia Encyclopedia, p. 1867, which notes that some species of mustard grow as weeds.

[10]Maimonides (Sabbatical, 4:2) and TYY, following Sifra Behar 1:3 and 4:5, understand sages' rule to refer to the question of harvesting and eating what grows on its own during the Sabbatical year. The pericope, however, nowhere mentions the issue of consuming this produce. The issue of buying it from those suspected of cultivating during the Sabbatical year, raised at A-B, provides the most logical reading of the entire dispute at C-G. Sifra's reading of G poses a further difficulty, for the view that people may not eat any produce whatsoever that grows uncultivated during the Sabbatical year contra-dicts the assumption of the bulk of the tractate's rules. In order to avoid this conclusion, both Maimonides (Sabbatical 4:3-4) and TYY must argue that sages do permit the consumption of certain types of produce that grow uncultivated during the Sabbatical year. This interpretation, however, in no way is supported by the language of G.

[11]All the traditional commentators introduce a further issue, that people should not buy produce of the Sabbatical year from someone suspected of transgressing the law, for this person cannot be trusted to use the proceeds of the sale in accordance with the restrictions of the law. The central issue of this unit of law, however, concerns buying produce that might have been cultivated in violation of the law, as A-B explicitly states.

[12]My interpretation of this rule, like that of Maimonides (Sabbatical, 4:5), assumes that the produce referred to at A has sprouted during the year following the Sabbatical from seeds that dropped during the harvest of the preceding year. See also Lieberman (TK, pp. 561-2) who interprets A-C as referring to produce that sprouts during the Sabbatical year itself. Even on Lieberman's view, however, it is clear that D refers to the year following the Sabbatical, unless the text is to be amended. This reading is problematic, for A-D comprise a formally unitary construction which strongly suggests that they should be interpreted as addressing a single issue throughout.

[13]Correns, Sabbatical, p. 141 claims that the "southern lowlands" refers to the Negev. I-J, however, makes it clear that the reference is to the coastal plain, for Lod is located between the coastal plain and the Judean mountains, far from the Negev.

[14]Maimonides (Sabbatical, 7:1) summarizes the law of removal as follows:

> Produce of the Sabbatical year may be eaten only as long as the particular species is available in the field, as it is said, And for the cattle and for the beasts that are in thy land, shall all the increase thereof be for food (Lev. 25:7), implying that as long as the wild beast can eat of that species in the field, you may eat of what there is of it in the house. Once there is no more of it in the field for the wild beast, you must clear out what there is of that species in the house (Klein, p. 374).

Maimonides' explanation of the law is taken from Sifre Behar 1:8. M.-T., for its part, never explicitly states the theory which underlies the law of removal. The explanation offered by Sifre, however, is entirely extraneous to Mishnah's interests. My explanation of the law is consistent with Mishnah's interest in assuring that produce of the Sabbatical year is treated as ownerless and thus available to everyone (see M. 5:7 and Chapter Eight).

[15]Mishnah never states explicitly that climatic conditions determine the division of the Land into distinct regions for purposes of removal. Nonetheless, the division of the Land into topographical areas, such as mountains and valley (D-H) is best understood in terms of the differences in climate from one region to the next.

[16]Maimonides (Comm. and Sabbatical 7:9) assumes that "Transjordan" refers to the area west of the Jordan River. Accordingly, he assumes that I-K spell out the areas which comprise this region. This interpretation is unacceptable for two reasons. First, both in Scripture and in M.-T., cbr hyrdn always refers to the area east of the Jordan River. Secondly, Maimonides assumes that I, J and K delineate three distinct geographi- cal areas. In fact, however, the area referred to at K incorporates those at I and J. Thus, I-J and K form a dispute, as my comment indicates.

[17]Correns (Sabbatical, p. 141), on the basis of y. Sheb. 9:2[38d] interprets K to mean that the area from Beit Horon to the sea constitutes a fourth region which itself is divided into three areas. This interpretation apparently is based on the occurrence of the word mdynh which appears nowhere else in the pericope. The problem with this reading, however, is that it contradicts A-B, which rules that there are three regions within the Land of Israel, not four. The authorities cited in y. Sheb. 9:2, realizing this problem, are forced to harmonize A-B with their reading of K. My interpretation avoids these unnecessary difficulties.

[18]Maimonides (Comm. and Sabbatical 7:9) interprets L-M as an explanation of A and so reads the ruling as follows:

> L.   And why have they stated [at A] that there are three regions [with respect to removal, despite the fact that C divides each region into three areas, making nine regions in all]?
>
> M.   That they may eat [produce of the Sabbatical year] in each [region, that is, in Judea, Galilee or Transjordan] until the last [produce of that region, whether in the mountains, the lowlands or the valley] is gone. [Thus, the areas which comprise these regions are mentioned at D-H only to clarify the boundaries of each region and are not to be understood as separate areas for purposes of removal].

According to Maimonides, then, the law does not take into account that produce growing in the mountains ripens later than that which grows in the valleys, where the climate is warmer. On this reading, however, there is no apparent reason for the division of the Land into distinct regions at all. My interpretation of L-M is preferable, for it makes intelligible the division of the Land into nine regions, delineated in accordance with the diverse climatic conditions that prevail in each.

19Lieberman, TK, p. 579, note 23, claims that Š'r is a mistake, caused by the occurrence of that word at M. 9:3.

20Tekoa is the name of two different places, see Freimark (Sabbatical, p. 259). The first is located in Judea, 7-1/2 km. south of Bethlehem. Freimark, however, claims that T. here refers to a town in the upper Galilee, 10 km. west of Safed.

21Freimark, ibid., identifies Gush Halab as being in the upper Galilee, south of the former location of Lake Huleh and notes that y. Sheb. 38d refers to Meron, west of Safed, as being included in this area.

22For a description of the manner in which olives are gathered, see M. Men. 8:4.

23Freimark, ibid., notes that Zoar is mentioned in Gen. 13:10 and was located on the southeastern edge of the Dead Sea. The sub-tropical climate there creates a long season for dates.

24My interpretation of šmwr follows that of Maimonides (Comm. and Sabbatical, 7:4), TYT, and Bert. Albeck, however, interprets B to refer to a case in which the householder did not initially renounce ownership of his produce, as the law requires, but subsequently did so. Since this produce was not dealt with initially as the law requires, it does not determine the point at which the law of removal takes effect. That is, the people may not retain produce in their homes on the grounds that such mishandled produce remains in the private possession of others. This interpretation is unacceptable, however, for M.-T. never mentions an obligation to renounce ownership of produce of the Sabbatical year other than the act of removal itself. Rather, Mishnah's laws everywhere assume that produce of the Sabbatical year is inherently ownerless.

25So Danby. See also Jastrow, p. 547, s.v., tpyh who translates, "stinted, poor grains."

26So Jastrow, p. 304, s.v., dypr'. Correns (Sabbatical, p. 144), however, claims that the word refers to the second crop of any fruit, not only figs. In either case, the point of the rule is the same.

27So Danby and Jastrow, p. 1030, s.v., štwwnyt.

28Freimark, ibid., p. 257 claims that the location of Beit Oni is uncertain, though he cites Dalman and Press who identify it with Bethany, near Jerusalem.

29Lieberman, TK, p. 577 locates Tobaniah near Beit Shean, in the lower Galilee.

30Lieberman, TK, p. 578-9, identifies this place as Abel-Keramim, mentioned in Judges 11:33, located west of Rabbath-ammon in Transjordan.

31Lieberman, TK, p. 578, following HD, notes that Yose at F-G qualifies his own rule at C, and suggests that F-G should be in the name of Judah rather than Yose. He misses the point of T.'s version, that Judah's ruling should dispute M. 9:4D-E, rather than qualifying it.

32So Jastrow, p. 64, s.v., 'ksygrwn, who translates "vegetables used for oxy- garum," i.e., all kinds of vegetables. TYT and TYY, on the basis of Maim. (Comm.), claim that snrywt refers to a type of purslane. So also, Correns, Sabbatical, pp. 156-7 who cites Loew, Flora, II, p. 486 and III, p. 71. I have followed Jastrow's translation, for this reading of G makes the most sense in light of F.

33Correns (Sabbatical, p. 146) locates Beit Netofah as N.E. of Sephoria. TYT and TYY, following Maim. (Comm.), note that this is an especially moist region.

34Freimark (Sabbatical, p. 256) notes that Klein (Erez Ha-Galil, p. 47) cannot identify this place, while Press, I, p. 79 identifies it as Beit Gan, 10 km. west of Safed.

35Though Lieberman identifies this plant, he offers no botanical information about it which would be useful in determining the point of T.'s rule.

[36]Freimark, ibid., cites Press, II, p. 666, IV, p. 910 who notes the Shimron is located west of Nazareth.

[37]So Danby and Correns (Sabbatical, p. 146). See, however, Jastrow, p. 860. s.v., mtwq, who translates "Bitter Apple or Cucumis" and Albeck, who translates mtwq as sweet herbs. The contrast between C and D, however, is that of fresh moist produce as against dried up produce of the same species. This suggests that A and B likewise refer to a single species of produce.

[38]My interpretation follows that of Sens, Bert., and TYY who read the issue of the pericope as that of removal. Maimonides (Comm. and Sabbatical 7:17), however, interprets the entire pericope as being concerned with the point at which people are no longer permitted to gather produce of the Sabbatical year. I prefer to read the pericope in the context of the chapter's discussion of removal, where its meaning is clear.

[39]See b. Ta. 6a, where the exact dates of the three seasonal rains are disputed. All parties to the dispute agree, however, that these rains come during the month of Heshvan, in the fall of the year.

[40]See M. Ned. 4:1ff. for the rules regarding vows not to benefit from one's fellow.

[41]See M. Peah 8:1 which states that after the second rainfall all people, not only the poor, may gather olives from the field.

[42]So TYY, TYT, Sens and MR. Bert., however, interprets the rule to refer to the time during the year following the Sabbatical when the poor may no longer go into the fields to collect produce of that year. Maim. (Comm.) and Correns (Sabbatical, p. 148) regard both interpretations as correct. The interpretation followed here is preferable, for our tractate nowhere indicates that there is a time after which people may not gather produce of the Sabbatical year. The issue of poor people's damaging a wet field, however, is raised at M. Peah 5:3 and T. Peah 2:20.

[43]So MR who reads M-N as referring to produce of the Sabbatical year lying in the field upon which it has rained. Bert. interprets the rule with respect to the law of removal. On his view, M-N rules that once straw of the field has rotted, the straw which remains in people's homes is deconsecrated and so can be used in any way people wish. But this interpretation contradicts the rule of M. 9:6B,D. When the straw or stubble in the field disappears, that which remains in people's homes becomes subject to removal; see MS, MR to M. 9:7.

[44]Jastrow, p. 657, s.v., kp translates, "top branch of a palm tree."

[45]So Jastrow, p. 1567, s.v., šys.

[46]So Jastrow, p. 13, s.v., 'gs.

[47]So Jastrow, p. 1414, s.v., qrwstmyl.

[48]So Jastrow, p. 1228, s.v., pryš.

[49]Jastrow, p. 1049, s.v., ᶜwzrd translates "medlar, crab-apple, sorb-apple."

[50]See Lieberman's note on the word, šlhyn; TZ, p. 199.

[51]See Sacks-Hutner, p. 88, note 68 and also Maimonides (Sabbatical, 7:3) which reflects this reading of the law. The bulk of MSS., as well as T. 8:1-2, however, support the reading that I have adopted here.

[52]My interpolation here relies on a view expressed in a dispute at y. Sheb. 9:6. Though the pericope does not explicitly mention removal, the redactor's placement of the rule at the conclusion of Mishnah's discussion of that law, makes this a plausible reading. Moreover, if the vegetables referred to at A were not given after the time of removal, there would be no apparent issue, for giving vegetables of the Sabbatical year as a gift is explicitly permitted; see M. 8:5. See, however, Maim. (Comm.), and Bert., and my comment on their interpretation (note 54 below).

[53]The referrent of "those who eat it" is unclear. According to Maim. (Comm.), TYY, MR, Cahati and Correns, the reference is to other people in general; that is, anyone who would eat produce after the time of removal. This reading, which makes sense of Eliezer's lemma, is problematic when we turn to sages' rule at C, where the phrase appears a second time. On this interpretation of the phrase, the procedure which sages propose serves no apparent purpose, for they first require the recipients of this gift or inheritance to sell the food "to those who eat it" and then to distribute the proceeds of the sale "among everyone," that is, to the very same people. My reading of the phrase eliminates this difficulty.

[54]Maim. (Comm.), Sens, Bert., Albeck and Correns, relying on y. Sheb. 9:6, interpret this dispute in light of the Houses dispute at M. Sheb. 4:2. The issue of that dispute, as read by the same commentators is whether or not one may gather produce of the Sabbatical year for another person as a favor. That issue, however, has no bearing on this chapter's discussion of the laws of removal and is in no way reflected in the wording of this pericope (which refers to a mtnh, not twbh, as does M. 4:2). The two pericopae clearly are unrelated.

[1] The word $\check{s}tr$ may refer either to a bond which specifies the security against the loan or simply to a document which states the amount of the loan. Both M. Git. 3:2 and M. B.B. 10:8 suggest that the word refers simply to a loan which is written. Nonetheless, M. B.B. 10:8 also rules that on the basis of a $\check{s}tr$ which does not specify security against a loan the creditor may collect the money owed him even from the debtor's mortgaged property. See also b. Git. 37a where the matter is disputed. In any event, within the present context the issue is of little importance. Our pericope's concern is with the distinction between loans and debts, not with the distinction between the two types of loans referred to at A.

[2] My interpretation follows that of Sens., Maim. (Comm.), Bert., and TYY, who base their interpretation on the discussion of y. Sheb. 10:1, offer an entirely different reading. They understand the phrase, $^{c}bwdh$ $\check{s}pwsqt$ $b\check{s}by^{c}yt$, to mean work which is forbidden during the Sabbatical year, such as plowing, and so which "ends with the beginning of the Sabbatical year." While this in itself is a plausible translation of I and K, their interpretation is suspect on other grounds. They understand Yose's point to be that wages not paid before the Sabbatical year begins are deemed a loan and for this reason are cancelled. Wages which are during the Sabbatical year, in their view, are not deemed a loan. They never account for such a distinction between debts and loans, however, nor does it have any apparent relation to the distinction as presented in the preceding rules. I prefer not to attempt to harmonize Yose's rule with the principle articulated above.

[3] Following V. Ed. princ. spells out both positions, preparing us for the rule which follows, thus, "A debt [owed to a] shopkeeper is cancelled [by the Sabbatical year]," the words of R. Judah. And sages say, "It is not cancelled [by the Sabbatical year]." E reverses the positions: "A debt [owed to a] shopkeeper is not cancelled [by the Sabbatical year]," the words of R. Judah. And sages say, "It is cancelled [by the Sabbatical year]." This, however, contradicts both Mishnah and the rule at B-C.

[4] See the extensive explanation of the working of the Hebrew calendar and especially of the rules governing intercalation in EJ, 5:43.

[5] TYT and MR correctly note that this rule contradicts M. 10:1B, which rules that debts to storekeepers are not cancelled by the Sabbatical year. On the basis of y. 10:2[39c] they argue that this debt is deemed a loan either because the butcher, unable to collect money on the festival, does not demand security or because he does not set a time for the collection of the debt. These interpretations clearly are attempts to harmonize this rule with M. 10:1, for the wording of the pericope in no way supports this reading. As at M. 10:1I-L, the point of the rule is expressed through the formal pattern, which here contrasts debts incurred during the Sabbatical year with those incurred afterwards.

[6] Jastrow, p. 101, s.v., 'pwtyq', translates "a note (contract) containing a mortgage obligation."

[7] The language of G is subject to two interpretations depending upon the way in which one translates mwsr. Albeck argues at length that it means "announce." Accordingly he understands that the substance of the prozbul is the announcement by a creditor that he is entitled to collect his debts at any time he wishes. This reading is supported by all manuscript evidence which reads, $\check{s}kl$, "I announce. . . that evey debt. . . ." I have chosen, however, to translate mwsr as "transfer" (see Jastrow, p. 810, s.v., msr), since this is its plain meaning in all other occurrences in Mishnah (see Kasovsky, Mishnah, III, p. 1147, s.v., mwsr). Accordingly, I drop the relative pronoun from $\check{s}kl$ and read, "I

transfer . . . every debt . . ." This translation of <u>mwsr</u> is further supported by the fact that the word is used exactly in this way in the pericope which immediately precedes this one (M. 10:2H-I). Though this slight difference in translation seems insignificant, it has important implications for one's understanding of the point of the <u>prozbul</u>. Albeck argues that, since a <u>prozbul</u> is merely a court-endorsed declaration on the part of the creditor, its power derives from its status as a court order. The repayment of a loan then takes on the status of a court enjoined payment which, in line with M. 10:2F-G, is not cancelled by the Sabbatical year. My interpretation of the pericope is guided by its context within the chapter. M. 10:2H-I, which immediately precedes the discussion of the <u>prozbul</u>, refers to the legal fiction that a court, but not a creditor, may collect outstanding loans after the Sabbatical year. The redactors placement of these two units of law strongly suggests that he understood the <u>prozbul</u> (M. 10:3-4) as an instance of this rule at M. 10:2H-I. Moreover, Maim. (<u>Comm.</u>), MR and MS, following Sifre Deut. 113, interpret the function of the <u>prozbul</u> in this way.

[8]Blackman (vol. IV, p. 221) gives a complete account of the manner of writing a folded document:

> The folded document was drawn up by writing one or two lines folding this part over and attaching the witnesses' signatures on the fold and sewing it down, then more lines added, the part folded down, a signature appended on the back, and again sewing down; this being repeated until the whole document was completed."

The result is a document which lies flat, but has pockets on the back side containing the signatures of the witnesses. See also Albeck to M. B.B. 10:1 who offers an alternative account of the procedure. Both positions derive from a dispute in b. B.B. 160b.

[9]TYY, TYT, Sens and Bert. all interpret A to mean that a <u>prozbul</u> may be written only if the borrower has secured the loan in question with a piece of his own real estate. Nothing in the language of A, however, suggests that this land must have been offered as security for the loan. Rather, as I have explained A, the function of the land is strictly symbolic. As I note in my comment, this reading of the law is supported by the rules at B-F, which permit the writing of a <u>prozbul</u> even if the borrower owns no real estate with which he could secure his loan.

[10]The principle that a minuscule amount of land has immeasurable value is not limited to our tractate. See, for example, M. Peah 3:7-8 and M. B.B. 9:6, which state that a man who gives his property to others as a gift, but retains some small amount of land for himself, indicates that he retains control of his entire estate.

[11]See Lieberman (TK, p. 590) who offers this reading of the facts of the case.

[12]Freimark (<u>Sabbatical,</u> p. 273) mistakenly adds R. Simeon b. Gamaliel's name here and omits it in T. 8:8, where it appears in all MSS.

[13]See M. Dem. 5:10 which explicitly rules that the soil within a perforated pot has the status of real estate. See also M. Kil. 7:8 and M. Shab. 10:6, which dispute this issue. Notably, in both of these pericopae, Simeon takes the position that perforated and non-perforated pots are subject to a single rule.

[14]Lieberman (TK, p. 592) interprets K as referring to the case of a woman who loans money, rather than to one who borrows it. They write a <u>prozbul</u> for her based on her husband's property, "since it is in the husband's interest that the wife collect outstanding loans; he certainly will allow her to transfer some of his property to the borrower (enabling her to write a <u>prozbul</u> and collect the loan)." But this reading ignores the fact that the phrase <u>lktwb prwzbwl l-</u> at M. 10:6F clearly refers to writing a <u>prozbul</u> on behalf of the borrower. My interpretation of K is consistent with this use of the phrase.

[15]This qualification, assumed by the dispute, is spelled out in detail at T. Uqs. 3:16:

> F.   "[If] it was attached [to the ground] with plaster, all [both Eliezer and sages] agree it is equivalent to immovable property in all respects.

G.   "[If] it was set on two pegs, all agree that it is equivalent to a [movable]
     utensil in every respect" (Neusner, _Tosefta_, vol. 6, p. 353).

[16]Bert., MS and TYT, following Rashi to b. Git. 37b, claim that A refers to the last
day of the Sabbatical year or to sometime after that year has ended. This reading is
necessary, they claim, since loans are cancelled only at the end of the Sabbatical year,
while during the Sabbatical year they still are collectable. This principle, which is
expressed nowhere in M.-T., appears to be based on the exegesis of Deut. 15:1 ("At the
end of seven years. . .") provided by Sifre Dt. 112. This is how Maimonides accounts for
the origin of this rule; see _Sabbatical_, 9:4. This interpretation of A, however, is
problematic. First, the usual meaning of bšbyCyt throughout the tractate is "during the
Sabbatical year," not afterward, as these commentators assume. (See, for example, M.
3:8, 4:10, 5:2 and 5:8). Moreover, as we have seen at M. 10:1I-L and 10:2A-E, Mishnah
assumes that debts incurred during the Sabbatical year are cancelled forthwith. My
interpretation avoids these problems by reading the rule before us in line with the simple
meaning of the words and with the thrust of these other rules. That is, M. 10:8A refers to
a person who wishes to repay an outstanding loan during the Sabbatical year itself, when
he does not have an obligation to do so.

[17]See b. Git. 37b which confirms that this is the rationale behind Mishnah's rule.
The Talmud claims that the borrower must explicitly acknowledge that his repayment has
the status of a gift. Until he does so, the lender must refuse to accept the payment.

[18]TYY, Bert., TYT, and Sens., relying on T. Mak. 3:8 interpret the point of the
verses somewhat differently. Since the word, _dbr_, is singular, the lender or murderer
must make the required statement only once. A-D and G-K, however, raise no question
about the number of times that the statement must be made. The point, rather, is that a
person must verbally acknowledge that he is not entitled to accept what he has been
offered.

[19]See also M. B.Q. 9:11, which likewise illustrates the principle that children born to
a convert prior to the time of his conversion do not inherit his property.

[20]See M. B.M. 4:2, which provides further details concerning the conditions under
which a buyer or seller may withdraw from a transaction. That rule also emphasizes that
both buyer and seller should stand by their word and conduct their transactions equitably.

[21]See Maim. (_Theft and Lost Objects_, 1:13 and _Borrower and Lender_, 4:5), who
makes this condition explicit in his restatements of this rule.

INDEX TO BIBLICAL AND TALMUDIC REFERENCES

SCRIPTURE

MISHNAH

MISHNAH (continued)

TOSEFTA

Abodah Zarah		Shebiit (cont.)	
2:8	239	3:10	97
		3:11-13	98-9
Baba Qamma		3:14-15	102-3
1:6	175	3:16	86
		3:17	103
Hallah		3:18	103
2:11	237	3:19	104-5
		3:20	105-6
Kelim Baba Qamma		3:21	107-8
1:5	239	3:22	109
		3:23	109-10
Moed Qatan		4:1	113
1:2	57	4:2	114
		4:3	115
Makkot		4:4	117
3:8	259	4:5	119
		4:6-11	123-4
Peah		4:12	125-6
2:20	254	4:13	127
4:6	239	4:14	128-9
		4:15	129
Shabbat		4:16-18	129-30
12:4	227	4:19	131
17:23	227	4:20	131-3
		4:21	133-4
Shebiit		5:1	135-6
1:1	44-5	5:2	136
1:2	48-9	5:3	141
1:3a	47	5:4	141-2
1:3b	49	5:5-6	142
1:4	55-6	5:7	142-3
1:5	56	5:8	144
1:6	56-7	5:9	145
1:7	57	5:10	145
1:8	57-8	5:11	146-7
1:9	58-9	5:12a	147-8
1:10	59	5:12b	147
1:11	59-60	5:13-14	149-50
1:12	62	5:15-16	153-4
2:1-2	74	5:17	154
2:3	60-61	5:18	154
2:4-5	64-6	5:19	155
2:6-7a	66-8	5:20	155-6
2:7b-8	68-9	5:21-22	164-5
2:9a	69	5:23	182
2:9b	69-70	6:1-4	156-7
2:10	70	6:5	154-5
2:11-12	73-4	6:6-7	157-8
2:13	70-71	6:8	158
2:14	77-8	6:9-15	158-60
2:15-18	80-82	6:16	160
2:19	82	6:17-19	161-2
2:20	82-3	6:20	162-3
3:1-2	84-5	6:21-2	165-6
3:3	85	6:23-25a	166-7
3:4a	87	6:25b	167-8
3:4b	89	6:26	168
3:5	91	6:27-29a	169-70
3:6	91	6:29b	172
3:7	92	7:1-9	172-5
3:8-9	95	7:10-12	184-6

TOSEFTA (continued)

Joshua
crops that grow over two years, 71, 114-115;
law of removal, 189-190;
repairing a public road, 90-91;
working a field during the sixth year, 47-49, 53-55, 57

Judah
appearing to cultivate the land, 76-78, 80-81, 84, 96-97, 101-104;
becoming an accessory to a transgression, 181;
cancellation of debts, 200-202, 206;
conducting business with sanctified food, 143-144;
crops that grow over two years, 112-113, 116-117, 133;
law of removal, 187-189, 195-196;
misusing produce of the Sabbatical year, 165-166, 169-170;
working a field during the sixth year, 44, 54-58, 60

Land of Israel
boundaries and regions of, 121-126, 179, 183-191;
sanctity of, 15-26, 98, 121-122

Lieberman
36, 44, 45, 68-70, 73, 89, 91, 95, 98, 104, 105, 109, 123, 128, 129, 132, 145, 153, 155,
162, 165, 169, 170, 172-175, 185, 186, 188, 189, 191, 193, 194

Maimonides
8-10, 68

Meir
appearing to cultivate the land, 76-82, 88-89;
law of removal, 139, 141-142, 146;
produce that grows over two years, 63-65, 113-114;
working a field during the sixth year, 44

Nehemiah
misusing produce of the Sabbatical year, 160-161, 165-166;
produce that grows over two years, 131-133;
working a field during the sixth year, 89

Shammai
enacting decrees, 97

Simeon
agricultural restrictions in Syria, 121, 134-135;
appearing to cultivate the land, 77-78;
becoming an accessory to a transgression, 109-110, 181;
crops that grow over two years, 133-134;
law of removal, 146-148, 153, 183-185, 190, 193-194;
misusing produce of the Sabbatical year, 169, 171-172;
working a field during the sixth year, 44-45, 52-55, 60, 63-64, 72-73

Simeon b. Eleazar
appearing to cultivate the land, 80-81;
conducting business with sanctified produce, 145;
law of removal, 135, 185, 193;
tending trees during the Sabbatical year, 59

Simeon b. Gamaliel
appearing to cultivate the land, 79-81, 84, 102, 105;
cutting down trees, 108;
heave-offering, 136;
law of removal, 185, 192-194;
misusing produce of the Sabbatical year, 158, 169;
produce that grows over two years, 66, 69, 132-133;
prozbul, 209-210;
working a field during the sixth year, 43-47

,